P9-CJH-173

Encyclopaedia of
ARCHERY

By the same author

Saracen Archery (with J. D. Latham)

Encyclopaedia of
ARCHERY

by

W. F. PATERSON

St. Martin's Press
New York

 For information, address St. Martin's Press, 175 Fifth Avenue, New York, N.Y. 10010.

Library of Congress Cataloging in Publication Data

Paterson, W. F. (William Forbes)
Encyclopaedia of archery.

1. Archery—Dictionaries. I. Title.
GV1184.5.P37 1985 799.3'2'0321 84-22335
ISBN 0-312-24585-8

First published in Great Britain by Robert Hale Ltd.

First U.S. Edition

10 9 8 7 6 5 4 3 2 1

To the memory of
Mrs Inger K. Frith, OBE,
as a small tribute to her outstanding achievements
in the field of
International Archery
over many years of successful endeavour.

Contents

List of Illustrations

PICTURE CREDITS

Victoria and Albert Museum, 1; W. F. Paterson, 2, 3, 4, 5, 6, 8, 9, 10, 11, 12,13, 14, 15, 16, 17, 19, 20, 29, 30, 31, 39, 40; Bob Thomas Sports Photography, 7; Enterprise Public Relations, 18; Roy Hungerford, 21; The Mary Rose Trust, 22, 23, 24, 25; W. E. Tucker, 26; Denis Jones, 27, 28; CADA, 32, 33; D. G. Quick, 34, 35, 36, 37, 38, 42, 43, 44, 45, 46, 47, 48, 49; The Associated Press, 41.

Acknowledgements

It is always a pleasure to offer thanks for the kind assistance that has contributed toward one's efforts. In the main, I can but express my gratitude to all those who have given me advice and help over more than thirty years, however inadequate this may be.

I am ever mindful of the wise words of a great master archer, Taybughā al-Ashrafi, who wrote in Damascus, around the year 1368, that no man will "have a complete grasp of all there is to know about shooting, and he will never be too old to learn. Authorities on archery say that, no matter how much knowledge in the art of shooting a man may acquire and no matter how long he lives, he will not achieve complete mastery." I humbly acknowledge my ignorance of some matters, but I hope that the pages which follow will be informative and of value to those who are interested in the sport of archery.

In compiling this encyclopaedia, a lengthy bibliography could be offered, but I would like to select three works that have proved to be of outstanding value.

First and foremost, I have made extensive use of Robert P. Elmer, *Target Archery*, published by Alfred A. Knopf, New York, 1946. When it first appeared it was the most complete and thorough work on the subject and its extensive glossary has been invaluable. Second is the work of an old friend, E. G. Heath, *A History of Target Archery*, David & Charles, Newton Abbot, 1973. His scholarly research has saved me much time and effort in checking many details. The third work that has greatly eased my task is that of F. Lake & H. Wright, *Bibliography of Archery*, The Simon Archery Foundation, Manchester Museum, 1974. Without this publication, many hours would have been spent searching for important references.

A few quotations are offered from Roger Ascham, *Toxophilus* (1545), where I have used the edition of W. A. Wright, *English Works of Roger Ascham*, Cambridge University Press, 1904.

Quoted regulations have been taken from FITA *Constitution and Rules* (1981), from the GNAS *Rules of Shooting* (1981), and NAA *Target Rules* (1981).

Though less frequently consulted, mention should be made of three further works of undoubted merit: E. G. Heath, *Archery: The Modern Approach*, Faber & Faber, London 1966; C. J. Longman & Col. H. Walrond, *Archery* (The Badminton Library), London 1894; T. Roberts, *The English Bowman*, London 1801.

References to all the above and to other works of importance are given under the related entry.

Abbreviations

Because of the frequency with which they appear, three abbreviations are used throughout:

FITA = Fédération Internationale de Tir à l'Arc, or International Archery Federation, which is the governing body for international contests.

GNAS = Grand National Archery Society, the governing body for the sport in Britain.

NAA = National Archery Association, the governing body for the sport in America.

Introduction

Archery is one of the oldest known sports. The bow, as an effective long-range weapon, contributed to the early survival of man, supplying him with meat, and leather and fur for clothing, as well as a means of both attack and defence when facing enemies.

The use of all weapons demands regular practice if a degree of proficiency is to be achieved and this leads to contests of skill between individuals. This work is *not* concerned with the history of the bow, interesting though it may be to many. That must be sought elsewhere. However, many forms and aspects of modern archery have their origins in the past, so references to earlier practices are needed if their present form is to be fully understood.

When the bow ceased to be a military weapon in England, its use continued for sport and recreation among a few groups of enthusiasts, following the old traditions. Interest grew in the last quarter of the eighteenth century, with many new clubs and societies being formed and this growth was encouraged by the personal interest and participation of the Prince Regent. He is credited with the first important steps taken to standardize rules and regulations, and he established the Prince's colours for the rings on targets and the Prince's lengths for the distances over which men should shoot. Early rules varied widely and often seem to be more concerned with costume and dress to be worn, when members of a club should dine, how many dishes should be provided and what wines should be available, rather than the conduct of formal shooting. Though there were always a number who seriously concerned themselves with skill in the art, for the majority it was mainly an excuse for elegant social occasions in the grounds of fine country houses. However, it was an important beginning.

In both Europe and America the traditional wooden longbow was the only form used in competitive shooting for many years. Alternative ideas began to develop around 1930 and after 1950 there was almost an explosion in new designs. This was brought about by two factors. The first was the studies from the scientific and engineering aspects of the bow and arrow, mainly pioneered in the USA, and the second was the availability of new materials, such as plastic-reinforced glass fibre and, more recently, carbon fibre. Aided by high-speed photography and other methods to obtain detailed analysis, many new factors came to light. The action of the bow and its arrow proved to be more complex than had previously been realized.

As a result of these developments, the modern target bow has only a small resemblance to its more simple forbear. With its relatively complex sights, stabilisers, torque flight compensators and counter-weights, it seems to be festooned with devices, strange to those not directly involved with the sport. But to the many who are involved, they add to their pleasure and enjoyment.

Archery, as a modern sport, is divided into contemporary and traditional forms. The latter still has an appreciable following with the wooden longbow in Britain and some other countries, and the Japanese *yumi*, as used in *kyudo*, which has adherents in several lands outside its area of origin. Many archers take part in both modern and traditional forms. The traditional equipment offers a serious but more relaxed atmosphere where scores, to a large extent, are of secondary importance. However, under the heat of major national and international contests, when every point counts, the archer needs every assistance that modern design can offer.

This may well be illustrated by the men's event at the World Target Archery Championships, held at Punta Ala in Italy in 1981 where, after four days of intensive effort and concentration, three points only separated the top four contestants. Under such circumstances, precision equipment—as allowed by rules and regulations—matters to those who take part and one point in a thousand can make the difference between a bronze or a gold medal in the final result.

If one's sole object is to hit a target as accurately as possible, then the rifle is the weapon to use. But how unromantic it is, compared with the bow! Archery today has so much to offer, from the traditional forms to the modern, from the simple to the complex. It is up to the individual to decide on the form they wish to pursue.

W. F. Paterson
Havant
1983

Encyclopaedia of

ARCHERY

ADHESIVES
While a majority of archers rely on the professional services offered by dealers and manufacturers of equipment, many amateur craftsmen gain added satisfaction from their own constructions and, for both bows and arrows, glues are involved.

There are several proprietary brands of waterproof adhesives that may be used to fletch (*qv*) arrows and to attach or replace their plastic nocks (*qv*). The choice available to the amateur bow-maker is more limited.

The problem arises with composite (*qv*) designs where a glue must not only adhere well to substances of very different character, but also have a degree of flexibility to withstand the repeated bending of a bow limb. This was recognized at least a thousand years ago in the construction of the oriental composite bows, where sinew and horn had to be bonded to a wooden core.

In those days, the best glues had an animal base, prepared by boiling hide, sinew, horn or hoof, or a mixture of these, in rain-water. To give added flexibility the Turks used isinglass from the sturgeon, while the Chinese employed a similar preparation from the air-bladder and other parts of a certain fish. Fish glue is more flexible than animal glue.

New materials present fresh problems as in the case of carbon fibre laminates, though experience and research eliminates them in due course. Equipment suppliers can offer well-tested products that are suitable for the construction of a bow, and advice on temperature control to achieve the correct setting rate of the adhesive.

AIM (*n*. and *v*.)
1. A mark at which an arrow is directed.
2. To direct an arrow.

Aiming is basically achieved by aligning the arrowhead with the mark or target. While this provides a form of foresight, the archer has no rear sight in the accepted sense, but brings the shaft in line with the target by lodging the tail of the arrow beneath the eye (see ANCHOR). The bowstring should always be pressed firmly against the same spot on the face so that its blurred image appears to bisect the arrow shaft. Added assistance may be given by the kisser (*qv*).

If the archer aligns the point of the arrow on the target, the bow being fully drawn and the drawing hand lodged beneath the chin, the arrow will have an elevation of about six degrees in relation to the line of sight. When the string is released, the arrow will fly toward the target in a parabolic path and above the line of sight. At a certain range, depending on the performance of the bow and the weight of the arrow, it will strike the target (see Figs A, B and C).

The elevation given to the arrow by lodging the drawing hand beneath the chin should be more than sufficient for the archer to cover all normal target ranges. It therefore follows that the arrowhead will be aligned below the centre of the target (see Fig. D). In the context of target shooting, the archer is aided by the use of a bowsight (*qv*), which is brought in line with the centre of the target and the arrowhead is then disregarded. It is, of course, important that the bow is held vertically as otherwise the arrowhead will not be directly below the centre of the target. Few target archers employ any other method.

The modern bowsight has the added advantage that it can be adjusted laterally to allow for the effect of a cross-wind, as well as indicating the needed elevation.

In addition to the bowsight, there are

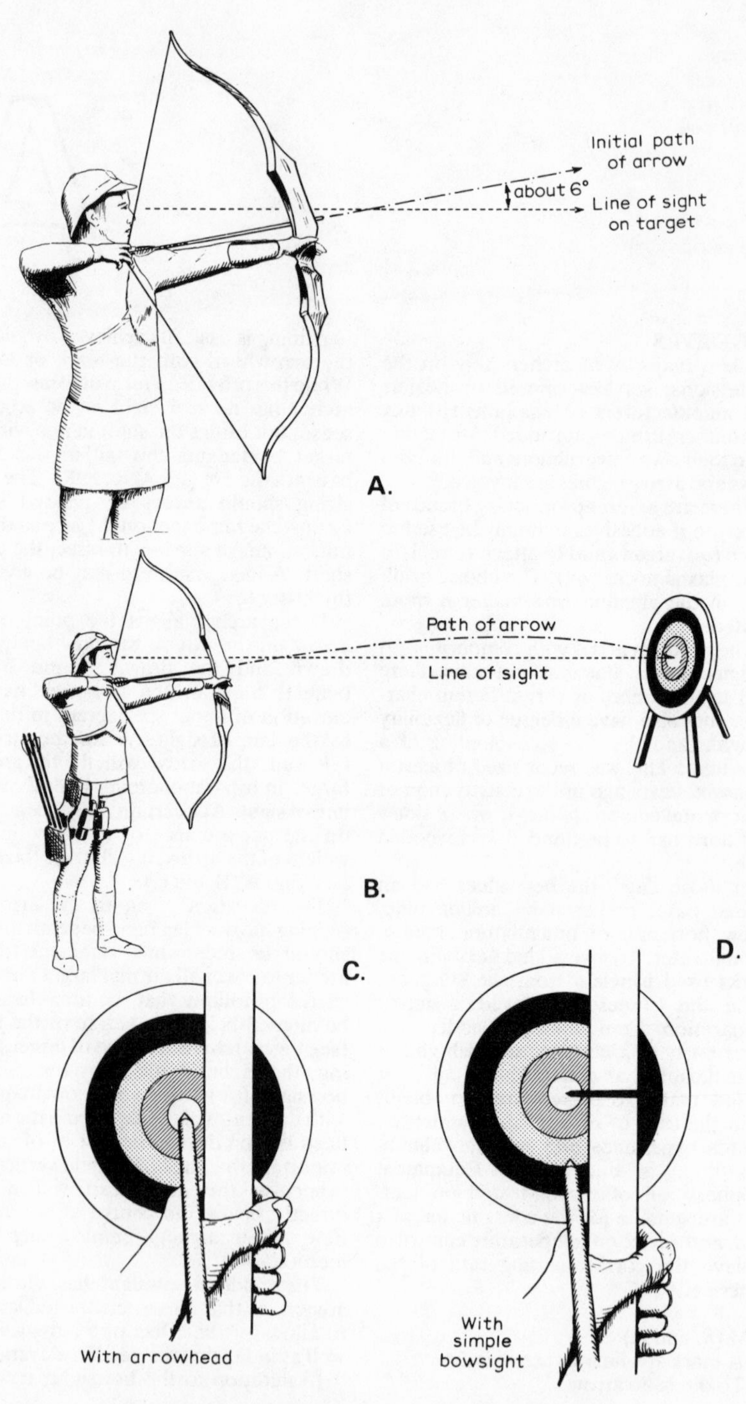
Initial path of arrow
about 6°
Line of sight on target
A.
Path of arrow
Line of sight
B.
C.
D.
With arrowhead
With simple bowsight

two other methods. One that is permitted under international regulations is the use of an **artificial point of aim**, consisting of a small disc, or triangle, on a peg. The archer places this in the ground, between the shooting line and the target and it enables the arrowhead to be sighted on this mark in order to hit the target. It was first allowed by the National Archery Association (NAA) in the USA in 1923. FITA Art. 504 (d) limits the diameter of such marks to 7.5 cm and they must not protrude more than 15 cm above the ground.

The APOA is rarely seen today. Its introduction goes back to the time when sighting marks were not allowed to project beyond the side of a bow and were thus limited to a simple mark, or line, on the upper limb above the grip. It then had advantages over what was thus permitted. With the eventual removal of this restriction, its purpose largely disappeared.

A variation of this technique can be used in field shooting (*qv*) in the *bare bow* class, where no sights are allowed. The archer, having determined from practice and experience how far below the target the arrowhead should be aimed, can then align it with some natural mark on the ground.

Lastly, aiming may be *instinctive*; this is the basic technique of the hunter, where the eyes concentrate on the target and not on the arrowhead. However, the hunter or the field archer should still be conscious of the position of the arrowhead in relation to the target and it must therefore be within the archer's field of vision. Howard Hill (*qv*) in *Hunting the Hard Way* (Chicago 1953), pp. 66–71, refers to this as split-vision aiming. It is achieved by using a high anchor against the side of the face and tilting the bow. Compared with the normal target shooting technique, this cuts down the angle between the line of vision and that of the arrow shaft to two or three degrees only. This greatly reduces any error from faulty estimation of range.

Howard Hill comments, "The one fault that defeats the efforts of many archers when using the method I advocate is that they allow their eyes to shift away from the target to the point of the arrow and back to the target again. If the archer allows himself to do this, he may just as well forget this type of aiming; it will not work that way. Anyone who desires to use this method must realize the importance of understanding it thoroughly, and must be willing to spend enough time to train both the eyes and the mind to perform rightly." He is supported in this view by Roger Ascham (*qv*) who says, "The cheife cause why men can not shoote streight, is bicause they loke at theyr shaft." And later, "For hauying a mans eye alwaye on his marke, is the only waye to shote streght."

The use of the term 'instinctive' for the method favoured by Howard Hill is open to argument, but there is no doubt concerning the technique employed.

It is of interest that Horace Ford (*qv*), to whom much credit is due for the development of modern archery, devotes thirteen pages in his book (1856) to the problem of aiming. This rightly emphasizes the importance of this aspect of archery.

AIM-CRIER

One who stands near a mark to advise the archer of the result of a shot. Such assistance is needed in clout shooting (see CLOUT) where the line of a shot can be seen but the distance it has travelled is difficult to gauge. The more modern terms of 'marker' and 'spotter' are favoured by certain societies and organizations, including the National Field Archery Society (*qv*) whose regulations require 'spotters' in their Game and Woodsman Rounds to indicate an archer's achievement against each target.

ALLOW

To aim an arrow to windward to allow for drift. The problem is eased for the target archer since the relatively complex modern bowsight (*qv*) has been permitted by regulations. This can be adjusted to allow for the effect of a side-wind. However, the wind is rarely steady and an archer on the shooting line may need to adjust the aim if a change in wind direction, or force, is sensed when time may not permit alterations being made to the sight.

For the many enthusiastic followers of the traditional English longbow, who shoot with no sights, and in hunting and field shooting (*qv*), the ability to allow for the effect of wind is most important.

AMERICAN ROUND

This round (*qv*) was adopted in the USA by the National Archery Association

(NAA) in 1879, since when it was used in their championships and in many of their major contests. It consists of shooting 30 arrows at 60, 50 and 40 yards – 90 shots in all.

There was also a **Junior American Round**, suited for the younger members of the archery fraternity, and adopted by the NAA in 1926, where 30 arrows were shot at 50, 40 and 30 yards.

Both rounds were shot at the standard four-foot target (*qv*).

ANCHOR (*n.* and *v.*)
In shooting at a mark an archer has a basic foresight in the arrowhead, which may be sighted on or below the target depending on the range. There is no rearsight in the accepted sense, though certain aids may be used, such as the image of the bowstring being brought into line with the head. To ensure the line of the arrow laterally, it is essential that the shaft, or drawing, hand (*qv*) is brought to a fixed position against the body. This is called the **anchor-point**.

In precision target shooting it is rare to see a good archer who anchors anywhere other than under the chin and against the jaw. The hunter and many archers when field shooting (*qv*) prefer the side of the face and some lodge the middle finger of the shaft hand in the corner of the mouth. The English longbowmen of old traditionally drew to the ear, while some Eastern archers, such as the Japanese, drew to the point of the shoulder.

The earliest recorded appreciation of the advantage offered by this technique would appear to be that of the Roman historian, Procopius, in his *De Bello Persico*, *c*. AD 350, when discussing the prowess and effectiveness of the horse-archers of his time, mainly drawn from the Teutonic tribes. "They draw the bowstring not to the breast, but to the face, or even to the right ear, so that the missile flies so strongly as always to inflict a deadly wound, piercing both shield and cuirass with ease."

ARBALEST
The crossbow (*qv*), from the Latin, *arcuballista*. Though the word implies a missile thrower, fitted with a bow, it is of interest that the modern Italian for a crossbow is *balestra* and in Spanish it is *ballesta*. However, in French the fuller term is preserved in *arbalète*. Archaic spellings, such as *arblast*, may be encountered in some old works.

The term is still favoured by some English crossbowmen and the user is termed an **arbalester**.

The alternative spelling, *arbalist*, is favoured by some and, indeed, was used by R. Payne-Gallwey in his noted work, *The Crossbow*, published in 1903.

ARBALESTRINA
The aperture in the wall of a castle or fort, in the form of a cross, from which crossbowmen could shoot at enemies below. There are many examples where the low height of the roof clearly suggests that the longbow could not have been used. While the longbow can be shot while holding it horizontally, little accuracy can be achieved by this method, so this aspect of a fortification was clearly introduced for the effective use of the arbalest.

ARCHER
One who shoots with or is skilled in the use of the bow and arrow; a bowman.

ARCHER'S CATALEPSY
Also known as **freezing, archer's paralysis** and **target shyness**, this physiological phenomenon is caused by involuntary muscular tensions that prevent the archer coming on aim. While the same problem can arise in other activities, it can strike in a particularly vicious manner in this sport.

Observation of one afflicted with this defect shows tightening of the neck and shoulder muscles as an attempt is made to bring the bowsight to the centre of the target. The application of will power and conscious effort merely makes the situation worse, but if the target is removed the tensions normally go.

The probable cause is the prolonged and repetitive actions demanded by modern target archery and, possibly, by 'trying too hard'. While emphasis is rightly put on the need to shoot in a relaxed manner, it is obvious that there are considerable tensions in the arm and shoulder muscles when handling a bow.

It is most difficult for an individual to solve this problem unaided, but modern coaching methods, with trained and qualified exponents, can usually deal with it in a short time.

As the whole process of target shooting is a rhythmic entity from the moment of taking one's stance on the shooting line to the follow-through after the loose (*qv*), an alteration in the shooting pattern can often help. A change in the archer's customary draw (*qv*) from 'V' to 'T', or vice versa, can often result in a cure. In some difficult cases a cure has been found by a right-handed archer learning to shoot left-handed and vice versa.

ARCHER'S RING
See THUMB RING.

ARCHERY (*adj.* and *n.*)
1. Pertaining to archery, as in 'archery equipment'.
2. The art of shooting with the bow and arrow.

Archery is one of the oldest sports still practised. Success demands regular training and exercise in the art, and in those times when the bow was a primary weapon for hunting and war, contests were held to improve and tax the skill of participants. Hunger is a stimulating taskmaster, so the proficiency of those who depended on a well placed arrow for their food is readily understood. Today there are still certain tribes and peoples in primitive communities who depend on their skill as archers for their food.

In medieval England the emphasis was on warfare and one may cite among several statutes, 12 Richard II in 1388, that required all servants and labourers to have bows, and to practise with them on Sundays and other holidays. With the development of effective firearms, interest in the use of both the bow and the crossbow slowly faded. This happened in England over a period of about 100 years, roughly between 1500 and 1600. One advantage of firearms was the comparatively short training period necessary – it took as many weeks to train a man to use a musket as it took years to train an archer. While a few enthusiasts endeavoured to carry on the old traditions, archery was ignored by the majority and laws were no longer enforced.

The revival of archery – as a sport or recreation in contrast to a military need – began in 1781, with the foundation of the Toxophilite Society (later 'Royal'), through the interest and enterprise of Sir Ashton Lever (*qv*). One of his employees, Thomas Waring, took up the use of the bow to rid himself of a chest complaint. Observing the beneficial effects of this exercise, he gathered together several friends and interest quickly spread.

The next milestone was the formation of the Grand National Archery Society (GNAS) (*qv*) in 1861, though the idea had been proposed sixteen years earlier. In the USA the National Archery Association was formed in 1879. These and similar organizations established rules and regulations within their respective countries that brought together their own various clubs and societies of archers. With the founding of the International Archery Federation (FITA) (*qv*) in 1931 agreement was eventually achieved between all affiliated associations for the conduct of competitive archery on a world-wide basis. The most recent major success was the readmittance of target archery to the list of approved sports at the Olympic Games (*qv*) in 1968. This led to a marked increase in the number of national organizations taking part in international events.

As a sport, target archery taxes serious contestants both physically and mentally. Consider a man's target bow with a draw weight (see WEIGHT) of about 40 lb or a woman's of about 30 lb; at major contests this force must be pulled 288 times (plus permitted sighting shots) and held for several seconds while final aim is taken. Such a contest may last as long as four days, during which full concentration must be maintained by the contestant who will be involved in some twenty hours on the shooting ground.

ARCHERY DARTS
A light-hearted amusement where archers shoot at an enlarged replica of a standard dart-board. Contests can also be arranged against dart players.

It is also a useful method of attracting the attention of spectators at appropriate fairs and exhibitions. Such a game, resolved in a few minutes, holds their interest and demonstrates the accuracy of the bow. It has led several into taking up the sport, of which they were previously ignorant, and thus can offer useful publicity, coupled with entertainment.

(See Appendix 1; page 000, for GNAS *Rule* 640).

ARCHERY GOLF
This provides a useful liaison and social occasion with a local golf club. Golfers

play their round, following the normal rules. An acceptable contest is provided where archers 'putt' by hitting a four-inch disc, after landing an arrow on the green. A shaft in a bunker adds one to the archer's score. Golfers have the privilege to place the 'putting disc' on the perimeter of the green and the archer shoots from where the last arrow landed, until the mark is hit.

This is another light-hearted entertainment for the benefit of those who take part.

(See Appendix 1; page 178, for GNAS *Rule* 620.)

ARCHERY GROUND
The field set apart for shooting with targets and measured ranges.

ARCHERY HALL OF FAME
Formed in the USA to honour Americans in all phases of archery for outstanding service to the sport, including those who have excelled as archers for a long period or who have been responsible for advancement in the design and quality of equipment. The first inductions were held in 1972.

1972: Fred Bear, Howard Hill, Russell B. Hoogerhyde, Ann Weber Hoyt, Karl E. Palmatier, J. Maurice Thompson, Ben Pearson.
1973: Saxton T. Pope, Rube Powell, Clayton B. Shenk, Arthur Young, Dr Robert P. Elmer.
1974: Dorothy S. Cummings, Harry Drake, Doug Easton, John Yount.
1975: Dr Paul Crouch, Mrs M.C. Howell, Jean Lee Lombardo.
1976: Mrs Henry 'Babe' Bitzenberger, Dr Paul E. Klopsteg, Louis Smith.
1977: Dr Clarence N. Hickman, Earl Hoyt, Jr, Myrtle K. Miller.
1978: Roy Hoff, Ann Marston, Homer S. Taylor.
1980: Florence Lilly, George Helwig.
1981: No award.
1982: Alfred K. Henderson.

ARCHERY: The Technical Side
A valued collection of published articles by scientists and engineers in the USA, who were also skilled archers. It was edited by three of the authors of the majority of the works, Clarence N. Hickman, Paul E. Klopsteg, and Forrest Nagler. It was published by the National Field Archery Association in 1947 and printed by the North American Press in Milwaukee, Wisconsin. The first of the articles was taken from *the Journal of the Franklin Institute* of October, 1929, and the last from the *American Bowman Review* of March, 1946.

Until the studies of the various authors appeared, there had been little development in the design of archery equipment since medieval times, though credit must be given to the Seefab Company in Sweden for the steel bow produced in the mid-1930s. The application of techniques, such as high-speed photography, to analyse what occurs when a bow is shot, revolutionized the thoughts of designers and it has played a very major part in producing the equipment that is available today.

ARMGUARD
See BRACER.

ARROW
The principal missile, shot from a bow. Pellets and other objects can also be projected. It may be given a variety of names, which may be related to the form of the shaft (*qv*), such as 'breasted', 'barrelled', etc.; to its purpose, clout, flight, target, etc.; to the form of its head, 'blunt', 'broad', etc. (see ARROWHEAD); or, in historical and ethnographic contexts, to a people, country or area of origin.

The length of an arrow can vary considerably, from the short varieties shot with the aid of an arrow guide (*qv*), to those still used in South-East Asia and in the Amazon Basin by hunters, which may be up to 8½ feet (2.7 m) long.

Modern suppliers of equipment offer shafts from 22–30 inches (56–76 cm) in length and their choice depends on the physical characteristics of the user. This is mainly related to arm length.

Types of arrow
The different forms of arrow are discussed in further detail under the appropriate heading. They are briefly listed below:

BARBED A war or hunting arrow, with a barbed head.
BEARING A heavy arrow used in warfare.
BEARDED The same as 'barbed'.
BLUNT Used against small game and birds in trees.

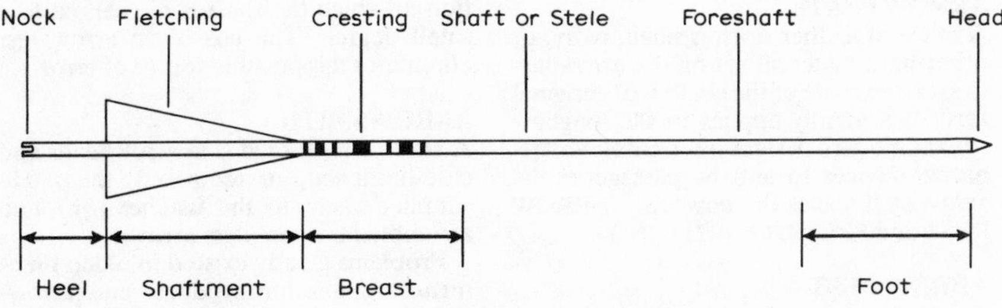

Parts of an arrow.

BREASTED An arrow which is largest at the breast.
BOB-TAILED An arrow whose shaft tapers from head to nock.
BROAD A wide, bladed head. It may, or may not, have barbs.
BULLET An arrow with a cup-shaped head for shooting bullets.
BARRELLED An arrow thickest at the centre of the shaft.
CLOUT A light arrow for clout shooting.
LIVERY or SHEAF The old English war arrow.
TARGET An arrow with a simple conical, or ogival, point, known as a pile, whose diameter is the same as that of the shaft.

FITA *Rules*, under Art. 504(f) allow that:

"Arrows of any type may be used provided they subscribe to the accepted principle and meaning of the word Arrow as used in Target Archery, and that such Arrows do not cause undue damage to target faces and buttresses.

"An Arrow consists of a shaft with head (point), nock, fletching and, if desired, cresting.

"The Arrows of each archer shall be marked with the archer's name, initials or insignia and all Arrows used for the same end of 3 or 6 arrows shall carry the same pattern and colour(s) of fletching, nocks, and cresting if any."

In the rules for Field Archery, Art. 808 B1(f) adds, "Each arrow shall be numbered."

ARROW-CASE

A box, usually of wood, in which arrows are kept. A simple rack mounting is fitted inside to protect the fletchings and prevent them from being crushed when stored or in transit. It is not a quiver (*qv*).

ARROW GUIDE

An extended shelf, or arrow rest (*qv*), to assist the passage of a shaft past the bow. Such a device is not permitted in target shooting, but it is allowed for use in flight shooting (*qv*), where it is often referred to by the old Turkish term *siper* (*qv*) (pronounced: *see-pur*). Its purpose is to allow a short arrow to be drawn inside the bow.

Various forms of guide were used in earlier times. (See Latham, J. D., & Paterson, W. F., *Saracen Archery*, 1970, chap. 26.)

ARROWHEAD

The striking end of an arrow, usually of steel, and fastened to the fore end of a shaft by a tang or a socket.

Ancient heads of flint and bronze are still occasionally found, while those of hardwood, horn and bone continue to be used by some primitive peoples.

In medieval warfare the **bodkin head** (*qv*) was the most effective form against mail and armour. Basically, it was a four-sided spike. Designs from Japan and India are legion and, though they are often elegant and artistic, their classification is outside the scope of this work.

For modern target shooting the form of head called a **pile** (*qv*) is used and, most commonly, is conical in form, though an ogival shape is sometimes seen.

The hunter uses a **broadhead** (*qv*) against most game, though **blunts** (*qv*) are of use against small animals and birds in trees, as well as for shooting at the popinjay (*qv*).

ARROWPASS

The place above the grip or handle where the arrow passes the bow.

ARROW PLATE
A piece of leather, tortoiseshell, ivory, or other hard material, set on the arrowpass to take the chafe of the shaft. In its original form this mainly applies to the longbow (*qv*) as modern designs often employ alternative devices to aid the passage of the arrow as it leaves the bow. (See ARROW REST and PRESSURE BUTTON.)

ARROW REST
A projection on the side of the bow on which the arrow is laid and drawn. This

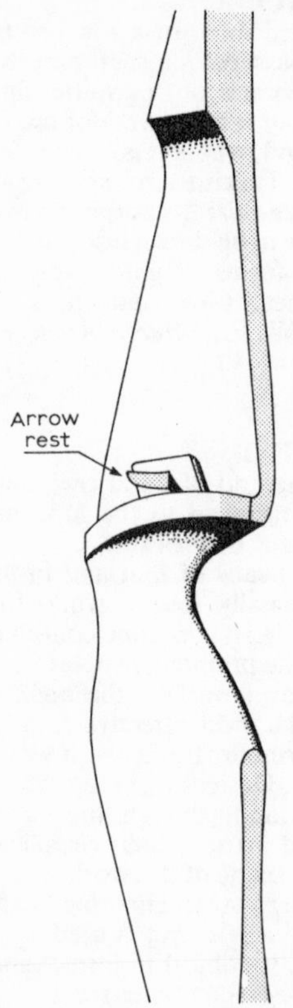

does not apply to the longbow (*qv*) where the shaft is rested on the knuckle of the forefinger, but it is an invariable fitting on the modern bow.

It is an aid to accuracy. When the arrow is rested on the hand that grips the bow, the fist can be moved fractionally up or down and this naturally affects the elevation at which the shaft is discharged to a small degree. The use of an arrow rest eliminates this possible source of error.

ARROWSMITH
A smith who forged iron arrowheads and case-hardened, or tempered, them. He supplied them to the fletcher (*qv*) who assembled the complete arrow.

Problems clearly existed in olden times regarding inferior products and arrowsmiths were threatened with forfeiture of goods and imprisonment by law as in 7 Henry IV. (See W. M. Moseley, *An Essay on Archery*, London 1792 (reprinted 1974), p. 234.)

ARROW STRAIGHTENER
The old expression, 'straight as an arrow', is very meaningful as a shaft that is warped or bent in any manner will never fly true. Arrows should always be checked before use. Most simply, this may be done by looking along the shaft or by the spinning test (*qv*), but these old devices do not offer the accuracy demanded by modern target shooting.

Wooden shafts may be heated and flexed by hand to remove any warp that may be observed, but to assist in the handling of a hot stele simple devices have existed from pre-history. This may be a block of stone with a hole through it or one of wood with a slot cut to take the shaft. These enable pressure to be applied where needed.

The more sophisticated devices, now available, can incorporate dial test gauges and pressure levers to correct any fault.

ARTIFICIAL POINT OF AIM
A mark placed on the ground in target archery, between the shooting line and the target, at which to aim with the point of the arrow, instead of using a bowsight (*qv*) or mark on the bow. (See AIM.)

ASCHAM
(Pronounced 'Askam'.) A tall, narrow cabinet or cupboard in which bows and arrows are kept and stored when not in use. It is named after Roger Ascham (see below).

ASCHAM, Roger (1515–1568)
He was an accomplished but impecunious university don, a Fellow of St John's College, Cambridge, where he took his

MA degree in 1537, and for some two years tutor to Princess (later Queen) Elizabeth. On hearing of his death she is reputed to have said, "Rather would I have cast ten thousand pounds into the sea than have lost my Ascham."

His most important work was *Toxophilus, The schole of shootinge conteyned in two bookes*, published by Edward Whitchurch in 1545. He wrote in English, which was unusual for a scholar at that time, but the clear straightforward simplicity of his prose has been admired by many. We are fortunate to have this legacy of shooting in the longbow, written at a time when it was still a primary weapon of war. Henry VIII was so delighted with the book that he awarded Ascham a pension of £10 a year. Much of its contents, recommendations and advice is as true today as when it was written.

On the history of Ascham see: A. E. Hodgkin, *The Archer's Craft*, London, 1951 (reprinted 1954), pp. 37–49; and on the numerous copies of his work: F. Lake & H. Wright, *A Bibliography of Archery*, Manchester, 1974 (*sv* 'Ascham'), which lists 28 different editions and reprints.

His celebrated *Five Partitions* have been quoted frequently: "Standynge, nockyng, drawyng, holdyng, lowsyng, wherby cometh fayre shotynge . . ." (Ascham is somewhat haphazard in his use of the verbal endings -yng and -ynge.)

Some modern authors have tried to add to the original list such items as 'aiming' and the 'follow through'. These detract from the basic and scholarly analysis offered by Ascham. As he viewed the problem, 'aiming' was part of the process of 'holding' and the 'follow through' was part of 'loosing'.

All the above terms are dealt with here under their respective headings, but Ascham's five partitions cover the fundamentals of shooting and they have stood the test of time. Nothing is gained by trying to complicate the essentials, although in the modern context added emphasis may be needed on certain aspects.

BACK (*n.* and *v.*)
1. The convex side of a strung bow that faces the target as the archer shoots. (See BOW.)
2. To attach a strip of material to the back of a bow that responds well to tension. A wooden bow may be backed with a different wood to improve performance while several American Indian tribes backed simple wooden bows with sinew set in glue. Similar techniques existed in other parts of the world (see BACKING).

BACKING
The material with which the back of a bow (see above) is reinforced. The backing may be *free* or *close*.

Free backing may be found, for example, on Eskimo bows where, in an environment lacking in natural resources, effective hunting weapons were produced that suited their particular purposes. Plaited sinew cords were ingeniously fastened along the back of inferior bow staves to give adequate performance.

For details of this unusual technique see: O. T. Mason, *North American Bows, Arrows, and Quivers* (The Smithsonian Report for 1893) Washington 1894, plates LXV – LXXVI, and related explanations. Also, T. M. Hamilton, *Native American Bows*, York, Pennsylvania, 1972, pp. 70–88 (Second Edition, Columbia, Missouri, 1982).

Close backing is achieved by gluing the material to the back of the bow. This technique existed from prehistoric times as a simple stave naturally tends to break under tension. Strengthening the back gave both greater security – as the life of a hunter might depend on the bow – and improved performance.

A backed bow is a reinforced bow and must not be confused with the composite (*qv*) designs which also employ a backing of sinew or other materials.

BACK QUIVER
A form of quiver designed to carry arrows on the back as opposed to one where they are carried at the side. It is usually hung over the shoulder with a strap or cord, in contrast to the belt quiver (*qv*).

It is a method that often suits the hunter as there is less chance of it becoming entangled in low undergrowth, though it precludes the selection of arrows with different heads as they cannot be seen. This may be of no consequence, especially if all are similar.

Arrows are normally withdrawn by grasping a nock (see ARROW) from over the shoulder and withdrawing the shaft by lifting it upward. An exception to this is found in some Japanese traditional forms where the quiver, on the back, has an opening near the base. The shaft is then grasped, near the head, lifted slightly and withdrawn with a forward and downward movement. (See also QUIVER.)

BALLISTIC PENDULUM
For those interested in the technical aspects of the bow and arrow, the measurement of arrow velocities is an important factor in assessing the performance and potential of different equipment.

Velocity measurement (*qv*) can be achieved by relatively simple means when electronic equipment is not available. In the December 1930 issue of the *Journal of the Franklin Institute* of Philadelphia, USA, F. L. English described a ballistic pendulum which he had adapted for measuring arrow velocities. After ten years of practical experience, resulting in certain modifications, a further paper was published by F. Isles, 'A Simple Route to

Arrow Velocities', *Bow & Arrow*, Covina, California, Nov.–Dec. 1966, pp. 42–5 and 64. Though the author was concerned with measurements relating to crossbows, the same method can be used with the hand bow.

The principle, in simple terms, is to hang a padded pendulum bob at the end of a wire, or strong thread, shoot an arrow into it, and see how far it swings. This enables the velocity of impact to be calculated.

For the bob, Isles used a pile of old magazines between two sheets of thick plywood, held together by threaded bolts secured by wing nuts. Experience showed that a bob weighing about 10–15 lb was well suited to the task. A comment might be offered that the stopping power of the packed magazines is a little violent for the longer arrow from a hand bow and can result in a broken or damaged shaft. A wooden box of about a 1-ft cube, open at the front and back, covered with two strips of old carpet and well packed with crumpled newspaper, offers a more gentle target for the long arrow.

The box requires a four-point suspension, and Dacron threads at each corner, about 40 in. long are satisfactory for this purpose, care being taken that the box is level and tensions on the threads are equal. A short, hinged arm is attached to the back of the bob, carrying a pen that rests on a sheet of paper (one with a fine felt tip is suitable).

The next step is to determine the effective length of the pendulum. The bob is swung about three inches off centre and the number of complete swings that it makes over a period of time is counted. Isles favoured two minutes or more. The arc of travel becomes smaller due to friction, but the period of each swing is constant. The time of each complete swing is then determined by dividing the total number into the time. Thus, if sixty swings were completed in exactly two minutes, the period *T* would be two seconds. The effective length of the pendulum *L* is given by:

$L = 0.817\ T^2$. As $T^2 = 4$, $L = 3.268$ feet.

Next, the weight of both the bob and the arrow must be measured as accurately as possible. The arrow is shot into the bob and the deflection recorded by the pen on a sheet of paper. The velocity is then calculated from English's formula, modified by Isles:

$$V = 0.2364\left(\frac{W - w}{w}\right)\left(\frac{D}{\sqrt{L}}\right) \text{ feet per second.}$$

where W is the weight of the bob in pounds,
w is the weight of the arrow in pounds,
D is the amplitude of the complete swing in inches
and L is the effective length of the pendulum in feet.

To compensate for friction and air resistance, Isles used the technique of drawing the sheet slowly to the side at right angles to the swinging pendulum after the arrow had struck. By measuring the reduction in amplitude of three or four swings, a correction could be applied to the first swing and greater accuracy in the results was achieved.

BALLOON FEATHER

A fletching (*qv*) cut with a curved outline, somewhat akin to that of half a balloon. Alternatively, it has been called a parabolic feather since the rear end is more strongly curved than the fore part.

BARB

A point that projects backward at the rear end of an arrowhead (*qv*). Though used in the past, and by some native peoples today, with the intention of preventing extraction, it is of note that a most experienced hunter, Howard Hill (*qv*), says in his book (*Hunting the Hard Way*, Chicago 1953, p. 117): "If the barbed-head type of broadhead is used and it is shot completely through the prey, there are ten chances to one that the protruding head will hang on some limb or brush in a short time and will pull the shaft out, so that if the game has not been hit in a vital spot, there will be left a clean wound which will heal quickly."

With fishing arrows (*qv*), where a line is attached to the shaft, barbs are essential to recover a fish that has been hit.

With some forms of broadhead the rear end of the blade may be cut away to reduce weight, thus leaving two barbs, even when the designer does not intend them to hang in game. Against this, some native designs, particularly in central Africa and in the Amazon Basin, are vicious in form and leave no doubt of their intended purpose.

BARE BOW
The term is mainly used in field shooting (*qv*) where there is a separate class for those who prefer to shoot instinctively with no form of sight nor other aid for aiming. The alternative method is known as Free Style (*qv*).

BARRELLED ARROW
An arrow shaft of curved form, thickest at the centre. The object is to offer adequate stiffness (see SPINE) and reduce weight. The design is only practical with wooden shafts.

BEARD
An old term for the barb (*qv*) of an arrow-head.

BEARING ARROW
The standard medieval English war arrow, also called the livery or sheaf arrow. As Ascham (*qv*) informs us in *Toxophilus* (1545), the bulk production shafts were of ash or aspen poplar. From the evidence of those recovered from the wreck of the *Mary Rose* (*qv*) their length from the nock to the shoulder of the tapered fore end, where the head was mounted by its socket, varied from about 27 to 32 inches, the majority being a little over 30 inches.

In the Fletchers' (*qv*) regulations for their trade, granted by the Mayor and Aldermen of the City of London on 11th May, 1484, arrows were of two types, 'bearing' and 'merke' or mark arrows, used for shooting at a mark or target. For ordinary bearing shafts of seasonable wood, well and cleanly made, notched, peeled and varnished, the workman was to receive 14*d*. for 100 shafts. For the same quantity of mark shafts, 20*d*. (See J. E. Oxley, *The Fletchers and Longbowstring-makers of London*, London 1968, pp. 15–16.)

A secondary meaning is shown when bearing arrows are mentioned in the Earl of Northumberland's expedition to Terrouenne, 5 Henry VIII: "Longe arrowes like standarts with socetts of stell for my Lord's foutemen to bere in their hands when they ryn with my Lorde." (See C. J. Longman and H. Walrond, *Archery* (Badminton Series), London 1894, p. 130.) Arrows carried as a symbol of office were not uncommon in medieval times. (See Helmut Nickel, 'Ceremonial Arrow-heads from Bohemia', *Metropolitan Museum Journal*, Vol. 1, New York 1968, pp. 61–90.)

BELLY
The side of a bow that faces an archer. It is thus the inner surface of a drawn bow.

BELT QUIVER
A quiver for arrows hung from a belt around the waist (*cf*. BACK QUIVER).

BEND
The distance between the braced bow and its string. Ascham (*qv*) says: "Let your bowe have a good, bigge bende, a shaft-ment and two fingers at the least." In this sense the term is rarely used today and **bracing height** (*qv*) is to be preferred.

BENDER
A lever for spanning (*qv*) a crossbow. Such devices were also known as spanners, but both terms are rarely used today. However, they may be encountered in older writings that relate to this subject.

BENDING BLOCK
A mould for setting a bow limb in a desired curvature. Modern bows are built and clamped on a former to give the desired shape, but the use of such a device continues with certain types, such as the traditional Japanese bow as used in *kyudo* (*qv*).

BEST GOLD
The shot nearest the exact centre of the target in an archery contest. When a special prize is awarded for this achievement the point is marked on each target. There are no fixed rules and the organizers of a tournament are at liberty to restrict the award to a particular distance during a round (*qv*).

BILLET
A rough length of wood from which a bow may be made.

BILSON, Frank Luther (1902–1980)
An eminent archer, author and bowyer, British target champion in 1948, President of the Southern Counties Archery Society, 1952–1962, and for several years a Vice-President of the GNAS (*qv*).

With the yew longbow and wooden

arrows he broke the British record for the single York Round (*qv*) in August 1943, which had been established by Horace Ford (*qv*) 87 years before. He proceeded to break the record on four further occasions, the last being in 1951 with a score of 813.

His work with the paraplegics started in 1948 at Stoke Mandeville and the beneficial exercise was highly praised by the late Sir Ludwig Guttman, Director of the Institute. Archery is now a standard sport in the Paraplegic Games.

A skilled craftsman, he started a business under the name of 'Jack the Yeoman', to design and make modern composite bows, a project that met with success. His activities included crossbows and the design of drugged darts to stun wild animals, which were used successfully by a Cambridge University team, led by Dr R. V. Short, in connection with the Kariba Dam project in 1963, when many animals were trapped by the rising waters.

His published works include: *English Archery* (1947); *Modern Archery* (1949); *Bowmanship* (1965); and *Crossbows* (1974). He wrote a series of articles that appeared in *The British Archer* (magazine) between 1950–1954.

BLACK
The fourth circle of a standard target (*qv*). Under English rules, with a five-zone target, a hit scores three points, while under FITA rules, where each colour is divided into two areas, to give a ten-zone target, the outer area scores three and the inner four points.

BLAZON
A square target that originated in Flanders, divided into fifty squares. The highest scoring area was at the centre, giving 26 points. The next highest areas were at the outer corners. There have been many variations in design and, though rarely met with today, some archery clubs still have a shoot at such a target where an inferior archer can often score more than the best shot. It provides amusement for all and encouragement for beginners.

BLUE
The third circle of a standard target (*qv*). Under English rules, with a five-zone target, a hit scores five points, while under FITA rules, where each colour is divided into two areas, to give a ten-zone target, the outer area scores five and the inner six points. In the latter half of the eighteenth century, the ring had been the 'inner white', but it was later standardized by the Prince Regent as blue (see PRINCE'S LENGTH AND RECKONING).

BLUNT
An arrowhead, usually circular in cross-section with a flat or slightly rounded fore end. It is used for shooting at the popinjay (*qv*) or for hunting birds and small game, which it can kill or stun. In woodland such a head will not embed itself in the branch or trunk of a tree and is therefore easy to recover. Horn is the most common material with a diameter of about ¾ in. or 15 mm.

BOB-TAILED ARROW
A shaft that is thickest adjacent to the head, and tapers toward the nock or tail. It has also been called 'rushgrown' in the past.

This type of arrow is rarely seen today, though it may be noted that many of the shafts recovered from the wreck of the *Mary Rose* are of this form.

BODKIN HEAD
Basically, an iron spike, fitted to the arrow shaft, to give an armour-piercing head. The term was originally applied to the English war arrow and the forms of existing examples in such institutions as the London Museum and the Tower of London Armouries show considerable variations in design. In cross-section they may be round, square, triangular or rhombic-shaped. Their length varies from about 2 inches (5 cm) up to 6 inches (15 cm), including the hollow socket to take the fore end of the wooden shaft, with odd examples in excess of this measurement. No bulk find has been made in Britain to reveal the more common form of the mass-produced article.

Roger Ascham (*qv*) says: "Our Englyshe heades be better in war . . . & I suppose if ye same lytle barbes which they haue, were clene put away, they shuld be far better."

Though many shafts have been recovered from the wreck of the *Mary Rose*, it is unfortunate that all their heads have completely corroded away. Rust marks in the sand suggest some were a little over two inches long. Some were stored in leather discs, punched with holes, and could not have been barbed as this feature would have hindered their withdrawal. Others in boxes or chests could have been fitted with heads of a different form.

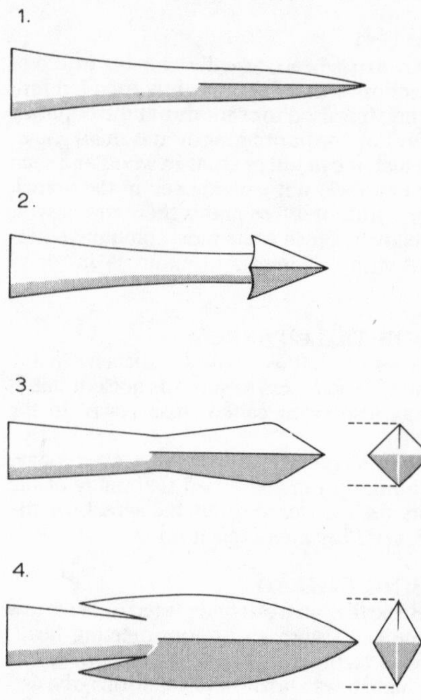

Bodkin heads.

The figure (above) shows four out of many, variations in design. The first is a true bodkin and, while highly effective against mail and other protective covering, the tip can be turned by plate armour, depending on the angle at which it strikes. The second offers a stronger tip and the third even more so, though heavier. It is akin to a form widely used for crossbow bolts. The fourth is an intermediate type, between the bodkin and the broadhead. It endeavoured to take advantage of the merits of both forms.

BOEHM, Hugo, Lt-Col, OBE, TD, JP, DL (b. 1911)
His outstanding ability in the field of organization and administration is reflected by his election as Chairman of the GNAS National Council for the 1956–1958 term of office and as President of that Society from 1958–1961. During that period he also served as Chairman of the GNAS Finance, Shooting and Target Selection Committees as well as being the Director of Shooting at the GNAS International Tournaments from 1957–1975. He was also the Tournament Secretary of the Southern Counties Archery Meeting from 1954–1975.

While many might consider the above duties, which he fulfilled in a most able manner, would be enough for any one man, he was also the Chairman of the Royal Toxophilite Society from 1958–1967, which included a most difficult period when their headquarters was moved from Albion Mews in London to Archers' Lodge in Burnham, and then as Hon. Secretary of that Society since 1967.

BOLT
The principal missile shot by the crossbow (*qv*). The majority of medieval examples are about 12 in. (30 cm) long and they are usually made from semi-hard woods such as beech, birch and chestnut. There are always exceptions, such as those in the Scott Collection, now in Glasgow Museum and Art Gallery, that are 34½ in. (87.6 cm) in length. Those made to carry inflammable material are also longer than average, so that the burning composition, wrapped around the fore end of the shaft, was well clear of the fore end of the tiller.

Most are fitted with vanes to ensure correct flight and these may be made of wood, leather, parchment or feathers, but examples fitted with bone or brass are sometimes found. Some have two vanes only, but three is more common. As many as five have been used. Those with two vanes may have them set at a slight angle on the shaft to make it spin as it flies through the air; this type is known as a *vireton* (from the French, *virer*: to turn). There are also those with no vanes, such as the German *Kronenbolzen* that were used in certain of their popinjay (*qv*) shoots, as well as those used with the Chinese repeating crossbows.

Modern bolts are about 9 to 10 in. long (23 to 26 cm). Regulations do not limit these measurements so the bowman has freedom of choice to select what is best suited to his requirements.

Bolt heads vary considerably. Of the old forms the pyramidical design was most widely used in Europe to pierce armour. Quarrels had a square form with points at the four corners. They were intended to be more difficult for armour to deflect. Broadheads were typically about 2¾ in. wide (70 mm) and many had long tails or barbs. Forked and crescent heads were often favoured in the hunting field, as well as blunt heads for use against small game and birds.

See R. Payne-Gallwey, *The Crossbow*, London, 1903 (reprinted 1958, 1964, 1967 and 1971), pp. 16–19; and Egon Harmuth, *Die Armbrust*, Graz (Austria), 1975, pp. 76–7.

BOSS

The base on which the target face is fixed. Most commonly it is a long and tightly bound bundle of straw, about four inches thick, wound in a coil with each turn stitched to the preceding one.

BOUNCER

An arrow that strikes and rebounds from the target face.

The rules relating to this problem have undergone several changes in recent years. Earlier, the GNAS laid down that an arrow had to be lodged in the target to be scored. However, it was understandably argued that a bouncer was not a fault of the archer, but attributable to the target boss and a factor outside the archer's control. As a result, it was decided that a bouncer would be awarded five points.

The present ruling under GNAS Rule 106 (f) is that, if an arrow is observed to rebound from a target the archer shall draw the attention of the Judge, or Field Captain, to this with a raised bow on the shooting line. After the completion of the end (*qv*) by all archers, and the rebound being confirmed, the archer concerned is permitted to shoot another arrow.

FITA regulations differ and under Art. 508 (h) and (i), unless all arrow holes have been suitably marked on each occasion when arrows are scored and drawn from the target – a normal procedure in major contests under FITA Rules – they cannot be scored. When previous hits have been marked, the archer stands with a raised bow on the shooting line as a signal to the Field Officers, who then inspect the target for any unmarked hole or mark and, if the point of impact can be identified, the appropriate score is awarded.

BOW

Basically, a bow is a simple machine where the potential energy put into it by the archer in drawing the string, relatively slowly, against the resistance of the two flexible limbs, is turned into kinetic energy, when the string is released, giving velocity to the arrow. The efficiency and effectiveness of a bow primarily depends on the resilience of the limbs. To this end various designs have developed in the course of time (see CLASSIFICATION).

FITA (*qv*), in their *Constitution and Rules*, Art. 504, defines the bow as "an instrument consisting of a handle (grip),

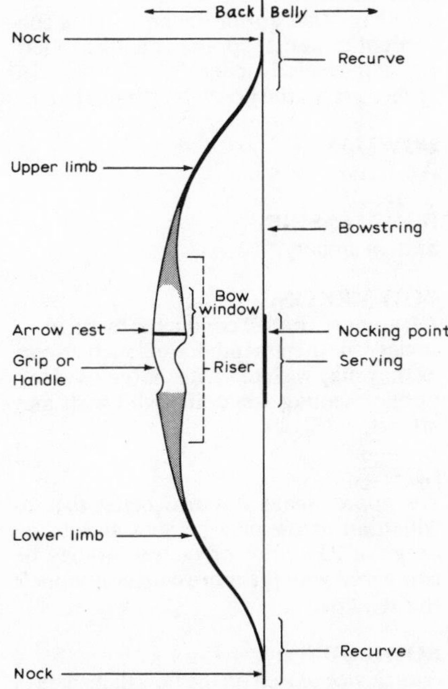

Principal parts of a modern bow. Various fittings may be added, see *BOWSIGHT, KISSER, STABILISER.*

riser and two flexible limbs each ending in a tip with a string nock.

"The Bow is braced for use by a single bowstring attached directly between the two string nocks only, and in operation is held in one hand by its handle (grip) while the fingers of the other hand draw, hold back and release the string."

This precludes the use of the modern compound bow (*qv*) and certain other designs and devices from international competition. (See also COMPOSITE, FLAT and LONGBOW).

BOW CASE
A long tube of material in which a bow can be carried and protected during transit.

In earlier times it might be described as a form of holster in which the strung bow was carried by the horse-archers of the mid-East and Orient and hung from the waist. It was shaped to fit the lower half of the bow, which could be grasped and withdrawn quickly when it was needed.

BOW HAND
The hand that grasps the bow. It is a convenient term that applies equally to a left- or right-handed archer. The right-handed archer grasps the bow with the left hand.

BOWMAN
An archer.

BOWMANSHIP
Skill in archery.

BOW MEETING
An archery contest conducted by a club or society for their members and such visitors as they may wish to invite, as opposed to a public meeting when any who wish may attend.

BOW SHOT
An approximate distance being that to which an arrow may be shot and in the order of 250 yards or metres. It may be compared with the more common 'stone's throw'.

BOWSIGHT
Any device placed on the bow that enables an archer to aim directly at the mark or target.

FITA (*qv*) regulations do not permit the use of a prism or lens, a levelling or electric device for this purpose, but facilities to allow for windage as well as elevation can be incorporated.

Until about 1950 the bowsight was a very simple device, consisting of a mark on the limb of a bow, an elastic band around it or a strip of cork, glued to it, in which a pin could be stuck. The modern sight is relatively elaborate with facilities for both vertical and horizontal settings.

BOW SLING
A strap, usually of leather, attached to the bow, below the grip, and to the wrist of the bow hand. As modern shooting techniques advocate a completely relaxed hold against the grip of the bow to avoid the possibility of any twist being applied at this point, it is possible that the bow could be dropped when shot. This could cause damage to the bow or, what is more likely, disturbance to the bow sight. It is thus a wise precaution to ensure that, if the bow is dropped, it will not strike the ground.

BOW STAVE
A wooden bow without its string. It may be the finished article or a roughly trimmed length from which the bow may be fashioned with added work. The term implies that the bow is not complete in some manner.

BOWSTRING
The string of a bow. It must be thin, light and of considerable strength. When shooting the instantaneous thrust upon it, as it checks the forward movement of the bow's limbs, is about five times the draw weight (*qv*) of that bow.

Various materials were used in the past, such as hemp, flax and silk, as well as gut, sinew and twisted rawhide. Modern strings are from man-made fibres, such as Dacron and kevlar. Some target crossbows use those made from steel wire, which some manufacturers also fit to compound bows (*qv*). Linen thread is still favoured by many for the longbow.

Making bowstrings is not a difficult task and many archers prefer to construct their own, rather than purchase the finished article. There are two basic methods for forming the end loops, which fit in the nocks of the bow tips. These are by *splicing* and by the *endless skein*.

Splicing is the normal method of making the end loop of the string for the longbow. While the common form of eye splice can be used (see Fig. A, also C. J. Longman & H. Walrond, *Archery* (Badminton Series), London 1894, p. 319), the spiral, or twisted, eye splice – also called a sailmaker's splice – is generally considered superior for this purpose.

The first step is to decide how many strands are needed in the string. A popular material for use with the longbow is Barbours No. 40 linen thread, which has a breaking strain of 7 lb. Suppose one is dealing with a bow having a draw weight of 40 lb, one must allow that the thrust on the string will be about 200 lb, as shown in paragraph 1 above, to which a safety margin needs to be added. About one quarter is a reasonable allowance, and the total number of strands should be divisible by three. Thus 36 strands, which should have a breaking strain of 252 lb would suit the task.

The strands are divided into three equal sets, in this case with twelve in each, which are then waxed together. While pure beeswax can be used, a better mixture can be achieved by melting it and adding one-third of resin. The length of the individual strands should be one foot longer than the bow, measured from nock to nock. The surplus can always be cut off, but it is better to have the string a little too long than to find it is too short when finished.

Initially, one foot of each set is waxed and, starting eight inches from the end, the three sets are laid together in the manner of a cord, by twisting to the left and laying to the right (Fig. B) for a distance of about three inches.

Some favour laying in a few extra strands in this section. This is achieved by taking the equivalent of one set – in this case twelve – dividing it into three parts, each two inches long, but slightly staggered to cover about 3½ inches, and waxing these into the sections laid together. This method offers a little added strength to an area where eventual breakage is liable to occur.

One is then left with about five inches of three separate strands at the end of the string, which are then laid in pairs with their opposite strands in the main body of the string (Fig. C).

So far, all strands have been laid 'right-handed'. The three pairs that have now resulted must then be laid together 'left-handed', by twisting to the right and laying to the left.

After about two inches, the end strands should start being thinned out as laying continues. This gives a pleasing and tapered effect to the form of the end loop.

The three sections of the main string, with even tension on each, are then twisted together, while holding the bottom ends. About twelve complete turns, 'left-handed', should be adequate. It is important that the tension on each strand of the finished string should be equal.

For the longbow the lower end of the string is secured in the nock by a timber hitch (Fig. D). For this purpose the bottom eight inches of the main string should be laid together in rope-form, which should be left-handed to follow the twist in the main body of the string.

To determine where this should start, the end loop, already formed, should be slipped over the upper end of the bow and slid down the limb so that the loop is about four inches below the upper nock. At the lower end a point should be marked two inches above the lower nock, where the laying should start.

It helps to pre-stretch the string, by securing a heavy weight to the end and hanging it up by the end loop. While so hanging the main length of the string should be waxed and this action will help to remove the initial stretch. With linen thread this is less than half an inch, but a little more will be found if Dacron is used.

For the **endless skein** a stringboard (*qv*) is needed. Basically, this consists of two pillars, or hooks, the appropriate distance apart, around which the thread is wound to give the number of strands needed. This method is superior to that described above when loops are needed at either end of the completed string, which is the form of fitting required by modern target bows.

After the skein has been formed, the opposite centre sections are individually whipped with thread for a distance of about three inches. The skein is then rotated around the pillars, or hooks, so that the whipped sections are around them. The ends are then whipped together and thus form the two end loops (Fig. E).

The most difficult problem that faces the string-maker is the distance between the pillars, or hooks, in relation to the bow concerned. Dacron, though relatively long-lasting, suffers from an appreciable amount of initial stretch, so the string needs to be constructed an inch or so shorter than the desired final length. At least a dozen arrows need to be shot from a bow with a new string to remove the stretch during which time the brace height (*qv*) must be closely watched until it settles

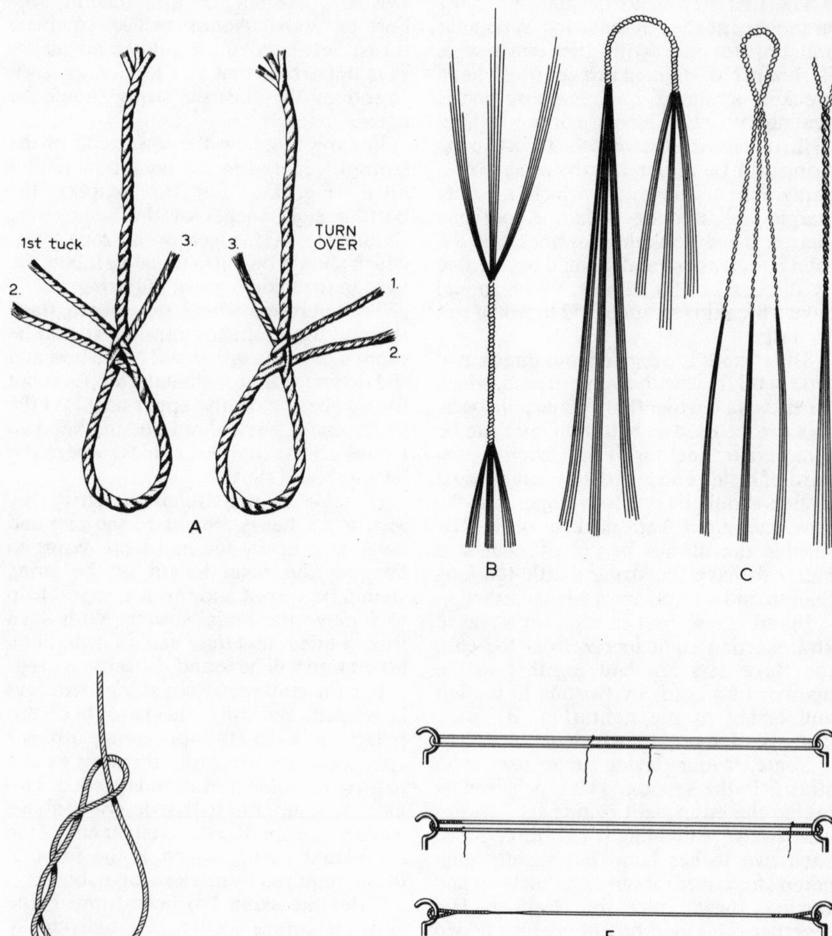

Bowstring loops.

down. Minor adjustments can be made by the number of twists in the main body of the string.

Kevlar, a carbonized fibre, has a shorter life but virtually no stretch. The setting of the distance between the hooks, or pillars, of the stringboard must therefore be adjusted to suit the material to be used.

It is important that once it has settled to the bow a string should have no stretch. For this reason past attempts to use Terylene and nylon have been failures.

A reason for experimenting with new threads is that a heavy bowstring detracts from the efficiency of the bow. A light string adds to its performance. In this respect, Dacron is superior to linen and kevlar is superior to Dacron. Other fibres will doubtless appear in time.

Finally, whatever the material, the centre section of the string requires serving (*qv*) and the nocking point (*qv*) adjusted to suit the arrows to be used. The whole string should be kept well waxed.

BOW WINDOW
With the modern bow it is the area above the grip that is recessed a little beyond the centre-line of the limbs and extends for about 6 in. (15 cm) above the arrow rest (*qv*). The object is to enable the arrow to travel through the vertical mid-line of the bow when it is shot. This design feature offers added accuracy in shooting above that of the older and traditional forms of bow, such as the longbow (*qv*), where the shaft is displaced from the centre-line by half the width of the limb.

BOWYER
A maker of bows. The Worshipful Company of Bowyers still exists in the City of London, mainly as a charitable organization, and their history goes back to the fourteenth century. They still support an annual shoot held by the Royal Toxophilite Society (*qv*).

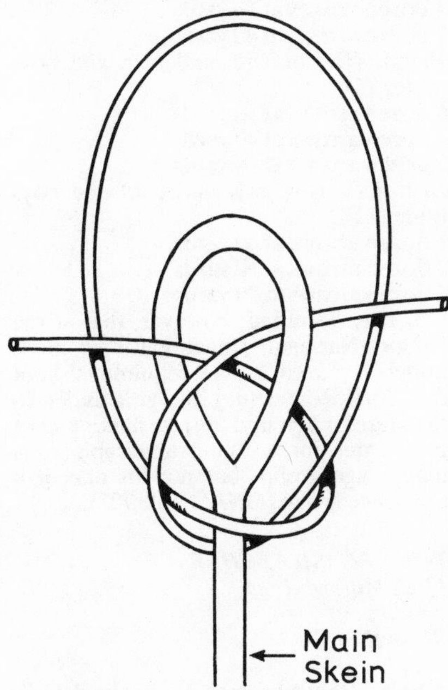

Bowyer's knot.

BOWYER'S KNOT
This title appears to have been given by Robert P. Elmer (*qv*) to the method of knotting a separate length of material to the main skein of certain oriental bowstrings. It provided the loop that fitted in the nocks of their bows. The term cannot be commended as it has no direct connection with the making of bows. It is better called an oriental bowstring loop knot.

BRACE
To flex a bow to fit the string. This is not always a simple matter and needs a degree of adroitness. Different types of bow require to be handled in different manners. Incorrect handling can result in damage or distortion to the bow.

The safest method is to use two padded pegs set in a wall or a board. The grip is placed against one peg and the end of the lower limb is hooked under the other. Pressure can then be applied to the end of the upper limb until the bow is sufficiently flexed for the upper loop of the bowstring to be slipped into the nock of the bow. This facility is rarely available, but can be found in the shops of some equipment dealers and in some club houses.

The next recommended method is by the use of a **bowstringer**. This consists of an auxiliary string that fits slackly between the tips of a bow. With the bow held horizontally at about knee height, it is long enough to allow the foot to be placed on it where it rests on the ground. The bow is then pulled upward by the grip to flex its limbs.

The most common method is to place the lower tip of the bow against the instep of the foot. While one hand pulls the grip of the bow, the other presses down on the upper limb while pushing the string loop upward toward the nock of the bow.

Another method which may be seen, but not generally recommended by manufacturers due to the chance of distorting the limbs, is the *step inside* method. One leg is placed between the belly of the grip and the slack string, so that the grip is against the back of the thigh. The back of the lower recurve of the bottom limb is set against the front of the ankle, or lower part of the shin, of the opposite leg. The end of the upper limb may then be pressed forward until the string loop can be set in the upper nock.

BRACER
A guard on the arm to protect the wrist against the slap of the bowstring. It is often called an armguard. The blow can be

severe and it is unwise for any archer to shoot without this protection. They are usually made of leather or plastic material. A few rare and old examples are made from ivory and the Tower of London Armouries has one made from tortoise-shell, with silver fittings, in its collection.

BRACING BOARD
A wooden board with padded pegs to assist the bracing of a recurved bow. The lower peg is placed against the lower curved section and the upper is against the grip or handle. The hand then draws back the upper limb until the bow is sufficiently flexed for the bowstring to be placed in the nocks. Its use virtually eliminates possible distortion to the bow limbs due to incorrect pressures being applied.

BRACING HEIGHT (or BRACE HEIGHT)
The distance between the bow and the string after it is braced. It normally varies between about 6 in. (15 cm) and 8 in. (20 cm), depending on the design of the bow. It is a factor that the archer needs to watch closely, particularly when a new string is fitted that may be subject to stretch and thus result in the lowering of the brace height. This change will affect the discharge of the arrow and the accuracy of the shot.

Incorrectly, the term 'fistmele' (*qv*) has been used to mean 'brace height' by certain authors, but this is a specific measure that may, or may not, apply to the bow in question.

BRAGANZA SHIELD
A small, but elegant, silver shield, subscribed for by members of the Finsbury Archers and entrusted to Sir William Wood, Marshal to the Regiment of Archers, in 1676. It was dedicated to Catherine of Braganza, Queen to Charles II. After Sir William's death in 1691, it was passed to succeeding Marshals until 1736. It now belongs to the Royal Toxophilite Society (*qv*), but it is on permanent loan to the Victoria and Albert Museum in London, where it is on display in the Department of Metalwork. (See E. G. Heath, *A History of Target Archery*, 1973, pp. 55–6 and pl. 6.)

BREAST
The area of the arrow shaft forward of the feathers and about six to nine inches from the nock.

BREASTED ARROW
An arrow shaft, tapered toward nock and head, that is thickest at the breast (*cf.* BARRELLED ARROW).

BRISTOL ROUNDS
Several rounds (*qv*) have been devised, suited to the junior archer (i.e. under 18 years of age) and approved by the GNAS (*qv*). A standard 4-ft target is used.
Bristol I (for boys under 18 years of age)
6 dozen arrows at 80 yards
4 dozen arrows at 60 yards
2 dozen arrows at 50 yards
Bristol II (for girls under 18 and boys under 16)
6 dozen arrows at 60 yards
4 dozen arrows at 50 yards
2 dozen arrows at 40 yards
Bristol III (for girls under 16 and boys under 14)
6 dozen arrows at 50 yards
4 dozen arrows at 40 yards
2 dozen arrows at 30 yards
Bristol IV (for girls under 13 and boys under 12)
6 dozen arrows at 40 yards
4 dozen arrows at 30 yards
2 dozen arrows at 20 yards

It may be noted, however, that at the Junior National Championships, boys under 18 years of age are required to shoot the York Round (*qv*) and girls under 18 the Hereford Round (*qv*). A junior archer may enter for a round applicable to a higher age group, but not for one of a lower age group (GNAS Rule 702).

THE BRITISH ARCHER
43/45 Milford Road,
Reading,
Berks RG1 8LG

A bi-monthly magazine, started by Patrick Clover (*qv*) in 1949 as a successor to *Archery News*. He edited this national archery magazine until 1976, when it passed to other hands. Its publication continues.

Without regular news being widely circulated among enthusiasts, the sport might well have died. This magazine has greatly encouraged and stimulated interest over many years.

BRITISH CROSSBOW SOCIETY
Founded in 1964 to organize and promote the use of modern crossbows in target and field shooting events, it went into decline and ceased to operate effectively after 1978. Its objects were taken over by the National Affiliated Society of Crossbowmen (*qv*) in 1980, but the original Society was re-formed in 1981.

BROADHEAD
Usually a triangular or leaf-shaped form of arrowhead with a cutting edge. It dates back to the Stone Age for both hunting and warfare, but the first serious study to find the best design for use against larger game, such as bear and deer, was made in the USA by Dr Saxton Pope (*qv*) during the second decade of the present century. The figure (overleaf) shows one of his recommended designs.

Forrest Nagler (*qv*) investigated the problem from his engineering knowledge. He suggested in *Archery Review*, Feb. 1933: "The overhang or unsupported tip should not be over one inch long; the thickness not less than .050″, if only of mild spring temper and not less than .035″ if of quite hard material. The width should not be over 1 1/8″ for heavy game.

"A length of 2″ is sufficient and the weight need not exceed 90 grains. The ferrule should be 1″ in length, since a long ferrule tends to break the shaft at the shoulder. Barbs are of little value and the points of the overhang should be cut off.

" . . . The ferrule should be taper bored to nearly a feather edge at 11/32″ diameter rear end, so as to avoid any shoulder on the shaft."

For more than twenty years Roy Case supplied hunters with a popular and successful design, made from surgical steel, and mounted in a slotted bullet jacket, secured by solder, as opposed to the use of a short length of steel tube, flattened and filed down at one end and secured with a rivet. The rear end of the blade was recessed to fit against the sides of the jacket, thus preventing any lateral movement of the head in relation to the socket.

A long, slim triangular pattern was developed by Howard Hill (*qv*) and successfully used both by him and Bob Swineheart against the largest game, including elephant and rhinoceros. (See Howard Hill, *Hunting the Hard Way*, Chicago 1953, pp. 120-1; and Bob Swineheart, *Sagittarius*, Covina, California 1970, pp. 92–3.)

Many different designs have appeared, including forms with three or four cutting edges. Slimmer broadheads are used against small game.

It should be noted that hunting with the bow is not legal in the UK, though there is no restriction in most other parts of the world. In the USA extended seasons are allowed in many states for the bow hunter.

BULLET CROSSBOW
A variety of stone bow (*qv*), designed to shoot a spherical lead bullet. It would appear to have originated in Germany at least as early as the second half of the sixteenth century, where it was known as the *Kugelschnepper*.

This type of crossbow has a steel lath, or bow, and a double string with crosstrees, or spreaders. There is a cradle of woven cord, or leather, at the centre to hold the missile. The tiller, or stock, contains a hinged lever, to which the mechanism is attached. When released and brought forward, the tumbler engages the loop at the centre of the string and the bow may then be spanned by forcing the lever backwards until its rear engages in a clip.

The bullet crossbow enjoyed a popularity in England from the last quarter of the eighteenth century until the mid-nineteenth century. Earlier forms had a straight stock that terminated in a flattened ball, while the later examples had a gun butt. They are equipped with both fore and rear sights and they are effective against small game up to about sixty yards – or metres. They had the advantage of relative silence when shooting, as compared with the gun.

The largest collection in the UK is that in Manchester Museum.

(See A. G. Credland, 'The Bullet Crossbow in Britain', *Journal of the Society of Archer-Antiquaries*, Vol. 15, 1972, pp. 22–36.)

BUTT
A mound of earth or stacked turves against which a shooting mark, or target, is placed. It was widely used from the Middle Ages onward and only gradually disappeared from normal use during the

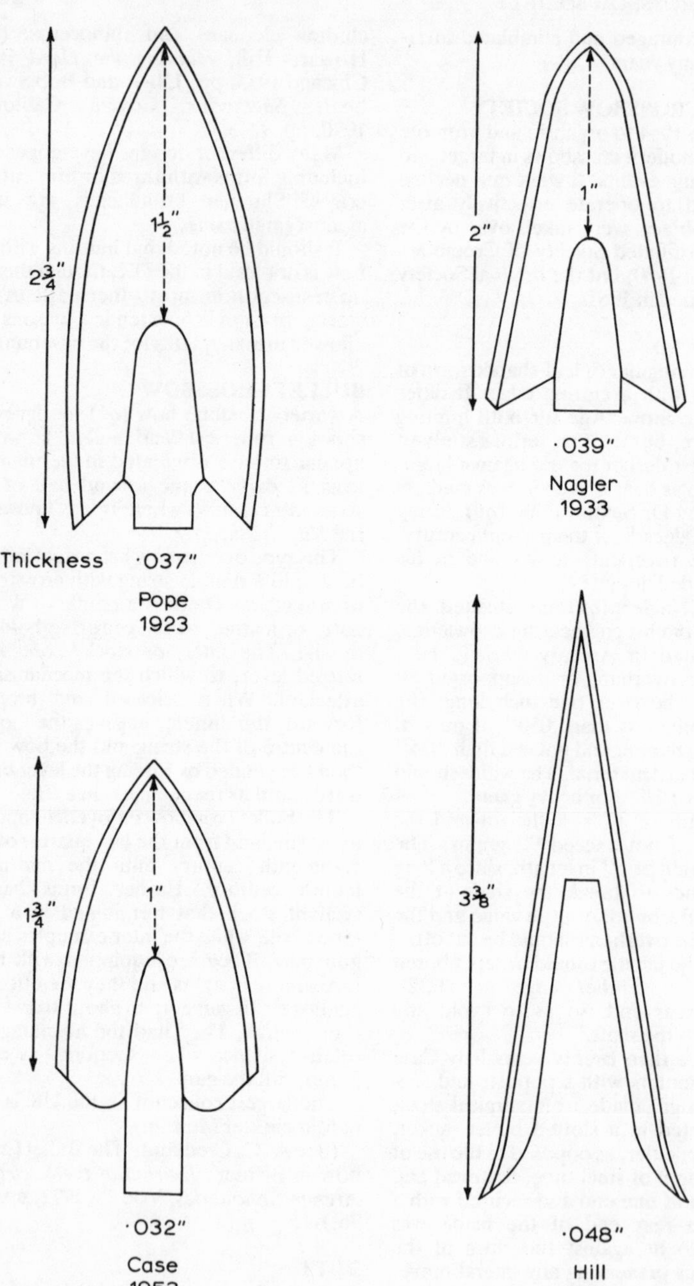

Examples of some of the earlier broadheads developed in the USA. All shown are actual size and have a maximum width of 1 1/8".

latter half of the nineteenth century with the introduction of the straw target boss. The term is also applied to a similar structure of straw bales, which are still used.

The term, **shooting at the butts**, is self-explanatory.

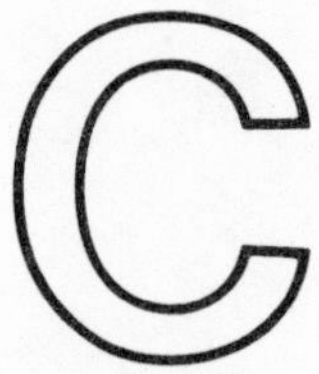

CAPTAIN OF NUMBERS
The archer who achieves the highest score in a contest. The term is scarcely used today, but it was not uncommon in the last century and some old medals are inscribed with this term.

CAPTAIN OF TARGETS
The archer who achieves the highest average score during a year. The term is little used today but some organizations, such as the Royal Toxophilite Society (*qv*), still make this award.

CARRIAGE BOW
A bow, jointed at the centre, so that it may be taken in two parts, thus making it easier to transport and carry to and from the shooting ground. (*cf.* TAKE DOWN BOW.)

CAST (*v.* and *n.*)
1. The ability of a bow to discharge an arrow in terms of velocity.
2. A twist, or warp, in the limbs of a bow.

CENTRE-SHOT BOW
Traditional bows, such as the longbow (*qv*), displace the arrow by half their thickness from the centre-line. Research has shown that if the upper limb of a bow, above the grip, is cut away to reduce this displacement, superior results can be achieved. The majority of modern bows are made in this manner. (See BOW WINDOW.)

For flight shooting (*qv*), modern designs of bow often include a hole through the centre of the upper limb of the bow and through which the arrow is shot.

CHAMPIONSHIPS
The following lists of champion target archers will be found in Appendix 2.

Olympic Champions
World Champions
British Champions
US Champions
European Champions

CHESTED ARROW
An alternative term for the breasted arrow (*qv*).

CHRYSAL
A line, somewhat akin to a crack in appearance, across the belly of a wooden bow. This is caused by wood fibres collapsing under pressure. If unattended it is likely that the limb will break at this point in due course. Longbows should be checked regularly in case this defect occurs, as early attention by a skilled craftsman is needed to preserve the bow.

CLASSIFICATION OF ARCHERS
Under GNAS Rules, Part IX, the use of the classification scheme is optional and its administration is in the hands of Club officials. Three rounds must be shot at approved meetings, within a calendar year, to qualify, except for the two highest categories of Grand Master and Master Bowman. These require four rounds to be shot which must include both FITA and the traditional English York and Hereford Rounds. (See GNAS Rules of Shooting, Appendix 1, page 184–6, for qualifying scores.)

Classifications are also awarded to juniors and for field shooting, flight shooting and crossbow shooting. The set standards may be seen by reference to the appropriate GNAS Rules, Appendix 1.

CLASSIFICATION OF BOWS
There is no fully accepted terminology. Attempts were made by C. J. Longman and H. Walrond in *Archery* (Badminton Series), London 1894, p. 27 and by O. T.

Mason in *North American Bows, Arrows and Quivers* (The Smithsonian Report for 1893), Washington 1894, p. 638, but their proposals are not entirely satisfactory.

The terminology used in this present work relates to the basic construction of bows:

a) **Simple**: bows made from a single material. This includes 'self' wooden bows, made from one length of wood, such as many English longbows, 'native' bows and modern glass fibre bows. Some bows are jointed, or spliced at their centre. Longbows are often made in this manner as well as south-east Asian horn bows.

b) **Backed**: bows using two layers, which may be of similar or dissimilar materials. Thus, a wooden bow may be backed (*qv*) with a different wood or with sinew or rawhide, to add to its performance. Backing may be 'close' or 'free'.

c) **Compound**: bows using three or more layers. This includes *laminated* construction, used with some longbows and, for example, the traditional Japanese bows whose main limbs have seven sections of wood and bamboo. There is the *composite* bow of three layers of dissimilar materials. The traditional composites employed horn and sinew on a wooden core, while the modern composites, also on a wooden core, use layers of plastic-reinforced glass fibre, or carbon fibre.

It must be noted that the modern so-called 'compound' bow (*qv*) is a composite, with added pulley wheels.

CLICKER (or Klicker)
A spring fitted in the bow window (*qv*) as a check on the archer's draw of the arrow. The arrow is placed between the spring and the body of the riser. When fully drawn, the pile of the arrowhead comes clear of the spring and a click is heard as it strikes the riser. Its object is to ensure that the arrow is fully drawn before release. Its use is permitted by international regulations.

CLOCKING (of arrows)
Those who favour the longbow and the use of wooden arrows are faced with a problem that, however carefully made, a set of wooden shafts are rarely similar when compared with metal alloy shafts.

The archer therefore needs to shoot the wooden shafts, repeatedly, at a target to assess any variation in their performance. Each arrow is numbered and its point of impact recorded. Thus each one may have to be aimed slightly differently in relation to the centre of the target. The process of determining these differences is termed 'clocking'.

CLOSE BACKING
See BACKING.

CLOTHYARD
The term 'clothyard shaft' is not uncommon in old records. Initially a merchant would measure cloth by taking the end of the roll and extending it to the length of his arm from the centre of his lips. This length naturally varied, depending on the stature of the individual concerned. While it is now equated with the statute yard of 36 inches, one may note that according to Acts 3 & 4, Edward VI, c.2, "cloth was to bee meten and measured by the yard, adding to every yard one inch of the rule."

There is, therefore, a degree of vagueness regarding the term and what it meant at a particular time. Shafts recovered from the *Mary Rose*, which sank in 1545, average about 30½ in. (77.5 cm) from the nock to the start of the taper that fitted in the socket of the head.

Specifications for the length of medieval war arrows is sadly lacking, but one may see in the Statute Rolls of Ireland (5 Edward IV, c.4) of 1465 that the King's subjects were required to have twelve shafts of three-quarters of the standard. It is suggested that the 'standard' referred to the English ell of 45 in., giving an arrow length of 33¾ in., presumably with the head, which would have been 3¼ in. long. This is not untypical for bodkin heads of that period, as may be seen, for instance, in collections such as those of the Museum of London.

CLOUT
Originally a piece of cloth, pegged to the ground at distances up to 12 score yards to exercise archers in long-range shooting. It is now a small circular straw target, with a white face, about 18 inches in diameter, that marks the centre of the target area. A small, light coloured flag may be used instead.

In **clout shooting** arrows have to be shot with a high trajectory to fall into a target area, marked by rings on the ground.

Under GNAS rules the radii of the rings are 18 inches, 3 feet, 6 feet, 9 feet and 12 feet. Within each ring the scores are 5, 4, 3, 2 and 1 point. Men shoot from 8 to 10 score yards, women from 6 to 8 score and a Clout Round consists of 36 arrows.

Under FITA regulations for international use, the Clout Round consists of 36 arrows shot at 165 metres for men and 125 metres for women. The circular target area is 15 metres in diameter and the centre is marked with a white triangular flag. It is divided into five equal zones with scores from 5 points to 1, as in the GNAS rules mentioned above.

In Britain the two leading exponents of this form of archery, using longbows and wooden arrows, are the Royal Company of Archers (*qv*) in Edinburgh and the Woodmen of Arden (*qv*).

CLOVER, Patrick (1911–1982)

After reading the classic work by Saxton T. Pope, *Hunting with the Bow and Arrow* (San Francisco 1923, reprinted 1925, 1928, 1930 and 1947) in 1944, Clover became interested in the art, obtained some simple bows and arrows and, with a few friends, founded the Portsdown Archery Club the next year. It was the first such club to be formed after the Second World War and it produced several British Champions in its earlier years.

In 1949 he started a noteworthy magazine, *The British Archer*, which he edited successfully for 27 years until 1976. Its publication still continues, but in other capable hands.

His efforts greatly stimulated the sport within Britain and he played a major part in the resurgence of the sport in this country by providing news to scattered clubs and a forum for the exchange of information and discussion.

He wrote extensively on the subject, which is amplified by the 42 entries under his name in F. Lake and H. Wright, *Bibliography of Archery* (see *Acknowledgements*). This included the production of *The Bowman's Handbook* in 1953, with further editions, successively enlarged, in 1954, 1955, 1957 and 1968.

COCK FEATHER

The feather that stands at right angles to the nock of western arrows, as opposed to the eastern arrow, where it was usually in line with the nock.

The longbow was normally loaded with the bow being held horizontally, except in the press of battle where space might not permit this action. It was thus the feather that was 'cocked upward' when the arrow was fitted to the string and it was – and still is – often of a distinctive colour. This enabled the remaining two *shaft* feathers to run evenly past the bow when the arrow was shot. The majority of arrows have three feathers.

This unfortunately led to certain authors in the USA to use the term 'hen feathers' for the shaft feathers, which their countryman, Robert P. Elmer, rightly slates in his valued work, *Target Archery*, New York 1946.

COLUMBIA ROUND

See under ROUND.

COMPOSITE BOW

A bow whose limbs are composed of three or more layers of *dissimilar* materials. The design appears to have originated in central Asia and the earliest depiction is on the stele of Naram Sin, in the Louvre Museum, dated around 2500 BC. It was widely used throughout the East from Korea to Turkey. It had a wooden core that provided the frame and basic shape of the bow. The back was coated with up to three layers of shredded sinew from either the Achilles' or the dorsal tendon of cattle, deer or horses and bonded to the core with glue. The belly, or face, of the bow was lined with horn to withstand compression as the bow was drawn. The design was flexible and efficient and enabled relatively short bows to be made that were well suited to the mounted archers of history.

The modern composite consists of a wooden core, for which Canadian maple is most favoured, between two layers of plastic-reinforced glass fibre. More recently, some designs are using carbon fibres for this purpose.

COMPOUND BOW

This term has two different meanings. For over a century it has been used to describe bows of complex construction (see, for instance, O. T. Mason, *North American Bows, Arrows and Quivers*, from the Smithsonian Report for 1893 where, on page 635, the COMPOUND BOW is defined as one "made of two or more pieces of wood, bone, antler, horn, or whalebone lashed or riveted or spliced together".)

The *modern* COMPOUND BOW has two flexible limbs, fitted with pulley wheels, and the bowstring is not attached to the tips of the bow. It offers several technical advantages as described below. The construction of the limbs is more simple than that of the recurved bows and, for a given effort, it discharges the arrow at a higher velocity.

Since it was first made available to archers in the late 1960s, it has found favour with many and several national archery rules and regulations allow its use under certain restrictions. As matters now stand, FITA Regulations, Art. 504 (a), require that the bowstring shall be directly attached between the two tips of the bow. The use of the modern compound bow is therefore not accepted for international contests.

The reason behind this would appear to be that because an instrument may eject an arrow, it does not mean it is a bow by definition. Arrows have been shot from muskets and from catapults or slingshots, as well as from other devices.

It may be noted that a designer submitted to a FITA committee at Interlaken in 1975 what might be described as two models of the Eiffel Tower, mounted base to base at either end of a central riser (*qv*), fitted with pulley wheels at either end. The motive power came from two coil springs, mounted within the 'tower' structure and whose tension could be adjusted. While not denying the ingenuity of the construction, the committee decided it was not a bow.

Regardless of the eminence of Tom Jennings in the production of the compound bow, the credit for the original concept and design rests with H. W. Allen of Kansas City, Missouri. This is supported by the grant of the United States Patent Office, filed 23 June, 1966, under patent no. 3,486,495, dated 30 December, 1969.

While legislation always takes time, the earliest announcement of this development in archery publications would appear to be that of Martin Haynes, 'Rigors for Riggers', *Bow & Arrow*, Covina, California, Nov–Dec 1967, page 72.

Discussion will doubtless continue on what constitutes a bow and what may be an arrow projector, but the increased interest and use of the *modern* compound bow cannot be denied.

In considering the bow as a machine, where the potential energy (PE) provided by the archer in drawing the string, is transformed into kinetic energy (KE) in giving the arrow velocity, certain conclusions result.

The stored energy in a drawn bow can be determined by the Force-Draw Curve (*qv*) where the area under the curve shows the amount. When a bow is shot it must expend energy in carrying forward its own limbs and the string. This is a loss that shows in terms of a reduction in the discharge velocity of the arrow. This latter factor is of great importance in target shooting. Modern design has endeavoured to produce bows that will give the arrow an increased velocity in relation to the maximum effort that an archer can exert in drawing the bow. This effort is limited as in most major contests 288 arrows need to be shot, which is a considerable physical task. The hunter may have a powerful bow under full control for a few shots, but if this equipment was used in a lengthy target contest, a marked drop in accuracy would occur as it proceeded due to fatigue.

Until the so-called *compound bow* appeared, improvement in discharge velocity was achieved by two means. First, the use of more resilient materials in the bow limbs and second, by curving the bow tips into *working recurves* (*qv*), which improved the force-draw curve and thus enabled greater energy to be stored for a given physical effort.

If one considers a simple bow with straight limbs, after it has been drawn and the string loosed, they accelerate forward and carry the string to which the arrow is nocked, until brought to rest. The centre of the string has to travel, very roughly, twice as far as the tips of the bow and must therefore move at about double the speed of the tips. The bending action of the working recurve adds to the rate of recovery of the tips and in this way to the velocity imparted to the arrow via the string, giving added efficiency and performance.

With the compound bow, not only are the tips carrying the string forward, but the action of the pulley wheels shortens the length of the string between the ends of the bow. An appreciable increase in the

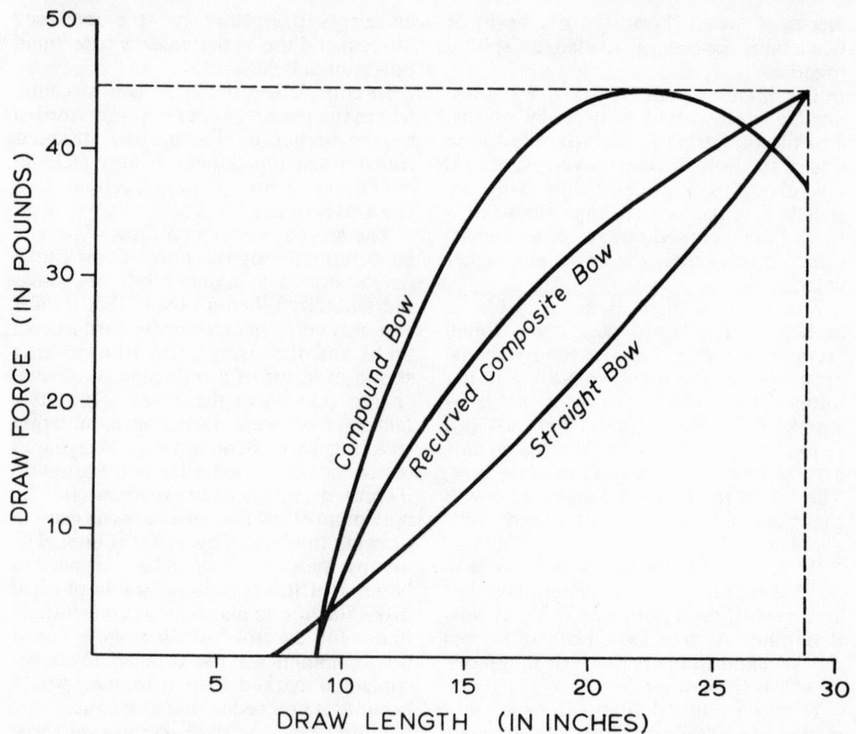

Simplified force-draw curves to illustrate the energy stored by different types of bow.

discharge velocity of the arrow is the result.

Another advantage of the compound bow is that it stores greater energy for eventual transfer to the arrow, as shown by its force-draw curve (see diagram). This curve is of special interest in that the draw weight of the bow reaches a peak before the arrow is fully drawn and thus eases the strain upon the archer during the hold (*qv*) while final aim is taken and the archer steadies before the loose (*qv*). For a given maximum effort in drawing the bow, the added velocity imparted to the arrow gives a lower point of aim at all target ranges. Alternatively, the archer can use a weaker bow to produce the same performance as regards arrow flight, thus reducing fatigue.

The higher arrow velocity, giving a lower time of flight to the target, reduces the effect of wind and weather and less allowance is needed to compensate for this.

A special class for the compound bow has been introduced into many major archery contests in recent years, though the users are not eligible for the main prizes. If and when its use may be permitted in international championships is a matter of interesting conjecture. There can be no doubt that the compound bow is here to stay.

It is now being constructed by several makers of bows and there are variations in design. Some have only one pulley wheel associated with each limb, while others have two, or even three. The use of eccentric wheels to enhance the effects is a refinement that is now generally employed.

While 'normal' target bows have their strings removed after use, to preserve their elasticity, compound bows are usually kept strung and use fine, stranded, stainless steel cables for this purpose.

CONTROL OF SHOOTING

There are minor differences between the

rules laid down by the GNAS and by FITA, mainly due to their respective organization of officials and the strict time control exercised under FITA's regulations. (See Appendix 1; page 164; for GNAS Rule 105 (a) to (n); also page 141, for FITA Article 505 (a) to (j).)

CRADLE
A small pocket, or pouch, fitted between the two parts of a double bowstring to hold the missile of a stone or pellet bow (*qv*).

CREEP
A slight edging forward of a fully drawn arrow immediately before the loose, normally considered to be a fault. It is due to a fractional loss of tension in the shoulder muscles during the hold (*qv*) while taking final aim. It causes the arrow to drop low on the target, compared with where it would hit if the full draw had been maintained.

Some successful archers may be observed to ease fractionally at this stage. Provided that this easement is slight and absolutely regular, accurate shooting is maintained, but Ascham's dictum that "good mennes faultes are not to be folowed" must be remembered.

CRESTING
Coloured bands painted around the breast of an arrow shaft as a means of identification. Its use is optional but under FITA Regulations, Art. 504 (f), revised in 1979, "The Arrows of each archer shall be marked with the archer's name, initials or insignia and all Arrows used for the same end of 3 or 6 arrows shall carry the same pattern and colour(s) of fletching, nocks, and cresting, if any."

The earlier practice for archers to adopt an individual design has been generally discontinued and that selected by the manufacturer to decorate a matched set is accepted.

CROSSBOW
A weapon formed by fastening a bow at right angles in a stock or tiller. The stock or tiller is fitted with a mechanism to hold the drawn string and then release it when a trigger is actuated.

For modern use, designs vary widely. There is no agreed international standard. They vary from societies who continue to use old, traditional designs, to those who make use of the latest techniques. The most sophisticated is the Swiss target crossbow, which the International Armbrust Union (IAU) (*qv*) is endeavouring to establish as a standard. At this time (1982) they have a following in fifteen countries.

The crossbow has a long history and those interested in this aspect should consult R. Payne-Gallwey, *The Crossbow*, London 1903, reprinted 1958, 1964, 1967 and 1971, and the 'International Crossbow Bibliography', by Sarah Bailey (Librarian of the Armouries, H. M. Tower of London), published by the Swiss Institute of Arms and Armour in *Rapport*, Vol. 3 & 4, Grandson (Switzerland) 1979, pp. 105–16. In contrast to the IAU design of match crossbow, a form for target shooting that is popular in both Britain and the USA is covered by Frank Bilson (*qv*), *Crossbows*, Newton Abbot 1974.

Background
Accuracy in shooting missiles in all their varied forms appeals to many. One may cite the establishment of many rifle clubs, whose members achieve satisfaction from the high precision offered by modern firearms. In the field of archery, the hand bow presents the greater challenge as it is more susceptible to human error. The crossbow, with its fixed length of draw and mechanical release, eliminates two of the major problems that face those who use the hand bow. The crossbow is inherently the more accurate weapon and, though smaller targets are employed at shorter ranges, it taxes the skill and art of those who favour its use.

Development
In Britain the main development must be credited to Frank Bilson (*qv*). As an enterprising designer of earlier composite bows (*qv*), his interest in the crossbow was stimulated by Dr R. V. Short of Cambridge University, Department of Veterinary Sciences, in his concern for animals trapped by the floods caused by the Kariba Dam project, completed in 1963. A drugged dart was needed to knock out animals, so that they could be transported to safe areas (see DRUGGED DARTS). He designed a crossbow for this purpose, which had considerable success. It appealed to those interested in this aspect of archery and it proved to be an effective target weapon.

Design
The bow lath, often called a 'prod' (*qv*), was about 32 inches in length and of modern composite design, employing plastic-reinforced glass fibre to face and back a wooden core. Frank Bilson did not favour the metal lath, whether of steel or aluminium alloy, which can break with repeated flexing and possibly injure the user. Metal laths should always be strongly bound with adhesive tape as a precaution.

The stock or tiller was about three feet in length, with the rear end akin to a gun butt. The bolt groove along the top surface had a central slot so that a shaft carrying three feathers at a hundred and twenty degrees could be set with one vane downward and be shot without damage.

Other makers have followed this basic design as well as introducing modifications and improvements as experience has been gained.

Mounting the bow in the stock needs care, as the string should only lightly touch the top surface at the end of its travel, or the velocity imparted to the bolt will be reduced.

The Latch or Lock (*qv*) which retains the drawn string and its trigger mechanism vary in design. Complete assemblies for mounting in a wooden stock can be obtained from suppliers of equipment.

Modern designs and mechanisms are well illustrated by the eminent authority on this subject in the USA, George M. Stevens, *Crossbows* (Desert Publications, Cornville, Arizona, 1980).

CROSSBOW ARCHERY DEVELOPMENT ASSOCIATION (CADA)
Founded in December, 1981, with the object of bringing together organizations and individuals interested in target shooting with the modern forms of crossbow, CADA has already played a significant role in the development of this sport. The association issues bi-monthly newsletters to members, with contributors and subscribers from many countries.

At the first World Championship, organized by the Finnish Archery Association at Mikkeli, the CADA team gained the bronze medal for Great Britain.

CROWN CLOD
An ornament of turf, usually urn-shaped, surmounting an archery butt (*qv*). As the butt is rarely seen today, the crown clod has disappeared, though it may sometimes be shown in old archery prints and paintings.

CRYSAL
See CHRYSAL.

CUT FEATHERS
A feather whose base is cut from the quill, as opposed to a stripped feather where the web is torn from the base. The latter offers an inferior form of fletching.

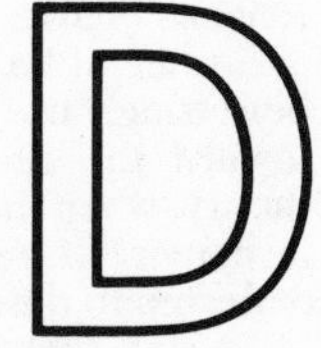

DAMP SAP
A greyish line between the heart and sapwood of yew (*qv*). Normally it is only a minor defect and a satisfactory bow can still be made from a stave where this appears.

DEAD LOOSE
A loose where the fingers of the shaft hand are relaxed gradually to free the bowstring. Though there is a slight loss of tension in the bow and a fractional reduction in the discharge velocity of the arrow, it has been favoured by several successful archers as being easier to perform with regular uniformity than its opposite, the *sharp* loose (*qv*). (See also LOOSE.)

DEAD SHAFT
An arrow that flies in a lifeless manner. It mainly applies to some wooden shafts that may appear to have adequate stiffness to stand in a bow, but lack resilience due to certain characteristics in the wooden section from which they are made. Such a shaft tends to drop short of the target.

Ascham (*qv*) remarks: ". . . Brasell, Turkiewood, Fusticke, Sugar cheste, & such lyke, make deade, heuy lumpish, hobblyng shaftes."

DIPS
A modification in the design of longbows, introduced by a noted bowyer named James Buchanan (*c.* 1850) of London. He found that improved performance could be offered by thickening the grip on the inside, or belly, of the bow with relatively sharply curved 'dips', either side of the grip, to the main limb. The object was to give added stiffness in the handle and avoid the kick that can be felt by the bow hand when the bow was shot and which can be caused by slight flexing of the stave at the centre when the bow is drawn.

DIRECTOR OF SHOOTING
Under international rules, the title given to the Field Captain (*qv*). The Director is appointed by the Organizing Committee, who may also nominate a Deputy, should they consider that assistance is needed in the execution of the duties imposed. (See FITA *Rules*, Art. 505.)

DISABLED ARCHERS
Shooting from a wheeled chair is permitted under both FITA and GNAS Rules. Archery is now a standard sport in the Paraplegic Games and some handicapped archers have reached very high standards with Willi Kocott of South Africa being a member of his national team at the World Championships held at Grenoble in 1973, and Neroli Fairhall representing New Zealand at this event at Punta Ala in Italy in 1981, and she was the Lady Champion at the Commonwealth Games in 1982.

While such achievements are possible for those who have full control of their bodies above the waist, others who suffer from greater disability have resorted to such techniques as drawing the bowstring with their teeth.

For those who cannot shoot standard rounds the GNAS has approved the Elizabethan Round (*qv*), with a scheme of awards to encourage contestants.

Credit for starting archery for the disabled must be given to Frank L. Bilson (*qv*) at Stoke Mandeville in 1948, whose achievements in this field were highly praised by the late Sir Ludwig Guttman, Director of the Institute. (See Alf Webb, *Archery*, Sport & Leisure for the Disabled series, 1982.)

DISCHARGE OF AN ARROW
Only in the 1930s was the behaviour of an arrow, when shot from a bow, fully under-

stood, following the advent of high-speed photography. This analysis was first published by Paul E. Klopsteg (*qv*) in *Archery Review*, (Tulsa, Oklahoma), April 1933.

Earlier, it had been presumed that the bowstring, on release, moved directly toward the centre-line of the bow. In theory, when the arrow leaves the string as it comes to rest, the shaft should be deflected to the side. (See Figure A.)

The fact that this does not occur is called the *paradox*. Various ideas had been put forward to suggest why this happened, but they were in error.

In the case of a right-handed archer, the pressure of the fingers on the string when it

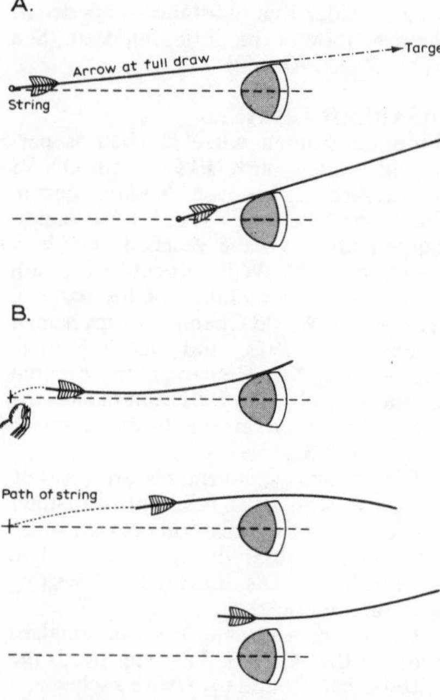

is released, causes it to move to the left. This causes the foreshaft of the arrow to press against the bow and the shaft bends. Its vibration period, as it moves forward, then results in the shaft bending the opposite way by the time it is about half way past the bow. It then flexes back again so that the tail swings clear as it leaves the bow. (See Figure B.)

For the arrow to travel along the line in which it was pointing at the moment of release, the vibration period of the shaft must be correctly related to the discharge time of the bow. This is mainly determined by the spine value (*qv*) and weight of the arrow, though other factors enter into the problem.

Subsequent research has now enabled the manufacturers of arrows to list the recommended characteristics of their varied products in relation to those of the bows with which they will be used. This has proved to be a valued addition to the accuracy and precision with which the modern bow may be shot.

In earlier times such tests were very rough and ready, compared with the attention now given. In H. A. Ford (*qv*), *Archery: Its Theory & Practice* (1856), p. 29, one may read, concerning an arrow: "To test its strength or stiffness, place the pile on any solid substance, holding it by the nock, and with the other hand press it gently downward in the middle. A very little experience will suffice to tell whether it be sufficiently stiff or no." Greater precision is demanded today to achieve a correct discharge.

DISTANCE

Synonymous with 'range' in yards or metres, but almost invariably used by archers in preference to the latter term.

The question is often asked by non-archers: "To what distance may an arrow be shot?" The answer is not simple and it depends on two main factors. First, the design and weight of the arrow, and second, the power and efficiency of the bow.

In the historical context, most war bows were intended to shoot a heavy arrow to give maximum penetration of whatever protective covering the enemy might be expected to wear. In simple terms this restricted the effective range to something in the order of 200 yards. To illustrate the effectiveness of a bow under these circumstances, one may consider an archer being charged by a horseman with lance, mace or sword. If the archer can pierce his adversary at a mere 30–40 yards, the archer has won the contest.

Archers often carried more than one form of arrow. In addition to the heavier design, an archer might have a light, long-range form, that would carry, perhaps, up to 400 yards. In contrast, modern target shooting equipment is designed to give optimum performance at the maximum distances of 100 yards or 90 metres. In most forms of archery the range to which an arrow can be shot is of no real interest, except in flight shooting (*qv*) and, to a lesser extent, in clout shooting (*qv*).

DOUBLE ANCHOR
Lodgement of the shaft hand against the face using two points of contact. In addition to the normal anchor where, more commonly, the knuckle and proximal phalanx of the index finger of the shaft hand are lodged beneath the jaw, the thumb can be extended and placed at the back of the jaw, beneath the ear. Though not often seen, several successful archers have favoured this variation of technique to avoid the risk of a creep (*qv*).

DOUBLE NOCK
An arrow with two nocks, cut at right angles to each other. It has been used for certain forms of trick shooting, but never for hunting nor for formal target shooting.

DOUBLE ROUND
A contest made by shooting two identical single rounds (*qv*). In the international field, regional championships are decided by a single FITA Round, while World and Olympic championships use the double round.

DOUBLE TARGETS
A contest using targets at either end of the range in 'two-way' shooting. The older English method of target shooting was in this form and its use continues with those who favour the traditional longbow (*qv*).

With this method, three arrows are shot against the targets at one end. When recovered and scored, they are then shot back at the targets placed at the other end of the range. This is the reason why the term 'end' (*qv*) appeared in the archer's vocabulary.

DOWN WIND
A wind that blows from the archer toward the target.

DRAW (*n.* and *v.*)
The action of pulling back the bowstring from its position at rest. Drawing is one of Roger Ascham's (*qv*) five 'partitions' of shooting and there are several ways in which it may be achieved.

Perhaps the most simple is the 'V'-draw where the archer starts with the bow held horizontally at waist height. With the bow hand pressing against the grip and the shaft hand pulling the string, the bow is raised smoothly until the full draw is achieved as the archer comes on aim. In the 'T'-draw, the archer again starts at waist height but while the bow is raised in line with the target, the draw does not begin until the sight has been brought roughly in line with the mark. The archer then draws back to the anchor point (*qv*).

Some archers favour raising the bow above the horizontal and complete the draw while lowering it to the line of the target. This method is also used in traditional Japanese archery (see KYUDO).

An extreme action of this type has been observed with some archers from North Korea, where the draw may start with the bow held almost horizontally above the head. A few exponents of this technique have achieved considerable success in major international contests.

The draw may be considered as the foundation of a good shot and Ascham rightly lays stress on this aspect. ". . . the best shootynge, is alwayes the moost cumlye shootynge . . . In drawyng some fet suche a compasse, as thoughe they woulde tourne about, and blysse all the feelde: Other heaue theyr hand nowe vp nowe downe, that a man can not decerne wherat they wolde shote, an other waggeth the vpper ende of his bow one way, the neyther ende an other waye. An other wil stand poyntinge his shafte at the marke a good whyle and by and by he wyll gyue hym a whip, and awaye or a man wite. An other maketh suche a wrestling with his gere, as thoughe he were able to shoote no more as longe as he lyued. An other draweth softly to y[e] middes, and by and by it is gon, you can not knowe howe.

". . . An other draweth his shafte well, vntyll wythin .ii. fyngers of the head, and than he stayeth a lyttle, to looke at hys marke, and that done, pouleth it vp to the head, and lowseth: whych waye although sume excellent shooters do vse, yet surely it is a faulte, and good mennes faultes are not to be folowed.

"Summe men drawe to farre, summe to shorte, sume to slowlye, summe to quickely, summe holde ouer longe, summe lette go ouer sone.

"Summe sette theyr shafte on the grounde, and fetcheth him vpwarde. An other poynteth vp towarde the skye, and so bryngeth hym downewardes . . .

"Drawynge well is the best parte of shootyng . . . In shootynge at the pryckes [i.e. 'targets'], hasty and quicke drawing is neyther sure nor yet cumlye. Therfore to drawe easely and vniformely . . . is best both for profit & semelinesse."

A little over three hundred years later, Horace Ford (*qv*), twelve times Champion of Great Britain, in *Archery: Its Theory and Practice*, London 1856, pp. 68–79, lists faults he had observed, very similar to those noted by Ascham.

He recommends ". . . the best system of drawing, that the pulling of the bow and the extension of the left arm be a simultaneous movement; that this be to the extent of drawing the arrow at the least three-fourths of its length before the aim be taken (if to such a distance that the wrist of the right hand come to about the level of the chin, so much the better); that the aim be found by a direct movement on to it from the starting-place of the draw; that the right elbow be well raised; and that the arrow be then pulled home, either with or without a pause, preference being rather given to the latter."

This is virtually the 'V'-draw as commended by Robert P. Elmer (five times Champion of the USA) ninety years later in *Target Archery*, New York 1946, pp. 385–92. Neither he nor Ford favour the 'T'-draw, due to the initial forward displacement of the rear shoulder.

While the foregoing emphasizes variations in the technique of the draw, it must be remembered that what suits one archer may not suit another.

The term *draw* is also used when describing the use of the fingers and/or thumb so that the arrow may be drawn. E. S. Morse (*qv*) in 1885 designated each varied method as a *release*, but this term, of course, means letting go instead of pulling back. Others have used the term *loose* for the same purpose.

Morse's *primary, secondary* and *tertiary* methods are variations of the pinch grip where the tail of the arrow is held between the thumb and the middle phalanx of the index finger. They may be discounted as far as modern archery is concerned and are of historical or ethnological interest only. Only two methods need to be considered, with their respective variations. The MEDITERRANEAN (*qv*), or three-fingered draw and the THUMB LOCK (*qv*), which Morse calls the Mongolian release.

DRAW CHECK
A device to inform the target archer that the arrow is fully drawn. In its early form it was a small strip of rubber attached to the fore end of the arrow rest at the top of the grip. The arrow held this down while it was being drawn and it flicked upward when full draw was achieved. It has now been replaced by the clicker (*qv*).

DRAW HOME
To draw an arrow fully so that it is ready for loosing.

DRAW THROUGH
To overdraw an arrow so that its tip comes inside the belly of the bow. This fault does not normally occur in target shooting, where the length of a shaft is selected to suit the action and physique of an individual. It can occur in flight shooting (*qv*), and may be dangerous if the string is loosed in this state. It can strike the bow, bend, buckle or break and rebound into the archer's face.

DRESS SHIELD
A triangular piece of leather, plastic, or other material, fitted with straps, to prevent the clothing from shoulder to chest catching the bowstring when it is released.

DRUGGED DARTS for Crossbows
An important development in the field of game preservation. While such devices had been designed for use with air-guns and with 12-bore shotguns, using a reduced charge to eject the missile, a crossbow has the advantage of relative silence. As the best times for dealing with animals in the wild is at dawn and dusk, it can be difficult to distinguish them against their natural background into which they blend by virtue of their protective colouring. Should the dart miss, the noise of a gun may scare them before a second shot can be made, while evidence shows that they are rarely disturbed by the slight twang of the string of the crossbow and a second, or even a third, shot has been achieved under practical conditions.

With many animals trapped by the floods caused by the Kariba Dam project

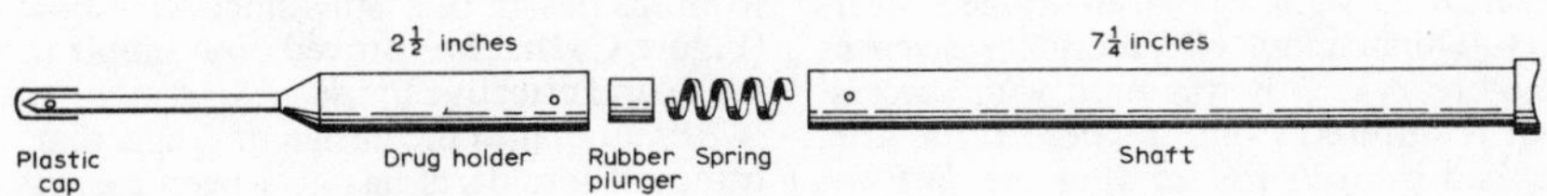

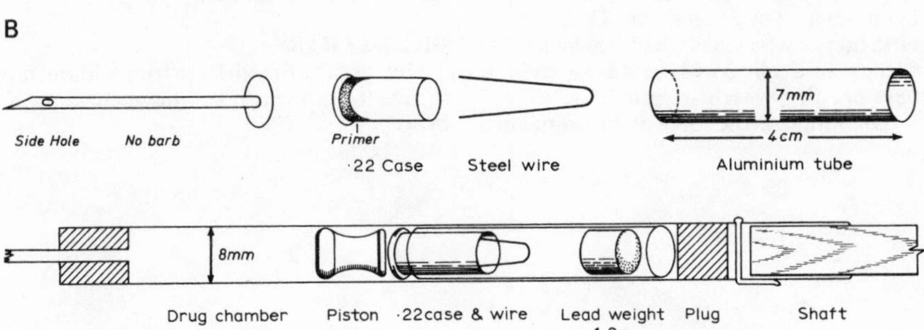

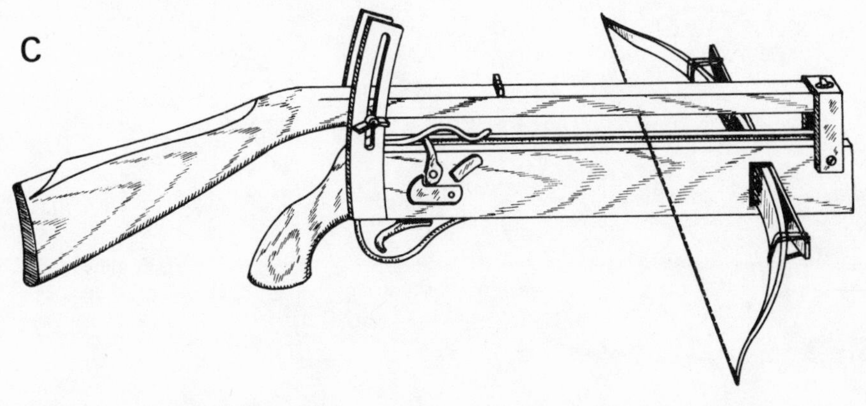

A: Early dart designed by Frank Bilson.
B: Outline plan of the drugged dart designed by Dr J. Fabian.
C: Outline of the split-stock crossbow fitted with an anti-hysteresis bow lath.

in Africa, completed in 1963, Frank L. Bilson (*qv*) designed a dart in consultation with Dr R. V. Short of Cambridge University, Department of Veterinary Sciences (Figure A). This was used with success, but it suffered from one defect: the drug leaked from its holder after the dart was assembled. A better dart was devised, following this experience, using gas pressure from a 'sparklet' bulb (see Frank Bilson, *Crossbows*, 1974, p. 108) and a further improvement (Figure B) has been devised by Dr Jules Fabian, a zoologist from the University of Gödöllo in Hungary, who has had considerable success in dealing with wild boar and red deer needing veterinary attention.

This employs the force of the primer of a .22 cartridge, triggered on impact with the target, to inject the drug. The dart is shot from his design of a 'split-stock' crossbow (Figure C) that has proved both simple to make and effective to use.

Research into the design of drugged, or tranquillizer, darts has also been carried out in the USA, first by Dr Crossett, with further developments by Carl Anderson and Thad Martin. This aspect of the subject is well covered by George M. Stevens, *Crossbows* (Desert Publications, Cornville, Arizona 1980), pp. 115–21.

DRY RELEASE

To release the drawn bowstring without an arrow. It can cause serious damage to a bow.

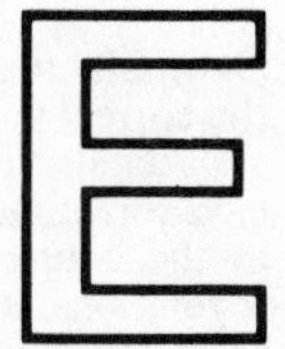

EAR (of a bow)
The virtually rigid end section of the limbs of the eastern composite bow, more generally referred to by the Arabic, Persian and Turkish term as the *siyah* (*qv*).

EDWARDS, Charles Bertram (1896–1974)
British target champion, 1946. Secretary of the GNAS (*qv*) from 1946 until 1962 and Secretary of the Royal Toxophilite Society from 1947 to 1968, when he was elected President of that Society.

His tireless effort, hard work and enthusiasm, coupled with sound administrative ability, did much to promote the growth of archery in Britain.

His book, *An Archer's Notes*, Leeds 1949 (reprinted in 1953 and 1960), is a model in clarity and briefness on how to shoot, as well as suggesting to new archery clubs how they might frame their rules. It includes the GNAS shooting regulations as they stood when his work was published (65 pp., 4 plates).

A later book in co-operation with E. G. Heath (*qv*), *In Pursuit of Archery*, London 1962, which covers the subject more widely, includes his original notes in pages 59–111.

EFFICIENCY (of a bow)
As with many machines, efficiency is determined by comparing the work put in with the work got out. It is normally expressed as a percentage.

In the case of a bow and arrow, the work put in is the effort exerted by the archer in drawing the string against the resistance of the two bow limbs. This is termed the *potential energy* (PE). The work got out is in the form of the velocity imparted to the arrow and this is the *kinetic energy* (KE). No bow can be 100% efficient, as energy must be expended in carrying forward its own limbs and the bowstring. This is a loss, as far as the arrow is concerned.

PE is determined from the force-draw curve (*qv*).

$$KE = \frac{1}{2}\frac{W}{g}V^2$$

where W is the weight of the arrow
g is the gravitational constant
and V is the velocity of discharge.

As an example, the figure shown under FORCE-DRAW CURVE illustrates a bow with a PE of about 35 foot-pounds. If there was no loss the bow would give an arrow of 350 grains an initial velocity of 212 feet per second. If the measured velocity was 170 f.p.s., this would give a KE of approximately 28 foot-pounds and an efficiency of 80%. (See also VELOCITY MEASUREMENT and VIRTUAL MASS.)

ELIZABETHAN ROUND
Devised by the GNAS for disabled archers (*qv*) unable to shoot standard rounds. It is shot at 15 yards at a 60-cm diameter face with five rings, as for the standard English target, with six ends of three arrows. The respective rings score 9, 7, 5, 3 and 1.

Badges may be awarded with different coloured backgrounds to indicate the standard achieved by the archer:

Badge Background	*Qualifying Score*
White	76–90
Black	91–110
Blue	111–130
Red	131–145
Gold	146–162

There is also a Green Award for the more severely handicapped, whose efforts deserve recognition, but who are unable to qualify for the White Award.

To qualify for a badge, an archer is required to shoot the Elizabethan Round on three separate occasions with at least 21 days between each round. Claims must then be forwarded to the GNAS Awards Secretary.

ELL

Originally the length of the arm and thus the correct length of an arrow shaft to suit a particular individual. Old records and laws sometimes relate to this measure but, in the course of time and revised legal regulations, it has become most difficult to ascertain what was meant by this quantity. Development resulted in the *English ell* of 45 inches, the *barony ell* of 42 inches, the *common ell* of 38 inches, the *Scottish ell* of 37.2 inches and the *Flemish ell* of 27 inches.

One may see in Act 3, *Henry VII*, c.7, "All merchandises . . . to be measured with Eln [*sic*] or Yard."(*OED*). Today the measure is almost meaningless though, it may be noted, the average length of the arrow shafts recovered from the *Mary Rose*, which sank in 1545, is 30½ in. (77.5 cm) from the nock to the start of the taper that fitted in the socket of the head.

ELMER, Robert Potter, Dr (1877–1951)

A medical doctor and winner of nine national target championships in the USA between 1911 and 1922, Dr Elmer also achieved the leading score for the double York Round six times, and for the double American Round ten times.

Among his written works are included *Archery* (Philadelphia 1926, with a second edition in 1933, reissued 1939); *Target Archery* (New York 1946, reprinted in London 1952 with an added appendix to cover the British GNAM); and with N. A. Faris, *Arab Archery* (Princeton 1945).

END

Six arrows are normally shot at an 'end' against a target in two groups of three, each archer shooting in turn, retiring and then returning to the shooting line for the second group. When all have completed the 'end', contestants advance to the targets, score and recover their arrows.

An exception to this is at the shorter ranges, such as the last distance in the FITA Round (*qv*) at 30 metres, where only three arrows are shot before scoring and recovery. This is to reduce the possibility of damage to arrows, already in the target, by those shooting after the first archer in the prescribed sequence.

Under FITA Rules an end is of three arrows (see Art. 506 (a), *passim*). Thus, when six arrows are shot before scoring and recovery, it is a double end.

ENGLISH ARCHERY FEDERATION

Formed in 1979 to enable an English team to take part in the Commonwealth Games where, under its constitution, Scotland, Wales and Ulster are entitled to enter their own contestants. The GNAS as parent organization for the whole UK could not act on behalf of England on its own and the object was to establish a firm base of administration and organization, as required by the Commonwealth Games Council for England.

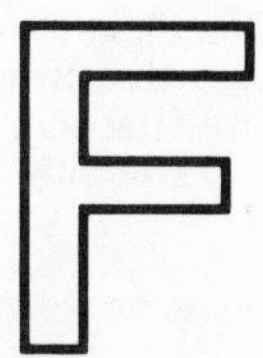

FAST
The traditional archer's cry to stop shooting should any person or animal stray in rear of the targets, or for any other reason during the conduct of a shoot when officials may need to advance in front of the shooting line.

From this is derived the expression 'to play fast and loose', which implies dangerous or risky behaviour. It originated from an archer loosing an arrow after the cry of 'fast'.

FEATHER
A wide variety of birds' feathers have been used in the past to fletch (*qv*) arrows. The wing pinions of the grey goose were those most widely used in English history as the toughest available, though both swan and peacock are mentioned in several early works. In the East, vulture tail and eagle were highly favoured.

From the mid-19th century, in both Europe and America, the availability of turkey wing pinions led to these being used, almost exclusively, as the strongest form of feather easily obtained.

In recent years the plastic vane (*qv*) has largely replaced the traditional feather as the means of steering and steadying the shaft during flight. The primary reason is that in rain a wet feather will collapse against the shaft and lose its effect. As a result it is rarely seen in major target shooting contests, though its use continues with those who favour traditional methods, such as exponents of the longbow (*qv*) and the Japanese art of *kyudo* (*qv*). Prepared feathers are available from equipment suppliers as well as complete feathers for those who wish to cut and trim their own fletchings.

The best feathers are the secondary wing pinions of the turkey, which may be white or bronze-barred, depending on the colour of the bird. A feather has a natural curve, its upper surface being slightly convex, and it is said to be right- or left-handed, depending on which side the barbs stand out from the quill. This, in its turn, depends on whether the pinion feather has been taken from the right or the left wing. It is essential that all fletchings on a shaft are of the same hand, as there is a lift on the upper surface, as the arrow flies through the air, so that the shaft rotates even when the base of the quill has been set straight along its line. If the feathers are mixed, unsteady flight results, with loss of accuracy.

Starting with the natural feather, the fore and rear ends can be discarded as being too weak, so that only one or, perhaps, two fletchings may be obtained from a single feather, depending on the length required for fitting to the shaft. The quill is first split down its centre with a sharp knife, which is also used to trim off surplus material and to cut the feather to the desired length. The section thus obtained should then be placed between two thin metal strips and held there with a spring clip. The base can then be carefully rubbed down on a sheet of fine sandpaper, leaving a little of the soft inner core still attached to the harder outer surface of the quill.

There is a second method, where the barbs and surface of the quill are torn away from the core. This is called a *stripped feather*, but this greatly weakens the feather and it cannot be commended for general use though, it may be remarked, it may be seen on old arrows from India, where tail feathers were often used.

The prepared sections may then be attached to the shaft, preferably with the aid of a fletching jig (see under FLETCH) and using one of the modern adhesives based on a solution of celluloid in acetone.

There are other good glues that are equally effective for this purpose. Those that are waterproof are to be preferred. Needless to say, the shaft must be clean and free from grease before the feathers are attached.

Trimming the feather to the desired shape, after it has been set on the shaft, can be a little difficult. The bulk of the surplus barbs can be cut away with a sharp pair of scissors, but due to their natural resilience it is best to clip templates, cut to the desired shape, either side of the feather to prevent the barbs moving under pressure from the scissors.

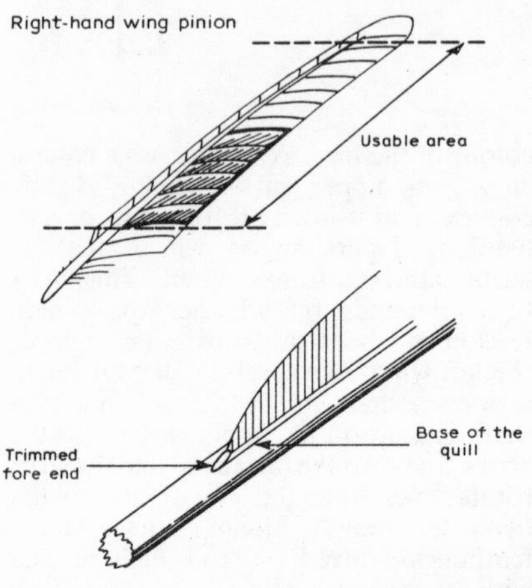

Where there is a regular need to trim feathers, it may be of advantage to make a feather burner, which is simple to construct, though a transformer is needed to step down mains voltage to give an output of about 6½ volts, 5 amps. It consists, basically, of a length of wire, as used in the element of an electric fire, bent to the shape of the finished feather. The arrow is fitted in a holder and the feathers are rotated against the wire after it has reached red heat. A design may be seen in *Bowman's Handbook*, Ed. Patrick Clover, fifth edition, Portsmouth 1968, pp. 103–4.

Whatever method may be used in trimming the shape of the feather, the final step is to trim the fore end of the quill so that it lies close against the shaft and to coat this area with a little glue. This will give the feather a smooth passage over the arrow rest (*qv*) or the bowhand, depending on the method and style of shooting employed by the archer.

FÉDÉRATION INTERNATIONALE DE TIR À L'ARC (FITA)

FITA Executive Bureau,
Via Cerva n. 30,
20122 Milan,
Italy.

The governing body for international target and field archery. It may be noted that there is also the International Field Archery Association which organizes rival regional and world championships. FITA rules include clout and flight shooting (*qv*).

FITA was founded in 1931 at Lwow in Poland, with representatives from Belgium, France, Poland and Sweden. The United Kingdom joined the following year and there are now (1983) 62 member associations.

It was a most important step in the modern annals of archery as, prior to its formation, there had been no agreed rules between countries and each followed its own traditional methods when international contests were held.

FITA rules and regulations took time to develop, but under the stimulating leadership, first of Mr Oscar Kessels (*qv*) of Belgium, President 1957–61, and then of Mrs Inger K. Frith, OBE, (*qv*) of Great Britain, President 1961–77, great progress was made that led to the Olympic Committee voting archery back into the Olympic Games (*qv*) at their meeting in Mexico City in 1968.

FITA Congress meets every two years when the World Target Archery Championships are held. It is also the authority that approves Olympic, World and Regional record scores that must be submitted for the consideration of their organization.

Details of regulations are published in the *Constitution and Rules*, adopted at the FITA Congress in 1959 and periodically republished to incorporate approved amendments (see Appendix 1). Reports on international contests and Congress resolutions are normally published every two years in the FITA *Bulletin*.

FIELD ARROW

A strong shaft, used in field shooting (*qv*), that may be fitted with a form of head or pile, better suited for this purpose than the standard target form.

FIELD CAPTAIN
The official responsible to the Judge for the conduct of archers on the shooting line in a target contest. Control is normally exercised with the aid of a whistle to start each end (*qv*) and, on completion, for those on the shooting line to advance, score and recover their arrows.

Under international regulations the duties are somewhat extended where the Director of Shooting (Field Captain), appointed by the organizing committee, is also required to watch for any incursion of photographers, Press or spectators that may in any way tend to inconvenience competitors. (For further details see Appendix 1, page 141, FITA *Constitution and Rules*, Art. 505 and GNAS *Rules of Shooting*.)

FIELD SHOOTING
A popular alternative to formal target archery. It is based on conditions that might be met when hunting, as nearly as the terrain permits, by shooting at targets that vary in size and range from a succession of different posts or shooting positions. If set in undulating woodland, a course can be both attractive and challenging to the archer.

Two classes of archers are recognized in all contests. Those who shoot in the **Instinctive** or **Bare Bow** class, where no form of sight, nor any other aiming aid, is permitted, and the **Free Style** class, where sights are allowed, as well as stabilisers (*qv*) and allied devices. Neither class permits the use of binoculars, or similar visual aids, nor may any form of range-finder be used.

Rules are somewhat complex and in a state of flux, with two international organizations, FITA (*qv*) and the IFAA (International Field Archery Association) failing to agree on certain important aspects, mainly concerning ranges and sizes of targets. Attempts have been made, and indeed continue, to reconcile the views of these two bodies. One can but hope that agreement will be achieved in due course.

While many archery clubs hold such shoots with the harmonious agreement of their members, it will be appreciated that where national and international championships are concerned, regulations must be clear and explicit. For such major contests the GNAS recognizes FITA Rules, though it also accepts other rounds (*qv*), provided they are conducted in accordance with the GNAS *Rules of Shooting*.

While the existing FITA Rules may be quoted, it must be emphasized that several major proposals and counter-proposals were tabled at the FITA Congress in 1981, but due to their number and complexity, time did not permit them to be resolved and decisions on the motions were postponed until the next planned Congress in 1983.

As matters now stand (1981) FITA recognizes two rounds, the **Field Round**, where 56 arrows are shot from 14 different shooting positions at specified ranges; and the **Hunters Round**, with a similar number of arrows to be shot and shooting positions, but at unknown ranges. Four different sizes of target face are used in both rounds. In the major championships double rounds are specified and thus require that archer to shoot a total of 228 arrows to complete both courses. Two days are allowed for the contest.

The Field Round consists of 14 shots (or different shooting positions), with four arrows at each distance:

15, 20, 25 and 30 metres at a 30-cm face
– a total of 16 arrows.

35, 40 and 45 metres at a 45-cm face
– a total of 12 arrows.

50, 55 and 60 metres at a 60-cm face
– a total of 12 arrows.

Then with each arrow shot from a different post or at a different target face:

35 metres at a 45-cm face(s)
– a total of 4 arrows.

6, 8, 10 and 12 metres at a 15-cm face
– a total of 4 arrows.

30, 35, 40 and 45 metres at a 45-cm face
– a total of 4 arrows.

45, 50, 55 and 60 metres at a 60-cm face
– a total of 4 arrows.

A total of 56 arrows are thus shot in the Field Round.

The Hunters Round also consists of 14 shots with one arrow only from each of four different posts for each target.

Two 15-cm targets placed between 5 and 15 metres, so that the total distance over which the 8 arrows are shot shall be 80 metres.

Four 30-cm targets placed between 10 and

30 metres so that the total distance over which the 16 arrows are shot shall be 320 metres.
Five 45-cm targets placed between 20 and 40 metres so that the total distance over which the 20 arrows are shot shall be 600 metres.
Three 60-cm targets placed between 30 and 50 metres so that the total distance over which the 12 arrows are shot shall be 480 metres.
A total of 56 arrows are thus shot in the Hunters Round.

Target faces consist of an outer and inner ring, with a central aiming spot. They may carry depictions of animals.
60-cm target has a 30-cm inner ring and a 10-cm centre spot.
45-cm target has a 22.5-cm inner and a 7.5-cm central spot.
30-cm target has a 15-cm inner and a 5-cm central spot.
15-cm target has a 7.5-cm inner and a 2.5-cm central spot.

Amendments submitted to FITA Congress include motions to increase both rounds to 60, or even 80, arrows, with corresponding increases in both posts and targets. Alterations to the dimensions of targets have also been tabled.

Since the first World Championship was held under FITA Rules in the United States in 1969, interest in this aspect of archery has steadily grown. There were then sixty competitors and in the VIIIth Championship, held in England in 1982, the figure had risen to 120 archers from 19 countries.

Both classes of field shooting feature in the championship – Instinctive (or Bare Bow) and Free style. Contestants shoot a 28-target course in the Hunters Round, where distances are unknown, and another 28-target course in the Field Round where distances are stated. The result of the two rounds, added together, decides the Championship, in each of the two classes. See Appendix 2 for list of World Field Champions. (See also NATIONAL FIELD ARCHERY SOCIETY.)

FINGER STALL or TIP

A leather cap, somewhat akin to a thimble, used to protect each finger of the drawing hand against the pressure of the bowstring. This item is rarely seen today, having been superseded by the shooting glove (*qv*) or the tab (*qv*).

FINSBURY FIELDS

A famous old shooting ground in London, where archers practised at rovers (see ROVING). Nothing now remains apart from the *Scarlet Lion* stone marker, now in the headquarters of the Honourable Artillery Company.

The most complete account, with maps and plans, is that given by the late Fred Isles (President of the National Crossbowmen of the USA), 'Locating The Ancient Finsbury Fields Archery Marks', in the *Journal of the Society of Archer-Antiquaries*, vol. 7, 1964, pp. 8–13.

FIRE ARROW

An arrow carrying an incendiary substance to set alight the mark at which it is shot. The term 'to fire an arrow' means to ignite it before shooting, but it is often used, in error, to mean discharging or shooting an arrow. The word only came into use with the introduction of early cannon when fire was applied to the powder and after the bow had already been in use for several thousands of years.

FISHER LOOSE

A three-finger draw where the fingers are at an angle to the bowstring, the deepest hold being taken by the index finger. It is named after Major C. Hawkins Fisher, an able exponent of this variation in technique and five times British Target Champion between 1871 and 1887. (See C. J. Longman and H. Walrond, *Archery* (Badminton Series), London 1894, pp. 377–9.)

FISHING ARROW

An arrow with a barbed head used for shooting fish. For this purpose a normal angler's spinning reel is usually attached to the bow and its line secured to the arrow shaft to enable the fish to be recovered after it has been hit.

A traditional variation is still used by certain native tribes in the Amazon Basin to catch fish. Their barbed heads are mounted on hollow reed shafts which may be some six feet, or two metres, in length that provide sufficient buoyancy to prevent the fish from escaping after the arrow is lodged in its body.

FISTMELE

For some fifty years this term, derived from the medieval word for 'fist measure', has been used by archers to mean the brace height of the longbow. The clenched fist, with the thumb extended, is placed on the grip. If the tip of the thumb just touches the string of the braced longbow, the string is correctly fitted. For the average man this distance is about six inches.

An extended meaning has been adopted by several authors who have used it as a synonym for 'brace height' which, for the modern bow, may be about eight inches.

The archer's definition does not accord with the *Oxford English Dictionary* (*sv* 'fistmeal') which is the simple measure of the fist, about four inches. That given with the extended thumb is under 'shaftment' (*qv*).

"Every English man . . . shall have an English Bow of his own length and one fistmele at least between the neckes." (From the Irish statute, 5 Edward IV.c.4.).

FITA ROUND

In international target archery, competitors shoot a FITA Round (see Fédération Internationale de Tir à l'Arc). This requires 36 arrows to be shot at each of the following distances:

Ladies and juniors: 70, 60, 50 and 30 metres.

Gentlemen: 90, 70, 50 and 30 metres.

At the two longer distances the ten-zone 122-cm target is used and one of 80 cm for the two shorter distances. Two of these rounds (*qv*) are shot for Olympic and World Championships (see Appendix 2), and a single round at European (see Appendix 2) and other regional championships.

For indoor shooting, which is popular during the winter where facilities exist, there are two international rounds which all can shoot:

FITA I : 30 arrows at 18 metres, at a 40-cm target.

FITA II : 30 arrows at 25 metres, at a 60-cm target.

Since the readmittance of archery to the Olympic list of approved sports (see OLYMPIC GAMES) in 1968, FITA Rounds have gained considerable added importance in planned national programmes and they have tended to replace certain older and traditional contests in both Britain and America.

FITA Star Badges may be gained at major tournaments, recognized by the member associations. A simple star is awarded for scores of 1,000 points, or more; on a black shield for 1,100, a blue shield for 1,200, and a red shield for 1,300.

FIVE PARTITIONS

Defined by Roger Ascham (*qv*) in *Toxophilus* (1545) as "Standynge, nockyng, drawyng, holdyng, lowsying, wherby cometh fayre shotynge . . ." His able analysis has stood the test of time and mastery of these five factors is still a primary requirement for successful archery.

FLAT BOW

A bow whose limbs are wide but thin, when compared with the traditional longbow (*qv*). Though this variation in design has been widely used in the past, its modern use has been derived from forms of certain North American Indian bows. The simple flat bow is rarely seen today, but the study of its merits was an important factor in the development of the modern bow.

FLEMISH LOOSE or DRAW

A variation of technique where the bowstring is drawn and released using the fore and middle fingers of the shaft hand, as opposed to the more widely used three finger method, where the ring finger also engages the string. It may be seen in many medieval paintings and older statues and carvings, which suggests a wide use in olden times. How and when this method became known as 'Flemish' is obscure.

FLETCH

To fit an arrow shaft with feathers or vanes. When fitted they are referred to as the fletchings.

A fletching jig is normally used for this purpose to ensure they are set and spaced accurately on the shaft. It consists of a locator, or holder, that can be rotated, in which the nock of the arrow is lodged. The fletchings are held in a spring-loaded clip and may be set straight or at an angle on the shaft after an adhesive has been applied to their base. There are several designs available from equipment suppliers.

Prior to about 1950 most target arrows carried straight fletchings, whose base was set in line with the shaft, but due to the natural curve of a feather (*qv*) the arrow rotates as it flies through the air. The rate of spin can be increased by mounting the fletchings at a slight angle so that it adds to the natural effect. Tests with a shooting machine (*qv*) show that closer grouping is achieved in a target by this means (see *The British Archer*, Vol. 5, No. 4, 1953–4, pp. 117–18). With the wide use of plastic vanes for fletching, an offset of about five degrees is needed to give adequate spin. An excessive offset gives no benefit and merely adds to the drag caused by air resistance which results in a drop in performance.

Fletchings are always liable to damage but, with the aid of a jig, a damaged feather or vane can easily be replaced. It is a simple repair that many archers are ready to carry out when the need arises.

Angled fletchings are usually favoured by the hunter when using arrows fitted with broadheads (*qv*) as the increased spin reduces the possible effect of wind on the arrowhead.

Fletchings are usually three in number and spaced at a hundred and twenty degrees around the shaft, with the cock feather (*qv*) at right angles to the nock of the arrow. An exception to this is found in flight shooting (*qv*) when using a 'keyhole', centre-shot, bow, when the oriental method of placing the cock feather in line with the nock is used. The object of both these methods is to give the two remaining shaft feathers a clear passage past the bow.

A few archers favour four fletchings in which case they are usually spaced at 75° × 105°, rather than 90° × 90°.

After the fletchings have been fitted, it is important to ensure that the fore ends sit closely against the shaft to avoid any risk of the base or quill of the lower fletching catching the arrow rest (*qv*) on discharge or, when shooting with the longbow, the knuckle of the index finger of the bow hand. When using feathers the fore end of the quill should be pared down with a sharp knife or razor blade and then covered with a little glue to give a completely smooth surface. Glue should be applied in a similar manner to plastic vanes.

The size and shape of fletchings vary but a parabolic shape is most common and a length of 2½ to 3 inches is adequate for target arrows. Hunting arrows need longer fletchings to balance the effect of wind on the broadhead and may be about 4 to 5 inches in length.

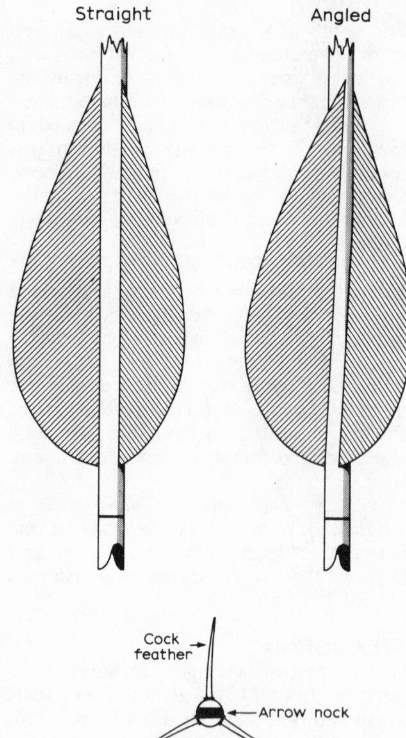

Methods of fletching.

Prepared fletchings, including feathers in natural colours or dyed, and plastic vanes are available from equipment suppliers. (See also FEATHER.)

FLETCHER

A craftsman who assembles the complete arrow in addition to fitting the feathers or vanes to the shaft.

In the City of London, among the several ancient guilds, the Worshipful Company of Fletchers is still active and has a distinguished history, dating back to 1371. (See J. E. Oxley, *The Fletchers and Longbowstringmakers of London*, 1968.)

FLIGHT SHOOTING

Shooting for maximum distance. There is no target. Under both FITA and GNAS Rules there are different classes for normal target bows and for special flight bows. These are further sub-divided into the draw weights of the bows used.

In the class of target bows the archer must use an arrow of standard length for target shooting, but shorter, very light, barrelled shafts are used in the flight class. They are drawn with the aid of an extended arrow shelf within the bow, generally referred to as a *siper* (*qv*), that enables an extended draw to be made.

There is an art and a perfection of technique needed to achieve maximum distance and the design and balance of the special flight arrows is critical.

International rules also recognize the foot bow (*qv*) in its appropriate class and distances in excess of 1,000 yards/metres have been achieved. (See Appendix 1, FITA *Rules*, Part V, Section E, and GNAS *Rules*, Part III.)

Modern flight shooting has a small, but very enthusiastic, following. The scope of the target bow class is very limited and their major interest is in the flight bow class. Very little has been published covering this specialized field, neither can retailers of equipment normally offer the articles needed for those wishing to take part in this aspect of archery. It therefore tends to be the province of the skilled amateur or professional craftsman who is prepared to devote time and effort to design and construction.

The flight bow is about half the length of a target bow, measuring about 34 to 36 inches around its curves. It has to withstand a draw of about 19 inches, to accommodate the modern flight arrow and the skilled designer will aim to stress all materials to the limit of their strength to give the maximum possible velocity to the arrow.

Though the centre-shot (*qv*) design may still be seen, with the bow-window (*qv*) cut away from the side, as with the modern target bow, the *key hole* – sometimes called the *hole in the heart* – design is more widely favoured. By using permitted release aids, such as the 'flipper' (see overleaf), the arrow can be shot through the centre of the bow through which a hole is cut to allow for its passage.

A design for a bow of this type by Jack Flinton (*qv*), with full construction details, well supported with nine figures, may be seen in *Bowman's Handbook* (ed. Patrick Clover), fifth edition, Portsmouth 1968, pp. 148–54.

The modern flight arrow is about 18 inches in length with a barrelled shaft, about ¼ in. thick at the centre, tapered smoothly to a point at the fore end, with a reinforced tip having a very small brass pile or a tiny point of horn, bone or ivory, to help withstand the impact in the ground at the end of its flight. The rear end tapers similarly to a small plastic nock, in front of which are set three small vanes of plastic film, or similar material, about ¼ in. high and 1 in. long. Contrary to the normal practice with 3-fletched target arrows, they are fitted in the oriental manner with the cock feather (*qv*) in line with the nock and the two shaft feathers, or vanes, at a hundred and twenty degrees either side. Drag, due to air resistance, must be kept to a minimum and the shaft must be well polished.

The design should give a point of balance about ¾ to ½ in. in rear of the centre of the shaft, as measured from the point to the base of the nock. Preliminary computer analysis by Dr David Clarke indicates that the point of balance is critical if sustained flight is to be achieved.

The flight behaviour of the flight arrow differs from that of the target arrow. The latter has a forward balance so that its centre of gravity is about 1½ in. in front of its mid-point. When shot it follows a parabolic path and, with the aid of its feathers or vanes, the line of the shaft is the same as that of the parabola. If shot at forty-five degrees, it will hit the ground at an angle of about fifty-five degrees, so that its line has rotated, or *pitched*, through a hundred degrees, and the *pitching rate* is the same as the rate of change of the curve in the parabolic path.

If the pitching rate is reduced by giving the shaft a rearward balance, it will fly point upward in relation to the normal flight path. With air pressure being exerted on the under side of the shaft, a soaring effect is achieved so that the flight arrow does not follow a normal parabola. This enables far greater ranges to be achieved than those theoretically possible from the initial velocity imparted to the arrow. However, distance will be lost if the point of balance is too far in rear of the mid-point and no advantage will be gained.

The weight of such arrows needs to be related to the draw weight (*qv*) of the bow to be used. Roy King in *Bowman's Handbook* (see above), p. 157, suggests as a guide, based on record achievements, 18-inch arrows should be within the following limits:

35-lb bow – 80-95 grains
50-lb bow – 95-110 grains
65-lb bow – 100-120 grains
unlimited – 120-135 grains

For the **arrow shaft** good quality pine or Port Orford cedar is suitable, though some suppliers are now offering carbon fibre for this purpose. With modern centre-shot bows and shooting techniques, spine value (*qv*) need not be considered, though the shaft should be as stiff as possible.

Certain **release aids**, not permitted in target shooting, are allowed in flight shooting. That most widely used is the 'flipper', either double or single. It consists of a leather strap, attached to the drawing hand, that is passed around the bowstring, below the nock of the arrow, and held between the thumb and forefinger. It enables a simple pinch grip to be used in drawing and releasing the string. The double form is needed with the more powerful bows; its design and method of use is illustrated by Jack Flinton in *Bowman's Handbook* (see above) pp. 154–6. Neither GNAS nor FITA Rules permit mechanical release aids.

Equipment and shooting techniques apart, an important reason for the limited interest in this form of archery is the problem that faces many in finding a suitable practice range on which to exercise the art. Failure to find an area nearly half a mile in length over which arrows can be shot has prevented many possible enthusiasts from involving themselves in flight shooting.

Historical Aspects

Modern flight shooting has evolved from the techniques developed by the Turks, with whom it was an honoured pastime in which Sultans and high-ranking officials took part. This naturally stimulated interest.

For this we are indebted to Mustafā Kānī and his treatise, *Telchīs resaīl er-rümat* (Summary of the Treatise of Archers), written at the command of the Ottoman sultan, Mahmud II (1809–39), himself a skilled bowman. The translation into German by Joachim Hein fortunately caught the attention of Paul E. Klopsteg (*qv*), who privately published a major extract in 1934 under the title *Turkish Archery and the Composite Bow*. Its success led to a revised edition in 1947.

An earlier account showing the prowess of the Turkish archers had appeared in Sir Ralph Payne-Gallwey, *The Crossbow*, London 1903, pp. 26–30, and in his attached 'Treatise on Turkish and other Oriental Bows of Mediaeval and Later Times'. P. E. Klopsteg had taken note of all this in preparing his own work. Stone pillars still exist on the Ok Meydan (Arrow Field) outside Istanbul, recording noted feats.

A degree of mystery surrounds what is said to be the greatest shot, made by the Sultan Selim in 1797, of 1,400 *gez* – a unit normally taken as being 24½ inches – giving a distance of 972 yards, 8 inches. This feat is often quoted in works on archery, but it is not listed by Mustafā Kānī in the *Telchīs* . . . There is no doubt that the Sultan was a highly skilled archer and his shot was seen by the British Ambassador, Sir Robert Ainslie, who reported the achievement to Sir Joseph Banks, President of the Royal Society. While a man of his standing would not have done so if he did not believe it to be true, it is strange that Kānī does not mention this record.

All this detailed information has given emphasis to the basic designs and techniques of the Turks and, it is not denied, they may be the best. Little or no research has been conducted into the performance of the sectional arrow, as recorded by Taybughā al-Ashrafī (*c.* AD 1368), (see J. D. Latham & W. F. Paterson, *Saracen Archery*, London 1970, pp. 104–10). This shows an alternative approach to the control of the pitching rate by concentrating the weight at the ends of the shaft, using relatively heavy material, joined together by a hollow reed. If the correct balance is achieved such an arrow would offer longer flight than one of conventional form.

Records

Enthusiasts in the USA have a unique advantage at the dry bed of Ivanpah Lake in California. It presents a large, flat area, devoid of vegetation and is thus ideal for flight shooting. Though some have argued that its elevation, some 3,000 feet above sea level, enables added distance to be achieved due to the lower air density, the skill of those who have set records cannot be denied.

In the Championship held on October 4th and 5th, 1980, in the professional Men's Unlimited handbow class, Don Brown shot 1,179 yards and 4 inches, using a bow of 130-lb draw weight. In the Women's Unlimited event, April Moon shot 923 yards, 1 foot, 6 inches. These almost incredible distances indicate what can be achieved with modern equipment. (See *Archery International*, December 1980, p. 59.)

A new World Record for a hand-held bow was set by Alan Webster of Sheffield at the American National Flight Shooting Championships held at Ivanpah Dry Lake in California in October, 1982. Using a bow of 100 lb draw weight, made specially for him by the veteran American archer, Harry Drake, he shot a 14-inch carbon fibre arrow 1,231 yards, 1 foot and 10 inches.

Alan Webster has been the British Flight Shooting Champion since 1968. His new bow, aided by ideal weather conditions, enabled him to exceed his British and National record of 798 yards, 1 foot and 9 inches set at Burton Constable near Hull in 1980, using an 80-lb bow. (See *The British Archer*, Vol. 34, No. 4, January 1983, p. 157.)

FLINTON, Jack (1893–1982)

He had a distinguished record in almost every branch of archery, since he took up the sport in 1927 when looking for some hobby and recreation within the physical limitations imposed upon him by serious wounds sustained during the First World War.

As well as having been a skilled target archer and a member of the British teams at the World Championships in 1939 and 1946, he was the National Flight Shooting Champion for eleven successive years.

After making his first longbow in 1928, he developed his skill as a craftsman and made several hundred bows of every type, including a few crossbows.

Among his other activities he was a coach and, with several other experienced archers, started the Coaching Certificate System from which modern British coaching has developed. He officiated at innumerable meetings as Judge or Field Captain and was an adviser to several film companies in productions involving archery.

In recognition for the assistance he had given over many years, he was an honorary member of seventy-two archery clubs, including several in the USA.

FLODDEN BOW

An old yew longbow in the possession of the Royal Company of Archers (*qv*) in Edinburgh and reputed to have been used at the Battle of Flodden Field in 1513. It was recovered from a house near the site of the battle, where it had been preserved, by Colonel J. Fergusson around 1830–40 and presented by him to Peter Muir (*qv*), bowyer to the Royal Company.

It is somewhat roughly finished, of squarish cross-section, measuring 1¼ × 1¼ inches at its centre, with an effective length of about 74 inches. The estimated draw weight has been given as 80–90 lb, but one may venture to suggest this figure is a little on the high side.

FLUTED ARROW

A wooden arrow, scored in lines along its length to prevent warping. It is rarely seen, but some of the popinjay (*qv*) arrows in Belgium are still treated in this manner.

FOLLOW THE STRING

Said of a bow that takes a permanent curve or set towards the belly from use. It is not unusual with a wooden bow and if the curvature is slight, there is little harm, though a fractional loss in performance may be experienced.

FOLLOW THROUGH

Maintaining the position of the bow, toward the target, after loosing the arrow. It is an important aspect of basic shooting technique. If neglected it can result in the bow arm beginning to drop before the arrow has, in fact, left the string. Inconsistent shooting may be the consequence.

FOOT -ED -ING

The foot of an arrow is the fore end of the shaft. It is not uncommon for wooden arrows to be reinforced by splicing a hardwood footing to the main shaft. Such an arrow is said to be footed.

FOOT BOW
A bow shot from a sitting position, with the two feet either side of the centre. The technique is of some antiquity and it is still used by some tribes in the Amazon Basin, as well as for modern flight shooting (*qv*) in its appropriate class. The added power that results from both hands being applied to the string has enabled the modern flight shooter to achieve distances in excess of 2,000 yards.

The term is also applied to certain forms of crossbow (*qv*), fitted with a foot stirrup at the fore end of the tiller to aid the process of spanning, or drawing the string back to the release mechanism of the weapon.

FORCE-DRAW CURVE
A curve plotted on squared paper of draw force against draw length to help assess the dynamics of a bow. It is of importance to those who are interested in the technical aspects of archery.

Such a graph is prepared with the vertical scale or ordinate marked in pounds weight and the base or abscissa in inches of draw, measured from the grip of the bow. The most simple method is to fit an arrow shaft, marked in inches along its length, to the bowstring. With the handle of the bow securely fixed, the string is then drawn with a spring balance so that the pull on the string can be read as the draw is increased. The readings are plotted and the points set on the graph are then joined together to give the force-draw curve for the bow being studied.

The area between the curve and the base line is then a measure of the potential energy (PE) stored in the bow by the action of the archer in bringing the string to full draw. In simple terms, a curve of a convex form shows more energy being stored, for a given maximum effort by the archer, than one of a straight – or even concave – form. It is desirable that the draw weight should build up relatively quickly in the early stages of the draw and that it should not become too steep toward the end. A slow build up at the start of the draw indicates a drop in performance,

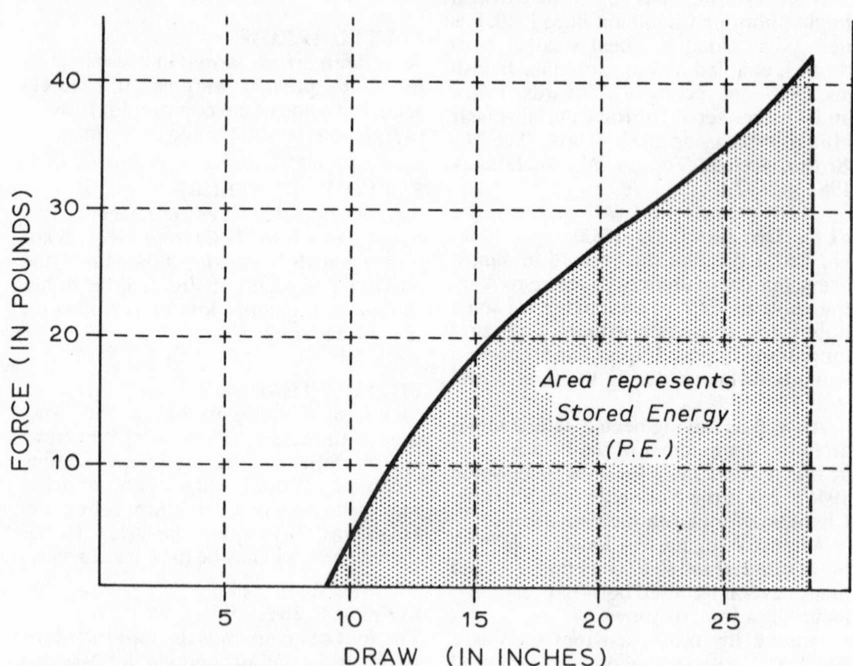

Force-draw curve taken from a modern composite target bow. The stored energy, in this example, is about 35 foot-pounds.

while a quick build up at the end of the draw can lead to inaccurate shooting as the velocity of discharge of the arrow is more affected by a slight variation in draw length than in the case of a bow showing a slower build up at this final stage.

The PE value, derived from the force-draw curve, is needed when assessing the technical efficiency of a bow, when it must be compared with the kinetic energy (KE) imparted to the arrow on discharge. (See also EFFICIENCY and VELOCITY.)

FORD, Horace Alfred (1822–1880)
Winner of the British Target Championship at the GNAM twelve times between 1849 and 1867, he is undoubtedly the greatest exponent of target shooting with the traditional English longbow (*qv*) on record. In 1854 he was the first to exceed 1,000 points at the GNAM for the double York Round (*qv*), his best score at this event being in 1857 with 245 hits on the target and 1,251 scored. For the single York Round his best score, as noted in *Archery*, (Badminton Series), p. 420, was 809 from 137 hits. This has never been equalled by any archer using the simple wooden bow.

His book, *Archery: its Theory and Practice* (1856), was a collection of eighteen articles, published in *The Field*, and led to Horace Ford being called 'the founder of modern scientific archery'. It went through four editions, with a further lithographic reprint in 1971 and it is a classic in its field. His logical and intelligent application of basic principles laid a sound foundation for future progress.

FOREHAND SHAFT
An arrow shot where the archer can view the mark or target above the bow hand (cf. *Underhand*). It applies to the majority of modern target contests, other than clout shooting (*qv*). However, those who favour the traditional longbow (*qv*) shoot underhand at the longer ranges.

FORESHAFT
The front half of an arrow shaft.

FORKED HEAD or FORKER
An arrowhead with two points in the form of the letter 'Y'. The basic design is of some antiquity and they were mainly used for hunting purposes with both hand bows and crossbows.

FREE BACKING
A form of backing (*qv*), usually of gut or sinew, that is not glued to the main stave, or core, of the bow. The best examples are those used by the Eskimos.

FREE STYLE
A class in field shooting (*qv*) allowing sights, stabilisers (*qv*) and torque flight compensators (*qv*) to be fitted on bows, in contrast to the instinctive or bare bow (*qv*) class where such devices are not allowed. (See Appendix 1, p. 150, for FITA Rule 548B.)

FREEZING
See ARCHER'S CATALEPSY.

FRITH, Mrs Inger Kristine, OBE (1909–1981)
President of FITA (*qv*) 1961–77, during which time, under her firm but diplomatic guidance and direction, archery gained a new dimension and flourished as never before in the international field. Its re-inclusion in the list of sports in the Olympic Games (*qv*) was the result of many years of unrelenting and determined effort. The event was staged in the 1972 Olympic Games in Munich and those of 1976 and 1980 in Montreal and Moscow. She was the first woman to be invited to address the International Olympic Committee (IOC) in session in 1963 and the only woman to head an International Sports Federation.

Hardly less were her other achievements. Largely through her efforts archery was accepted in the Pan-American, Mediterranean, Asian and Commonwealth Games; she also inaugurated the FITA target championships – European (1968) and of the Americas (1972) – and the field championships of the World (1969) – European (1971) and of the Americas (1973).

For her inspiring and successful leadership she was awarded the OBE in 1971, the Silver Medal of the Olympic Order in 1977, and the Avery Brundage Foundation Gold Medal of Merit in 1973.

Mrs Frith took up archery in 1948 and she was a member of the British teams at the World Target Championships in 1950 and 1952. This gave her a personal insight and understanding of the stresses that face archers, and indeed all sportsmen and women, in major contests. This influenced many of her later rulings and decisions. From 1953–61 she was the GNAS delegate to FITA. In 1954 she started the British international trials and for ten years she was the British team manager. From 1955–61 she was a FITA Vice-President. Her subsequent selection and re-election as President for four successive terms of office showed the outstanding confidence in her ability held by all FITA member associations. Following her retirement in 1977, she was elected an Honorary President of FITA.

GAFFLE
The earlier English name for the lever used for spanning (*qv*) certain types of crossbow. (See also GOAT'S-FOOT LEVER.)

GLOVE
See SHOOTING GLOVE.

GOAT'S-FOOT LEVER
A form of lever for spanning (*qv*) certain types of crossbow, with two curved prongs whose shape is evocative of the leg and thigh of a goat, or a similar animal. The appellation has been applied in Europe to forms of lever with straight prongs, where the terms *pied de biche* or *pied de chèvre* may be met.

Such levers offer a power advantage in the order of 5:1 and they were used for both military and sporting purposes. The medieval English term for this device was *gaffle*.

GOLD
The central circle of an archery target. While the rifleman uses the term 'bull's-eye' for this area, the archer prefers the word 'gold', which refers to its colour. In target contests a special prize is normally awarded to whoever gains most hits in the gold and, when deciding a result of a tie in the number of points scored, the archer with most 'golds' is the winner.

Older targets were invariably coloured with gold paint, but in more modern times it has been replaced by yellow to simplify printing. With the standard English target a hit in the gold scores 9 points, while for the 10-zone FITA target it is divided into two equal parts, the centre circle scoring 10 points and the outer ring 9 points. Hits on the inner circle only are recorded as 'golds'.

GRAND NATIONAL ARCHERY SOCIETY (GNAS)
The governing body for target archery in Britain. Its rules also cover field, flight, and clout shooting (*qv*). It was founded in 1861, though the idea had been suggested sixteen years earlier.

With a permanent headquarters within the National Agricultural Centre, Stoneleigh, Warwickshire, it is affiliated to the British Olympic Association and to the International Archery Federation (FITA).

The Grand National Archery Meeting (GNAM), which included the British Target Championship until 1970, has records dating back to 1844. From 1971 a separate British National Championship was instituted and divorced from the GNAM for the first time after 126 years.

GREASE BOX
A small container of grease, usually attached to the belt of the quiver. The grease was applied to the finger stalls, tab or shooting glove to give a sharper release to the bowstring. It has been out of favour for many years and may be regarded as a collector's piece, rather than being an item of practical value. Even as early as 1856, Horace Ford (*qv*) casts doubt on its use in his book, *Archery: Its Theory and Practice* (p. 46).

GRIP (*n.* and *v.*)
The handle of the bow or the method of holding the bow for which there are variations.

With the traditional longbow a firm grip on the handle was the general practice. The modern method, sometimes called the *hammock grip*, merely supports the bow in the fork between the thumb and index finger, without pressure on the sides of the grip.

GROUND QUIVER
A holder placed on or stuck in the ground to hold the arrows. It usually incorporates a support or rest for the bow where it may be left while an archer is waiting to shoot.

GROUP -ING
A number of arrows together in the target. Close grouping is an indication of good shooting and steadiness of technique.

GUILDS
In medieval times guilds of craftsmen were formed, mainly to set standards and ensure the excellence of their products. Many still exist in the City of London, though they have departed from their original purpose and are mainly concerned with charitable and other works. However, both the Worshipful Company of Bowyers and the Worshipful Company of Fletchers give their support to certain archery contests in Britain. Similar active guilds exist in several European cities and give their support to the modern use of the bow and the crossbow.

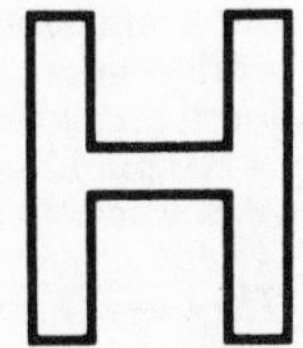

HAMMOCK GRIP
The method of supporting the grip of the bow in the crotch between the thumb and forefinger, with no positive grasp on the handle. The object is to avoid putting any twisting moment into the bow; it is a technique widely favoured by modern target archers. A strap is used to attach the bow to the wrist so that it will not fall to the ground after the arrow is released.

HAND BOW
Any bow whose grip is held or supported by the hand, as opposed to the crossbow or the form where one, or both feet are applied at or near the centre.

HANDICAP
A system of adjustment to scores achieved in a round (*qv*) to enable archers of different abilities to compete on equal terms. The GNAS (*qv*) provides tables on request to any who wish to operate the scheme. (See Appendix 1, GNAS *Rules of Shooting*, Part IX.)

HANDLE
See GRIP.

HANGER
An arrow that fails to penetrate the target boss adequately and, as a result, hangs down across the face. Shooting is stopped if this occurs and the Judge or Field Captain (*qv*) attends to the offending shaft and determines the score it has achieved.

HANSARD, George Agar
Author of *The Book of Archery* (London 1840, with reprints in 1841, 1845, and 1876), an important contribution to archery literature. Its main interest may be considered to lie in the numerous historical anecdotes that it contains.

HARPOON ARROW
An arrow with a detachable, barbed head to which a cord is fastened, so that the fish or animal may be recovered after it has been hit. Several interesting forms are associated with the Alaskan Eskimos. (See O. T. Mason, *North American Bows, Arrows and Quivers*, Washington 1894.)

HARROW or HERCE
The traditional formation of the medieval English archers on the battlefield, drawn up in several staggered ranks, that allowed as many men as possible to stand and shoot with a reduced frontage. It enabled the archers to be given maximum protection from flanking infantry or cavalry without reduction of their output of arrows against the enemy. (See Robert Hardy, *Longbow: A Social and Military History*, Cambridge 1976, pp. 67–8.)

HEAD
The point of an arrow. They have existed in hundreds of different forms from antiquity. The most prolific variations in design are those from Japan, but India does not lag far behind.

Modern target arrows are fitted with a pile (*qv*), while several variations of broadhead (*qv*) are favoured by the hunter. (See ARROWHEAD.)

HEARTWOOD
The inner substance of a tree, beneath the outer bark and sapwood. Its use is of importance in the design of the traditional yew longbow (*qv*).

HEATH, Ernest Gerald, BA (b. 1920)
Author and founder member of the Society of Archer-Antiquaries, whose *Journal* he edited from 1958–76. He has also acted as an adviser and consultant on exhibitions and television programmes as

well as organizing the GNAM (see GNAS) for several years.

He successfully stimulated the interest of certain publishers to reprint thirteen old works on archery and wrote appropriate forewords to each.

His published works include, *In Pursuit of Archery* (with C. B. Edwards – 1962), *Archery: The Modern Approach* (1966), *The Grey Goose Wing* (1971), *A History of Target Archery* (1973), *Brazilian Indian Archery* (with Vilma Chiara – 1977), and *Archery: A Military History* (1980).

HEDGELEY MOOR BOW
A longbow, probably of yew, preserved at Alnwick Castle and reputed to have been used during the Wars of the Roses at the Battle of Hedgeley Moor in 1464. The stave is 65½ in. in length, though the two tips are slightly damaged. A suggested draw weight of 45–50 lb has been offered, which is below that of a man's war bow. (See H. Gordon & A. Webb, *Journal of the Society of Archer-Antiquaries*, Vol. 15, 1972, pp. 8–9.)

Because of its shortness and light draw weight, when compared with preserved examples of English medieval war bows, the opinion may be offered that it was made for a youth before he gained his full stature and strength as a man. In one of the recorded sermons given by Bishop Latimer before Edward VI in 1549, he said: "I had my bows bought for me according to my age and strength; as I increased in them so my bows were made bigger, for men shall never shoot well, except that they be brought up in it."

HEEL (of an arrow)
The section of the shaft between the rear end of the feathers and the nock. (See also ARROW, Parts of.)

HEIGHT (of a bowstring)
See BRACING HEIGHT.

HELWIG, George Charles (b. 1917)
George Helwig holds a long and distinguished record in the field of archery administration and organization, not only in the USA, but also with FITA in the world-wide context.

Within the USA he was elected to the Board of Governors of the NAA (*qv*) in 1955; he served as a Vice-President from 1957–72 and was their President during the 1972–76 term of office.

Among his many international activities, he has been the USA's representative to FITA Congress since 1963 and officiated as a judge in several World Championships, as well as being the Tournament Director when the event was held at Valley Forge in 1969.

As instigator and director of the National Junior Olympic Archery Development in the USA, his efforts have shown conspicuous success in the achievements of young archers in both World and Olympic contests.

HEREFORD ROUND
A round (*qv*) that consists of shooting 72 arrows at 80 yards, 48 arrows at 60 yards and 24 arrows at 50 yards against a standard four-foot target. A double round of a total of 288 arrows has been used since 1947 to decide the ladies' championship of Great Britain and that of several other major contests.

HERSE (or HERCE)
See HARROW.

HICKMAN, Clarence Nichols (1889–1981)
An archer and scientist in the USA who made noted contributions to the study of the design of bows and arrows. In October, 1929, his first paper on the subject appeared in *The Journal of the Franklin Institute* on 'The Velocity and Acceleration of Arrows, Weight and Efficiency of Bows as affected by Backing of Bow'.

Having taken up archery as a recreation, and being a research physicist, he investigated many problems, both mathematically and experimentally, with some surprising and interesting results. His earlier articles in journals and archery periodicals have been collected in *Archery: The Technical Side* (1947), with those of F. Nagler, Paul E. Klopsteg and others.

Until revealed by his studies, it had been rare to see anything other than the traditional English longbow on the shooting line, but he found that better performance could be obtained with bows having reflexed limbs. His submission in June, 1935, 'A New Bow of Radical Design, Construction and Performance' (U.S. Patent No. 2,100,317), revolutionized the subject and led directly to the sophisticated modern construction of the sporting bow, though this took time and the availability of new materials to develop.

HILL, Howard (1900–1975)
A redoubtable American archer, mainly noted for his achievements in the hunting field, but an exponent in both target and flight shooting (*qv*). His skill was also employed by film companies in historical contexts to show the power and effectiveness of the bow.

Among his several published works, *Hunting the Hard Way* (1953 – reprinted 1954 and, with certain alterations, in 1955 and 1956), and *Wild Adventure* (1954 – reprinted 1955 and, with certain alterations, in 1959) remain classics for those who hunt with the bow.

HIT
The striking of an arrow on the mark or within the target area. At the GNAM, between the first meeting in 1844 and 1848, the British men's target championship was awarded for most hits on the target, and until 1852 this was also the practice for the ladies' target championship. After these dates the prizes were awarded on points scored.

In the event of a tie in points scored, the winner is the archer with most golds (*qv*). If these are equal the prize then goes to whoever has most hits on the target. (For details see both FITA and GNAS *Rules* in Appendix 1.)

HOLD
A pause made by the archer, with the arrow fully drawn, while final aim is taken. It is one of the five 'partitions' originally laid down by Roger Ascham (*qv*) in *Toxophilus* (1545) on which good shooting depends.

Ascham, concerned with the powerful longbow (*qv*) for use in warfare, says: "Holdynge must not be longe, for it bothe putteth a bowe in ieopardy, & also marreth a mans shoote, it must be so lytle y[t] it may be perceyued better in a mans mynde when it is done, than seene w[t] a mans eyes when it is in doyng." The modern target archer, however, may hold as long as ten seconds to ensure the accuracy of aim.

HOOD, Robin
The legendary outlaw and master bowman of Sherwood Forest, who has epitomized the fight of free men against oppressive authority through the ages. In this he has a counterpart in William Tell (*qv*). (See P. V. Harris, *The Truth About Robin Hood* – 1973.)

HORN
A piece of carved horn, normally fitted to each tip of the longbow (*qv*) and carrying the nock – or notch – for the bowstring.

HOYLE SHOOTING
A form of roving (*qv*), now superseded by field shooting (*qv*). It is of historical interest as an old method by which archers trained, by shooting at marks at varied and uncertain distances, but at relatively short ranges when compared with roving.

The rules are set out by Thomas Roberts, *The English Bowman* (1801) p. 236, where he states that *hoyle* is an old north-country word, signifying small eminences, as mole-hills, or thistles, docks, and other prominent marks. He adds that ranges may sometimes be as short as fifteen yards but the mark given is never to exceed *six score*.

HUNTING
Though not legally permitted in Britain with the bow and arrow, there are few or no restrictions in most other countries. In the USA many states have special seasons for the bow-hunter.

For bigger game more powerful bows are needed than those used for target shooting, and arrow shafts are normally fitted with broadheads (*qv*). The primary works devoted to this aspect of archery are: Saxton T. Pope, *Hunting with the Bow and Arrow*, 1923; Howard Hill, *Hunting the Hard Way*, 1953; and Bob Swineheart, *Sagittarius*, 1971.

HYSTERESIS (of a bow)
The difference in the stored energy in a bow, as shown by the static force-draw curve (*qv*) and the dynamic curve, when the bow is released. The latter runs a little below the former and represents a small added loss to the energy imparted to the arrow when it is shot.

INNER WHITE
Before the adoption of the modern colours of the target rings, the third ring was often white, as was the fifth or outer ring. It is now blue as specified at the Grand National Archery Meeting at Knavesmire, York, in 1844. (See also TARGET and PRINCE'S RECKONING.)

Under FITA Rules, where the five coloured rings of the target face are each divided into two zones, the inner white scores 2 points (see Appendix 1, page 138, Article 502).

INSTINCTIVE SHOOTING
Shooting without any form of sight. It is the basic technique of the hunter and it is also employed in the 'bare bow' class of field shooting (*qv*).

INTERNATIONAL ARCHERY FEDERATION (FITA)
See under FÉDÉRATION INTERNATIONALE DE TIR À L'ARC.

INTERNATIONAL ARMBRUST UNION (IAU)
A federation founded in 1956, concerned with crossbow target shooting. After organizing eleven European Championships, they held the first Crossbow World Championship in 1979 in which teams from nine countries took part.

The primary concern of the IAU is that, while users of the crossbow shoot in many countries, there have been no agreed rules and regulations. Their objects have stimulated considerable interest and there has been a steady growth in their membership.

Under their regulations, shooting is carried out at 10 and 30 metres, with restrictions on both the weight and the draw weight of the crossbows used.

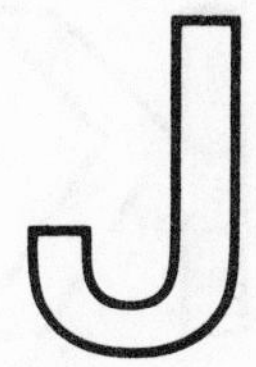

JAPANESE ARCHERY
See KYUDO.

JERSEY ROUND
An archery round (*qv*) in the USA, adopted for men by the New Jersey State Archery Association in 1930 and consisting of 36 arrows shot at 80, 60, 50 and 40 yards; 144 arrows in all, against a standard five-zone target. The Jersey Round for women, adopted in 1945, consists of 36 arrows shot at 70, 60, 50 and 40 yards.

JUNIOR ARCHER
An archer under 18 years of age (GNAS Rule 700). A variety of suitable rounds (*qv*) has been devised for Junior contests, listed under their respective headings. They include four different *Bristol* Rounds, four different *Metric* Rounds, the *St Nicholas* Round, the *Short Windsor* Round and the *Junior National* intended for girls under 13 and boys under 12 years of age.

JUNIOR NATIONAL CHAMPIONSHIP MEETING
GNAS Rule 702 specifies that the Meeting shall be of one day's duration and that the following rounds shall be shot:

Boys under 18 years of age – York
Girls under 18 years of age – Hereford
Boys under 16 years of age – Bristol II
Girls under 16 years of age – Bristol III
Boys under 14 years of age – Bristol III
Girls under 13 years of age – Bristol IV
Boys under 12 years of age – Bristol IV

(Details of rounds are given under their respective entries.)

An archer may enter for a round applicable to a higher age group, but not a lower one. The minimum age for competitors shall be 9 years on the day of the Championships.

The winners of the York and Hereford Rounds shall be designated, respectively, as National Junior Boy and Girl Champions.

KEEPING A LENGTH
To shoot arrows consistently to a desired range. An important aspect for the medieval archer in war, as emphasized by Roger Ascham (*qv*) and still of concern to those who engage in clout shooting (*qv*).

KEMBER-SMITH, John (b. 1924)
National Coaching Organizer and Chairman of the GNAS National Coaching Committee, he has been actively involved in the training of archers since he qualified as a GNAS coach in 1954.

He has written extensively on this subject and his 'Coaching Notes' have appeared regularly in *The British Archer* (*qv*) for more than twenty years. As a result he has played a major part in the study and development of training methods and techniques in Britain.

He is also an international judge and has officiated at World Championships.

KESSELS, Oscar (d. 1968)
A unique combination of international champion, indefatigable administrator and one of the finest ambassadors of the sport of archery. A Belgian, Oscar Kessels began shooting in a bow in 1930 and, from the beginning of international archery in 1931, out of twenty-four world championships during his lifetime, he was selected twenty-one times for the Belgian team. This is an unequalled record.

He was elected President of FITA in 1957 and held the post until 1961. Although he failed to realize his constant ambition to re-establish archery as an event in the Olympic Games, the firm foundation he had laid enabled this to be achieved by his successor, Mrs Inger K. Frith, OBE (*qv*), in 1968.

(For further biographical details see E. G. Heath, *A History of Target Archery* (1973), pp. 152–3.)

KISSER
A small, bulbous projection, fitted to the bowstring. At full draw it is brought between the lips to ensure the accuracy and exactness of the anchor (*qv*) of the shaft hand beneath the chin. It is also called a lip mark and, under international rules, its diameter is limited to 1 cm.

KLICKER
See CLICKER.

KLOPSTEG, Paul E. (b. 1889)
A distinguished physicist in the USA, who has held many important posts in both government and civil scientific organizations, he became interested in archery around 1930 as a relaxation, and applied his technical knowledge to the study of bows and arrows for more than fifty years. The design and development of the modern bow owes much to his published works on this subject, where he put forward reasoned ideas that were revolutionary in their time.

His earlier papers, together with those of C. N. Hickman and F. Nagler and others, were collected and published under the title of *Archery: The Technical Side*, 1947. His other major work in this field is *Turkish Archery and the Composite Bow* (Evanston, Illinois 1934, reprinted in 1947). In addition to several other articles in journals and magazines, he has written the definitive entry, *sv* 'Archery' in the *Encyclopaedia Britannica*.

(See also VIRTUAL MASS.)

KYUDO
The formal Japanese art of archery that follows their traditional methods and techniques. It is a branch of Zen Buddhism where the physical and mental disciplines of the bow and arrow are used as an aid in achieving a spiritual goal.

The famous Samurai warriors of old were competent archers, as well as swordsmen. They could shoot on horseback, as well as on foot with their long seven-foot laminated bamboo bows. (See YUMI.)

When compared with the technique of international target archery, the main differences in *kyudo* (*kyu* = 'bow'; *do* = 'the way of') are (i) the use of the thumb lock, which was widely employed

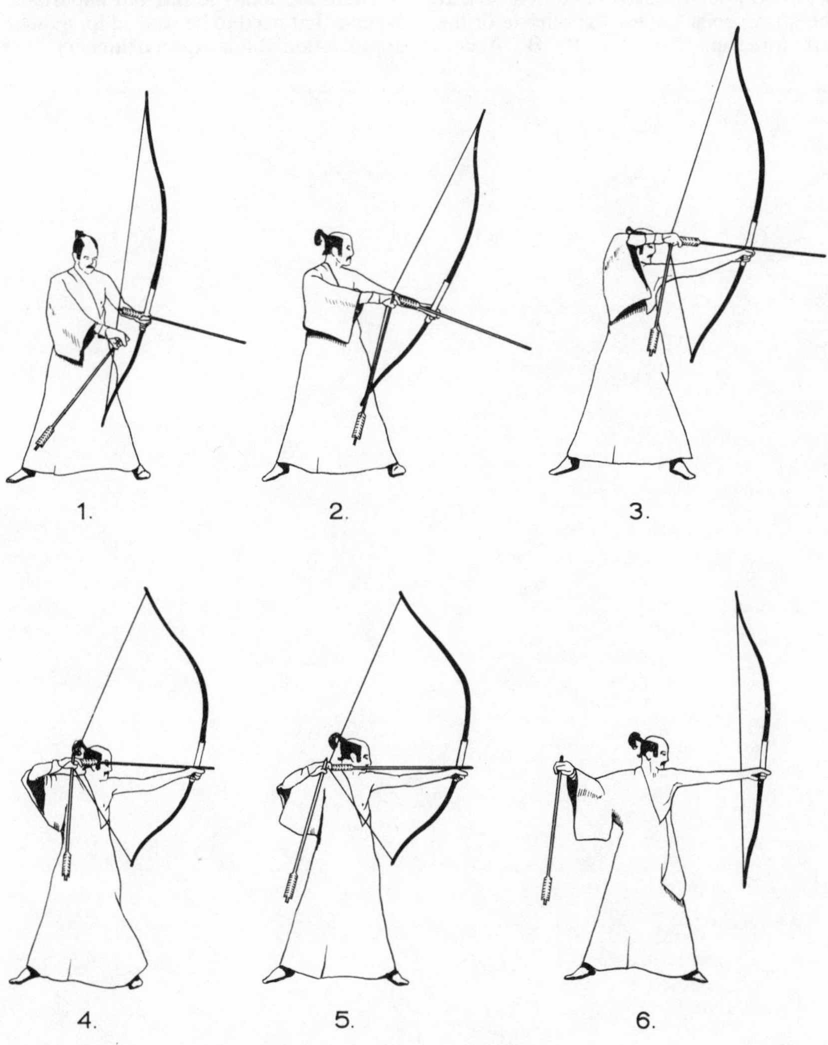

Kyudo.
1. Tsurugarami, *or Gripping the String.*
2. Monomi, *or Viewing the Mark.*
3. Uchiokoshi, *or Raising and Drawing.*
4. Dai San, *or Consummation of the Draw.*
5. Jiman, *or Holding at Full Draw.*
6. Zanshin, *or Posture after the Release.*

by eastern archers, the shaft hand being protected by a leather glove having a heavily reinforced thumb piece, and (ii) the arrow is drawn to the point of the right shoulder. The bow is allowed to rotate in the hand when the arrow is loosed, so that the string ends against the outside of the left forearm. (See W. R. B. Acker, *Japanese Archery*, Tokyo 1965; E. Herrigel, *Zen in the Art of Archery*, 1953, reprinted 1956, 1959, 1964 and 1968; A. Sollier and Z. Györbiro, *Japanese Archery: Zen in Action*, Tokyo 1969.)

There are many lesser, but important, aspects that need to be studied for a fuller appreciation of this aspect of archery.

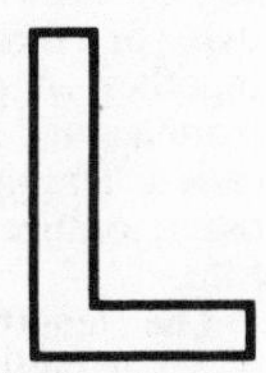

LADY PARAMOUNT
In Britain, the patroness of an archery meeting or tournament. She is the final arbiter in any dispute that may arise and she presents the prizes at the conclusion of the contest.

LAMINATED (bow)
A bow constructed from several layers of basically similar materials, in contrast to COMPOSITE (*qv*) designs where dissimilar components are used. Modern English longbows of traditional form are often made from three layers of different woods, while the Japanese traditional bow, as used in KYUDO (*qv*) has a central core made from bamboo flanked by strips of a deciduous wood and sandwiched between two long, flat strips of bamboo.

LEAK
A target is said to 'leak' when an arrow passes completely through the boss at a weak point.

LET DOWN
A reduction in the power and performance of a bow usually resulting from long and continued use. The term is also used when an archer, from full draw, relaxes and eases down the bowstring, without releasing the arrow.

LEVER, Sir Ashton (1729–1788)
Founder member and first President of the Toxophilite Society in 1781, which was later permitted the prefix 'Royal'. (See Thomas Roberts, *The English Bowman*, London 1801, p. 79; and E. G. Heath, *A History of Target Archery*, Newton Abbot 1973, pp. 61–2.)

LIMB
The parts of the bow from the handle to each tip, and further distinguished by the terms 'upper' and 'lower' limb. There is also the 'working part' of the limb, when dealing with the oriental COMPOSITE (*sv*) bows, which refers to the section between the grip and the rigid ends or 'ears', where all flexing takes place as the bow is drawn.

LIP MARKER
See KISSER.

LIVERY (arrow or bow)
The standard issued equipment to the medieval English archer.

LOCK (*v.* and *n.*)
1. To secure the thumb on the bowstring for drawing (see THUMB LOCK), as widely practised by oriental archers, including exponents of *Kyudo* (*qv*).
2. A general term for that part of a crossbow's mechanism that retains the drawn string. There are many variations in design.

LONGBOW
In Europe many examples of long, straight, wooden bows have been excavated dating back to the Neolithic period, 4–5,000 years ago. A summary of these, with drawings, is included in Gad Rausing, *The Bow: Some Notes on its Origin and Development*, Lund, Sweden 1967 (text in English).

In the context of modern target archery, the traditional English wooden longbow still has a strong following among those who favour the older methods and techniques, as opposed to the use of modern designs, even though the latter offers greater accuracy and better performance. A special class is included in many tournaments for those who wish to shoot in the longbow.

Yew (*qv*) is considered to be the best wood, though others are used. Due to the difficulty in finding good staves, modern construction often employs the splicing together of two half lengths or the use of two or three different woods glued together. A good longbow can be made from a stave of hickory or dagame (often called 'lemonwood'), while in the USA osage orange offers an excellent substitute.

The length of the English longbow depends on that of the arrow to be drawn and may vary from about 5 ft 6 in. to a little over 6 ft. The traditional cross-section is a 'D' shape, the flat side forming the back of the bow, which faces the target when shooting. Some old longbows are almost square in cross-section, as in the case of the Mendlesham bow (*qv*), while others are almost circular, with a slightly flattened back, as may be seen in the two examples salvaged from the *Mary Rose* (*qv*), and exhibited in the Tower of London Armouries.

For details of construction see: Robert Hardy, *Longbow: A Social and Military History*, Cambridge 1976; A. E. Hodgkin, *The Archer's Craft*, London 1951 (reprinted 1954); and the series by Roy King, 'Making a Longbow', *The British Archer*, vol. 22, Nos. 3, 4 & 5, 1970–1.

Making a longbow can be a pleasing task for which only simple tools are needed. A problem that may face the amateur is when a full length stave is not available and two half sections have to be spliced together in the centre. This calls for the accurate cutting of about a 3½-inch double fishtail.

It is generally recommended to start with dagame as there is no need to follow the run of the grain as is necessary with yew and osage. If a stave is obtained 6 ft long and 1 in. × 1 in. in section, it should result in a bow with a draw weight of about 45 lb.

First, rule a line across the centre of the stave. The upper limb is a little longer than the lower so two more lines are needed to mark the grip or handle. These should be one inch above the centre and three inches below. Next, mark a centre-line along the length of the stave. From the limits of the grip, the width is tapered to half an inch at the ends. The thickness is reduced to the same measure but the back (*qv*) is left alone, all surplus wood being removed from the belly.

After the traditional 'D' shape, with a flat back and rounded belly, is achieved, nocks for the bowstring can be cut in the tips and the bow may be strung. The final adjustment is made with the aid of a tiller (*qv*), surplus wood being carefully scraped away until the desired curve in the two limbs is achieved. While stiffness is needed in the grip, the rate of curvature of each limb should increase slightly toward the tips and present an elliptical, rather than a circular bend.

From mathematical analysis, ideal limb dimensions are shown in R. P. Elmer, *Target Archery*, New York 1946, pp.

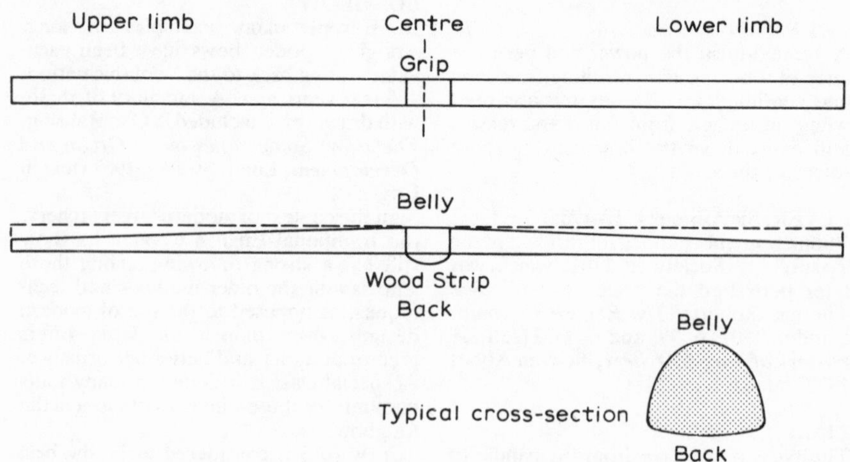

207–8, and also in P. E. Klopsteg, 'Bows and Arrows: A Chapter in the Evolution of Archery in America', *Smithsonian Report for 1962*, pp. 567–92, Washington 1963.

At the finishing stages an additional piece of wood needs to be added to the back of the grip so that it will be nearly circular when it is covered. The ends can either retain their 'self nocks', cut into the wood, or they may be tapered and fitted with traditional horn nocks, which are more pleasing and available from some suppliers of equipment.

Fine steel-wool will give a good finish to the limbs, which can then be polished.

The yew longbow is made in the same way, but after the stave has been tapered for width, the sapwood (see YEW) must be patiently scraped away, following the run of the grain, and leaving a layer of about 1/8 inch. The shaping of the belly depends on the irregularities found after preparing the back. Rules cannot be offered as it is an art that is best acquired by practice and experience. Many amateur craftsmen have been very successful in their efforts to produce effective yew longbows.

The term 'longbow' is occasionally used in error to mean any form of bow that is held in the hand, for which the term 'hand bow' is correct. There are several forms of short bow, also held in the hand, from the early medieval Saxon short bow to the later Turkish composite bows and the modern flight bows. Some of these are in the order of only three feet in length and thus cannot be called 'longbows'.

The British Long Bow Society, under Rule 7, states: "A longbow is defined as the traditional type with the limbs of wood only (laminations of wood may be used) the belly is 'stacked' (D-shaped) the back is straight or slightly convex and the sides convex, the nocks are horn. The length between nocks is not less than 5 ft for arrows up to 26″ long and not less than 5′ 6″ for arrows over 26″. The thickness of the limb measured from belly to back is at no point less than three-fifths of the overall width of the limb at the same point."

LOOSE (*n.* and *v.*)
The action of releasing the bowstring. It is one of Roger Ascham's (*qv*) five 'partitions' of shooting and it may be classified as 'sharp' or 'dead'.

Both methods have their exponents. Whichever is used, the criterion in modern target shooting is that it must be regular and consistent if repeated accuracy is to be achieved. A sharp loose is achieved by drawing back the shaft hand, as the string is released by relaxing the fingers, but without altering the length of the draw. The latter consists of merely relaxing the fingers until the string leaves, which results in a slight loss of draw length and a consequent small loss in the velocity imparted to the arrow.

A good and steady loose of the bowstring is one of the most difficult aspects of shooting to master but one that is vital to success.

MARK
Any object at which an archer shoots.

MARKER
One who observes and signals the result of another's shot. Though not needed in target shooting, the service is of value in clout shooting (*qv*). While the archer can observe the line of the arrow, range is difficult to determine.

The marker, using a flag, first signals if the shot is over or short and then the number of bow's lengths from the clout, up to four. The task is not without hazard and the marker should be provided with a shelter in the form of a board behind which cover can be taken. (See also AIM-CRIER.)

MARKHAM, Gervase (1568?–1637)
Author of *The Art of Archerie*, London 1634 (reprinted 1968). Though the bulk of this work is a repetition of Roger Ascham's (*qv*) *Toxophilus B* (*The Seconde Booke of the Schole of Shotyng*), with minor additions and amendments, it is important as an attempt by an evident enthusiast to preserve the use of the longbow (*qv*) for military purposes at a time when it had been superseded by fire-arms.

'MARY ROSE'
Built 1509–11, she gave distinguished service until 1545 when, as flagship of the Vice-Admiral, Sir George Carew, she sank in the Solent with heavy loss of life. The ship was going into action against an attempted landing by the French, and there seems little doubt that she was over-loaded with some 300 extra soldiers on board to engage the enemy. With this added topweight she appears to have heeled over excessively when tacking, and with the lower gunports open and loaded guns run out, water poured in, causing the ship to capsize.

Before the remains of the hull were raised in October, 1982, in a most remark-able feat of underwater excavation, its contents had been recovered by divers.

First, the Deane brothers, pioneer helmet divers, worked on the wreck between 1836 and 1840 recovering several yew longbows, among other objects. Two of these are on display in the Tower of London Armouries.

Since 1978, divers have brought to the surface over 100 yew longbows, more than 2,000 arrow shafts and 12 bracers (*qv*). The importance from the archery aspect is that traditions, handed down from the time when the bow and arrow was com-pletely superseded by firearms, had become distorted after bulk supplies, held by arsenals, were destroyed to make room for muskets. Nothing remained that could be positively dated.

The average overall length of the bulk store longbows is about 6ft 6in. They had all been fitted with horn tips, which have disintegrated due to micro-biological action. Their effective length from nock to nock might have been about 6ft 4in. A broken stave that has been examined shows a closer grain, with some fifty annual growth rings to the inch, than can be found in England. This superior and more resilient wood was probably imported from Italy. Calculations and trials, which continue, suggest a wide variation in draw weights from as little as 55 lb to well in excess of 100 lb.

The arrowheads have completely rusted away. The average length of the shafts to the start of the taper that fitted in the socket of the head is about 30½ in. Examined shafts show they were made from aspen or white poplar, which Statutes of the Realm reserved for the construction of livery or sheaf arrows, used for war (see 4 Henry V of 1416 and 4 Edward IV of 1464–5). The tails of the shafts were reinforced with slim horn inserts, about 2in. long and most are tapered from about ½in. at the head to about 3/8 in. This form was called 'rush-grown' or 'bob-tailed'.

Arrows in chests were tied together in bundles of 24, while a few were inserted in leather discs, with 24 holes, making it easy to issue standard quiver-loads to archers on deck.

Much work and research remains to be done before final reports can be issued on the archery equipment (see Margaret Rule, *The Mary Rose*, Conway Maritime Press, 1982, pp. 168–83.)

MASTER BOWMAN
See CLASSIFICATION.

MASTER EYE
The dominant eye that controls the aim. It can present a problem where a right-handed archer has the left eye as the master, and vice versa. In target shooting it is overcome by closing one eye or by shielding it, but in the hunting field, where it is desirable to keep both eyes open as an aid to the instinctive estimation of range, it is a slight handicap. If the 'wrong' eye is the master it can still be closed an instant before shooting to ensure the accuracy of the aim.

MEASURING CARD
Carried by the Judge or Field Captain (*qv*) to record the distance of an arrow shaft in the gold from the 'pinhole' in the centre. In most contests a prize is awarded for the 'best gold', or shot nearest the centre.

The card has a small square cut out of a corner, equal to the radius of a shaft, to facilitate the accuracy of the measure.

MEDITERRANEAN Draw, Loose or Release
The three-finger draw on the bowstring, as used by the majority of modern archers, and so designated by E. S. Morse (*qv*) in his noted work, 'Ancient and Modern Methods of Arrow-Release' (*Essex Institute Bulletin*, 1885). It was certainly used by the medieval English archers and in other European countries, with the two-finger variation, known as the FLEMISH LOOSE (*qv*), while the major part of the Mediterranean area, in historic times, used the THUMB LOCK (*qv*).

MENDLESHAM BOW
A yew longbow, preserved in the armoury attached to the parish church of the village of Mendlesham in Suffolk. Records show that it was placed there, with other weapons for arming the train-band, in the time of Elizabeth I.

At some time in the past it has been broken. What remains is a stave about 53 inches long with a cross-section that is approximately square, with rounded corners.

It differs from the bows recovered from the *Mary Rose* (*qv*) in that the grip is defined by extra wood left in that area to give a round section. The horn tips are missing, but the total original length would not have exceeded six feet and a draw weight in the order of 80 lb can be suggested from the available dimensions of the bow.

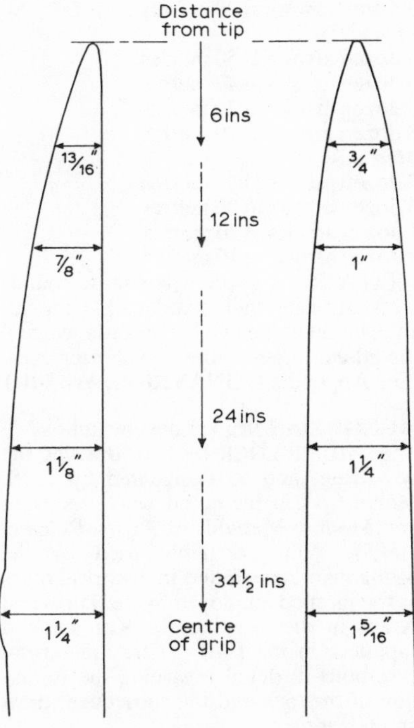

Approximate form of the Mendlesham yew longbow (irregularities smoothed out).

METRIC ROUNDS
The GNAS has approved certain shoots when time does not permit a full FITA Round to be shot. They are, in effect, half FITA Rounds:
Long Metric (men)
3 dozen arrows at 90 metres
3 dozen arrows at 70 metres
Long Metric (women)
3 dozen arrows at 70 metres
3 dozen arrows at 60 metres
Short Metric
3 dozen arrows at 50 metres
3 dozen arrows at 30 metres

Four further rounds are recognized for junior archers (*qv*).
Metric I
3 dozen arrows at 70 metres
3 dozen arrows at 60 metres
3 dozen arrows at 50 metres
3 dozen arrows at 30 metres
Metric II
3 dozen arrows at 60 metres
3 dozen arrows at 50 metres
3 dozen arrows at 40 metres
3 dozen arrows at 30 metres
Metric III
3 dozen arrows at 50 metres
3 dozen arrows at 40 metres
3 dozen arrows at 30 metres
3 dozen arrows at 20 metres
Metric IV
3 dozen arrows at 40 metres
3 dozen arrows at 30 metres
3 dozen arrows at 20 metres
3 dozen arrows at 10 metres

FITA Rules apply when these rounds are shot, using their standard 122-cm, 10-zone target at the two longer distances and the 80-cm target at the two shorter ones. (See Appendix 1, GNAS Rules, Art. 701.)

MONGOLIAN Draw, Loose or Release
The THUMB LOCK (*qv*) for drawing the bowstring, and so designated by E. S. Morse (*qv*) in his noted work, 'Ancient and Modern Methods of Arrow-Release' (1885). While certainly used by the Mongolians, it is found in historical times as the method employed by the Turks and Arabs in the West to the Koreans and Japanese in the East. There are several variations in detail regarding the formation of the lock and the subsequent draw and release.

MORSE, Edward Sylvester (1838–1925)
Author of a noted contribution toward the history of archery in his work, 'Ancient and Modern Methods of Arrow-Release', *Essex Institute Bulletin*, 1885. He followed this, thirty-seven years later, with *Additional Notes on Arrow Release*, Salem, Mass., 1922.

Though criticism may be made of the term 'release' instead of 'draw', his classification has been quoted by several authors of books on archery, with particular regard to "primary, secondary, tertiary, Mediterranean and Mongolian" draws (*qv*).

MUIR, Peter (1799–1886)
He became a qualified bowyer (bowmaker) in 1827 at the age of 18, having learnt the trade from his father in Kilwinning, Ayrshire. He continued to work until 1877, after moving to Edinburgh in 1829, where he also made bows for the Royal Company of Archers (*qv*).

It is recorded by C. J. Longman and Col. H. Walrond, *Archery* (Badminton Series), London 1894, pp. 284–5: "As a bow-maker, Mr Muir (his arrows being remarkably good) was known wherever archery was established, and he was also an archer of no mean ability." He won the National Championship in 1845, 1847 and 1863.

His fine longbows, which are collector's items, are marked P. MUIR/EDINBURGH or just MUIR/EDINBURGH.

MUSKET ARROW
An arrow shot from a musket. Evidence suggests they were not more than two feet in length, and fitted with bodkin heads (*qv*) or, as in the form known as a *spright*, sharpened wood only. The shafts were fletched.

The earliest evidence of its use is during the latter half of the sixteenth century, in the ordnance account compiled by Sir Francis Drake in 1577–8; in Sir Richard Hawkins, *Voiage in the South Seas*, 1593; and in the Royal Commission report of 1599. (See A. G. Credland, 'Crossbow Guns and Musket Arrows', *Journal of the Society of Archer-Antiquaries* 1977, pp. 5–19.)

NAGLER, Forrest (1885–1952)
A skilled archer, mainly concerned with the field of hunting in the USA, and engineer. He applied his sound technical knowledge to many equipment and design problems. In co-operation with C. N. Hickman and P.E. Klopsteg, most of his earlier articles were republished in *Archery: The Technical Side* (1947).

NATIONAL ARCHERY ASSOCIATION of the UNITED STATES (NAA)
Founded in January, 1879, as the governing body for target archery in the USA. Later in the same year, the NAA held its first championship in Chicago and it had five very successful years until 1883 when, for various reasons, interest in target archery began to decline. Membership remained somewhat static until the mid-1920s, after which it steadily expanded to become a well administered and successful organization.

A detailed history of the NAA has been published by Robert Rhode: Vol. I, 1879–1945, and Vol. II, 1946–1978; the period up to 1945 has been well covered by R. P. Elmer, *Target Archery*, New York 1946, pp. 37–119. (See Appendix 2 for the Champion Archers of the United States.)

NATIONAL CROSSBOW FEDERATION (of Great Britain)
At its meeting on 5 February 1983, National Council approved the formation of the NCF and its affiliation to the international body—the International Armbrust Union (*qv*).

The NCF incorporates the British Crossbow Society (Field Division); the British Match Crossbow Association (Match Division) and the Crossbow Archery Development Association (Field Division), from whom membership details are available (see p. 198).

NATIONAL FIELD ARCHERY SOCIETY
An independent British organization, constituted in 1973 to foster and promote Field Archery (*qv*), using targets at unknown distances, set in natural, undulating woodlands with few, or no, clear-laned marks. The lay-out of courses takes full advantage of peculiarities of the terrain and natural obstacles, with the object of providing as much pleasure as possible from the challenge presented to the archers.

The Society holds an annual Championship whose success may be judged by the 300 to 400 competitors who attend. From published figures it may claim to be the biggest field archery organization in Europe.

Among the more usual shoots organized by the NFAS are:

Game Round (also called the Animal or Big Game Round): Target faces carry depictions of animals, having an 'inner' or *kill* zone, and an 'outer' or *wound* zone within the outline of the animal. Archers shoot a single arrow from three different positions, marked by pegs. The highest scores are made from successful shots made from the first peg and their value reduces for those made from the second and third pegs. The basic unit consists of 14 targets.

Woodsman Round: This only differs from the above in that an archer stops shooting at the target when a *kill* is achieved.

Forester Round: Shot against a ringed target, superimposed on the animal background of the face. It also carries a centre spot, giving three scoring zones, as opposed to two.

There is also a *Bushman Round* and a *Poacher's Round*, basically similar to the *Forester*, but differing in sizes of targets and the number of shooting stations related to each.

NATIONAL ROUND

A round (*qv*) where 48 arrows are shot at 60 yards and 24 at 50 yards. It was first introduced by the GNAM at Derby in 1849 for the Ladies' Championship and continued until 1948, after which it was superseded by the Hereford Round (*qv*). In the USA the double National Round was part of the Ladies' Championship from 1881.

NOCK (*n.* and *v.*)

1. The notch in each tip of a bow to take the string.
2. The notch in the tail of an arrow in which the string is fitted.
3. To set the arrow on the string.

There is little to be said of the nocks of a bow other than sharp edges that may damage the bowstring must be avoided. The tips of a modern bow have added layers of material into which the nocks are cut, while the longbow is usually fitted with horn tips for the same purpose. Those cut into the wood of the bow are called *self nocks*.

The bulk of modern arrows, apart from those with wooden shafts, are fitted with plastic nocks. The most popular form has the internal width at the base of the nock fractionally larger than at its entrance. In this way it may be gently clipped to a correctly fitted bowstring and avoid any danger of falling off the string during the draw. Those with straight internal sides to the slot are fully satisfactory, provided they have sufficient depth which should be, at least, double the diameter of the bowstring. As Ascham (*qv*) comments: "The depe and longe nocke is good in warre for sure kepyng in of the strynge."

For wooden shafts, such as those associated with the longbow, a *self nock*, cut directly into the wood, must be made directly across the grain of the wood as otherwise the shaft is likely to split under the impact of the string when it is loosed. To avoid any chance of this happening, wooden arrows of the best quality are fitted with slim 'V' horn inserts to give them added strength at this point.

Nocking, or setting the tail of the arrow upon the string, is one of Ascham's five points, where he says: "To nocke well is the easiest poynte of all, and there in is no cunninge, but onelye dylygente hede gyuyng, to set hys shaft neyther to hye nor to lowe, but euen streyght ouertwharte hys bowe."

To shoot a bow without the load of an arrow on the string (see DRY LOOSE) can cause damage or even breakage of the bow. It follows that the arrow's nock must be securely lodged upon the string, but without excessive pressure. A very minor error can cause this to happen and there are few archers who have not experienced this fault. They are fortunate if no damage has resulted. The archer cannot pay too much attention to the correct adjustment of the NOCKING POINT (*qv*) on the bowstring.

NOCKING POINT

The place on the bowstring where an arrow is nocked (see NOCK). The body of a bowstring (*qv*) consists of a number of strands. The area opposite the arrow rest (*qv*) is served, or bound, with thread to protect it against the abrasion of the protected fingers and the arrow nock.

The point must be carefully and accurately adjusted. Its centre should be about ¼ inch above the arrow rest and on no account must it be below. Added thread binding is then applied, equal in length to the diameter of the arrow nock, to a thickness that offers a gentle push-fit to the arrow nock.

As an alternative to a thread binding, equipment suppliers can offer a variety of fittings that may be clipped to the string. Determining their exact position is described under TUNING.

NUT

A string retaining and release device, widely used in older crossbows but still found fitted in those favoured by certain European societies of crossbowmen who follow traditional designs of equipment.

It consists of a rotating cylinder of ivory, bone or metal. A transverse section is cut out and shaped to hold the drawn string, and a further section is removed so that the tail of the bolt (*qv*) may rest against the string between two raised lugs (see Figure).

On the underside a slot is fitted to take the sear of the trigger mechanism. Where the nut is made of ivory or bone the fore-end is usually reinforced with an iron peg to take the wear of the sear.

In many old crossbows, up to those of

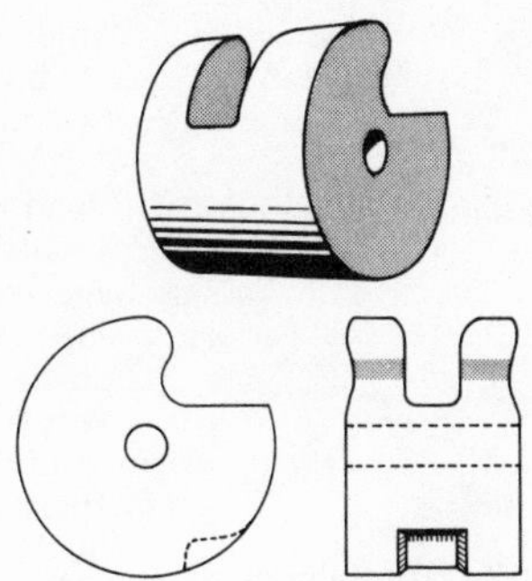

the eighteenth century, the nut was held in the stock or tiller by strong twine, through the centre and around the body of the tiller. Even rawhide, knotted at either end, has been found, though the opinion may be ventured that this was not the best material for this purpose.

Some crossbows from the seventeenth century had metal nuts, often of brass, mounted in well fitting saddles. They needed no central spindle or pivot.

Other fittings and forms exist but the majority are as described above.

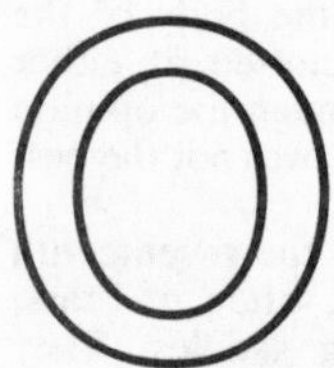

OLYMPIC GAMES

Following the establishment of the Olympiads of the Modern Era, due to the effort and enthusiasm of Baron Pierre de Coubertin, archery events were included in the Games held in 1900 (Paris), 1904 (St Louis), 1908 (London), and in 1920 (Antwerp). (See Appendix 2, page 194.)

With no international organization each contest was different and followed the national rules of the country where the event was held. Only a few countries were interested in this sport and, with demands for the inclusion of more widely popular events, archery was understandably dropped from the list of approved sports after 1920.

The establishment of the International Archery Federation (FITA) (*qv*) in 1931 began a new era in international archery. The number of affiliated associations steadily grew as world-wide interest expanded. Due mainly to the sustained and unrelenting efforts of Mrs Inger K. Frith, OBE, during her notable four terms of office as President of FITA, archery was once again included in the list of Olympic sports at Mexico City in 1968. In its modern form, with well-established rules, supported by 51 national associations, archery reappeared as an Olympic event at Munich in 1972. This success was continued in the Games held in Montreal in 1976 and in Moscow in 1980.

At Munich each Member Association of FITA could nominate up to three contestants in each event, the men's and the women's, provided that all had submitted four minimum qualifying scores to their respective national organizations. The numbers were cut to two in each event at Montreal and Moscow. In addition any Member Association could nominate a single contestant in each event, regardless of qualifying scores. A double FITA Round (*qv*), totalling 288 arrows, is shot over a period of four days.

The reduction in numbers was the result of a problem facing the International Olympic Committee (IOC): they had to keep the total entry and costs within a reasonable budget. Archery suffered no more than several other sports.

While Munich saw 95 contestants (55 men and 40 women), the figure fell to 64 at Montreal (37 men and 27 women). At Moscow it rose slightly to 67 (38 men and 29 women), in spite of a few countries declining to take part including the USA, Japan and Federal Germany. All three could have put first-class competitors into the field, which might have produced different results to those achieved.

There are no team events in the Olympic archery contest. (See Appendix 2 for Olympic Medal Winners.)

The results of the earlier Games are listed by E. G. Heath, *A History of Target Archery*, Newton Abbot 1973, pp. 182–5 (see Appendix 2) where the author notes: "Data for the archery events at the Games of 1900, 1904 and 1920 are incomplete, and no comprehensive results have been published. The information presented for those years has been collated from scattered sources, and . . . any errors or omissions result from conflicting or non-existent records."

ORIENTAL DRAW or LOOSE

See THUMB LOCK.

OUTER WHITE

An old term for the fifth or outer coloured ring on the target to distinguish it from the third, which is now blue, but originally also white and called the 'inner white'. The term is now obsolete, but it may be encountered in old records and accounts.

(See also PRINCE'S LENGTH and RECKONING.)

Under FITA Rules, where the five coloured rings of the target face are each divided into two zones, the outer white scores 1 point (see Art. 502).

OVERBOWED
Said of an archer using a bow that is too strong for the individual concerned to shoot under full control. It is the opposite to being underbowed (*qv*).

Experienced coaches are right in starting beginners with a light bow, as the initial emphasis must be to develop a correct shooting technique. While many archery clubs provide light equipment for the beginner, after achieving a good basic grounding – and wishing to continue with the sport – the tyro archer then purchases suitable personal equipment before the shoulder, arm and finger muscles are fully developed. The opinion is ventured that, at this stage, the archer should be a little overbowed. In a month or two normal physique will accommodate the added effort that is needed and the new bow will then be under full control.

A few extra pounds in draw weight offers an advantage under adverse weather conditions, particularly when strong winds are encountered.

OVERDRAW
An arrow is overdrawn when its head or pile has been drawn back too far so that it is inside the bow. The position can be dangerous and, while it should not occur with an experienced archer, it can happen with a tyro. It is almost impossible with the modern bow, due to the thickness of the riser (*qv*) but, with the simple bow or the traditional longbow (*qv*), the fault may be encountered. The danger is, if the string is released, the point of the arrow can strike the belly of the bow, the shaft will break with the rear half being driven through the bow hand.

It should be noted, however, that certain exponents in art of flight shooting (*qv*) are mentioned by Taybughā al-Ashrafi (*c.* 1368) as deliberately overdrawing their arrows to achieve extra distance and without the aid of any guide or protective device, such as the *siper* (*qv*).

OVERHAND
See FOREHAND.

PADDLE BOW
A form of native bow with broad limbs of an appearance somewhat similar to the two-bladed paddle as used by canoeists.

The best known are those from the Andaman Islands, whose form and construction has been described in detail by C. J. Longman (*Archery*, Badminton Series, London 1894, pp. 31–41). Others of this form have been found in East Africa and some American designs are similar, such as certain Eskimo constructions and that from Sudbury, Massachusetts (*c*. 1660), now in the Peabody Museum (see T. M. Hamilton, *Native American Bows*, York Pa. 1972, pp. 30–2, and O. T. Mason, 'North American Bows, Arrows and Quivers', *Smithsonian Report for 1893*, Washington 1894, pl. 65–73).

PAIR OF ARROWS
Under the old shooting rules at the end of the eighteenth century, two arrows only were shot at an end (*qv*). T. Roberts, *The English Bowman*, London 1801, p. 154, observes: ". . . in *archery*, *three* arrows are called a *pair*; that, if one is broke, lost, or injured, the archer may have two (the number used at a time) left of equal weight." The term is now archaic.

PAPINGO
See POPINJAY.

PARADOX
See DISCHARGE OF AN ARROW.

PARALLEL ARROW
An arrow whose shaft is of a constant diameter throughout its length. Cf. BARRELLED, BOB-TAILED and BREASTED.

PATTERSON, Stan (b. 1928)
After taking up the sport of archery in 1950, he became deeply involved in the organization and administrative aspects. He is a national judge and coach, a member of the GNAS National Council (since 1969) as well as being chairman of their International Committee, and a past President. During his term of office, he successfully organized the European Target Archery Championships, held at Stoneleigh, Warwickshire, in 1978.

In the international field he has been a member of the FITA Administrative Council and chairman of their Technical Committee since 1979, as well as being the GNAS Representative to the National Olympic Committee.

PEEP-SIGHT
A rear sight fitted in the bowstring, consisting of a ring with a small hole through it, as an aid to aiming. This fitting is not permitted either by FITA or GNAS Rules.

PELLET BOW
A hand bow whose string has a divided centre section, held apart by one or two small spreaders, and fitted with a cradle near the mid-point to hold and shoot clay pellets or small stones. It is also called a stone bow for this reason.

It may still be found in India and parts of South-East Asia for shooting birds and it is shot with a twisting force on the grip so that the pellet is thrown past the side of the bow and does not strike the hand.

This type of hand bow had limited use in Europe until the seventeenth century, when it was generally replaced by the lighter pellet crossbow and the heavier bullet crossbow. A form of the latter, fitted with a slotted barrel, is still used for target shooting by certain societies of crossbowmen in Belgium. (See A. G. Credland, 'The Pellet Bow in Europe and the East', *Journal of the Society of Archer-Antiquaries*, Vol. 18, 1975, pp. 13–21; and H. L. Blackmore, *Hunting Weapons*, London 1971, pp. 164–9.)

PERFECT END
In target shooting an end (*qv*) of six successive arrows, all hitting the central gold circle.

It had been a long-standing custom at major contests for all shooting the same round to pay one shilling to the archer achieving this feat. It was a rare demonstration of skill in those days when the traditional wooden longbow dominated the target range but, with modern equipment offering far greater accuracy, it became somewhat meaningless, except for those who still favour the longbow (*qv*). Rules have been modified and the GNAS now offers a *Six Gold Badge*. It may be claimed by members of the Society if it is achieved by men at a distance of at least 80 yards, and by women at a distance of at least 60 yards. In the FITA Round (*qv*) it applies to the 90- and 70-metre distances for men and the 70- and 60-metre distances for women. The National Archery Association (NAA) in the USA has similar rules. (See GNAS Rule 290 and, for Juniors, 507.)

PETTICOAT
The edge of the painted or printed target face outside the scoring area.

PIECING
An old term for a section of hardwood spliced to the fore-end of a wooden shaft to give added strength. Today the word 'footing' (*qv*) is preferred.

Ascham (*qv*) (1545) was familiar with the technique and says: "Peecynge of a shaft with brasell and holie, or other heauy woodes, is to make ye ende compasse heauy with the fethers in fliyng, for stedfaster shotyng . . . Two poyntes in peecing be ynough, lest the moystnes of the earthe enter to moche into the peecinge, & so leuse the glue. Therfore many poyntes be more plesaunt to the eye, than profitable for the vse."

PILE
The head of a target or field arrow. The majority have a point that is conical or ogival in form and their diameter is the same as that of the shaft to which they are fitted. They are socketed for wooden arrows and fitted with inserts for use with tubular metal alloy shafts.

A long-nosed variant is often favoured for field shooting (*qv*) as the slimmer point is more likely to stick in the ground, should an arrow miss the target, than the more usual forms which may be deflected on impact and disappear into the undergrowth in rough ground. Most ogival forms are catalogued as 'bullet piles', though they have a pointed tip. A true bullet-form, with a rounded tip, is sometimes used by those using wooden shafts in association with the traditional longbow.

Conical or chisel pile

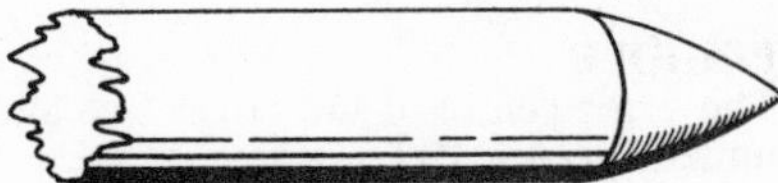

Ogival or bullet pile

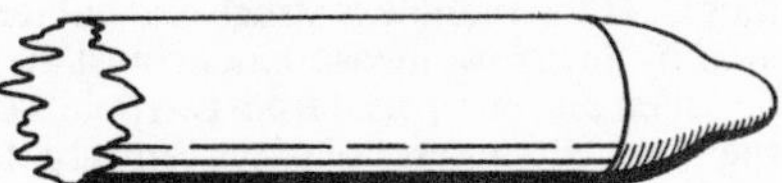

For use with the clicker (q.v.)

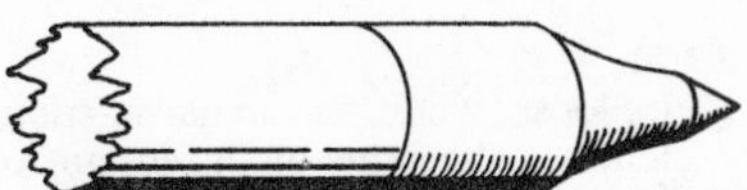

Field pile

Another form that is basically ogival, but with a small, protruding nose, has proved popular with a number of archers who use the clicker (*qv*), as it offers a more definite action in ascertaining the exactness of the draw.

PIN
A small blemish, like a tiny knot, in a yew (*qv*) bow where a twig has grown through the outer trunk of the tree.

PINCH
Excessive pressure on either side of the arrow nock, from the first and middle fingers, during the draw. It can affect the accuracy of a shot.

There is a natural tendency, due to the angle of the string at the arrow's nock when the shaft is fully drawn, to press the fingers toward the nock. Archers troubled with this fault can obviate its effect by the use of a separator on the glove or tab (*qv*) to keep the fingers apart. The problem is an old one and Ascham (*qv*) (1545) comments: "For this there be .ii. remedyes, one to haue a goose quyll splettyd and sewed . . . betwixt the lining and the ledder (of the shooting glove), . . . the other way is to haue some roule of ledder sewed betwixt his fingers . . ., which shall kepe his fingers so in sunder, that they shal not hold the nock so fast as they did."

PINCH DRAW
See PRIMARY RELEASE.

PINHOLE
The exact centre of the target face and, under GNAS Rules where a prize is awarded for the best gold (*qv*), it is marked with a pinhole from where the Judge or Field Captain takes measurements. If the pinhole is struck and obliterated by an arrow, measurement must then be taken and compared from two points of the outer circumference of the central gold circle to decide how far off the centre the hit has been made or, indeed, if it is a perfect central shot.

PLUCK
A faulty loose, where the archer fractionally increases the draw at the instant of releasing the string. The arrow will then, normally, hit high on the target.

POINT-BLANK
The term derives from the French *point à blanc* and it is the range at which the point or head of the arrow was aimed (see AIM) directly at the piece of white (*blanc*) cloth, placed against the earth butt, as a mark at which to shoot. With a traditional longbow (*qv*) and the medieval style of shooting, where the arrow was drawn to the cheek or ear, this would have been in the order of 60 yards or metres.

POINT OF AIM
The place or object at which an archer aligns the tip of the arrow to achieve the correct elevation that results in a hit on the target. (See also ARTIFICIAL POINT OF AIM.)

POISON
A variety of different poisons have been used to impregnate arrowheads and, in some areas, they are still used. It is of interest to note that where bodies of effective archers used powerful bows in organized warfare, poison was virtually unknown.

Curare is the best known of these substances and is mainly confined to the Amazon and Orinoco Basins in South America. It kills by relaxing muscles and, indeed, has been used medically for this purpose in small doses. The action of a heavier quantity on the heart and lungs can cause death in a very short time. (See E. G. Heath and V. Chiara, *Brazilian Indian Archery*, Manchester 1977, pp. 133–41, Appendix I, by N. G. Bisset.) It is a vegetable poison from the sap of the wourali vine, which is boiled with other ingredients to produce a sticky form that will adhere to the arrowhead, and to increase its effect.

Ouabain is another vegetable poison, mainly found in central Africa, which also acts on the heart and lungs, but through muscular contraction. Varieties of *Acocanthera* are the main source and it is used by native archers in East Africa to kill rhinoceros and elephant in their illegal ivory poaching.

The **Upas** tree, which grows widely in South-East Asia, provides a virulent poison from its bark, known as *ipoh*.

In addition to other poisonous plants, deadly extracts have been prepared from the skin of certain toads, the salamander, spiders and from snake venom. (See W. F. Paterson, 'A Survey of Arrow Poisons', *Journal of the Society of Archer-Antiquaries*, 1971, pp. 21–4.)

POPE, Saxton T. (1875–1926)
A medical doctor who was introduced to archery through his professional contacts with Californian Indians and, in particular, with Ishi of the Yana tribe from the year 1911. This stimulated his interest in the traditional longbow (*qv*) and its application in the hunting field. His

exploits, often in company with his fellow enthusiast, Arthur Young, are almost legendary.

His published works include, *Hunting with the Bow and Arrow*, New York 1923 (reprinted 1925, 1928, 1930 and 1947), *The Adventurous Bowmen*, New York 1926, and *A Study of Bows and Arrows*, University of California 1923 (reprinted 1930 and 1962).

POPINJAY

Originally a mark, in the form of a bird, set on a mast as a target for archers to knock down with blunt arrows. It is also known as the *papingo* or *papegai*.

This form of near vertical shooting has never had a great following in Britain, though it has been popular in Holland, Belgium and Northern France, where several societies or guilds of archers hold annual contests. It may be noted that, among several events included in the archery programme of the Second Olympic Games (*qv*), held in Paris in 1900, *Tir à la perche* with a 30-metre mast was included. It appeared again in the Seventh Olympic Games, Antwerp, 1920, with 20 arrows allowed to each competitor at a 31-metre mast, with individual awards being made for shooting at 'high birds' and at 'small birds'.

The form and conduct of such shoots has varied greatly, involving both those who use the hand bow and others with the crossbow. Perhaps the most splendid was the annual gathering of the Dresden crossbow, whose history goes back to medieval times. They shot at a replica of the Imperial German eagle, 13 feet in length and 8 feet in breadth across its extended wings, hoisted to the top of a mast, 136 feet (41 m) high. Each feather and other parts had to be knocked down in succession and awards were made accordingly. (See R. Payne-Gallwey, *The Crossbow*, London 1903 (reprinted), pp. 231–6.) A small replica of the bird is displayed in the White Tower of the Tower of London as part of their presentation of crossbows. It must be recorded, with regret, that the annual Dresden shoot was prohibited in 1961 and has not been held since.

While several societies follow their own established traditions in the rules and conduct of their shoots, the general principle is that the 'birds' are small wooden blocks, decked with coloured feathers and mounted on spikes. At the top of the mast is the cock bird, which is the largest and most resplendent. Below the cock are smaller hen birds and below them and even smaller are the chicks, all mounted on yards secured to the mast.

GNAS Rules, Arts. 600–606, cover popinjay shooting in Britain. It specifies that the full complement of a 'roost' shall consist of 1 cock, 4 hens and a minimum of 24 chicks, all with a body size of 1½ in. by ¾ in. Emphasis is correctly laid on the safety precautions to be observed, to protect both contestants and spectators from possible injury from falling arrows, whose blunt heads must be ¾ in. to 1 in. in diameter.

PRESSURE BUTTON or PLUNGER

A spring-loaded device, fitted through the riser (*qv*) of a bow to absorb the pressure from an arrow shaft during discharge (*qv*). Its use is permitted under both GNAS and FITA Rules.

The button assembly can be adjusted in two ways. First, it can be moved in or out which enables it to be set so that the line of the arrow appears to be divided by the bowstring. Second, the internal pressure of the spring can be adjusted and this will affect the amount to the right or left to which the arrow is deflected on discharge. Its correct setting is an important part in tuning (*qv*) the modern bow.

PRICK

A simple white mark, placed on a post or butt (*qv*), as a target for archers. The term is archaic; it is derived from the Anglo-Saxon word for *point* and thus implies a point at which to aim.

Prick shooting was practised by medieval English archers at relatively short ranges, using lighter prick shafts, as opposed to the heavier sheaf arrows (*qv*). Existing records give little information on this aspect of shooting, but it may be considered as the forerunner of modern target shooting.

Prick marks had their place in roving (*qv*) though under the Act, 33 Henry VIII, c.9, ". . . no man under the age of four and twenty shall shoot at any standing prick, except it be at a rover, whereat he shall change at every shoot his mark . . .". The penalty for failing to comply with this regulation was a fine of four pence for each shot, but the large sum of six shillings and eightpence for those who were older. (See T. Roberts, *The English Bowman*, London 1801 (reprinted), pp. 230–3 and 241–2.)

PRIMARY DRAW or LOOSE
Achieved with the simple pinch grip on the tail of the arrow, between the thumb and first finger. E. S. Morse (*qv*) classified it as 'primary' in his noted work on arrow release.

It is a very simple method by which an arrow can be drawn and shot, but it can only be used with weak bows. However, in the past, it has suited the purpose of certain native peoples who did not need power in their shooting.

PRINCE'S LENGTH AND RECKONING
The first standardization of distances, target size and colours, and values of hits, prescribed by the Prince of Wales – an enthusiastic archer – in 1792 and adopted as rules at the Grand National Archery Society's formation at York in 1844.

Following the revival of archery as a sport in the last quarter of the eighteenth century, various clubs and societies – doubtless enthusiastic and well organized – produced their own rules which naturally resulted in many variations. With the increasing popularity of the sport, agreed standards were clearly needed.

Length referred to what became the York Round (*qv*) for men. It must be appreciated that, at the time, archery was a man's sport and, while the ladies might 'play' with the bow and arrow, their endeavours were not taken seriously. This situation, of course, has changed drastically.

Reckoning concerned the target colours and the score awarded for hits in the various rings: gold – 9, red – 7, blue – 5, black – 3 and white – 1, equally divided with an outer diameter of 4 feet.

These specifications have been of lasting importance as, apart from being followed in Britain, the FITA target at longer ranges is 122 cm, which is virtually 4 feet, and the colours of the rings are the same.

It may be mentioned, in this context, that though each colour on the FITA target has been divided in two, to give ten zones, as opposed to the original five, arrows are still shot in 'dozens' – with odd exceptions – and clearly shows that the Prince's rulings provided a vital standard on which modern target shooting is based.

PRISM SIGHT
A form of sight, attached to a bow, that enables an archer to see the target, even though the direct line of sight is blocked by the riser (*qv*) and bow hand due to the range at which the intended shot is to be made. Its use is not permitted under GNAS and FITA Rules.

PROD or PRODD
1 A light sporting crossbow that shot balls of clay or lead, also termed a stonebow. The name stems from an error or misprint that first appears in Francis Grose, *Treatise on Ancient Armour* (London, 1786), p. 59, in referring to the great inventory of all King Henry VIII's possessions, drawn up in 1547 on the order of his son, Edward VI, which includes "Cross-bowes called prodds". The original document reads "rodds", but the faulty spelling was followed or copied by several reputable authorities such as S. R. Meyrick, *Critical Enquiry into Antient Armour* (London, 1842), J. Skelton, FSA, *Engraved Illustrations* . . . (Oxford, 1833) and R. Payne-Gallwey, *Crossbow* (London 1903). As a result the word 'prod' (or 'prodd') has crept into common usage.
2. The bow of a crossbow. The term originated in the USA in the early 1950s in an endeavour to distinguish this item from the hand-drawn bow. It has no historical support. Lath would have been more correct (see *Oxford English Dictionary*).

QUARREL
A form of crossbow bolt (*qv*) with a head having a square cross-section. The tip is slightly hollowed to leave four short spikes, one at each corner.

It was primarily intended for the penetration of plate armour as it was more difficult to deflect, when striking at an angle, than the widely-used ogival form of head though, it may be noted, the latter design had a higher penetration, given a reasonably square hit against the curved surface of the armour.

Several authors have offered the origin of the term from the Latin 'quadrus', or the French 'carreau', overlooking the medieval French word, *quarrel*, meaning 'square'.

QUIVER
A container to hold arrows or crossbow bolts conveniently for shooting. Among the modern forms there is the *belt* or *side* quiver, hung from the waist and often with separate holes or compartments for the six arrows normally carried. There is the *back* quiver, hung over the shoulder, often used by both hunters and field archers, the *ground* quiver, basically consisting of a ring at the top of a rod, planted in the earth on the shooting line, which some target archers find more convenient than the belt quiver, and the *bow* quiver, attached to the bow with the arrow shafts held by spring clips. This latter form is popular with hunters.

RANGE
1. The distance of the mark or target from the archer. The term 'distance' (*qv*) is more generally favoured.
2. The ground over which shooting takes place.

REBOUND
An arrow that strikes but fails to lodge itself in the target so that it rebounds from the face (see BOUNCER).

RECURVE
A curve built into the tips of a bow, inclined toward the back. Many modern composite bows are constructed in this way with *working recurves* that partially straighten out as the string is drawn. Their recovery after the loose adds to the velocity imparted to the arrow and thus the performance of the bow (cf. REFLEX).

In addition to the added speed achieved by the tip of the bow, the effective length of the string is shortened at the instant of discharge of the arrow as it comes to rest against the curve of the bow tip. This also adds to the discharge velocity.

The traditional Japanese bow or *yumi* (*qv*) is also constructed with recurved tips, which add to performance, though they lack the flexibility of the working recurves.

RED
The circle surrounding the central gold ring of a standard target (*qv*). Under GNAS rules, with a 5-zone target, a hit scores seven points, while under FITA rules, where each colour is divided into two areas to give a 10-zone target, the inner area scores eight points and the outer seven points.

REFLEX
The curvature of the limbs of an unstrung bow toward the back, which is the opposite way to that in which they will be flexed to fit the string. The effect is to increase the initial tension in the string before it is drawn and, while not generally favoured

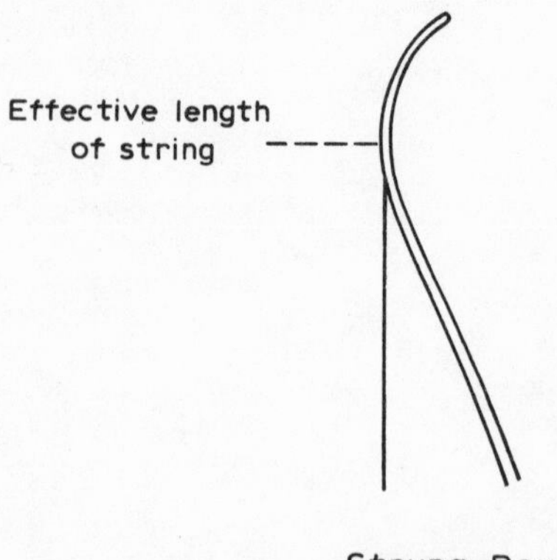

Strung Bow
at rest

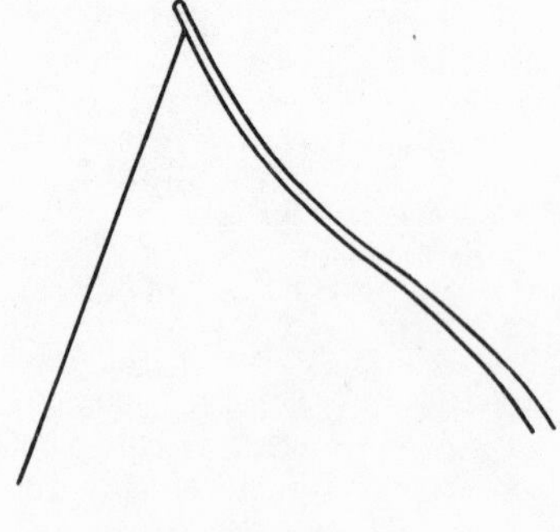

Bow drawn

by modern designers it was a primary feature in the traditional oriental composite bows made from horn and sinew on a wooden central core.

RELEASE
To loose (*qv*) or let go the drawn bowstring.

As a result of the manner in which this term was used in the noted papers by E. S. Morse (*qv*) on arrow release (1885 and 1922), it can also apply to methods of drawing or retracting the bowstring. Most modern writers are agreed that Morse was incorrect in the application of this term for his intended purpose, though this in no way detracts from the merit of his two works.

RETROFLEX, RETROVERT
Terms occasionally encountered in modern writings, often without adequate definition to explain their intended meaning. R. P. Elmer (*qv*) in his comprehensive glossary in *Target Archery* (1946), understood the former as synonymous with 'recurve' (*qv*) and the latter as the relatively sharp backward angle in the knee of the traditional oriental composite bows.

RISER
Originally a short piece of wood glued to the belly of the grip or handle of a wooden bow to reinforce the centre section and to give a better fit to the hand.

With the modern composite bow it has become more elaborate and offers a rigid centre section up to about 20 inches in length, shaped to fit the hand in a form somewhat akin to a pistol grip, and with clip or screw fittings at either end by which the limbs of the bow are attached. They are made both from hardwood, which is usually laminated, and from metal alloy.

ROD or RODD
A name given to certain forms of light, hunting crossbows that became corrupted to *prod* (*qv*) or *prodd*.

ROUND
A specified number of arrows shot at given distances. Of the British target rounds, the two most important are the York and Hereford, used respectively for the men's and ladies' championships. The rounds recognized by the GNAS are listed under Rule 108 (see Appendix 1, page 166–7).

For Junior archers under 18 years of age, several additional rounds are recognized under Rule 701 (see Appendix 1, page 179).

ROVING
Also known as 'shooting at rovers', roving was the main method of exercise and training used by medieval English archers. A group of bowmen would walk over the countryside, shooting at natural marks, usually at long range. The archer with the best placed arrow was said to have 'gained the up shot' and nominated the next mark at which the group should shoot.

With the regular practice of archery being compulsory under several laws as, for example, 12 Richard II of 1388, requiring all servants and labourers to have bows, and to practise with them on Sundays and holidays, roving ranges were set up adjacent to some of the more populous districts. The best documented example is the Finsbury Fields in London (see F. Isles, 'Locating the Ancient Finsbury Fields Archery Marks', *Journal of the Society of Archer-Antiquaries*, Vol. 7, 1964, pp. 8–13, with an addendum, giving added captions to the maps, in Vol. 9, 1966, p. 36). F. Lake has reconstructed the layout of the archery marks in St George's Fields, Southwark (see F. Lake, 'New Light on the Honourable Artillery Company and Archery in Southwark', *JSA-A*, Vol. 10, 1967, pp. 21–8.)

The rules to be observed in roving are recorded by T. Roberts, *The English Bowman*, London 1801 (reprinted 1973), pp. 230–5.

ROYAL COMPANY OF ARCHERS
Founded in Edinburgh in 1676 to encourage archery, it was granted a charter by Queen Anne in 1704, making it a *Royal* Company that provides the Sovereign's Body Guard in Scotland, when it takes precedence over all other guards and troops who may be concerned in such ceremonial occasions. In return for this and other favours the Royal Company could be called upon, when asked, to render to Her Majesty and her successors "one pair of barbed arrows". (See PAIR, which is three arrows.) This is known as the *Reddendo*.

Membership is coveted, exclusive and largely hereditary, and numbers about 400. It is selected from the nobility and from military and civil officers who have played a worthy part in Scottish life.

A number attend regular shooting practice, which mainly concentrates on clout shooting (*qv*) at 180 yards with the traditional longbow. The Royal Company of Archers has close association with the Woodmen of Arden (*qv*) and the Royal Toxophilite Society (*qv*) in England.

Among the annual trophies which are contested is the King's Prize, instituted in 1787; the Musselburgh Arrow, whose history goes back to 1603, before the Royal Company was formed; the Peebles Arrow, 1628; the Selkirk Arrow, 1660; the Edinburgh Arrow, 1709; the St Andrew's Cross, 1801; the Flopetoun Vase, 1823; the Dalhousie Sword, 1834; and the Biggon Jug, 1852.

The uniform, unchanged since 1863, is of dark green with Balmoral bonnets, trimmed with golden eagle feathers. The Captain General wears three feathers, officers wear two, and other members one. (For details of their history see Ian Hay, *The Royal Company of Archers*, 1676–1951, Edinburgh and London 1951.)

ROYAL TOXOPHILITE SOCIETY
Founded in 1781 as the Toxophilite Society, with Sir Ashton Lever elected as the first President, the Society played a major part in the revival of archery as a sporting pastime and stimulated interest throughout the country. The prefix 'Royal' first appears on the scores list of the first GNAM in 1844, and may have been granted by William IV, who took an interest in the Society and presented several prizes and trophies from 1831 until his death in 1837.

A brief account of its history was compiled by C. B. Edwards, Honorary Secretary from 1946–68, when he was elected President of the Society, under the title *The 'Tox' Story*, privately published in 1968.

Several of the early trophies were brought to the 'Tox' by members of the Finsbury Archers, who joined the Society. The most valued possession is the shield, dedicated to Catherine of Braganza, Queen to Charles II, entrusted to the care of Sir William Wood, Marshal to the Regiment of Archers, in 1676. It is on permanent exhibition at the Victoria and Albert Museum.

After using various shooting grounds within London, the Society moved to a permanent headquarters to the north of the village of Burnham, Buckinghamshire, in 1967, where its activities continue.

RUN ON THE BOW
Said of a feather or vane that presses excessively against the bow during the discharge of an arrow. It can occur with faulty nocking (*qv*) when the cock feather (*qv*) is set toward the bow, instead of away from it, or if the fletching is incorrectly set on the shaft.

RUSHGROWN ARROW or SHAFT
An old term for the bob-tailed arrow (*qv*), whose shaft tapers from head to tail.

the nocking point (*qv*) to about four inches below to protect the strands from the abrasion of the fingers of the drawing- or shaft-hand and from the impact against the nock of the arrow when it is loosed.

Complete bowstrings, as purchased, may occasionally need this fitting to be replaced and it is a minor repair of which all archers should be capable. For those who prefer to make their own strings, it is an essential feature. In addition to the centre section, the end loops of bowstrings (*qv*) made on the endless skein principle also need to be served.

The material for serving is thicker than the strands forming the string. Flax carpet thread is well suited to linen strings as often used with the traditional longbow, but nylon or monofilament thread is better for Dacron or kevlar strings as used for most modern composite bows.

To serve the centre section, the bowstring should be fitted to the bow to keep it taut. A mark should be made about one inch above where the nocking point will be fitted; this is where the binding process starts. About six feet of serving thread is needed. The end two or three inches are laid along the string from the mark, and the first six turns or so should be wound on by hand, each turn being drawn very tight. After that one can continue by hand or a serving tool (*qv*) can be used until near the end of the covered section. To finish the serving, the end of the thread must be passed back through the last half dozen turns (see diagram) which must be drawn very tight, and the slack is then pulled through before being cut off.

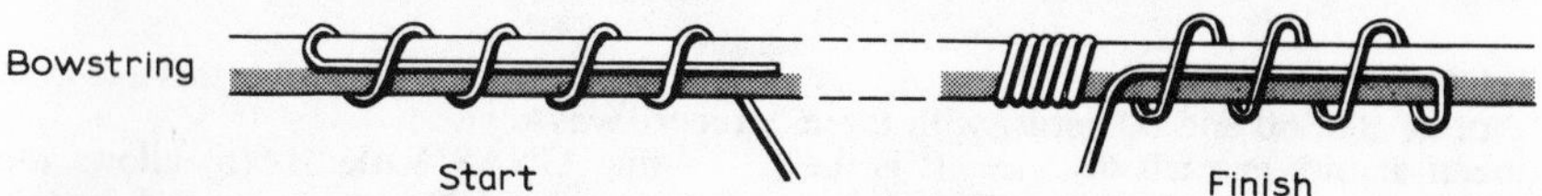

There must, of course, be no gap between successive turns of the serving thread around the string.

SERVER, SERVING TOOL
A simple device carrying a spool of thread that enables a serving (*qv*) to be applied more quickly and easily than by hand.

SET BACK IN THE HANDLE
Said of a bow where the grip projects inward toward the string instead of following the line of the two limbs. While this feature is not used by modern bow designs it may be found, in varying degrees, in certain traditional oriental composite bows, the most marked being the Korean bow as still used for archery contests in that country.

SHAFT
1. An arrow.
2. The main, rod-like body of an arrow, without fletching or head.

SHAFT FEATHERS
The two feathers that lie next to the bow when the arrow is correctly placed on the string. (Cf. COCK FEATHER). It is wrong to call them 'hen' feathers, a term which still seems to persist in America in spite of R. P. Elmer (*qv*) recording in his glossary that it is a "bastard offspring of ignorance that should be squelched".

SHAFT HAND
The hand that draws the bowstring. This is the right hand for the right-handed archer and vice versa. It is a convenient term that embraces both.

SHAFTMENT
1. The section of the shaft occupied by the feathers or vanes.
2. A measure of about six inches given by the clenched fist with the thumb extended (see the *Oxford English Dictionary*; cf. FISTMELE). This was the approximate length of the fletchings on medieval arrows, fully supported by the evidence from shafts recovered from the *Mary Rose* (*qv*).

SHAKE
A longitudinal split or crack in a wooden stave.

SHARP LOOSE
A fast, clean release of the bowstring with a quick backward movement of the shaft hand (cf. DEAD LOOSE).

S

St GEORGE'S ROUND
Shot at 100, 80 and 60 yards, with three dozen arrows at each distance. It is the oldest round (*qv*) which is still shot and was adopted by a club called the Fraternity of St George which flourished between 1835 and 1845, with a shooting ground in St John's Wood, London.

Under the classification scheme (*qv*) it is recognized by the GNAS for men up to first class and it is favoured for some club shoots when time may not permit a full York Round (*qv*), which is shot over similar distances, to be on their programme.

St NICHOLAS ROUND
A round devised for Junior archers (*qv*) under 12–13 years of age and consisting of 4 dozen arrows shot at 40 yards and 3 dozen at 30 yards against a standard 5-zone, 4-ft target.

SAP WOOD
The wood of a tree that is found next to the bark. Its use is important in the construction of the traditional yew bow (*qv*).

SCORE
1. A record of the points gained in target or field shooting.
2. A unit of twenty yards, often used to specify distances for clout shooting (*qv*) and, in old times, for the distance of roving (*qv*) marks and in the laws of England relating to the training of archers.

SCORER
One who records the points gained by each archer when an end (*qv*) has been completed, together with the number of hits and golds (*qv*).

Under earlier rules this duty was carried out by No. 3 on each target, the Target Captain, No. 1, assisted by the Lieutenant, No. 2, being responsible that a correc record was kept.

While GNAS Rule 106(b) allows th duty of entering the scores to be shared b the archers on each target, the old custom is still widely followed.

For major FITA contests, Rule 414 requires that the "organizers shall appoint scorers in sufficient numbers to ensure that one for each target in Target Archery and one for each group in Field Archery shall always be on duty: such scorers shall not take part in the shooting."

SECONDARY DRAW or RELEASE
A method of drawing and releasing the bowstring, found among the Chippewa Indians of northern Wisconsin and classified as *secondary* by E. S. Morse (*qv*). The tail of the arrow is grasped between the thumb and forefinger with the second and, sometimes, the third fingertips applied to the string to assist in the draw. It was also observed among the Ottawa and Zuñi Indians in North America.

SELF
Applied to a bow made from one piece of wood. This is derived from one meaning of the word: natural, unmixed or pure condition.

SEPARATOR
A piece of padding between the index and middle fingers, attached to the shooting glove or tab (*qv*) to prevent the archer from pinching the nock of the arrow during the draw.

SERVE, SERVING (*v.* and *n.*)
1. To bind or whip with thread.
2. The binding or whipping applied to the bowstring.

The centre section of a bowstring is invariably served from about one inch abov

SHEAF
The standard issue of 24 livery arrows to the old English longbowmen.

SHEAF ARROW
Also known as the livery arrow, it was the standard war arrow issued to the old English longbowmen.

From the evidence of the shafts recovered from the *Mary Rose* (*qv*) which sank in 1545, the old Statutes of the Realm and the writings of Roger Ascham (*qv*), aspen or white poplar seems to have been most widely used, though ash was also employed. In 1416 the Statute 4 Henry V required aspen to be used for arrows only, though it was slightly relaxed in 1464–5 under 4 Edward IV that permitted aspen not fit for arrows to be used for pattens, which were clogs or wooden shoes.

The average length of the shafts found is 30½ inches (80 cm) from the base of the nock to the shoulder that fitted against the socket of the head. The conical, tapered end that was inserted into the socket is about one inch long. The diameter of the shaft would appear to be about 7/16ths inch (12 mm) for parallel shafts, but tapering from about ½ inch at the socket of the head to 3/8ths inch at the tail when bobtailed. From marks on the green-tinted coating over the shaftment (*qv*) the length of the fletching was 6 – 6½ inches. Slim horn inserts were fitted at right angles to the nock to a depth of about 2 inches.

The heads (*qv*) of the *Mary Rose* arrows have, sadly, completely corroded away, though rust marks in the sand and mud suggest a length a little over 2 inches. While a variety of arrowheads may be seen in such collections as those of the Tower of London Armouries and the Museum of London, there remains uncertainty regarding the design of the bulk production for military purposes. It is not unlikely that in different areas of the country the smiths who forged the heads used slightly different patterns.

SHENK, Clayton B. (b. 1908)
An organizer and administrator who has played a major part in the development of the National Archery Association in the USA, holding the office of President in 1947, 1950, 1959 and from 1960 to 1967 inclusive. He then became Secretary from 1967 to 1980 as well as being a member of FITA Administrative Council since 1961.

In recognition of his work he was awarded the NAA 'Maurice Thompson Medal of Honor' in 1959 for distinguished service and he was inducted into the Archery Hall of Fame (*qv*) in 1973. In the international field he was awarded the FITA Silver Plaquette in 1979.

He is now (1982) an Honorary President of the NAA, which organization he continues to represent at FITA Council meetings.

SHILLING
The basic unit for the weight of wooden arrows and equal to 87.2 grains (7,000 grains = 1 lb, avoirdupois; 1 gram = 15.432 grains). Such arrows, many of which are still in use, have their weight in silver coin stamped on the shaft close to the nock or on the shaftment (*qv*). It appears for example, in the form, 4 3, meaning four shillings and threepence, which is 370.6 grains.

While arrows have been weighed or, at least, matched for weight for hundreds of years, it is uncertain when silver coin was first used for this purpose. The practice is certainly recorded by T. Roberts, *The English Bowman*, (London 1801) p. 153, where he notes: "Arrows are now weighed with the same weights as standard silver, and marked accordingly: so that an arrow equal to five shillings troy or silver-weight, is called an arrow of *five shillings*."

SHOOT
To discharge an arrow from a bow. To 'fire' an arrow means to set alight to an inflammable substance or mixture, attached near the head, when dealing with incendiaries.

SHOOT IN A BOW
The older and more correct expression for the practice of archery than 'shoot a bow'.

SHOOTING GLOVE
To protect the first three fingers of the shaft hand, some archers prefer a shooting glove, with its strengthened finger-tips, to the more simple tab (*qv*).

Ascham (*qv*) comments: "A shootynge Gloue is chieflye, for to saue a mannes fyngers from hurtynge, that he maye be able to beare the sharpe stryng to the vttermost of his strengthe."

The Japanese shooting glove, as used in *kyudo* (*qv*), differs in giving primary protection to the thumb, which is heavily padded and reinforced with bone or antler inside the leather. The index and middle fingers are also covered as these are placed across the end of the thumb to form the lock when drawing the string.

SHOOTING LINE
The line from which archers shoot. Under FITA Rules the shooting line is fixed and the targets are moved at each change of distance, while under GNAS Rules the targets are fixed and there is a different shooting line for each distance.

SHOOTING MACHINE
A stand in which a bow can be secured and shot by mechanical means for the purpose of dynamic studies.

A design, based on one devised by Tracey L. Stalker in the American magazine *Archery*, is fully illustrated by Patrick Clover, *Bowman's Handbook*, 5th Edition, Portsmouth 1968, pp. 115–17.

It is of interest to note that a manufacturer of archery equipment in the 1950s used such a machine to match sets of wooden arrows. They were shot at a target and those that grouped closely together were selected to make sets.

SHORT WINDSOR ROUND
A round devised for junior archers (*qv*), suited for girls under 16 years of age and boys under 14. It consists of 3 dozen arrows at 50 yards, 3 dozen at 40 yards, and 3 dozen at 30 yards against a standard 5-zone 4-ft target.

SIMON ARCHERY FOUNDATION
Established in Manchester as a result of the collection donated by H. Ingo Simon (*qv*) (d. 1964) and supported by a generous financial contribution, further enhanced by Mrs Erna Simon (d. 1973), it includes the Simon Archery Collection at the Museum.

The available funds have enabled further acquisitions to be made to the collection which now (1983) stands at 140 composite bows (*qv*), 23 Japanese laminated bows, 70 crossbows (*qv*), many arrows, quivers and related objects. Recent donations include an extensive collection of archery material from parts of the Amazon Basin, given by Dr Vilma Schultz, and a selection of oriental thumb rings given by Dr Charles E. Grayson.

The Trust has also given financial support for the initial publication of two works of importance in the archery field, F. Lake & H. Wright, *Bibliography of Archery*, 1974, and E. G. Heath & Vilma Chiara (Schultz), *Brazilian Indian Archery*, 1977.

SIMON, H. Ingo (1875–1964)
Archery was one of his many and varied interests, probably stimulated by his early acquaintance with Sir Ralph Payne Gallwey. He formed a noted collection of mainly oriental equipment which he donated to Manchester Museum, together with supporting funds, that enabled the Simon Archery Foundation (*qv*) to be formed.

He was a leading authority on flight shooting (*qv*) and set the British record of 462 yards 9 inches on June 26th, 1914, using an old Turkish bow, arrows, *siper* (*qv*) and thumb ring, that clearly demonstrated his expertise in this eastern technique. His record stood until 1953.

While he did not concern himself with competitive target shooting he was, nevertheless, an expert shot and records, for instance, hitting a matchbox, swinging at the end of a cord, with four successive shots at 20 yards, using a big Sino-Tatar composite bow (see *The British Archer* Vol. 8, No. 6 (1957) p. 231). However, he actively encouraged those to whom target shooting appealed, including his wife, Mrs Erna Simon, who became Lady World Target Champion in 1937.

He was elected as President of the Royal Toxophilite Society (*qv*) in 1955 and he was the first President of the Society of Archer-Antiquaries, which has a worldwide membership of those interested in the history of archery, following its formation in 1956.

SIPER
The Turkish term for a shallow horn groove, strapped to the wrist of the bow hand and held over the thumb by a ring or a cord, to enable the tip of a short flight arrow to be drawn up to about two inches inside the bow. The horn groove then guides the arrow past the bow when the string is loosed. The term comes from the Persian *sipar*, or 'shield'.

As an extension to the original meaning it is used in modern flight shooting (*qv*) terminology to refer to the extended arrow shelf, as fitted above the grip, of the centre-shot flight bow. It may be noted that the term is incorrectly transliterated in both GNAS Rules (Art. 302) and FITA Rules (Art. 583) as *sipur*.

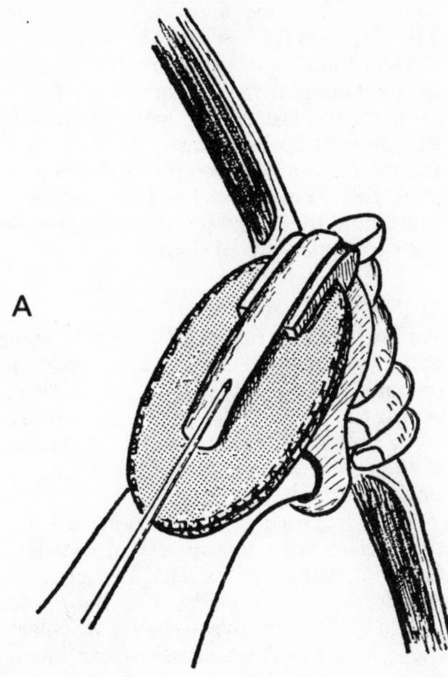

The original Turkish siper.

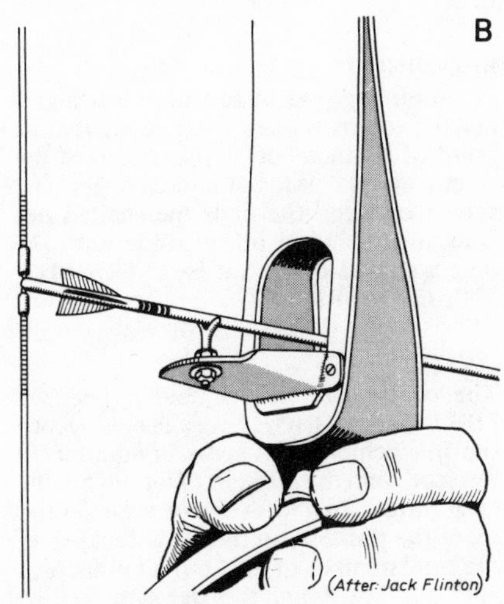

A form of modern siper.

SIX GOLD AWARDS
Under GNAS Rules a badge is awarded to members of the Society for six successive arrows into the gold at one end during a contest recognized by the Society (see Rule 110). For men the distance must be at least 80 yards and for ladies 60 yards or, if shooting a FITA Round (*qv*), 70 metres and 60 metres respectively. An archer is entitled to only one such badge. A similar award can also be gained by juniors at not less than the middle distance in the National Championship Round for each age group (Rule 110 (g)).

Six gold awards are also made by the NAA in the USA. In both cases it is purely a national award and it is not covered under FITA Rules.

SIYAH
The relatively rigid end of most traditional oriental composite bows (*qv*) that acts as a lever to aid the flexing of the working section of a limb when the string is drawn. It adds appreciably to the efficiency of the design and to the discharge velocity of the arrow. The term is found in old archery literature throughout the mid-East.

SKELETON GLOVE
A protective device for the three fingers of the drawing hand. It consists of cylindrical tips for each finger, usually made of leather, connected by straps across the back of the hand to a wristband.

SLASH -ING
A vigorous plucking action on the bowstring at the end of the draw, that incorporates its release. It adds to the velocity of the arrow but not to its accuracy. The technique is of value in flight shooting (*qv*).

SLUGGISH LOOSE
A loose in which the fingers of the drawing hand are relaxed gradually to release the string. Though arrow discharge velocity is lost, the technique has been favoured by some successful target archers. If applied in a regular and consistent manner, accuracy can be achieved.

SPANNING
The action of retracting the string of a crossbow to the latch or lock mechanism, where it is held when fully drawn.

With the less powerful crossbows this

may be done by hand while stronger examples, such as the Swiss match crossbow, employ a hinged lever for this purpose. Other traditional aids to spanning include the windlass and the rack or cranequin.

SPECTACLES and SUNGLASSES
Archers are permitted to wear these provided they are not fitted with microhole lenses or marked in any way to assist aiming under both GNAS Rules (Art. 102 (viii)) and FITA Rules (Art. 504 (h)).

SPINE and SPINE VALUE
The term *spine* is commonly used when *spine value* is intended.

True *spine* is a measure of the dynamic properties of an arrow and it depends on several factors. The more important are the stiffness or *spine value*, total weight, weight distribution and external diameter of the arrow shaft. Any of these can affect to a greater or lesser extent the dynamic behaviour of the arrow on discharge (*qv*) apart from what may be caused by the archer's style of shooting. Other factors relate to the bow, such as its draw weight, the width at the arrow pass, the weight of the bowstring and the bracing height.

Spine value is a static measure of stiffness and it is defined by the GNAS as the deflection at the centre of a shaft, measured in hundredths of an inch, when a weight of one and a half pounds is hung at that point, with the arrow supported at the base of the nock and at the shoulder of the pile. The value is given as so many GNAS units of spine.

For precision target shooting, manufacturers of arrows offer tables of specifications that relate the characteristics of their shafts to bows of various draw weights. The selection for individual needs will always present archers with a problem. While a correct relationship between spine value and weight of an arrow is essential, the lighter shaft offers advantages under calm conditions, but the heavier one is superior when shooting into a strong headwind.

As explained *s.v.* DISCHARGE the shaft of an arrow flexes when it is shot. A heavy arrow has greater inertia than a light one and it will tend to bend more during this phase. Thus for a given bow the heavier arrow will need to be stiffer, or have a lower spine value, than the lighter one, if both are to be correctly matched to the bow.

One manufacturer, whose tubular metal alloy arrows are very widely used, employs an alternative method of grading the physical characteristics of their shafts. A four-figure coding is used, such as 1616. The first two figures give the diameter of the shaft in sixty-fourths of an inch which, in the example, would equal a quarter of an inch; the last two figures give the wall thickness in thousandths of an inch. Most major dealers offer conversion tables to give the weight for finished arrows in grains and their related GNAS spine units for varying lengths of shafts.

SPINE TESTER
An instrument that measures the spine value (*qv*) or stiffness of an arrow shaft. In essence it consists of two supports on which the ends of the shaft rest and provides a method of measuring the deflection at the centre when a weight is hung at that point.

Since relatively few archers concern themselves with this aspect of matching and comparing arrow shafts, no such tester is offered commercially. For those who like to make their own arrows, particularly those with wooden shafts, such an instrument is essential if a matched set is to be produced. It is thus left to individual ingenuity to devise a tester suited to their needs.

SPINNING TEST
A simple method of testing the straightness of an arrow shaft by spinning it at its point of balance between the nails of the thumb and the index or middle finger. If it rattles between the nails the shaft is not true and it should be set aside until the defect can be corrected (see STRAIGHTENING AN ARROW).

SPOT
The centre circle on a field target (see FIELD SHOOTING). Score sheets record the hits achieved on spots in addition to the score and the number of hits within the target area. In the event of a tie on the score the position on the list is decided on the total number of hits, but if both scores and hits are equal the decision is then given in favour of the archer with most hits on the central spot. Should all three

factors be equal the archers concerned tie for the position achieved.

STABILISER

A weight attached to a bow to dampen the effect of twists and torque that occur in the limbs during the discharge of an arrow. The weight or weights are more usually attached to the end or ends of rods that project from the back of the modern composite bow.

The object of this fitting is to achieve added accuracy in target shooting and the need arises mainly from involuntary turning effect applied to the grip of the bow by the archer's hand. An initial movement to the side by the bowhand as a result of the slight pressure of the arrow shaft against the bow during discharge is virtually eliminated by the use of the pressure button or plunger (*qv*). This latter effect was first noticed by Dr Clarence Hickman (*qv*) and reported by Paul E. Klopsteg in *Archery Review* in January, 1934 (see *Archery: The Technical Side*, 1947, p. 141).

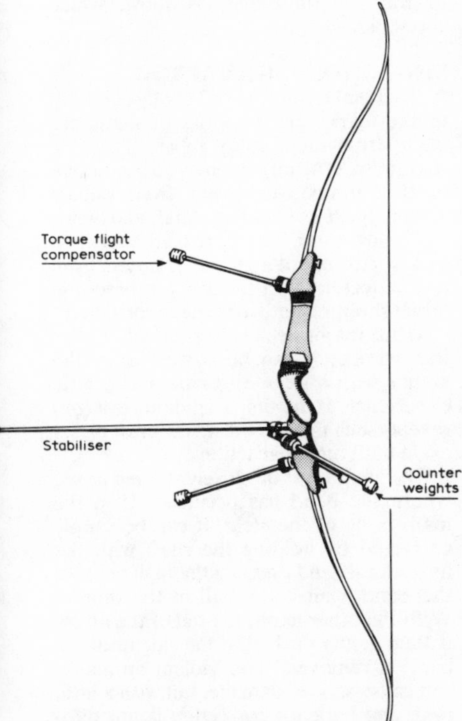

Both *stabilisers* and their allied *torque flight compensators*, together with balancing counterweights on the inside of the bow, are permitted under FITA Rules, Art. 504(e) and GNAS Rule 102(v), provided they do not: (1) serve as a string guide, (2) touch anything but the bow and (3) represent any obstacle to other archers as far as place on the shooting line is concerned.

STACK

1. To form the belly of a longbow (*qv*) in a high rounded arch.
2. A bow is said to stack when the weight or draw force increases with added rapidity toward the end of the draw. A slight increase is not unusual, but if excessive the discharge velocity of the arrow will vary with fractional differences in draw length that results in inaccurate shooting.

STAMP, Don (b. 1920)

Introduced to archery in 1949, Don Stamp has a distinguished record as a coach, organizer and administrator in both the national and international aspects of the sport. He has also written extensively on the subject and is the author of *Challenge of Archery* (1971) and *Field Archery* (1979) as well as being a regular contributor to *The British Archer* (*qv*) and a member of the Editorial Board of *Archery International*, in which several of his articles have appeared.

He was elected as President of the GNAS for the term of office commencing in 1980, after being a Vice-President from 1966–80. For his work for the Association of Archery in Schools and his management and coaching of the British Field Team over some ten years, he was awarded the Queen's Silver Jubilee Medal in 1977.

An International Judge since 1977, he was a member of FITA Rules and Regulations Committee from 1977–9, Chairman of their Target Archery Committee in 1979 and also a member of the Field Archery Committee.

In all this he has been well supported by his wife, Fionnavar (b. 1927), who shares his interest and enthusiasm, as well as being a qualified coach and regional judge in her own right.

STAND

A simple device on which a bow can be rested, clear of the ground, while an archer is waiting to shoot. It usually consists of a spike to go into the earth, with a horizontal support at the top for the bow and it may also incorporate a ring in which arrows can be placed to serve additionally as a ground quiver (*qv*). Some designs incorporate tripod legs for added sturdiness.

STAND IN A BOW
Said of an arrow whose shaft is sufficiently robust to withstand the impact of the bowstring in its nock, when the bow is shot. Though not of concern to the modern target archer, whose matched shafts can be selected to suit the bow in use, it was of concern in the more simple days of the traditional longbow, and it still applies to the fine, slender shafts used in flight shooting (*qv*).

STANDARD ARROW
The medieval English war arrow, also known as the sheaf arrow (*qv*).

STANDING
The first of Roger Ascham's (*qv*) 'partitions' or points of shooting. He says: "The fyrste poynte is when a man shoulde shote, to take suche footyng and standyng as shal be both cumlye to the eye and profytable to hys vse . . . one fote must not stande to far from the other, leste he stoupe to muche whyche is vnsemelye, nor yet to nere together, leste he stande to streyght vp, for so a man shall neyther vse hys strengthe well, nor yet stande stedfastlye."

The archer stands sideways to the mark, with feet a comfortable distance apart and in line with the target or point of aim. The weight of the body should be equally distributed on each foot, in a relaxed and easy manner. Though Horace Ford (*qv*) recommended that the heels should be about six or eight inches apart, not further, most modern target archers employ a slightly wider stance. In the Japanese art of *kyudo* (*qv*) the feet are placed even further apart, sometimes as much as 30 inches (75 cm), depending on the archer's stature (see W. R. B. Acker, *Japanese Archery*, 1965, p. 22 and A. Sollier & Z. Györbiro, *Japanese Archery*, 1969, p. 48).

Some favour advancing the rear foot slightly where this offers a more relaxed and comfortable position.

STELE
The shaft or main body of an arrow, excluding the fletchings, head etc.

STONEBOW
A bow that shoots a round stone, clay pellet, or even a small metal ball. The term incorporates the pellet bow and the bullet-shooting crossbow.

The handbow has been used over a wide area for this purpose against birds or other small game. The bowstring is divided into two parts with one, or two, spreaders or crosstrees, with a cradle fitted at the centre to hold the missile. It is shot with a twist on the grip to throw it past the bow as, without this action, it would strike the bow hand. As a simple pinch grip must be applied to the cradle or pocket, such bows are relatively weak, but effective at close range for their intended purpose.

A similar string construction is found with two basic forms of crossbow, the light pellet crossbow, with a down-curved fore end of the stock, which shoots a clay ball, and the German *Kugelschnepper* that led to the English bullet crossbow, which shoots a lead ball.

STRAIGHTENING AN ARROW
A shaft that is not true will not fly correctly to the mark. The majority of shafts are made from metal alloy tubes; if such a shaft misses the target it may strike a stone in the ground, or suffer from impact against the leg of a target stand, and bends can easily result. These are commonly of a minor nature, but a shaft that suffers from this defect is of little use for precision target shooting until it has been corrected.

While major dealers in equipment offer this service, it can be corrected by the archer with a degree of care and a little experience. If the simple spinning test (*qv*) reveals such a fault, the arrow must be set aside until remedial action can be taken.

The shaft must be closely studied to see where the bend has occurred. If in the main body of the stele, it can be simply corrected by holding the shaft with the index finger and pressing the high point of the bend against the ball of the thumb. With the other hand, the tail of the arrow is then gently pushed to the side until the bend is removed. Too violent an action can cause serious damage, but with a little time and patience correction is not difficult to achieve.

Bends near the pile can be more difficult. They can be dealt with by drilling a hole on a small block of softwood, inserting the head and applying correcting pressure. Alternatively, dealers offer a simple instrument, somewhat akin to a pair of pliers, that is effective for this purpose.

Wooden shafts present a different problem. If they have become warped for any reason, then one has to resort to heat treatment. The shaft must be heated over a stove or in front of a fire, until it is hot. Correcting pressure can then be applied until the shaft is true. Again, patience is needed as the final result may not be achieved at the first attempt.

STRING (*n.* and *v.*)
1. A bowstring.
2. To fit a string to a bow.

STRINGBOARD
A device for making bowstrings (*qv*). It consists of a wooden base with two or four recessed pillars around which the thread forming an endless skein may be wound. The distance between the pillars is adjustable to allow for the differing amount of stretch in different materials, and also for the construction of strings for bows of different lengths. The length of the skein can be adjusted by sliding the right-hand pillar, secured by a wing-nut underneath the board, in or out to compensate for the different amounts of stretch incurred with different materials.

With wooden pillars and the facility to turn these on a lathe, their lower section can be made in a conical form to provide a firm base on the board. Metal pillars will need a suitable washer on their bases for this purpose. The four-pillar stringboard provides the facility to reinforce the end loops of a bowstring with added strands. The two cross-bars, each carrying two pillars, are secured to the base by wing-nuts.

First, the cross-bars are rotated so that they are in line with the board. The thread skein is then wound around the two outer pillars, after which the cross-bars are turned back so that they are at right angles to the base of the board. Extra strands can

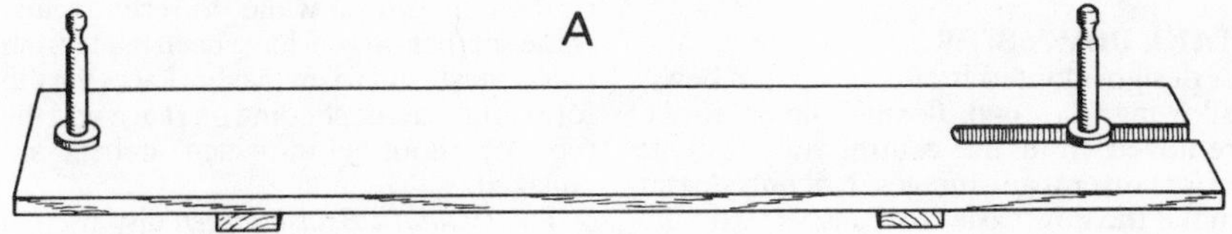

Simple, two-pillar stringboard.

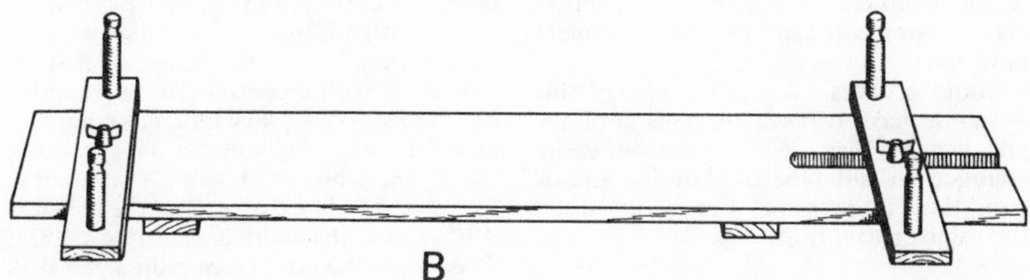

A four-pillar stringboard.

then be added around each pair of pillars. (See E. G. Heath, *Archery: The Modern Approach*, London 1966, pp. 201–5.)

STRINGER
A maker of bowstrings. Roger Ascham (*qv*) comments: "But here in you muste be contente to put youre truste in honest stringers . . . An ill stringe brekethe many a good bowe, nor no other thynge halfe so many. In warre if a string breke the man is loste and is no man, for his weapon is gone . . . therfore god send vs good stringers both for war and peace."

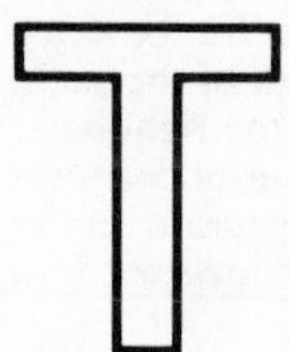

TAB
A simple device, usually of leather, to protect the fingers of the drawing hand against the abrasion of the bowstring. It is slotted between the index and middle fingers so that the tail of the arrow may go between them and it is fitted with one or two holes for the finger(s) to go through. Some designs incorporate a separator (*qv*) to prevent the fingers from pinching the nock of the arrow.

TAIL
The rear end of an arrow, including the shaftment (*qv*), heel and nock.

TAKE DOWN BOW
A design adopted for many modern bows, allowing the two flexible limbs to be removed from the central riser (*qv*). It offers several advantages. Not only does it make the bow easier to transport with the three sections often being mounted in a fitted case, but in the event of a defect or damage occurring to one limb only, a replacement can be obtained at an appreciably lower cost than that of a complete new bow.

Some archers take advantage of this design to have two sets of limbs of different weights (*qv*) which can be easily changed to suit type of shooting and/or conditions under which they shoot, using the same central riser.

TANG
A metal spike that is part of an arrowhead, enabling it to be mounted on the fore-end of a shaft by insertion into the body of the stele, as an alternative to fitting the head with a socket that fits over the outside of the shaft.

It is rarely found in examples of old English arrowheads, but was more widely used in the Orient, where it was well suited for bamboo shafts and it is, therefore, the normal method employed in Japanese construction for their target arrows, as used in *kyudo* (*qv*).

TAPERED ARROW
See BOB-TAILED.

TARGET
The mark at which the archer shoots. It normally consists of a boss, made from a coiled straw rope, to which a face is attached, marked with scoring rings or areas. Straw bales or boards of compressed straw are sometimes used in place of the coiled rope while, in recent years, some smaller targets have been made from nylon mesh and foam plastic. Faces vary in form and size, depending on range and the type of shooting in which archers are engaged.

The *standard British target*, also used in America, dates back to the formation of the Grand National Archery Society (*qv*) in 1844. Prior to this time there had been no national rules and the size and colours varied with different clubs and societies. It was standardized as being 4 feet in diameter, with a central gold surrounded by four rings of equal width, coloured red, blue (though originally the inner white), black, and white, with scoring values of 9, 7, 5, 3 and 1. The diameter of the gold was 9 3/5 in. and the width of each ring 4 4/5 in. The size of the target face is the same at all ranges.

The *standard FITA target* is 122 cm in diameter at the longer ranges. Both its size and colours were adopted from the British target, though each colour is divided into two equal parts to give 10-zone scoring, each ring having a width of 6.1 cm. At 50- and 30-metre ranges the target diameter is 80 cm and the width of each ring is 4 cm (see FITA ROUND).

TARGET ARCHERY
Shooting at the standard, ringed targets, as opposed to the several other forms of contest in which archers may participate. See GNAS Rules 100–185 and FITA Rules 502–504.

TARGET ARROW
An arrow used for target shooting. Both GNAS Rule 102 (vi) and FITA Rule 504 (f) allow that: "Arrows of any type may be used provided they subscribe to the accepted principle and meaning of the word Arrow as used in Target Archery, and that such Arrows do not cause undue damage to target faces and buttresses.

"An Arrow consists of a shaft with head (point), nock, fletching and, if desired, cresting. The Arrows of each archer shall be marked with the archer's name, initials or insignia and all Arrows used for the same end of 3 or 6 arrows shall carry the same pattern and colour(s) of fletching, nocks and cresting (if any)."

A target arrow may be recognized by the form of its head (point), known as a pile (*qv*).

TARGET DAY
A day set aside by a club or society for formal shooting.

TARGET SHYNESS
An archer's inability to aim at the target due to involuntary muscular tensions (see ARCHER'S CATALEPSY).

TARGET STAND
A tripod on which the target is placed. It is usually of wood and the legs below the target are often padded against the impact of arrows that may fall short. Both GNAS and FITA Rules require that the target shall be inclined at about fifteen degrees from the vertical and be securely anchored by cords attached to a peg in rear of the stand to avoid any chance of it being blown over by a strong wind.

The height of the stand and the position of the struts on the legs that support the boss are such as to allow the centre of a standard target (*qv*) to be 130 cm (4 ft 3 in) above the ground.

TASSEL
Made from woollen yarns, it is hung from the archer's belt or quiver to wipe the shafts of arrows that may strike the ground and to which dirt or mud may adhere.

Some clubs and societies favour the adoption of a specific colour for the use of their members.

TELESCOPE
A visual aid for spotting arrows, permitted under both GNAS Rule 102(a)(viii) and FITA Rule 504(h).

TELL, William (*fl. c.* 1300)
The legendary Swiss crossbowman who, during the period of Austrian oppression, was forced to shoot an apple from his son's head by Gessler, administrator of the canton of Uri.

While argument will continue over whether he really existed or not, he is a symbol of freedom and his memory and spirit is still held in high regard. (See G. Gibson, 'Origins of William Tell', *Journal of the Society of Archer-Antiquaries*, 1975, pp. 6–8.)

THOMPSON, James Maurice (1844–1901)
With his younger brother, Will (see below), their efforts were largely responsible for the founding of the National Archery Association (*qv*) in the USA. Among his several published books, *The Witchery of Archery* (1878) is a classic in its field and it inspired many to take up the sport.

The founders of the NAA elected him as their first President at their inaugural meeting in 1879.

In his memory the Board of Governors of the NAA established the Maurice Thompson Medal of Honor in 1939, awarded to archers who had made outstanding contributions to the sport and it still remains as their highest and most prestigious award.

His literary efforts were considerable and they are listed in F. Lake & H. Wright, *A Bibliography of Archery*, Manchester 1974, where they take nearly four pages.

THOMPSON, Will Henry (1846–1918)
The younger brother of Maurice (see above) and the more skilled archer of the two, winning the National Championship five times, including the first in 1879. His last victory in this event was in 1908 and until 1913 he was never placed out of the top ten in any major tournament.

He wrote a series of articles, published

in *Forest and Stream* between 1878 and 1915, listed by Lake and Wright (see above), and, together with his brother Maurice, published in 1879 a manual on how to train in archery.

THUMB LOCK

The technique of drawing the bowstring with the thumb of the shaft hand, as opposed to the use of the fingers for this purpose. Its use has been found throughout most of the Orient, from Turkey in the west to Japan and Korea in the east. The method is still used by exponents of the Japanese art of *kyudo* (*qv*) and thus has an application in modern archery, as well as its continued use by certain native tribes and by those in the East who continue to follow their old traditions in the use of the bow.

The term 'lock' is correctly used in that, after the thumb has been hooked around the string, below the arrow, it is locked in position by the index finger being placed

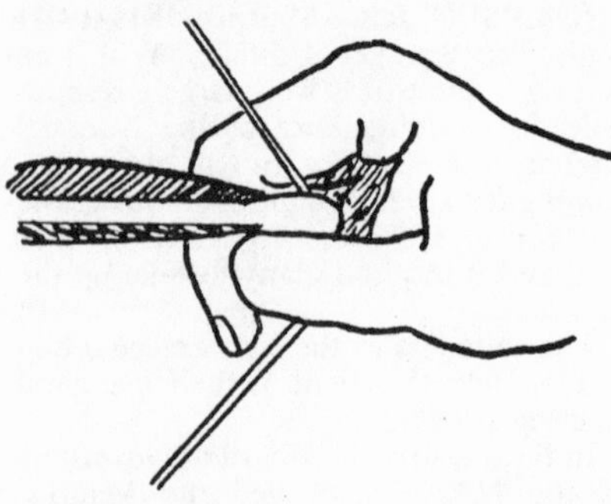

Basic thumb lock.

across the nail. As a variant, known in the mid-East as the *pillion* lock, both index and middle fingers are fastened across the end of the thumb. This method was and still is used in the Japanese technique of shooting.

Its origin may well have resulted from the development of the short, composite Eastern bow, where the angle of the string at full draw would have caused unacceptable pinching of the fingers. Though history attests its effectiveness in both hunting and war, for the repeated precision demanded by modern target archery, the finger loose has been shown to offer greater sustained accuracy.

The formation of the thumb lock can vary in detail, depending mainly on the physical characteristics of the user (see J. D. Latham & W. F. Paterson, *Saracen Archery*, London 1970, pp. 51–5 and figs. 22 and 41).

THUMB RING

Used by archers shooting with the thumb lock (*qv*) for protection against the abrasion of the bowstring.

There are two basic forms, the cylindrical Sino-Tatar type favoured in China and Mongolia, and the more widely used type with a lip that partially covers the inside of the tip of the thumb.

There are appreciable variations in design details and those made for persons of wealth and importance were often finely carved in jade or other hardstones and, in some cases, inlaid with gold and precious stones. Rings of metal, ivory and horn were more commonly used.

TILLER (*n.* and *v.*)

1. The earlier term for the stock of a crossbow, derived from the medieval English word for a bar or beam.
2. A simple, notched bar, used by a bowmaker or bowyer, to study and adjust the curvature of the limbs of a bow, in a process known as *tillering*.

When the bow is nearing its final form, it is strung and the tiller is placed against the grip. By lodging the string in successive notches in the bar, the bow may be drawn an inch or two at a time so that the shape of the flexed limbs may be studied and adjusted by careful scraping away of surplus material. The process should continue until full draw is achieved and the bowyer is satisfied with the even balance of the two limbs.

TIMBER HITCH

The knot used to secure the bowstring in the lower nock of a traditional longbow. It will not slip under tension and it is very simple to adjust should the length of the string need modification (see BOWSTRING).

TIR AU BEURSAULT

An old and traditional form of target shooting in France that dates back to the Middle Ages. In some old works it is called *tir au berceau*. It is still used for selected target contests.

Archers shoot at 50 metres at a white target, marked with black circles to give three scoring zones, values 1, 2 and 3. The scoring area is 450 mm in diameter, ringed by a black circle 15 mm wide. The inner zone 3 of 125 mm diameter is also ringed by a heavy black circle 11 mm wide, known as the *petit cordon* (a hit within the area of this circle is called a *chapelet*).

The centre of the target is a white circle, 8 mm in diameter, surrounded by a black ring, 17 mm wide, called the *petit noir*.

The system of scoring records the total hits within the target area, known as *honneurs*, the hits within the *petit cordon* (*chapelets*) and the *points* achieved by hits in the three scoring zones. Thus a hit in the central area gains an archer: 1 *honneur*, 1 *chapelet*, and 3 *points*. Prizes are usually awarded for the best scores in each of the three categories as well as for the shot nearest the centre of the target or *la plus belle flèche*.

The traditional rules are basically similar to the modern method where hits, score and golds are recorded and the 'best gold' measured, though they are of far greater antiquity. (See F. Avon-Coffrant, *Tir à l'Arc*, Paris 1977, pp. 98–103.)

TORQUE FLIGHT COMPENSATOR
See STABILISER.

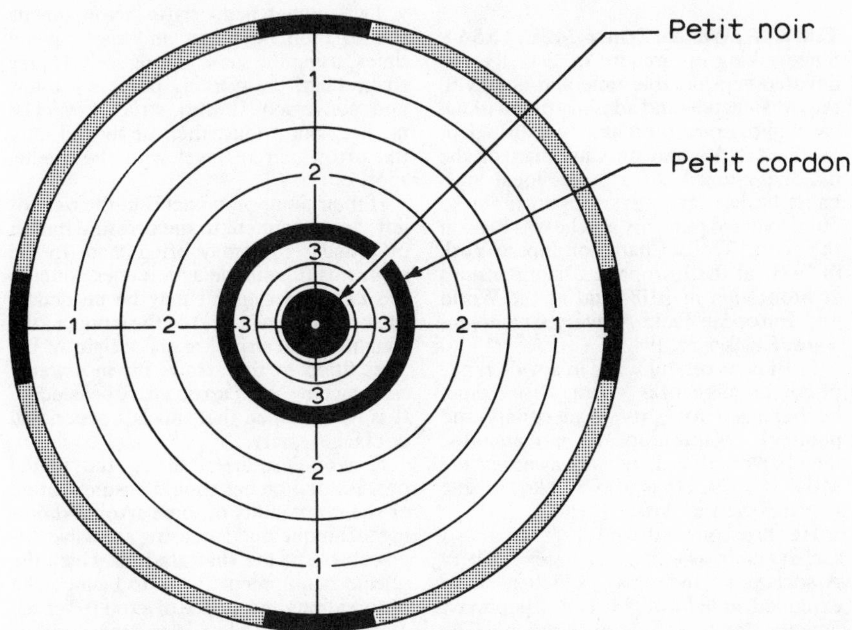

The Tir au Beursault Target.

Centre white	8 mm diameter
Inner black ring (*Petit noir*)	17 mm wide
Inner circles	55 mm and 92 mm diameter (internal)
(Circle lines	2 mm wide)
Zone 3	125 mm diameter (internal)
Black surrounding circle (*Petit cordon*)	11 mm wide
Zone 2	292 mm diameter (internal)
(Circle lines	2 mm wide)
Zone 1	450 mm diameter (internal)
Outer black ring	15 mm wide

TOXOLOGY
The study of archery, from the Greek – *toxon*, a bow.

TOXOPHILITE
An archer, *lit.* – 'a lover of the bow'. The use of the term continues with such institutions as the Royal Toxophilite Society (*qv*).

TOXOPHILY
The art of archery. While the use of the bow and arrow is still considered to be an art, there are those who feel that many of the devices, permitted under both national and international regulations, are tending to turn it into a science.

TUCKER, William Ernest, MBE, FRSA
Since taking up archery in 1946, he has devoted considerable time and energy to the organization and administration of the sport and served both as a Vice-President of the GNAS and as Chairman of the national council. As a professional journalist he has taken every opportunity to obtain valued publicity and he was PRO at the World Target Championships at York in 1971, at the European Championships at Stoneleigh in 1978, and at the World and European Field Archery Championships, Kingsclere, 1982.

For his successful work in a wide range of community works where, at one time, he belonged to thirty local county and national organizations as a committee member or official, he was awarded the MBE in 1979. He is also a Fellow of the Royal Society of Arts.

He has founded and organized two archery clubs as well as the Essex Archery Association and his activities have extended to field, flight, clout, popinjay, novelty shoots and demonstrations. The Society of Archer-Antiquaries, which is concerned with the history of the bow and arrow, owes its existence to his original proposal and positive efforts that established it in 1956. He has been President of the Society since 1977.

TUNING a bow
With the development of the modern bow, bowstring materials and the use of stabilisers (*qv*), torque flight compensators and relatively complex sights, as permitted by both national and international regulations, the need for fine adjustment to a bow has arisen where the archer seeks to make the maximum possible score. For those who wish to involve themselves in competitive success, particularly in the international field where every point scored is of importance, accurate *tuning* is essential.

The first adjustment is to set the nocking point (*qv*) in the correct position. This should initially be set on the bowstring between 1/8 and ¼ inch above the line at right angles to the arrow rest. With a target at about 10 or 15 yards range, the bowsight is adjusted so that a normal, fletched arrow strikes as near as possible to a selected aiming spot on the target. The sight must not then be moved.

Two unfletched, bare arrow shafts should then be taken and shot several times, using the same aiming spot. If they strike high, the nocking point is too low and conversely if they strike low. The nocking point must then be moved until the arrows strike level with the aiming spot.

If their point of impact is to the right or left, an adjustment to the pressure button or plunger (*qv*) may bring them to the centre. If this simple action does not cure the fault, adjustment may be needed to the bracing height (*qv*) of the string, to the weight of the string, to the weight of the piles fitted to the arrows or, in extreme cases, a new set of arrows may be needed. It is to be hoped that this last action will not be necessary.

If problems arise during the tuning process, the archer should ensure that he or she is not guilty of some error in shooting technique that is causing excessive displacement of the shaft and for which the selected equipment is not to blame. The observations and advice of a trained coach or, at least, that of an experienced archer may well provide a simple solution.

Assuming that no major problems arise, following the correct adjustment of the nocking point, if the bare shafts of the right-handed archer hit left of centre the spring tension of the pressure button needs to be reduced and vice versa.

The final stage of adjusting the pressure button is achieved by placing the aiming spot near the top of a target boss and moving back in five-yard steps, shooting fletched arrows. As the range increases the arrows will hit progressively lower on the target, as the sight must not be moved during this phase of the test. If successive hits are vertically below the aiming spot, then an ideal adjustment has been achieved. If they move to the left the plunger should be brought in a little toward the bow and conversely if they move to the right.

It is important that tuning is carried out under calm weather conditions and it must be appreciated that the results can be no better than the shooting ability of the archer. However, adequate tuning, even when not perfect, should result in improved scores and, with the added confidence this gives, the archer's ability should increase.

TURTLE-BACK SHOOTING

Shooting at a high elevation or with a nearly vertical trajectory to hit a mark or target on the ground. It is rarely seen today.

UNDERBOWED
Using a bow that is too weak for the archer. It is the opposite of overbowed (*qv*). While the beginner will tend to start with a light bow and concentrate on the development of a correct technique, a stronger bow will be needed when the rudiments have been mastered, as otherwise faults and problems may result, particularly in the loose.

UNDERHAND
Shooting at a mark that is sighted and aimed at below the bowhand. At the maximum ranges when shooting at normal targets under GNAS and FITA Rules this aspect of aiming does not arise, but in variations, such as clout shooting (*qv*), the archer cannot sight the mark *overhand*, due to the elevation needed to reach this particular form of target. It is usual to use simple marks or bands on the lower limb of a bow as an aid to aiming at these longer ranges.

UNDERSTRUNG
Said of a bow where the bracing height – or distance between the bow and the string – is less than it should be.

UNSTRING or UNBRACE
To remove a string from a bow by flexing it and easing the upper loop of the bowstring from the nock. A bow is invariably unstrung when shooting for the day is over, with the exception of the modern compound bow (*qv*).

UPSHOT
Though the word is established in the English language to mean the 'conclusion' or 'end', it originated from the archery practice of rovers (*qv*).

When, in medieval times, a group of archers would wander through the countryside, shooting at random marks, whoever was nearest the nominated target was said to have 'gained the upshot', and had the right to select the next mark at which the archers were to shoot.

VANE

A general term for the steering device on the rear end of an arrow, irrespective of the material from which it is formed. It embraces the feather, widely used throughout thousands of years, the plastic fittings, popular with modern archers, and even the sections of razor blade, fitted to some modern flight arrows.

Old crossbow bolts may be seen in certain museums, fitted with vanes of wood or horn, and some of the old Turkish flight arrows used parchment for this purpose.

The term 'flight' is sometimes used as a synonym.

VELOCITY MEASUREMENT

To the archer with an interest in the technical aspects of equipment this can present a difficult problem.

The most accurate method of measurement is by the use of electronic equipment, using photo-electric cells and a time counter. With such a device there are two photo cells about 18 inches apart with beams of light falling on them. When the arrow is shot and breaks the first beam of light, it operates a 'trigger' that starts the time counter. It is then stopped when the second beam of light is broken. The time taken for the arrow to travel from one beam to the next can then be read from the counter and converted to velocity.

Since the construction of such a device is beyond the skill of the average archer, it is worth noting a simple method of obtaining a very close approximation, as described by J. D. Seagrave. He has determined that with an average target arrow, shot almost vertically upwards, the total time of flight from the instant of loosing to when it returns and hits the ground, multiplied by a factor of 17 – which is ½g (the gravitational constant) plus an error percentage found by checking against an electronic device – will give an answer that is sufficiently accurate for most practical purposes. Thus, an arrow which is in flight for 10 seconds had an initial velocity of about 170 feet per second.

Velocity measurements are needed to determine the *kinetic energy* (KE) imparted to an arrow by a bow when calculating its efficiency (*qv*).

VIRTUAL MASS

A method of assessing the relative merits of different bows, devised by Paul E. Klopsteg (*qv*) from studies of their efficiency (*qv*).

The problem with 'efficiency' is that it varies with the weight of the arrow and it is not a constant. A given bow will discharge a heavier arrow at a lower velocity than a lighter one. The theory assumes that the bow and its string have no weight and thus all the potential energy (PE), stored in the bow by the archer in drawing the string, is available for transfer to the arrow as kinetic energy (KE). Theoretically, a bow might shoot an arrow of 350 grains at 200 feet per second but, in fact, it could be found that it gives the shaft an initial velocity of 150 fps. It is as if the 'weightless' bow and string was shooting an arrow of 500 grains until, of course, the arrow has left the string.

The difference between the true and apparent weights of the arrow of 150 grains – in this example – is a quantity called the *virtual mass*. It is a unique characteristic of the bow in question.

The figure is small for modern bows of high efficiency, while it is large in the case of the traditional wooden longbow (*qv*) with its relatively heavy limbs absorbing more of the PE in carrying themselves forward.

An important aspect of this study was to

impress on the designers of bows the need to keep the weight of the limbs to a minimum as this is the factor that has the greatest effect on the virtual mass. (See P. E. Klopsteg, 'Virtual Mass of a Bow', *Archery: The Technical Side*, 1947, pp. 167–72.)

In mathematical form the mass-velocity relationship is expressed in the form:

$E = \frac{mv^2}{2} + \frac{Kv^2}{2}$ or, in simplified form:

$E = \frac{1}{2}(m + K)v^2$.

Where E is the potential energy in the drawn bow, $\frac{1}{2}mv^2$ is the kinetic energy in the discharged arrow and $\frac{1}{2}Kv^2$ represents the part of E which failed to be transferred from the bow to the arrow. It is that part of the energy that is left behind when the arrow leaves the string. The term employs the same velocity v as that of the arrow, and the quantity K, which has the dimensions of mass, is termed the *virtual mass* of the bow. (See P. E. Klopsteg, 'Bows and Arrows: A Chapter in the Evolution of Archery in America', *Smithsonian Report for 1962*, Washington 1963, pp. 588–90.)

VISUAL AIDS

Field glasses, telescopes and other visual aids may be used for spotting arrows under GNAS Rule 102 (viii) and FITA Rule 504 (h), but note should be taken that an archer is required to retire behind the waiting line immediately after the group of three arrows have been shot, as required under GNAS Rule 104 (c) and FITA Rule 505 (h).

Ordinary spectacles or shooting spectacles are allowed, provided they are fitted with the same lenses normally worn by the archer, and sun-glasses may also be worn. None may be fitted with microhole lenses, glasses or similar, nor marked in any way which can assist in aiming.

WAND SHOOTING
Shooting with the object of hitting a stick, placed upright in the ground, at an agreed range. Splitting the willow wand is linked with traditions going back to the annals of Robin Hood, and while some clubs hold a light-hearted shoot in this manner, it only has a small following today. As a result there are no national rules and regulations for such a shoot, though R. P. Elmer in the glossary of *Target Archery* (New York 1946) offers the information that, in America, it was a round of 36 arrows at 100 yards for men and 60 yards for women.

WEIGHT – of a bow
The force in pounds on the bowstring needed to draw an arrow to a specified distance in that bow. For the modern target bow this is in the order of 30 lb for women and 40 lb for men, though there are appreciable variations, depending on the stature and strength of the individual archer.

For those who favour the traditional longbow, greater weight is needed to give adequate performance at the recognized target ranges.

WHIP, WHIPPING
Synonymous with *serving* and *lapping*, for the binding applied to the end loops and central section of a bowstring (*qv*) to protect the strands against the abrasion of the bow nocks and of the arrow nock and fingers, when the bow is drawn, as well as impact against the bracer (*qv*) when the shot is made. (See also SERVE, SERVING.)

WHISTLING ARROW
A shaft fitted with a hollow, bulbous head, usually with four holes around its periphery, that emits a whistling sound when shot.

While history makes no mention of this device being used by the English in medieval times, it was well known in the Eastern world for signalling purposes. As an example, sentries patrolling an encampment would carry them to raise the alarm should they sight anything suspicious, while the Japanese archers would often open an engagement with massed flights of such arrows, commonly fitted with forked heads (*karimata*), to strike terror in their enemies.

There is also mention of their use by commanders on Mongol cavalry squadrons, each carrying whistling arrows with their own note, and using them to indicate the target to be engaged by the horsemen they commanded.

In England, from the seventeenth century, they have occasionally been used at the start of an archery contest for the amusement of spectators.

WHITE
The outer circle on the standard target, where a hit scores one point or, with the FITA (*qv*) target where each colour is divided in two, the outer white scores one and the inner two points.

WINDPLANE
A condition that can occur with a broadhead (*qv*) hunting arrow when the effect of wind on the head overcomes the steadying balance of the fletching and results in erratic flight.

This emphasizes the importance of mounting the head exactly in line with the shaft and of having an adequate size of fletching to overcome the pressure on the head from a strong crosswind.

WING
1. The fletching or vane on the shaft of an arrow.

2. The barb on certain forms of arrow-head.
3. A military formation of medieval archers, extending at the side of the main body of infantry.

WOODMEN OF ARDEN
A society of archers, founded in 1785 at the Bull's Head, Meriden, whose shooting ground is near the spot that is reputed to be the exact centre of England. Their main interest is in clout shooting (*qv*) with the traditional longbow and every three years they meet in contest with the Royal Company of Archers (*qv*) at the clouts. Membership is restricted to eighty 'Gentlemen of Warwickshire' and they shoot up to twelve score yards, which is close to the limit of a good longbow. Their uniform is of white trousers and shoes, with a green tail-coat, except for clerical members, who wear black. The senior Woodman, or Lord Warden, is the Earl of Aylesford.

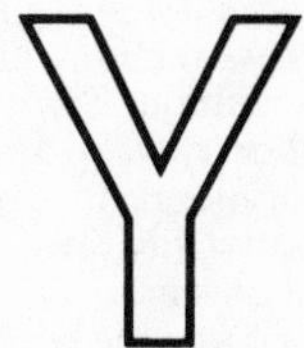

YEOMEN OF THE GUARD

Formed in 1485 as a royal bodyguard of archers. The contemporary historian, Edward Hall, records that in 1513 at the siege of Terrouenne, Henry VIII had the six hundred archers of his guard all in white gaberdines and caps.

YEW

European yew (*Taxus baccata*) is and was the best wood for the traditional English longbow, though it can vary appreciably in quality. Trees grown under hard conditions in hill and mountain country offer a closer grained wood that is normally superior to that grown near sea level.

Its excellence lies in the very different quality of the ivory or cream coloured outer sapwood, and the inner, reddish heart wood. The former has an almost rubbery consistency, with a high tensile strength, while the dark heart withstands compression. The better bows are made from the main trunk of the tree. As Roger Ascham (*qv*) comments, "Euerye bowe is made eyther of a boughe, of a plante or of the boole of the tree. The bough comonlye is verye knotty, full of pinnes, weak, of small pithe, and sone wyll folowe the stringe, . . . yet for chyldren & yonge beginners it maye serue well ynoughe."

The native North American yew (*Taxus brevifolia*) is virtually indistinguishable from the European yew as regards the quality of the wood. (See R. P. Elmer, *Target Archery*, New York 1946, pp. 123–35.)

YORK ROUND

A round (*qv*) that consists of shooting 72 arrows at 100 yards, 48 at 80 and 24 at 60 yards against a standard four-foot target. A double round of a total of 288 arrows has been used since 1844 to decide the men's championship of Great Britain and that of several other major contests.

It originated from the Prince's Lengths (*qv*), which specified the distances given above, while its name was adopted from the first organized British championship, held at York, on the Knavesmire ground, in 1844.

YUMI

The long, traditional Japanese bow. Though the written character for 'bow', when it stands on its own is read as *yumi*, when it is qualified it is read as *kyu*, as in KYUDO (*qv*), the way, or art, of using the bow.

The construction of the *yumi* is unique and it has no resemblance to any other form. Its origin is obscured in the mists of time, but the design is very old. In the same way as the longbow achieved fame in England during the Hundred Years War, so the *yumi* is honoured for its performance in the hands of the Samurai warriors during the long civil war between the Taira and Minamoto in the twelfth century AD.

The main component of the *yumi* is bamboo. The term 'bamboo' is in itself vague, as there are about a thousand species, of some fifty genera in the world. The most common variety in Japan is the *Phyllostachys bambusoides*. There are others and the makers of both bows and arrows carefully selected the growths best suited to their arts.

The bow is about seven feet in length, needed to allow an arrow to be drawn up to about 34 inches (87 cm) in following the Japanese technique of drawing level with the point of the shoulder. Seasoned bamboo is selected with nodes, or joints, about 12 inches (30 cm) apart, that will give seven nodes along the length of the bow. The main stave consists of two lengths of this bamboo, comprising the back and belly with the position of the nodes alternating. Between these two lengths is a third section, consisting of three bamboo strips, roughly square in cross-section, flanked by two strips of a deciduous wood, such as mulberry, cherry, waxwood or sumac. The tips, with shoulders to carry the end loops of the bowstring, are scarfed and pegged to the main stave.

After the components have been glued together, using a fish glue, and it has been given time to set, the bow-maker puts

HIMEZORI
(Lit: 'Little curve'.)
End reflexed section.
Upper = *Ura*.

TORIUCHI
(Lit: 'bird beater'.)
Upper convex curve.

YAZURITO
Rattan binding of the arrow-pass.
(About 10 cm. in length.)

NIGIRI
Grip.

TESHITA
(Lit: 'beneath the hand'.)
Lower convex curve.

HIMEZORI
End reflexed section.
Lower = *Moto*.

A

Parts of a Japanese bow.

reflexed curves into the stave with the aid of heat and a bending block that ensures the correct shape is achieved.

The majority of older, traditional bows are coated with black lacquer and bound at intervals with rattan, painted red. On just one bow as many as seventy-four separate bindings have been found, while other bows may have only five. While modern bows of traditional design have the same laminated form of construction, they are usually coated with a clear varnish and lack the rattan bindings except, perhaps, those at either end where the tips are fitted to the main stave and another immediately above the grip.

Another unique feature of the *yumi* is that the grip is about two-thirds of the way down the stave from the upper end. The explanation for this is conjectural. It has been suggested that the very early bows were made from a simple length of bamboo which, naturally, would taper toward the top and it was found that better performance was achieved by grasping it well below the centre. Another idea that has been mentioned is that the warrior, when on foot, might require to shoot from a kneeling position and if the lower limb of the bow was too long it might strike the ground. Also, when shooting from horse-back it would be liable to hit the horse. Neither reason is convincing, but the fact

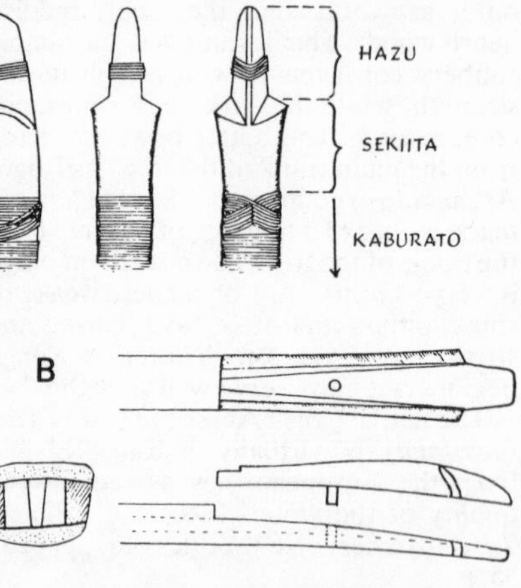

Top: *The upper end of a bow*. Hazu = *Tip*. Sekiita = *Shoulder*. Kaburato = *Binding*. Left: *Section taken from the centre of a limb*. Right: *Construction of the shoulder and tip*.

remains that tradition requires the grip to

be below the centre of the stave.

This aspect, coupled with the considerable length of the bow, resulted in the development of an unusual shooting technique (see KYUDO) to give effective performance and there is no doubt that, in the hands of the Samurai, it was a highly effective weapon during their periods of war.

Appendix 1
Rules

FÉDÉRATION INTERNATIONALE DE TIR À L'ARC CONSTITUTION AND RULES INTERNATIONAL ARCHERY FEDERATION (1981)

Contents

Part I
CONSTITUTION

101 Name
The name of the Federation shall be "Fédération Internationale de Tir à l'Arc" and shall be abbreviated "F.I.T.A."

102 Objects
The objects of F.I.T.A. shall be:
(a) To promote and encourage Archery throughout the World in conformity with the Olympic principles;
(b) To frame and interpret F.I.T.A. Rules and Regulations;
(c) To arrange for the organization of World Championships and such Continental or Regional Championships as Congress may establish in any branch of Archery;
(d) To confirm and maintain:
(i) World Record Scores,
(ii) World Championships Record Scores,
(iii) Olympic Games Record Scores;
(e) To maintain complete lists of scores from:
(i) World Championships,
(ii) World Championships Record Scores,
(iii) Olympic Games.

103 Membership
(a) Members of F.I.T.A. shall be National Amateur Archery Associations, one only from each country;
(b) The name of National Associations must reflect the territorial extent and tradition of that country;
(c) Members shall recognize F.I.T.A. as the sole International Federation for Amateur Archery, shall be bound by its Rules and submit to its jurisdiction and shall undertake to implement its aims;
(d) No discrimination in the practice of the administration of Archery shall be allowed against any country, association or person on grounds of race, religion or politics;
(e) Member Associations shall deposit with the General Secretary of F.I.T.A. a copy of their Constitution, together with a certified translation in one of F.I.T.A.'s official languages and communicate similarly any changes therein.

104 Affiliation
(a) A National Archery Association wish-

Note: Appendices 1–7 of the FITA handbook detailing championship entry forms etc. are omitted.

ing to become a member of F.I.T.A. must submit a written application stating clearly the acceptance of the present Constitution;
(b) The application must be accompanied by:
(i) a copy of their current Constitution with a certified translation into one of F.I.T.A.'s official languages;
(ii) the letters of two Member Associations supporting the application;
(iii) the membership fee for the current year;
(c) The Executive Committee, satisfied that the application is in order, will announce it to all Member Associations and to all Members of Council. If no serious objections are raised in writing within 60 days of this announcement, temporary membership will be granted until the next Congress, when final affiliation will be submitted to a vote: in case of objections, the Executive Committee will examine them and decide on temporary membership;
(d) Congress may decline an application: in that case the fee paid shall be returned.

105 Organization
(a) Congress is the Senior Administrative body of F.I.T.A.: to it belong all powers that are not specifically attributed to other offices by this Constitution;
(b) Congress elects, and to it are responsible, the following offices of F.I.T.A., namely:
(i) The President,
(ii) The First Vice President,
(iii) The Vice Presidents,
(iv) The Council,
(v) The Board of Justice,
(vi) The Permanent Committees;
Responsible to Congress are also:
(vii) The General Secretary,
(viii) The Treasurer,
who are appointed by the President and approved by Congress.
(c) The President, General Secretary and Treasurer form the Executive Committee. They may be assisted by an Executive Secretariat appointed by the Executive Committee, approved by Council and paid for by F.I.T.A. funds;
(d) All offices have a term of four years, except Committees and the Executive Secretariat;
(e) Retiring officers are eligible for re-election;
(f) The President, two Vice Presidents and three Members of the Council shall be elected at the Congress held the year after the Olympic years; the First Vice President, another Vice President, four other Members of the Council and the Board of Justice shall be elected at the Congress held three years after the Olympic year.

106 Congress
(a) Congress is formed by the delegations of Member Associations as well as Members of the Permanent Committees together with Council. Delegations are qualified to attend Congress only if the member association they represent have paid their membership fees up to and including that of the current year;
(b) Each Member Association shall be represented by one voting delegate and no more than two other delegates;
(c) Each member Association shall have one vote. The vote of a Member Association may be cast by proxy. No delegation may carry more than one proxy vote. Each voting delegate and proxy shall table written authority from the Member Association represented before the meeting starts.
(d) A Congress session shall be valid if at least half the Member Associations qualified to attend have answered the roll call at the beginning of the session.
(e) The President or Chairman shall have a casting vote in the event of a tie. Other Members of the Council shall have no vote unless acting also as properly appointed voting delegates or proxies of Member Associations. Neither the General Secretary nor the Treasurer may serve as voting delegate or proxy.
(f) Congress decisions are final and can only be changed by the vote of a following Congress. Amendments to the F.I.T.A. Constitution or Rules of Shooting shall require a two-thirds majority of the votes cast; whereas other Rules, Regulations and Matters shall be decided by a simple majority.
(g) The President shall preside at all meetings of Congress at which he is present. In the absence of the President, the First Vice President shall preside. If he is not present, one of the other Vice Presidents shall preside, or, if none are present, a Member of the Council other than the General Secretary or the Treasurer. If

none of these are present, then a voting delegate shall be elected as Chairman.
(h) Congress shall be convened by the Executive Committee in Ordinary Session at the time of every Target World Championship.
(i) The Executive Committee shall convene an Extraordinary Session of Congress on written request of:
(i) Council;
(ii) at least the majority of Member Associations.
(j) The notice convening an Extraordinary Session of Congress shall state clearly the object for which the meeting is being called. The only business which may be transacted at an Extraordinary Session of Congress shall be the special business for which such a meeting is called.
(k) Motions for consideration by Congress may be submitted only by Member Associations, or by the President, or the Council, or Permanent Committees within their terms of reference, at least 6 months before Congress.
(l) At least four months before Congress, the General Secretary shall collate all Motions and distribute them to all Member Associations Honorary Officers, Members of the Council and Members of the relevant Permanent Committees together with nomination forms for offices that may be vacant at that Congress.
At least two months before Congress, the General Secretary shall collate and distribute to all Member Associations, Honorary Officers and Members of the Council:
(i) the Congress Agenda,
(ii) the President's Report,
(iii) the audited accounts for the period since the previous Congress,
(iv) the financial programme for the period until next Congress,
(v) the Auditors' Report,
(vi) the Permanent Committees' Reports, and comments on motions,
(vii) the lists of nominations for offices received.
(m) The Congress Agenda, the Treasurer's Report, the audited income and expenditure account and balance sheet, the financial programmes, the Auditors' Report, the Permanent Committee's Reports and list of nominations received shall be distributed at least two months before any Ordinary Session of Congress.
(n) Nominations for offices that reach the General Secretary at least three months before the date of the Congress will be circulated together with the Agenda. Nominations however are acceptable from the floor until the opening of each vote. Anybody nominating a candidate for office must confirm, presenting a written statement by the candidate that he belongs to a Member Association and is willing to accept such office, if elected.
(o) Congress Sessions shall be recorded. The General Secretary shall, within six months distribute the Congress Minutes to all Member Associations, Honorary Officers, Members of the Council, as well as Members of the Permanent Committees and F.I.T.A. Judges.
(p) Every participant in Congress may request to have his words minuted in full: in this case he must present a written and signed text before the end of the session at which he has spoken.
(q) Translation services in at least the official languages of F.I.T.A. shall be available at all sessions of Congress.
(r) The costs of Congress accommodation, facilities, recording and translation services and of delegates' meals in the intervals of sessions shall be borne by the organizing Member Association.

107 President

(a) The President represents F.I.T.A., presides over Congress, Council and Executive Committee meetings and is "ex officio" Member of all Committees.
(b) At every Congress, the President shall present a report on the administration and activities of the Federation and a programme of activities for the period up to the next Congress.
(c) The President may delegate a Vice President or, if that be impractical, another officer of F.I.T.A. to represent the Federation at significant events or meetings.

108 Vice President

(a) There shall be one First Vice President and three Vice Presidents.
(b) The First Vice President will act as substitute for the President if he is unable to attend a function and has appointed no other delegate.

109 General Secretary

(a) The General Secretary is the officer responsible for the correct and efficient functioning of F.I.T.A.'s administration.

(b) In particular his primary tasks are:
(i) The preparation of Congress meetings;
(ii) The keeping and distribution of Congress Minutes;
(iii) The preparation of Council meetings;
(iv) The keeping and distribution of council minutes;
(v) The preparation of Executive Committee meetings;
(vi) The keeping of Executive Committee minutes;
(vii) The processing of temporary affiliation;
(viii) The keeping of records as specified in Art. 102.d;
(ix) The keeping of scores as specified in Art. 102.e;
(x) The award of F.I.T.A. Star Badges;
(xi) The supervision of the Executive Secretariat;
(xii) The timely distribution of relevant information to Member Associations and Members of the Council;
(xiii) The editing of the Official Bulletins.

110 Treasurer
(a) The Treasurer, under responsibility of the President, will keep orderly accounting of F.I.T.A. finances.
(b) In particular his primary tasks are:
(i) The keeping of income and expenditure accounts;
(ii) the keeping of balance sheets;
(iii) the keeping of accounts relative to each Member Association;
(iv) The keeping of accounts relative to each chapter of the budget;
(v) The preparation of the financial information necessary for Congress, Council and Executive Committee meetings;
(c) The Treasurer shall annually prepare a detailed budget for Council approval;
(d) The Treasurer shall annually present a report and audited accounts to Council as well as to Congress every two years.

111 Council
(a) The Council shall comprise:
(i) The President,
(ii) The Vice President,
(iii) The General Secretary,
(iv) The Treasurer,
(v) Seven other Members;
Except for the Members of the Executive Committee, there shall not be more than two members from any one Member Association.
The General Secretary and Treasurer shall have no vote, except as under (c) below;
(b) Council shall be responsible for the government of F.I.T.A. between Congresses: it shall meet at least once a year.
(c) Council shall be convened to an extraordinary meeting on request of the Executive Committee or of at least the majority of the total number of its members.
(d) Convocation, including the Agenda for the meeting, will be sent with at least 40 days' notice.
(e) The quorum for a Council meeting or vote shall be the majority of its Members with voting powers.
(f) Council decisions shall be made by simple majority of votes expressed.
(g) Council may decide by postal or telegraphic vote; votes reaching the General Secretary after the date given shall be considered as not expressed.
(h) Council shall:
(i) Approve yearly a programme of activity along the lines established by Congress;
(ii) Approve a yearly budget allocating funds for the implementation of such programme;
(iii) Consider for approval the yearly report of the Treasurer;
(iv) Consider for approval any appointment to the Executive Secretariat.
(v) Appoint Members of the Jury for Olympic Tournaments.
(vi) Appoint Judges for the Olympic Tournament on recommendation from the Judges Committee.

112 Executive Committee
(a) The executive officers of the Council shall form the Executive Committee as follows:
(i) The President,
(ii) The General Secretary,
(iii) The Treasurer.
Any two of these shall form a quorum.
(b) Committee decisions shall be made by a simple majority.
(c) The Committee shall handle all routine business and make decisions of a routine nature.
(d) The Executive Committee shall cause proper books of accounts to be kept.

113 Board of Justice
(a) Congress shall elect a Board of Justice of five Members to investigate alleged breaches of F.I.T.A. Constitution and

Rules by Member Associations or Members thereof.
(b) No two Members of the Board of Justice can belong to the same Member Association.
(c) The Board shall elect a Chairman among themselves.
(d) Cases can be submitted to the Board of Justice only by:
(i) The President,
(ii) The Executive Committee,
(iii) Member Associations,
(iv) Judges or Juries for cases arising in tournaments under their supervision.
(e) The examination of a case shall include a fair hearing of all parties involved.
(f) Members of the Board of Justice cannot belong to the F.I.T.A. Council or be President of a Member Association.
(g) Every case is to be presented through the General Secretary.

114 Sanctions
(a) The Board of Justice shall submit on each case examined a detailed report that shall also propose:
(i) Dismissal of the case as irrelevant or
(ii) acquittal or
(iii) sanctions to be imposed.
(b) Sanctions can be:
(i) public reproach;
(ii) withdrawal of record recognition;
(iii) withdrawal of awards and prizes;
(iv) temporary suspension up to one year;
(v) expulsion from F.I.T.A.;
(c) An expelled Member Association can apply again for membership after one year has elapsed.
(d) Refund of costs sustained by F.I.T.A. for the investigation of a case may be claimed from a party found guilty.
(e) Board of Justice proposals of sanction shall be ratified by Council except in cases brought against elected officers for alleged misuse of office or, if expulsion of a Member Association is proposed, in which cases the proposal shall be circulated to all Member Associations and submitted for ratification by Congress.
(f) Council or Congress decisions, as the case may be, are final.

115 Permanent Committees
(a) There shall be the following Permanent Committees:
(i) Constitution and Rules Committee,
(ii) Technical Committee,
(iii) Target Archery Committee,
(iv) Field Archery Committee,
(v) Judges Committee,
(vi) Medical Committee.
(b) Permanent Committees and their Chairman shall be elected by Congress and shall submit a report for adoption at every Congress meeting.
(c) No more than two Members of a Committee can belong to the same Member Association.
(d) Their term of office is two years (from Congress to Congress).
(e) Should any vacancy occur in a Committee, the Executive Committee, in consultation with the relevant Committee, shall appoint a new member whose term of office will extend until the next Congress.
(f) The Chairman is responsible for seeing that the tasks of his committee are being properly performed, in cooperation with all other members.
(g) Committees shall reply to queries concerning interpretation of rules within their field of competence.
(h) Such queries can be submitted by Member Associations or by Members of Council through the Executive Committee that will forward them to the appropriate committee(s).
(i) If a query covers a matter pertaining to more than one committee, the relevant Committees shall examine it jointly, with the coordination of the Chairman of the Constitution and Rules Committee.
(j) All replies by other Committees shall be submitted to the Constitution and Rules Committee who will check they are not contrary to existing rules or Congress decisions and will forward them to the General Secretary for immediate distribution to Member Associations, Members of Council and Committees and to all F.I.T.A. judges.
(k) Such interpretations shall be accepted until confirmed or amended at the next session of Congress.
(l) Congress motions submitted by member associations shall be passed to the appropriate committees for comments by the General Secretary.

116 Terms of Reference for Committees
(a) A Constitution and Rules Committee of three shall deal with matters covered by F.I.T.A. Constitution and by Rules concerning eligibility, Championships, Tournaments, Records and Awards.

(b) A Technical Committee of five shall deal with matters concerning Archers' equipment.
(c) A Target Archery Committee of three shall deal with the following matters concerning Outdoor and Indoor Target Archery Tournaments:
(i) organization and safety;
(ii) shooting rules;
(iii) field equipment and layout;
(iv) dress;
(v) mail matches.
(d) A Field Archery Committee of three shall deal with the following matters concerning Field Archery Tournaments:
(i) organization and safety;
(ii) shooting rules;
(iii) course equipment and layout;
(iv) dress.
(e) A Judges Committee of five shall deal with Congress motions and interpretation of rules concerning judging at official F.I.T.A. Tournaments and the government of the judging activities.
This Committee shall also be responsible for:
(i) organizing and implementing the education of new F.I.T.A. judges and the training of approved F.I.T.A. judges through courses and seminars;
(ii) examining applications of candidates and re-applications of judges;
(iii) keeping an up to date list of F.I.T.A. judges;
(iv) appointing judges for F.I.T.A. Championships, Regional and area Games (Art. 307 (c)).
(f) A Medical Committee of three shall deal with matters concerning such medical tests as may be required at Tournaments recognized by F.I.T.A. and any other medical matter concerning F.I.T.A.
At least two Members of this Committee should be Doctors of Medicine.

117 Honorary Offices
Congress may elect Honorary Presidents and Honorary Vice Presidents, who shall be distinguished persons whom F.I.T.A. desires to honour, or persons who have distinguished themselves by their work for International Archery.

118 Awards
(a) Gilt and Silver Plaquettes
Congress may award gilt or silver Plaquettes to individuals in recognition of their service to International Archery.

Recommendations covering awards of these Plaquettes may be put forward by Member Associations or Council Members and a detailed exposition supporting such recommendations should reach the General Secretary at least 6 months before a Congress meeting.

A citation covering each award shall be submitted to Congress for approval and publication in the Bulletin. F.I.T.A. shall bear the cost of these awards.
(b) Bronze Plaquettes:
Individuals who have rendered good service towards International Archery particularly within their own Associations, may qualify for the award of a bronze Plaquette. Recommendations for this award shall emanate from Member Associations, and shall be sent to the General Secretary. These awards shall be subject to approval by the F.I.T.A. Executive Committee and shall be paid for by the Member Association making the recommendations.

119 Subscription and Levies
(a) The financial year of F.I.T.A. shall run from 1st January to 31st December.
(b) Congress shall decide the amount of the yearly subscription fee paid by every Member Association and the currency in which it shall be paid.
(c) Subscriptions are payable in advance and shall be paid to the F.I.T.A. Treasurer by 31st January of each year.
(d) Congress may establish levies to be paid by Member Associations.

120 Revenue from F.I.T.A. Events
(a) F.I.T.A. shall have the sole right to arrange and to receive all revenue from all commercial promotion, media coverage and reproduction of F.I.T.A. Championships. The member association responsible for staging any such competition shall ensure that no arrangements in respect of television, film, or photographic coverage or advertising associated with such competition or its locations shall preclude F.I.T.A. from concluding agreements in respect of the same at its sole discretion.
F.I.T.A. may assign or delegate this right to a Member Association or other organizations at its sole discretion.
(b) F.I.T.A. shall have sole intellectual property rights (trade mark, design and/or copyright) to:
(i) any design, symbol, logo or text

adopted by the Federation from time to time as an official mark or legend or as the mascot or emblem of a specific competition staged under the authority of the Federation and such mark or legend or mascot or emblem shall not be reproduced or displayed except with the prior written consent of F.I.T.A.
(ii) any cups, sculptures, designs, pictures or other items intended to be used or used as prizes or trophies in any competitions or other events staged under the authority of the Federation and such prizes or trophies shall not be reproduced or displayed except with the prior written consent of F.I.T.A.
(iii) any competition rules or codes of conduct or training material issued by F.I.T.A. from time to time in respect of Archery. Such rules or codes shall not be reproduced in the original languages or in translation without the prior written consent of the Federation.

F.I.T.A. shall have right to require payment of royalties in respect of any such reproduction. F.I.T.A. may arrange commercial promotion and reproduction of any of the above marks, prizes or trophies or rules or codes of conduct or training material and may transfer its rights to any other entity. Any revenue or benefits arising from any such promotion or reproduction or transfer shall be the sole property of F.I.T.A.

121 Auditing
(a) The income and expenditure account and balance sheet are to be audited yearly.
(b) Auditor(s) shall be appointed by the Executive Committee and such appointment confirmed by Congress.
(c) The auditor(s) must be properly qualified and member(s) of a body of accountants recognized for this purpose in the country concerned.

122 Emblem, Flag and Fanfare
(a) The official emblem of F.I.T.A. is adopted by Congress, belongs to F.I.T.A. and may be covered by copyright.
(b) The F.I.T.A. flag shall be light blue in colour (Target colour: blue) with the F.I.T.A. emblem in colour surmounted by the letters F.I.T.A. centrally placed.
(c) Member Associations may fly the F.I.T.A. flag only at Tournaments recognized for World record and/or F.I.T.A. star badges and may display it at Member Associations' National Congresses.
Each Member Association to provide its flag for this purpose.
(d) F.I.T.A. has as its official fanfare that composed by Mr Jiri L. Bastar for the World Championship held in Prague in 1957.

123 Offices and Archives
(a) The address of the Official Headquarters of F.I.T.A. shall be decided by Congress.
(b) An Executive Office Committee with approval by Council.
(c) The Executive Committee shall be responsible for keeping orderly files and archives and for transmitting them *in toto* to the succeeding Executive Committee.

124 Official Languages
(a) The official languages of F.I.T.A. shall be English and French.
In the event of there being difference of interpretation between the English and French texts in any document, the original draft of such document shall be referred to for the correct interpretation.
(b) Working languages, besides the official languages, may be adopted for Congress Sessions.

125 Official Publications
The Executive Committee shall be responsible for the publication and distribution of:
(i) up-to-date editions of the F.I.T.A. Constitution and Rules;
(ii) the official organ of the Federation called: "Bulletin Officiel de la Fédération Internationale de Tir à l'Arc"; this shall be issued at least after each Target World Championship and after Olympic Games;
(iii) a circular called "F.I.T.A. Information" that shall be issued at least six times a year and at every Change of World Records, F.I.T.A. directory and after every Council meeting.

126 Resignation from Membership
(a) A Member Association may resign F.I.T.A. membership by registered letter to the General Secretary.
(b) Subscription fee for the current year is due in full whatever may be the date of resignation.

127 Dissolution of F.I.T.A.
In the event of F.I.T.A. becoming defunct for any reason, the net assets of the Federation shall be divided equally amongst those National Associations which are Members of the Federation at the time of such occurrence. Indebtedness due to the Federation, but not paid by any Member Association, shall be brought to account before any distribution is made.

Part II
ELIGIBILITY

201 Definition of an Amateur
(a) An amateur in Archery, for the purpose of participation in Championships, Games, International and National Tournaments, which are recognized, controlled or directed by F.I.T.A., practises the sport in all or one of the various branches adopted by F.I.T.A. as a leisure pursuit by the established Rules and Regulations governing Archery within F.I.T.A.
(b) To be eligible to participate in the Olympic Games, Regional or Area Games, F.I.T.A. Championships, Awards and World Record Tournaments and such other events as F.I.T.A. may concede and specify, Archers must be amateurs and must comply with Rules and Regulations laid down by F.I.T.A.
(c) Archers shall be liable to sanctions if participating in International Archery Championships, Games or International Tournaments other than specified above and therefore not recognized, controlled or directed by F.I.T.A. or a Member Association.
(d) Irrespective of what is said in 201 (c), participation in events organized by an Archery Association or Club not affiliated to F.I.T.A., is permitted subject to approval by the Executive Committee for the purpose of promoting Archery for F.I.T.A. purpose and affiliation in the organizer's area. The Executive Committee may require a vote by Council if they deem the consequence of such participation to exceed a routine nature.

202 Olympic Eligibility
F.I.T.A. adopts as a base for its Rules on eligibility Rule 26 and its Bye-Laws A + B of the Olympic Charter of the International Olympic Committee: Rule 26 I.O.C.:
To be eligible for participation in the Olympic Games, a competitor must:
– observe and abide by the Rules of the I.O.C. and in addition the rules of his or her International Federation, as approved by the I.O.C., even if the federation's rules are more strict than those of the I.O.C.;
– not have received any financial rewards or material benefit in connection with his or her sports participation, except as permitted in the bye-laws to this rule.
– Bye-laws to Rule 26:
(1) Be a physical education or sports teacher who gives elementary instruction.
(2) Accept, during the period of preparation and actual competition which shall be limited by the rules of each International Federation.
(a) – assistance administered through his or her NOC or national federation for:
– the costs of food and lodging,
– the cost of transport,
– pocket money to cover incidental expenses,
– the expenses for insurance cover in respect of accidents, illness, personal property and disability,
– the purchase of personal sports equipment and clothing,
– the cost of medical treatment, physiotherapy and authorized coaches;
(b) – compensation authorized by his or her National Olympic Committee or National Federation, in case of necessity, to cover financial loss resulting from his or her absence from work or basic occupation, on account of preparation for, or participation in the Olympic Games and international sports competitions. In no circumstances shall payment made under this provision exceed the sum which the competitor would have earned in his work in the same periods. The compensation may be paid with the approval of the National Federation or N.O.C. at their discretion.
(3) Accept prizes won in competition within the limits of the rules established by the respective International Federations.
(4) Accept academic and technical scholarships.

203 Specification of I.O.C. Eligibility Code
The I.O.C. Eligibility Code (Rule 26) and its Bye-Laws are to be observed with the

following qualifications applying to ARCHERY:
(a) In any one calendar year
– the period of preparation shall not exceed 18 continuous days of organized full time training.
– Participation in outdoor target tournaments with assistance administered through the National Olympic Committee (N.O.C.) or National Archery Association (N.A.A.) may not exceed 15 championships/tournaments whether international or national.
Direct financial assistance other than that approved by N.O.C. and N.A.A. to individual archers is not permitted.
(b) Trophies or Prizes to be retained are not to exceed the value of S.F. 700 (Seven hundred Swiss Francs). No Prizes can be in cash.
(c) Sponsorship in order to support or promote archery must safeguard the archers' eligibility when involving publicity or advertising.
(d) Advertising material must not be carried or worn by archers participating at any F.I.T.A. tournament. The emblem and/or the name of the archers' country, or association approved by F.I.T.A., N.O.C., N.A.A., other relevant National Sport Governing Body or affiliated Society/Club may be worn on uniform and shooting clothes.
(e) Normal trade marks on personal technical equipment (such as bow and arrow etc.) are permitted provided these do not conflict with equipment specifications laid down in the rules (max. trade mark size 3 cm square and letters/figures max. 1 cm high). Bags, cases and boxes carrying advertising are not to be taken onto the tournament field beyond the waiting line.
(f) A competitor must not have allowed his person, name, picture or sports performance to be used for advertising, except when F.I.T.A. or his National Olympic Committee or his National Association enters into a contract for sponsorship or equipment.
(g) An official tournament, emblem, or name of venue or sponsor may be added to competitors' target back numbers and to official armbands, but must not distract from the numbers and letters. Any such addition must be confined to a lower part not exceeding 4. by 25 cm.
(h) Commercial installations and advertising signs shall not be permitted on the tournament field, but must be confined to the spectators' area. If a stadium displaying permanent advertising is the only available venue, this will be admissible but any extra advertisement must follow the above rule.
(i) Trade marks on technical equipment set up in the tournament field must be limited to one mark on each piece (max. trade mark size 3 cm square and letters/figures max. 2 cm high), such marking must not constitute advertising; on target faces the marking must not be in the scoring zones.

204 Services to Mass Media and Lecturing

An amateur archer cannot accept compensation above refund of normal expenses for writing, lecturing or broadcasting on sports matters unless professionally engaged in such activities as part of his/her normal work duties.

205 Medical Provisions

(a) Amateur archers competing in Championships, Games, International and National tournaments recognized, controlled or directed by F.I.T.A. must agree to submit to such Medical tests or examinations as may be required by F.I.T.A., by the organizers of the event or by the laws of the country in which the event takes place.
(b) Doping is the use by and/or the distribution to a competitor of certain substances, which could have the effect of improving artificially the competitor's physical and/or mental condition and thereby augmenting his performance as an archer. Doping is forbidden in archery whenever shooting for F.I.T.A. purposes. In addition, for competing in the Olympic Games the I.O.C. Rule 27 Medical Code applies in its entirety.
(i) Doping substances not permitted include:
– the current list issued by the International Olympic Committee and published by F.I.T.A.
– that group of drugs known as Benezodiazepines
– any other drug or group of drugs the I.O.C. or the F.I.T.A. Medical Commissions may see fit, from time to time, to include.
(ii) At F.I.T.A. Championships (and other tournaments as may be announced)

competitors are liable to doping control in conformity with the rules of the I.O.C. Medical Commission.
(iii) Doping control at any F.I.T.A. Championships will be by request of Congress with the advice of the F.I.T.A. Medical Commission providing it does not constitute an unacceptable financial burden for the Organizing Committee. The Laboratory and control Centre facilities must be approved by the Medical Commission and their guidance accepted through the official channels.
(c) Any competitor refusing to take the required Medical tests or proved to have broken the above provisions shall be disqualified. Any records or Championship title won by such archer shall be returned for redistribution. Accreditation shall be withdrawn to any official found guilty of breaking the above rules. Their cases shall be submitted to the Board of Justice by the National Association responsible for the organization of the event.

Part III
COMPETITIONS

301 Disciplines
Competitions in the Sport of Archery are classified in the following disciplines:
(a) Target Archery;
(b) Field Archery;
(c) Clout Archery;
(d) Flight Archery.

302 Events and Tournaments
(a) A competition, for which a separate list of results and separate sets of prizes and/or titles can be given, is called an event.
(b) A tournament is an organized competition consisting of one or more events. No archer, other than a member of a National Archery Association affiliated to F.I.T.A., may compete in tournaments to be recognized by F.I.T.A.
(c) Where tournaments consist of events belonging to more than one discipline, as specified in Art. 301, the programme will follow the order in which the disciplines are listed therein.

303 Classes
(a) F.I.T.A. recognizes the following classes:
(i) Women;
(ii) Men;
(iii) Junior Women;
(iv) Junior Men.
(b) Separate events for Junior Women and Junior Men can be recognized by F.I.T.A. in the disciplines of Target Archery.
(c) An archer may participate in the Junior Classes in tournaments when the competition starts before the 17th birthday of such archer.
(d) A Junior archer may choose to compete in the Senior class at his/her discretion.

304 F.I.T.A. Events
Only tournaments consisting of one or more of the following events, as described in detail in the relevant article of the shooting rules, can obtain official recognition by F.I.T.A.:
(a) in the discipline of **Target Archery**:
(i) the Outdoor FITA Round for Women;
(ii) the Outdoor FITA Round for Junior Women;
(iii) the Outdoor FITA Round for Men;
(iv) the Outdoor FITA Round for Junior Men;
(v) the Outdoor FITA Round for Women's Teams;
(vi) the Outdoor FITA Round for Junior Women's Teams;
(vii) the Outdoor FITA Round for Men's Teams;
(viii) the Outdoor FITA Round for Junior Men's Teams;
(ix) the double Outdoor FITA Round for Women;
(x) the double Outdoor FITA Round for Men;
(xi) the double Outdoor FITA Round for Women's Teams;
(xii) the double Outdoor FITA Round for Men's Teams;
(xiii) the 25 mt. Indoor FITA Round for Women;
(xiv) the 25 mt. Indoor FITA Round for Junior Women;
(xv) the 25 mt. Indoor FITA Round for Men;
(xvi) the 25 mt. Indoor FITA Round for Junior Men;
(xvii) the 18 mt. Indoor FITA Round for Women;
(xviii) the 18 mt. Indoor FITA Round for Junior Women;
(xix) the 18 mt. Indoor FITA Round for Men;

(xx) the 18 mt. Indoor FITA Round for Junior Men;
(xxi) the Combined Indoor FITA Round for Women;
(xxii) the Combined Indoor FITA Round for Junior Women;
(xxiii) the Combined Indoor FITA Round for Men;
(xxiv) the Combined Indoor FITA Round for Junior Men.
(b) in the discipline of **Field Archery**:
(i) the Bare Bow Hunters Round for Women;
(ii) the Bare Bow Hunters Round for Men;
(iii) the Bare Bow Hunters Round for Junior Women;
(iv) the Bare Bow Hunters Round for Junior Men;
(v) the Free Style Hunters Round for Women;
(vi) the Free Style Hunters Round for Men;
(vii) the Free Style Hunters Round for Junior Women;
(viii) the Free Style Hunters Round for Junior Men;
(ix) the Bare Bow Field Round for Women;
(x) the Bare Bow Field Round for Men;
(xi) the Bare Bow Field Round for Junior Women;
(xii) the Bare Bow Field Round for Junior Men;
(xiii) the Free Style Field Round for Women;
(xiv) the Free Style Field Round for Men;
(xv) the Free Style Field Round for Junior Women;
(xvi) the Free Style Field Round for Junior Men;
(xvii) the Bare Bow Combined Field Event for Women;
(xviii) the Bare Bow Combined Field Event for Men;
(xix) the Bare Bow Combined Field Event for Junior Women;
(xx) the Bare Bow Combined Field Event for Junior Men;
(xxi) the Free Style Combined Field Event for Women;
(xxii) the Free Style Combined Field Event for Men;
(xxiii) the Free Style Combined Field Event for Junior Women;
(xxiv) the Free Style Combined Field Event for Junior Men.
(c) in the discipline of **Clout Archery**:
(i) the Clout Event for Women;
(ii) the Clout Event for Men;
(d) in the discipline of **Flight Archery**:
(i) Target Bow Shoot for Women;
(ii) Target Bow Shoot for Men;
(iii) Flight Bow Shoot for Women;
(iv) Flight Bow Shoot for Men.

305 Official Recognition of Tournaments
(a) F.I.T.A. gives official recognition to tournaments for one or more of the following purposes:
(i) competition for World titles (World Championships);
(ii) competition for Continental or Regional titles (Continental or Regional Championships);
(iii) competition for Olympic titles (Olympic Archery Tournament);
(iv) registration of World records;
(v) competition for F.I.T.A. Star awards;
(vi) inclusion in the official calendar of major international Archery events;
(vii) the gaining of Olympic qualification;
(viii) participation in the F.I.T.A. Mail Match.
(b) The organization of F.I.T.A. Championships (paragraph (a), (i) and (ii)) is prescribed separately in Part IV.
(c) In order to obtain official recognition, tournaments must conform to the standards of organization set out in the following articles for each type of recognition in respect of:
(i) registration with F.I.T.A.;
(ii) announcement and/or invitations;
(iii) participation of archers from other Member Associations;
(iv) order of shooting (target/group list);
(v) judging;
(vi) publication of results.
(d) Member associations, wishing to obtain official F.I.T.A. recognition for a tournament, must announce it in writing to the General Secretary within the prescribed term specifying:
(i) the name of the tournament if any;
(ii) the events it includes;
(iii) a clear geographic indication of the venue (e.g. town and province);
(iv) whether or not the tournament is open to teams and/or individual members of other Member Associations.
(e) Changes, in the information requested under paragraph (d), can only be accepted by the General Secretary if announced at least 30 days before the first day of shooting.

306 World Record and F.I.T.A. Star Tournaments

(a) F.I.T.A. can recognize, as valid for the gaining of F.I.T.A. Star badges and the registration of World Records, a number of tournaments organized by each Member Association not exceeding the number for which that same Member Association can obtain recognition for F.I.T.A. Star awards, as stated in point (c).

(b) The F.I.T.A. Star Badges may be gained at Major Tournaments recognized by Member Associations or any Tournament recognized by F.I.T.A. as an International Tournament and are provided as follows for shooting a single F.I.T.A. Round:

(i) Score at least 1000 points: the F.I.T.A. Star;

(ii) Score at least 1100 points: the F.I.T.A. Star imposed on a black shield with the figures 1100;

(iii) Score at least 1200 points: the F.I.T.A. Star imposed on a blue shield with the figures 1200:

(iv) Score at least 1300 points: the F.I.T.A. Star imposed on a red shield with the figures 1300;

(v) Score at least 1400 points: the F.I.T.A. Star imposed on a yellow shield with the figures 1400.

(c) (i) Each Member Association may recognize in any one calendar year the following number of basic tournaments valid for F.I.T.A. Star and World Record purposes in relation to the number of its individual members:

10/100 Members: 2 basic tournaments,
100/1000 Members: 10 basic tournaments,
1001/10000 Members: 15 basic tournaments,
10001/plus Members: 20 basic tournaments.

(ii) Member Associations may recognize over the number stated in (c) the following number of extra tournaments valid for F.I.T.A. Star and World Record purposes in any one year, subject to payment to F.I.T.A. for each extra tournament of a tax that shall be decided by Congress:

10/100 Members: 3 extra tournaments;
100/1000 Members: 5 extra tournaments;
1001/10000 Members: 10 extra tournaments;
10001/plus Members: 15 extra tournaments.

(iii) Each Member Association may recognize the following number of indoor tournaments valid for World Record purposes in any one year, subject to payment to F.I.T.A. for each tournament of a tax that shall be decided by Congress:

10/100 Members: 2 tournaments,
100/1000 Members: 10 tournaments,
1001/10000 Members: 15 tournaments,
10001/plus Members: 20 tournaments.

(d) A Member Association intending to organize such a tournament must:

(i) mail the announcement to the General Secretary at least one month before the first day of shooting;

(ii) mail the announcement to other Member Associations, if the tournament is international, at least 60 days before;

(iii) provide a Director of shooting and Judges to the number of one for every ten targets and, in the case of International Tournaments, a Jury of appeal of three members: all Judges must be approved by their National Association or by F.I.T.A.;

(iv) mail within one month of the tournament to the General Secretary and to each Member Association whose archers have competed, at least one copy of the complete results list.

(e) Applications for 1000 Point Stars and 1100 Point Badges will be sent to the Member Association to which the Archer is affiliated, that shall be responsible for:

(i) requesting yearly from the General Secretary and holding in stock a sufficient number of such awards;

(ii) noting the name or description, place and date of the tournament;

(iii) noting the name and sex of the applicant;

(iv) controlling that the tournament was shot according to F.I.T.A. shooting rules;

(v) controlling that all archers whose application are submitted were affiliated to a Member Association at that time;

(vi) controlling the correctness of the original score sheets or properly witnessed copies that shall accompany each application;

(vii) send to the General Secretary at the end of the year a complete list of the badges so awarded with a declaration signed by a responsible officer of the Association that the conditions under points (iv), (v), (vi) were complied with.

(f) (i) Applications for 1200, 1300 and 1400 Point Badges indicating the name and sex of the applicants and the names,

places and dates of the tournaments must be sent on behalf of the applicants by their member associations, supported with a declaration that conditions under points (e) (iv, (v) have been complied with and accompanied by the original score sheets or properly witnessed copies;
(ii) the General Secretary, if satisfied with the documentation received, shall forward the badges through the Member Association free of charges and shall publish periodically nominal lists of the badges awarded.

307 International Calendar Tournaments
(a) F.I.T.A. recognizes every year an official calendar of international tournaments.
(b) Member Associations may apply for the inclusion in the official calendar of tournaments organized by them, in each calendar year, and no more than one in each of the disciplines specified in Art. 301, on the following conditions:
(i) the tournament shall be announced to F.I.T.A. and to other Member Associations, whose archers will be invited at least six months before the first day of shooting;
(ii) at least 3 other Member Associations shall be invited to send archers to each of the events on the programme;
(iii) the tournament shall be organized and held in full conformity with the rules for F.I.T.A. Championships under Articles 409, 410 (f), 413 and 415.
(iv) the judges shall be appointed by the Member Association organizing the tournament and at least ⅓ of them shall be judges approved by F.I.T.A.
(v) Within 30 days of the tournament, a complete list of results shall be mailed to the General Secretary and to each Member Association whose archers competed.
(c) In the Official Calendar may be included tournaments belonging to the programme of Regional or Area Games (e.g. Asian, Pan-American, Mediterranean, etc.) providing they comply with the following conditions:
(i) the tournaments shall be organized and held in conformity with the Olympic principles and F.I.T.A. Constitution and Eligibility Rules;
(ii) at least one technical delegate shall be appointed by F.I.T.A. in order to advise the organizers and to check that all preparations are in accordance with F.I.T.A. rules: the expenses for at least one visit, at an agreed date during the period of preparation, and for his presence during the Games, will be borne by the organizers;
(iii) the Judges and the Jury of Appeal shall be appointed by F.I.T.A. according to F.I.T.A. Championships standards and procedures as specified in Articles 412 and 413.
(iv) the chosen archery events (see Art. 303) to be included in the programme of the Games, their rules and regulations and the list of National Archery Association to be invited, shall be communicated to F.I.T.A. at least one year before the opening of the Games.

308 Olympic Qualification Tournaments
Any target tournament that the Organizing M.A. guarantees as shot in accordance with F.I.T.A. rules is valid for establishing Olympic qualification scores.

309 The F.I.T.A. Mail Match
(a) the F.I.T.A. Mail Match shall normally be held once each year.
(b) The Match shall be determined on the basis of a single F.I.T.A. round shot on one day under F.I.T.A. Target Shooting Rules, in a Tournament recognized by a Member Association.
(c) Member Associations wishing to participate, shall specify a month during which its members may shoot for the F.I.T.A. Mail Match.
(d) The Mail Match shall be held for the following categories:
(i) Women,
(ii) Men,
(iii) Junior Women,
(iv) Junior Men.
(e) Member Associations shall submit their entries to the General Secretary to reach him by not later than 31st December of the year of the Mail Match, together with a declaration covering:
(i) the name or description, place and date of the Tournament,
(ii) confirmation that the Tournament was shot under F.I.T.A. Target Shooting Rules,
(iii) confirmation that all archers, whose scores are submitted, were members of the Association at the time,
(iv) the following details for each competitor:

– name and sex of archers,
– category,
– score for each distance,
– hits,
– number of Golds.

(f) Not more than 12 scores shall be submitted from any Member Association.

(g) Teams shall consist of the first three Women and the first three Men respectively from each Member Association.

(h) F.I.T.A. Mail Match Diplomas shall be awarded as follows:

(a) A Diploma to the ten best Women, Men, Junior Women, Junior Men individually;

(b) A Diploma to each Member of the three best Women's Teams and Men's Teams.

(i) Results and complete scores lists shall be circulated by the General Secretary to all Member Associations and to Members of Council.

310 Responsibility

F.I.T.A. shall in no circumstances accept liability for damages resulting from injury to spectators or to members of any member association or from the damage or loss of property whilst participating in or attending any Championship, tournament or other function organized, sponsored or recognized by F.I.T.A.

Part IV
F.I.T.A. CHAMPIONSHIPS

401 World Championships and Titles

F.I.T.A. arranges for the organization of the following world championships:

(a) **Outdoor Target World Championships** for the titles of:
(i) Woman Champion of the World;
(ii) Man Champion of the World;
(iii) Women's Champion Team of the World;
(iv) Men's Champion Team of the World.

(b) **Field World Championships** for the titles of:
(i) Woman Champion of the World Bare Bow;
(ii) Man Champion of the World Bare Bow;
(iii) Woman Champion of the World Free Style
(iv) Man Champion of the World Free Style.

402 Regional Championships and Titles

(a) F.I.T.A. recognizes the following three regions:
(i) Europe and the Mediterranean;
(ii) the Americas;
(iii) Asia and Oceania.

(b) A Member Association may belong to one region only; if its territory is situated in more than one region or in a border area, it may choose. If such Member Association chooses to be listed in another region, notice must be mailed to the General Secretary at least three years before the congress at which this change will be announced and become effective.

(c) If the belonging of a Member Association to a region is disputed, F.I.T.A. will decide after hearing the Member Association concerned.

(d) F.I.T.A. arranges for the organization of the following regional championships:

(i) **Target Championships of Europe and the Mediterranean** for the titles of:
– (i) Woman Champion of Europe and the Mediterranean;
– (ii) Man Champion of Europe and the Mediterranean;
– (iii) Women's Champion Team of Europe and the Mediterranean;
– (iv) Men's Champion Team of Europe and the Mediterranean;

(ii) **Target Championships of the Americas** for the title of:
– (i) Woman Champion of the Americas;
– (ii) Man Champion of the Americas;
– (iii) Women's Champion Team of the Americas;
– (iv) Men's Champion Team of the Americas.

(iii) **Target Championships of Asia and Oceania** for the titles of:
– (i) Woman Champion of Asia and Oceania;
– (ii) Man Champion of Asia and Oceania;
– (iii) Women's Champion Team of Asia and Oceania;
– (iv) Men's Champion Team of Asia and Oceania.

(iv) **Outdoor Target Junior Championships of Europe and the Mediterranean** for the titles of:
– (i) Junior Woman Champion of Europe and the Mediterranean;
– (ii) Junior Man Champion of Europe and the Mediterranean;
– (iii) Junior Women's Champion Team

of Europe and the Mediterranean;
– (iv) Junior Men's Champion Team of Europe and the Mediterranean.
(v) **Indoor Target Championships of Europe and the Mediterranean** for the titles of:
– (i) Woman Champion of Europe and the Mediterranean;
– (ii) Man Champion of Europe and the Mediterranean;
– (iii) Women's Champion Team of Europe and the Mediterranean;
– (iv) Men's Champion Team of Europe and the Mediterranean.
(vi) **Field Championships of Europe and the Mediterranean** for the titles of:
– (i) Woman Champion of Europe and the Mediterranean Bare Bow;
– (ii) Man Champion of Europe and the Mediterranean Bare Bow;
– (iii) Woman Champion of Europe and the Mediterranean Free Style;
– (iv) Man Champion of Europe and the Mediterranean Free Style.
(vii) **Field Championships of the Americas** for the title of:
– (i) Woman Champion of the Americas Bare Bow;
– (ii) Man Champion of the Americas Bare Bow;
– (iii) Woman Champion of the Americas Free Style;
– (iv) Man Champion of the Americas Free Style.
(viii) **Field Championships of Asia and Oceania**
– (i) Woman Champion of Asia and Oceania Bare Bow;
– (ii) Man Champion of Asia and Oceania Bare Bow;
– (iii) Woman Champion of Asia and Oceania Free Style;
– (iv) Man Champion of Asia and Oceania Free Style.

403 Dates

(a) F.I.T.A. Championships shall be held every two years as follows:
(i) Target World Championships: in odd years;
(ii) Field World Championships: in even years;
(iii) Outdoor Target Championships of Europe and the Mediterranean: in even years;
(iv) Outdoor Target Championships of the Americas: in even years;
(v) Outdoor Target Championships of Asia and the Pacific: in even years;
(vi) Outdoor Target Junior Championships of Europe and the Mediterranean: in odd years;
(vii) Indoor Target Championships of Europe and the Mediterranean: in odd years;
(viii) Field Championships of Europe and the Mediterranean: in even years;
(ix) Field Championships of the Americas: in odd years;
(x) Field Championship of Asia and Oceania: in even years.

404 Championship Tournaments

(a) Target Championships shall be decided on the Double Round, shot over four consecutive days.
(b) Target Junior Championships shall be decided on the F.I.T.A. Round shot over two consecutive days.
(c) Indoor Target Championships shall be decided on the Combined Indoor F.I.T.A. Round shot over two consecutive days.
(d) Field Championships shall be decided on the Bare Bow Combined Field events and on the Free Style combined Field events, shot as follows:
(i) on the first day the free style archers will shoot the hunters round with unmarked distances, while the bare bow archers will shoot the field round;
on the second day archers will rest while the organizers will modify courses so as to eliminate all likelihood of archers benefiting from the experience of the first day of shooting;
on the third day the free style archers will shoot the field round while the bare bow archers will shoot the hunters round with unmarked distances.
(ii) if the number of preliminary entries (see Art. 408, (a), (i)) is less than eighty, at the discretion of the organizers all competitors will shoot; on the first day the hunters round with unmarked distances and on the second day the field round.
Such decision shall be announced by the organizers to the General Secretary and to all Member Associations eligible for that championship no later than forty days before the first day of shooting.

405 Allocation of Championships

(a) The organization of F.I.T.A. Cham-

pionships shall be entrusted by Congress to a Member Association (M.A.).
(b) A Member Association must have been affiliated to F.I.T.A. for at least two years before it can apply for permission to organize a F.I.T.A. Championship.
(c) Application must be submitted in writing to the General Secretary and must give:
(i) the dates;
(ii) the venue;
(iii) an assurance that, as far as can be reasonably foreseen, no difficulties will be raised for the participation of archers, teams and officials from any eligible Member Association on grounds of nationality, race, religion or politics or for free passage through customs of equipment or trophies.
(d) Congress shall endeavour to allocate championships in turn to different M.A.s and with due attention to the convenience of all M.A.s.
(e) If a M.A., has been entrusted with the organization of a F.I.T.A. Championship, and is unable to hold it or to uphold the commitment under (c) (iii), the General Secretary and all M.A.s must be immediately informed by cable.
(f) The possible reallocation of such a championship will be decided by Congress at its next meeting if there is at least one year between the date of Congress and the beginning of the year in which the championship in question is to be held; otherwise council shall make the decision.

406 Responsibilities of the Organizing M.A.
(a) The M.A. entrusted with the organization of a F.I.T.A. Championship, hereafter called the organizers, may appoint an organizing committee but the M.A. shall be directly responsible to F.I.T.A.
(b) The Organizers shall submit to every Congress, between the date of allocation and that of the championship, a report on progress made in the preparations.
(c) The organizers shall be totally responsible for making financial arrangements for the championship allocated to them such as:
(i) deciding the amount of Entry Fees;
(ii) bearing the cost of striking and engraving F.I.T.A. medals;
(iii) covering the cost of food, lodging and necessary local transportation for the Judges and Members of the Judges Committee and of the Jury of Appeal;
(iv) providing commemorative badges for all competitors and officials;
(v) providing non-challenge trophies and prizes at their discretion.
(d) The Organizers shall communicate to F.I.T.A. 60 days before the Championship the number of press accreditation cards they intend to issue.

407 Invitations
(a) At least six months before the first day of shooting, the Organizers shall issue:
(i) invitations, to all other eligible M.A.s, to compete as well as to Honorary Officers and members of the Council to attend.
(ii) detailed information on the amount of Entry Fees.
(b) At least three months before the first day of shooting, the organizing M.A. shall send, to all the eligible M.A.s, confirmation that the Championship shall be held as announced and:
(i) preliminary entry forms requesting the numbers of expected participants in each event and of officials;
(ii) final entry forms requesting names of participants entered for each event, and of officials.
(iii) Information on accommodation, booking arrangements, meals, etc. with information on costs.

408 Entries
(a) All Member Associations in good standing may enter competitors.
(b) Member Associations wishing to enter competitors in a F.I.T.A. Championship shall return the completed entry forms to the Organizers as follows:
(i) no later than sixty days before the first day of shooting for the preliminary entry form;
(ii) no later than twenty days before the first day of shooting for the final entry form;
(c) Entry forms submitted after the above terms may be refused by the organizers; however, if the cause of the delay is due to circumstances beyond the possibility of control by the M.A. concerned, the organizers may still accept that entry. The General Secretary must be informed at once of this late acceptance and of the reasons for the delay.
(d) The submission of entry forms implies a declaration that the F.I.T.A. member-

ship fee for the current year has been paid, or will be paid before the start of the competition. If this is not the case, archers from that M.A. shall be disqualified from the Championship.

(e) At Target Archery Championships a M.A. may enter no more than four archers in each class.

(f) At Field Championships a M.A. may enter no more than three archers in each class in both the bare bow and the free style events.

409 Accreditation

(a) The organizers shall issue, to each participant and official, appropriate nominal accreditation for one oi following categories:

(i) F.I.T.A. Officers;
(ii) F.I.T.A. guests;
(iii) Judges, Field officers;
(iv) Jury of Appeal;
(v) Presidents and Secretaries of M.A.s;
(vi) Team officials;
(vii) Competitors;
(viii) Organizing Committee;
(ix) Scorers;
(x) Field party, communication;
(xi) Medical personnel;
(xii) Mass media at the discretion of the organizers in accord with F.I.T.A. Executive Committee.

(b) The proof of accreditation must be carried at all times on the competition area and be shown on request of responsible officials.

(c) Only holders of appropriate accreditation shall be allowed on to the relevant parts of the competition area.

410 Championship Documents

(a) The organizers are responsible for producing the following documents:

(i) a programme of the championships indicating dates, times and localities of all competitions, ceremonies, occasions and services of interest to competitors and officials; such programme must have been approved by the executive committee;

(ii) a list of competitors, prepared by M.A., with the indication of team officials and their championship address and according to target group and competition numbers;

(iii) Interim results lists, to be published at least daily and distributed as early as possible and, in any case, before the beginning of the shooting the next day, to at least each competitor and official;

(iv) A final detailed results list with the indication of all title winners to be distributed within a month of the closing day of the Championships. The scores of all competitors and teams shall be listed in descending order of final result. Individual results shall be specified for round, distance and double distance as applicable. The final results list to be distributed by the organizers to all M.A.s, Honorary Officers, Members of the Council and to Competitors and Officials, through their National Associations.

(b) Within two months of the closing day of the Championship, the organizers shall submit to the General Secretary a report on the Championship accompanied by a copy of all the above documents as well as samples of posters, commemorative badges, accreditation cards, photographs, press cuttings and any other item that may be of interest to the archives of F.I.T.A.

(c) Within six months of the closing day of the Championships, the organizers shall send to the General Secretary a copy of the detailed income and expenditure sheet of the Championships. The General Secretary shall circulate it to all M.A.s. and F.I.T.A. officers.

411 Field Officers

(a) The organizers shall appoint a Director of Shooting, a Deputy Director of Shooting and, if necessary, one or more Assistants to perform the duties specified in Part V.

(b) Their names shall be mailed to the General Secretary at least one month before the beginning of the Championships.

(c) The organizers shall provide the Field Officers with a raised platform or a central post, as applicable, with adequate weather protection and seating accommodation and with the necessary signal and communication equipment.

(d) The Director of Shooting shall be responsible for enforcing respect of Art. 505.

(e) The Field Officers shall not have other tasks during the hours of competition or take part in the shooting.

412 Judges

(a) F.I.T.A. Championships shall be controlled by Judges numbering no fewer than

one for every seven targets in Target Championships and no fewer than seven Judges in Field Championships.
(b) They shall be appointed by the J.C. who shall communicate the names to these Judges, the General Secretary and the organizers no later than ninety days before the first day of the competition. The J.C. must receive confirmation of judges availability before making the appointment.
(c) The J.C. shall appoint one of these Judges as Chairman.
(d) If possible, no more than two Judges should be drawn from any one M.A.
(e) If possible, only Judges approved by F.I.T.A. should be appointed for F.I.T.A. Championships.
(f) The Judges shall present to congress for the outdoor target World Championship and to the General Secretary for other championships, a report on the tournament.
(g) At Field Archery Championships each Judge shall be connected by audio communication equipment to the central post (see 422 g).
(h) The organizers shall provide Judges with stop watches, tape measures and magnifying glasses.
The International Judges are expected to be in possession of field glasses.

413 Jury of Appeal
(a) A Jury of Appeal of three Members shall be appointed by Council for every F.I.T.A. Championship Tournament.
(b) Appeals against rulings by the Judges must be presented by Team Captains in writing: no appeals can be made against the value of an arrow.
(c) The Jury must be available at the Tournament grounds at all times during the Championship including the day of Official Training until 30 minutes after the end of the shooting.
(d) Their decisions shall be minuted and submitted to the appealer, the Chairman of the Judges and the organizers before the awarding of prizes.

414 Scorers
(a) The organizers shall appoint scorers in sufficient numbers to ensure that one for each target in Target Archery and one for each group in Field Archery shall always be on duty: such scorers shall not take part in the shooting.
(b) The scorers shall work under the supervision of one or more officials, appointed by the organizers, who shall be responsible for the correct conduct of the scoring.
(c) One or more score-boards, of sufficient size to show the target number, name, code for Member Association and progressive score of at least the first five in each event, must be maintained.
(d) In Target Championships, the progressive total for each competitor must be displayed on the field after each distance.

415 Team Officials
(a) At F.I.T.A. Championships, each Member Association's team taking part shall be represented by a Team Captain who may or may not be a competitor.
(b) The Team Captain shall:
(i) contact the organizers as soon as possible on arrival;
(ii) attend the Team Captains' meeting that may be called by the organizers, the Judges or the Jury;
(iii) accompany his team at the inspection of equipment;
(iv) approach whenever necessary organizers, Judges or Jury on behalf of the archers of his team;
(v) generally represent his team in all matters pertaining to the Championship.
(c) A Team Captain may be helped by up to three assistants or coaches, but the total number of officials must not exceed the number of archers of that team.
(d) In Target Archery, Team Officials can be on the field only behind the waiting line and must behave so as not to disturb the archers.
In Field Archery they must be confined within the spectator area, unless requested by a judge to enter the competition area.
(e) In Target Archery, archers may delegate authority, to score and collect their arrows, to their Team Captain or to another archer of their own Target, provided the archer concerned does not move up to the Target.

416 Draw for Shooting Numbers
(a) The draw for shooting numbers, and for the order of shooting, shall be arranged by the organizers as follows:
(i) an urn will contain as many cards as there are M.A.s competing; each card bearing the name of one M.A.;
(ii) the chairman or secretary of the

Organizing Association will first draw one card;
(iii) from another urn the names of all competitors of that Member Association will be drawn: these will be allocated on each target in the order in which they are drawn;
(iv) having finished with one Member Association, another is drawn and so on until all names have been drawn;
(b) Competitors shall be numbered as they are drawn:
1A 2A 3A 4A 5A 6A . . . to the last name
1B 2B 3B 4B . . . to the last name
1C 2C 3C . . . to the last name etc.
Women and men and, when applicable, bare bow and free style archers, shall be drawn separately.
(c) In order that archers from the same team may all be placed on adjoining targets, alterations to the drawn order may be made by the organizers if possible: such alterations shall be minuted and the minutes given to and approved by the Judges before the competition.
(d) Lists of competitors, according to target/group order and alphabetical order indicating the Member Association of each competitor, shall be made available to all officers, judges and competitors and officials at least two days before the first day of competition.
(e) Substitutions of entries will be allowed until the day before that of official practice.

417 Control of Equipment
(a) On the day before the first day of competition, the organizers shall arrange, on or near the practice field, for the inspection by the Judges, of all the equipment that each archer intends to use during the competition.
(b) Teams will be called in alphabetical order and all archers accompanied by their team captain, shall submit all the equipment they intend to use, including spares and accessories.
(c) Judges may request equipment to be modified or changed if found in contravention of F.I.T.A. rules.
(d) If an archer is compelled, in the course of the competition, to use equipment which has not been submitted to inspection, it is his duty to show such equipment to the Judges before using it.
Any competitor contravening this rule may have his scores disqualified.

418 Practice
(a) At Target Championships, the Tournament field may be used by competitors for practice only on the day prior to the beginning of the competition.
(b) Other practice facilities must be made available to competitors at least five days before that day.
(c) At Field Archery Championships no practice shall take place on the courses set out for the competition: a practice ground shall be made available nearby or elsewhere at least a week before the first day of competition.

On the days of the Tournament, some practice targets must be set up near the assembly point(s) for the archers.
(d) A number of targets equal to one fourth of that of the entries, arranged at all the different competition distances, shall be provided to permit practice during all times announced by the organizers.
(e) Should the practice field be insufficient for such number, the organizers may arrange two or three practice sessions a day, of at least four hours each: attendance at these sessions may be booked up to 24 hours in advance. Bookings for more than one session a day for the same competitor may only be accepted if this does not prevent any other competitor booking his first practice period at his chosen session.
(f) A Director of Shooting must be in charge of the practice field at all times: he will give acoustic signals to indicate when all shooting must stop, in order to allow archers to collect their arrows, and when shooting can be resumed.
(g) All archers will move forward together to collect their arrows, whatever the distance at which they may be shooting: no archer shall shoot during this time or collect arrows at any other time.
The Director of Shooting may bar from the practice session any archer contravening this rule.
(h) Any change in the distance at which targets are set, must be by permission of the Director of Shooting, who may ask practising archers to assist him in moving and rearranging targets, should he so require.
(i) On the days of competition, before the competition is over, targets on the practice field shall only be placed at 40 m. distance with 122 cm. target faces except for two buttresses without faces at 10 m. distance.

Such targets may be used before the sighter arrows are shot and during the intervals between distances.

419 Programme and Protocol

(a) The second day before the tournament a meeting of all Team Captains shall be held jointly by the Chairman of Judges and a representative of the organizers for the purpose of conveying detailed information on the Tournament and facilities and of answering possible requests. Team Captains may delegate others but no M.A. may be represented by more than one person: they may however be accompanied by an interpreter.

(b) The day before the Tournament the following will take place:

(i) at Target Championships competitors shall be allowed to practise on the tournament field or in the tournament hall;

(ii) control of tackle;

(iii) Opening Ceremony: the competing Teams, headed by their Captains and formed up in alphabetical order of nationality (according to choice of language of the organizers) will march in, preceded by the F.I.T.A. Flag and accompanied by the reigning Champions if present. The Team from the Host Member Association shall be last. The procession will march onto the Field and past the stand for the Officials and Dignitaries. The President of the Organizing M.A. or his appointed representative shall then greet all present and introduce the President of F.I.T.A., who will declare the Championship open. The flag of F.I.T.A. shall be raised at the sound of the F.I.T.A. fanfare. The Teams will then march out in the same order.

(c) Shortly after the end of the Tournament and on the Tournament venue the award ceremonies will take place: a podium with three steps indicating, from left to right from to the spectators' viewpoint, second, first and third place shall be put in front of the spectators' main stand. The team will march as in the opening ceremony. The President of F.I.T.A. or his deputy shall award the medals to first, second and third place in each event in the order in which the events are listed in point (c). After the awards in each event, the national flag of the first three competitors may be raised while the national anthem of the first may be played. After each award, the receivers of the medals will take their places near the main stand facing the podium.

(d) When all medals are awarded, the President of F.I.T.A. will thank the organizers and competitors and declare the championships closed: The flag of F.I.T.A. will be lowered at the sound of the F.I.T.A. fanfare, then the flag of the host country or M.A. will be lowered and the flag of the country or M.A. that will host the next round of the same championship, will be raised; the teams will then march out past the winners who will receive their salute.

(e) A reception, banquet or refreshments will be organized preferably on the day following the closing ceremony, during which all other prizes and trophies will be awarded.

(f) The President of F.I.T.A., if unable to attend, may delegate another F.I.T.A. officer to be his deputy at F.I.T.A. Championships and may, at opening and closing ceremonies, invite some local Personality to award some medals and/or declare the Championships open or alternatively closed.

420 Medals

(a) F.I.T.A. Championships medals shall be awarded to the first, second and third highest scorer in each event of the Championships.

(b) The medal shall bear on the face the emblem of F.I.T.A. and on the reverse the name of the championship, the venue, the year, the indication of the placing of its winner (e.g. woman champion or second men's team) and, when necessary that of the event for which it is awarded (e.g. bare bow man champion or free style third woman or second junior man).

(c) The medals for world championships shall be surrounded by a wreath.

(d) Individual medals shall have a diameter of 40 mm, team medals of 30 mm.

(e) The medal shall be suspended on a ribbon in a colour chosen by the organizing M.A., as wide as the diameter of medal, one metre long, sewn in the form of a loop so that it can be hung around the neck of the winner.

(f) 30 mm above the medal, the ribbon shall be held by a bar brooch 42 mm × 10 mm for 40 mm medals and 35 mm × 10 mm for 30 mm medals and bear the year of the

championship. Bar brooches shall be gilt, silver or bronze to suit the medals.
(g) All medals and bar brooches shall be supplied by the Executive Committee at least two months before the date of the championship and shall be paid for by the organizers, who shall provide the ribbons.

421 Prizes and Trophies
(a) The following prizes shall also be presented at F.I.T.A. championships:
(i) at Target Archery championships the 30 mm F.I.T.A. medal without ribbon, bar brooch or wreath in gilt, silver and bronze to the 3 highest scorers for each separate distance in each individual event.
(ii) at Field Archery championships the 30 mm F.I.T.A. medal without ribbon, bar brooch or wreath in gilt silver and bronze to the 3 highest scorers for each separate round in each event.
(b) The archers receiving these gilt medals shall be referred to as *winners* and not as *champions*.
(c) Council may receive for F.I.T.A. the donation of Challenge Trophies for F.I.T.A. Championships. Such challenge trophies shall remain the property of F.I.T.A., held in trust by their respective winners until the next similar championship.
No more than one challenge prize shall be made available for any one title.
(d) The winner's M.A. is responsible for seeing that the trophy is returned to F.I.T.A. at that championship.
Should no such championship be held for four consecutive years, the Trophy shall be returned to the General Secretary. The M.A. shall also have the name of the winner, the venue and the year of the championship appropriately engraved on the Trophy.
The winner's M.A. shall be responsible for the safe custody and freight of the Trophy and shall cover all the necessary expenses.
(e) Challenge Trophies received by F.I.T.A. are listed in Appendix 7 to these rules, with mention of the donors and the conditions of donations as accepted by council.
(f) The organizing Member Association may award other prizes at its discretion, to individual participants or to teams. These prizes shall become the property of the winners. The value of such prizes must not exceed the limit set in Art. 203.

422 Championship Venue, Equipment and Facilities
(a) At all F.I.T.A. Championships the tournament grounds shall be clearly divided between:
(i) the shooting field or course, as appropriate;
(ii) the practice field;
(iii) the spectators and amenities area or areas. The spectators' area is to be clearly defined by a barrier.
(b) At Target Championships the tournament must be held on an open field and not in an arena or stadium closed in on all sides.
(c) At Target Championships seating accommodation for all competitors, team officials and judges shall be made available close behind the waiting line.
(d) Behind the waiting line at Outdoor Target Championships and near the assembly point at Field Championships, the organizing M.A. shall provide adequate shelter against the weather for competitors and their equipment.
(e) Adequate toilet facilities for women and men respectively shall be provided within reasonable distance of the shooting field or along the ranges.
(f) At Outdoor Target Championships the Director of Shooting shall be positioned on a raised platform situated on the shooting line at the separation between the women's and the men's parts of the field.
(g) At Field Championships a central post for the Chairman of Judges, with adequate shelter and communication equipment, shall be located in a suitable position along the range.
(h) A stand with seating accommodation and adequate weather shelter shall be provided for F.I.T.A. officers and Honorary Guests in a central position in the spectators' area, behind the waiting line at Target Championships or at the venue of the opening and closing ceremonies at Field Championships.
(i) In the vicinity of this main stand shall be placed, in a prominent position, two flag poles for the flags of F.I.T.A. and the flag of the host country or M.A., and three flag poles, the central one higher than the other two, where the flags for the medal winners will be hoisted.
(j) The Organizing M.A. shall provide a podium to be erected in front of the main stand for the award ceremony; the central

step shall be 60 cm, the other two 30 cm high; all steps to be wide enough to accommodate three persons when there are team events.
(k) The organizers shall make available to F.I.T.A., at the Tournament grounds, at least two rooms or adequate temporary shelter (e.g. tents or caravans) for the use of the President, the Executive Committee, the Judges and the Jury of Appeal.
(l) Where shooting rules prescribe the use of field or range equipment in different alternatives, the equipment of the highest quality shall always be adopted for F.I.T.A. Championships.

423 Meals and Refreshments
(a) The organizers shall arrange for the distribution of drinks and a light midday meal to all competitors, team officials, field officers, judges and members of the Jury of Appeal.
(b) Such meals and drinks may be charged for: in that case, prices must be indicated on the invitation.

Dress Regulations
(a) The World Championship Tournament as well as the Continental Championships are majestic occasions honoured by the attendance of many dignitaries. It is therefore respectful and fitting that all Archers, Team Captains, Officials, etc. participating in the Opening and Closing Ceremonies, should be properly and fully dressed in the uniform dress of their respective Associations.
(b) During Target Tournaments women are required to wear dresses, skirts or trousers (slacks), and suitable blouses or tops, and men, full length trousers and long or short sleeved shirts. Sweaters/cardigans may be worn.
In adverse weather suitable protective clothing may be worn.
During Field Tournaments the same Regulations apply as above.
(c) Footwear must be worn by all competitors at all times during the Tournament.
(d) Shorts for women and sleeveless singlets, underwear vests or shorts for men, as well as track suits, will not be allowed at any time.
(e) No advertising of any kind whatsoever shall appear on clothing worn by the competitors or officials at any time during the Tournament.
(f) Competitor's target number to be worn on the middle of the back and to be visible at all times while shooting is in progress.
(g) Archers are permitted to wear clothing, etc. on which appears the name and/or the official insignia, flag or emblem of the country they represent, without restriction as to size.

Part V
RULES OF SHOOTING
A) OUTDOOR TARGET ARCHERY

501 The F.I.T.A. International Outdoor Target Round
The F.I.T.A. Round consists of 36 arrows from each of the following distances:
90, 70, 50 & 30 metres for Men.
70, 60, 50 & 30 metres for Women.
Shooting shall be in one direction only, and will commence at the longest distance and finish at the shortest distance in the order set out above.
A Round may be shot in one day or over two successive days. If a Round is shot over two days, the two longer distances shall be shot on the first day and the two shorter distances shall be shot on the second day.
The double F.I.T.A. Round shall be shot over four consecutive days, the third and fourth being the repetition of the first and second. Two ends of three sighter arrows are permitted preceding the commencement of shooting each day. These are to be shot under the control of the Director of Shooting and shall not be scored.
In the event of a Programme including a F.I.T.A. Round as well as some other Rounds to be wholly or partly shot during the same day, the F.I.T.A. Round shall always be shot first.

502 Target Faces (See illustration on next page)
Description:
(a) There are two Standard circular F.I.T.A. Target Faces 122 cm and 80 cm in diameter.
Both these faces are divided into five concentric colour zones arranged from the centre outwards as follows:
Gold (Yellow), Red, Light Blue, Black and White.
Each colour is in turn divided by a thin line into two zones of equal width thus making

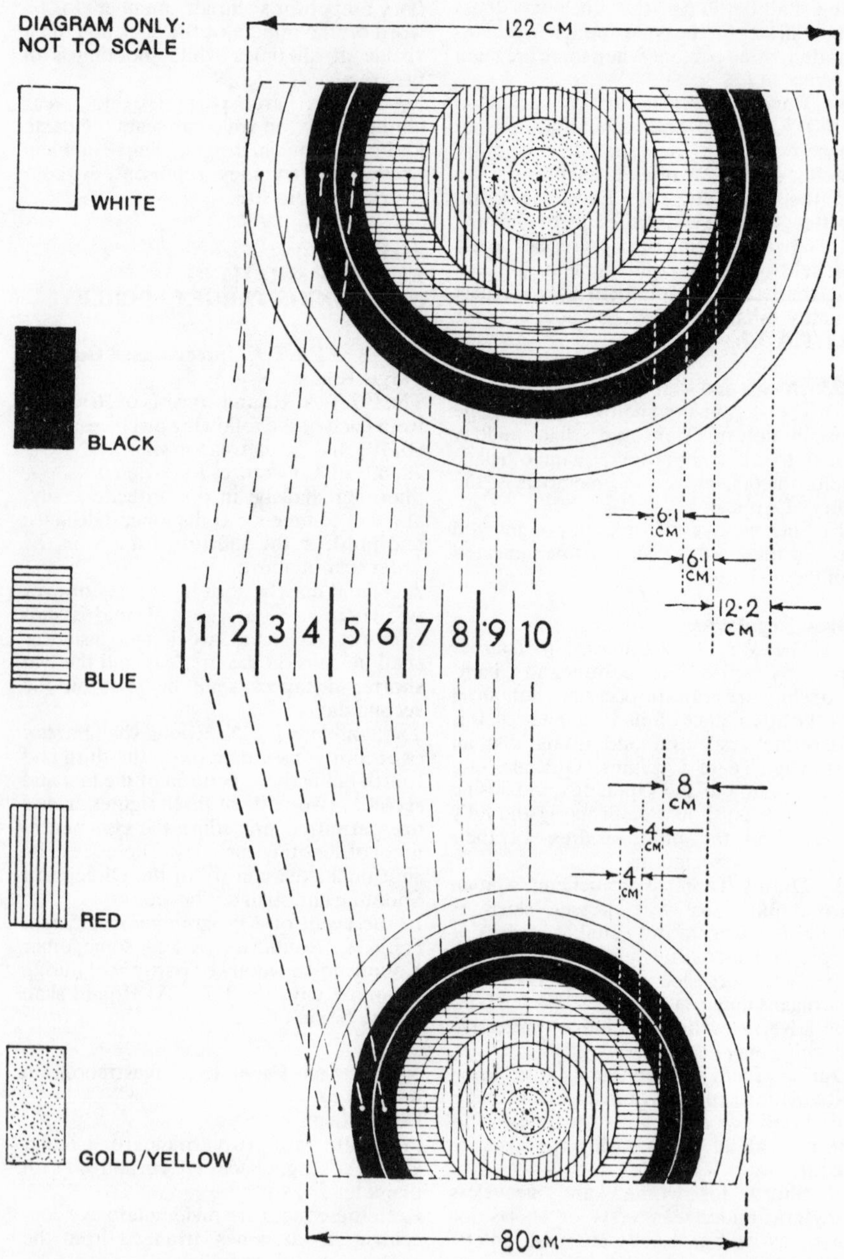

in all ten scoring zones of equal width measured from the centre of the Gold:
6.1 cm on the 122 cm target face
4 cm on the 80 cm target face

Such dividing lines, and any dividing lines which may be used between colours, shall be made entirely within the higher scoring zone in each case.

Any line marking the outermost edge of the White shall be made entirely within the scoring zone.
The width of the thin dividing lines as well as the outermost line shall not exceed 2 mm on either the 122 cm or the 80 cm target faces.
The centre of the target face is termed the "pinhole" and shall be indicated by a small "x" (cross) the lines of which shall not exceed 2 mm.
(b) **Scoring Values and Colour Specifications:**

Scoring Values			Colour	Munsell Colour Scale Notations
Zone	Inner	10	GOLD/ YELLOW	5 Y 8/12
	Outer	9		
	Inner	8	RED	8.3 R 3.9/13.5
	Outer	7		
	Inner	6	LIGHT BLUE	5 B 6/8
	Outer	5		
	Inner	4	BLACK	N 2
	Outer	3		
	Inner	2	WHITE	N 9
	Outer	1		

(c) **Tolerance of Measurements**
The permissible variations in dimensions of the target face in each of the 10 zones shall be measured by the diameters of each separate circle enclosing each of the 10 zones. The tolerance of each such diameter shall not exceed plus/minus 3 mm on the 122 cm target face and plus/minus 2 mm on the 80 cm target face; i.e. measured through the centre outwards:

Zone	Diam. 122 cm Face	Toler. plus/ minus	Diam. 80 cm Face	Toler. plus/ minus
10	12.2 cm	3 mm	8 cm	2 mm
9	24.4	3	16	2
8	36.6	3	24	2
7	48.8	3	32	2
6	61.0	3	40	2
5	73.2	3	48	2
4	85.4	3	56	2
3	97.6	3	64	2
2	109.8	3	72	2
1	122	3	80	2

(d) **Size of Target Faces at different Distances**
For distances of 90, 70 and 60 metres, the Target Face of 122 cm shall be used.
For distances of 50 and 30 metres, the Target Face of 80 cm shall be used.
The size of the buttress, whether round or square, must be not less than 124 cm in any direction to ensure that any arrow hitting the buttress and touching the outermost edge of the target face remain in the buttress.
(e) Target Faces may be made of paper, cloth or any other suitable material.
All faces shall be uniform and of the same material.

503 Field Layout
(a) The Range shall be squared off and each distance accurately measured from a point vertically beneath the Gold of each Target to the shooting line.
(b) A waiting line shall be indicated at least five metres behind the shooting line.
(c) Each Buttress shall be set up at an angle of about 15 degrees.
(d) The Centre of the Gold shall be 130 cm above the ground. A tolerance of measurement shall not exceed plus/minus 5 cm.
(The height of the centres of the Golds in a line of buttresses on the Field should at all times look straight).
(e) All competitors shall be accommodated on one Field.
The women's portion of the Field shall be separated from the men's portion of the Field by at least five metres.
(f) Provision shall be made, if at all possible, for sufficient Target Buttresses to allow for not more than three archers to each target. If the Field does not allow this, four archers shall be the maximum at each Target.
(g) Buttresses shall be pegged securely to the ground, to prevent them from being blown over by wind. Any portion of a buttress likely to damage an arrow shall be covered.
(h) Each buttress shall be numbered. The numbers shall be 30 cm. square and shall be black figures on a yellow background, alternating with yellow figures on a black background. (e.g., No. 1 Black on Yellow, No. 2 Yellow on Black, etc.).
Target Numbers shall be affixed above or below the centre of each buttress, so as to be clear of the Target face.

(i) Points on the shooting line directly opposite each buttress shall be marked and numbered correspondingly.
(j) Lines at right angles to the shooting line, and extending from the shooting line to the target line, making lanes to contain one, two or three buttresses may be laid down.
(k) Suitable barriers shall be erected around the field to keep spectators back. Such barriers should be at least ten metres behind the waiting line, at least ten metres away from each side of the field; and as far beyond the target base line as necessary to prevent members of the public from moving past an archer's line of vision or shooting.

504 Archers' Equipment

This Article lays down the type of Equipment archers are permitted to use when shooting for F.I.T.A. purposes.
Items of equipment not mentioned or covered in this Article are consequently not allowed to be used without prior approval of F.I.T.A. Congress. Further it will be necessary to place before Congress any Equipment or part thereof for which approval is requested.
(a) A Bow of any type may be used provided it subscribes to the accepted principle and meaning of the word Bow as used in Target Archery; e.g. an instrument consisting of a handle (grip), riser and two flexible limbs each ending in a tip with a string nock.
The Bow is braced for use by a single bowstring attached directly between the two string nocks only, and in operation is held in one hand by its handle (grip) while the fingers of the other hand draw, hold back and release the string.
(b) A Bow String may be made up of any number of strands of the material chosen for the purpose, with a centre serving to accommodate the drawing fingers, a nocking point to which may be added serving(s) to fit the arrow nock as necessary, and to locate this point one or two nock locators may be positioned, and in each of the two ends of the Bow String a loop to be placed in the string nocks of the Bow when braced. In addition one attachment, which may not exceed a diameter of one centimetre in any direction, is permitted on the String to serve as lip or nose mark.
The serving on the String must not end within the archer's vision at full draw.
A Bow String must not in any way offer aid in aiming through "peephole", marking or any other means.
(c) An Arrowrest, which can be adjustable, any moveable Pressure Button, Pressure Point or Arrowplate and Draw Check Indicator may all be used on the Bow provided they are not electric or electronic and do not offer any additional aid in aiming.
(d) A Bowsight, a Bowmark or a Point of Aim on the ground for aiming are permitted, but at no time may more than one such device be used.
(i) A Bowsight as attached to the Bow for the purpose of aiming may allow for winding adjustment as well as elevation setting is subject to the following provisions:
– It shall not incorporate a prism or lens or other magnifying device, levelling or electric devices nor shall it provide for more than one sighting point.
– An attachment to which the Bowsight is fixed is permitted.
– The length of any sight (ring, barrel, conical etc.) shall not exceed the minimum inside diameter of the aperture. A hood is not to exceed a length of 1 cm irrespective of shape.
(ii) A Bowmark is a single mark made on the Bow for the purpose of aiming. Such mark may be made in pencil, tape or any other suitable marking material.
A plate or tape with distance marking may be mounted on the Bow as a guide for marking, but must not in any way offer any additional aid.
(iii) A Point of Aim on the ground is a marker placed in the shooting lane between the shooting line and the target. Such marker may not exceed a diameter of 7.5 cm and must not protrude above ground more than 15 cm.
(e) Stabilizers and Torque Flight Compensators on the Bow are permitted provided they do not:
(i) serve as a string guide;
(ii) touch anything but the Bow;
(iii) represent any obstacle to other archers as far as place on the shooting line is concerned.
(f) Arrows of any type may be used provided they subscribe to the accepted principle and meaning of the word Arrow as used in Target Archery, and that such Arrows do not cause undue damage to target faces and buttresses.

An Arrow consists of a shaft with head (point), nock, fletching and, if desired, cresting.

The Arrows of each archer shall be marked with the archer's name, initials or insignia and all Arrows used for the same end of 3 or 6 arrows shall carry the same pattern and colour(s) of fletching, nocks, and cresting if any.

(g) Finger Protections in the form of finger stalls or tips, gloves, shooting tab or tape (plaster) to draw, hold back and release the String are permitted, provided they are smooth with no device to help to hold and/or release the String.

Shooting tabs may be built up of several layers of any materials suitable for their use and allow for the part of the tab behind that used for drawing the string to be stiff using different materials for this build-up (the latter can be leather, plastic, metal, etc.). No shapes have been specified and no limitations in respect of sizes.

A Separator between the fingers to prevent pinching the arrow may be used.

On the bow hand an ordinary glove, mitten or similar may be worn.

(h) Field Glasses, Telescopes and other visual aids may be used for spotting arrows.

Ordinary Spectacles as necessary or Shooting Spectacles provided they are fitted with the same lenses normally used by the archer, and Sun Glasses. None must be fitted with microhole lenses, glasses or similar nor marked in any way, which can assist in aiming.

(i) If it becomes necessary for an archer to use tackle which has not been inspected by the Judges, the onus is on such archer to show such tackle to the Judges before using it.

Any competitor contravening this rule may be excluded from the shooting.

505 Director of Shooting

The Organizers shall appoint a Director of Shooting who shall not participate in the shooting, and whose duties shall include:

(a) Controlling the shooting with a whistle, regulating the timing of ends, and the order in which Competitors will occupy the shooting line.

(b) Instituting and enforcing any reasonable safety measures he considers necessary.

(c) Exercising control over the use of Loudspeakers, the activities of Photographers, etc., so that the comfort and concentration of competitors is not disturbed.

(d) Ensuring that Spectators remain behind the barriers enclosing the shooting field.

Assistants may be appointed as necessary at the discretion of the Organizers to assist the Director of Shooting in the execution of his duties.

(e) The Director of Shooting shall ensure the observance of the 2½ minute Time Limit for shooting an end of three arrows.

The Director of Shooting shall control the shooting with a whistle or other acceptable audible device.

One sound-signal will be the signal for shooting to start.

Two sound-signals will be the signal for archers to move forward to score and collect arrows.

A series of sound-signals for all shooting to cease.

If shooting is suspended during an end for any reason, one sound-signal will be the signal for shooting to recommence.

(f) Under the control of the Director of Shooting, two ends of three sighter arrows are permitted preceding the commencement of shooting each day. No other trial shots are allowed, in any direction, on the shooting field during the days of any competition.

(g) No archer may draw his bow, with or without an arrow, except when standing on the shooting line.

If an arrow is used, the archer shall aim towards the Targets but only after being satisfied that the field is clear both in front of and behind the Targets. If an archer, while drawing his bow with an arrow before the shooting starts or during breaks between distances, looses an arrow, intentionally or otherwise, such an arrow shall count as part of the next end of scoring arrows to be shot.

The Scorer shall make a note to this effect on the archer's scoresheet and enter the values of all hits for that end (3 or 6 arrows as the case may be), but the highest scoring arrow will be forfeited. This also applies to sighter arrows shot before or after the signal indicating the 2½ minutes allowed to shoot an end of three arrows. Such action must be initialled by a judge and the archer concerned.

(h) While shooting is in progress, only those archers whose turn it is to shoot may

be on the shooting line. All other archers with their tackle shall remain behind the waiting line. After an archer has shot his arrows, he shall immediately retire behind the waiting line.
(i) No archer may touch the tackle of another without the latter's consent. Serious cases may lead to disqualification.
(j) An archer arriving after shooting has started, shall forfeit the number of arrows already shot, unless the Director of Shooting is satisfied that he was delayed by circumstances beyond his control, in which case he may be allowed to make up the arrows lost after the distance then being shot has been completed.
(k) The Director of Shooting has authority to extend the 2½ minute Time Limit in exceptional circumstances. The Director of Shooting shall consult Judges beforehand. Any such special ruling introduced must be announced to the competitors before having effect. Final result lists to be endorsed to this effect, giving reason.
When visual time controls are in use the 2 minutes section will be prolonged and the 30 seconds section remain unchanged.
(l) For visual time control, methods by lights or plates may be used under the control of the Director of Shooting at any tournament at the Organizer's discretion as may a flag or other simple device.
(m) Archers may not raise the bow arm until the signal for shooting to begin is given (i.e. when the light changes to Green and/or the whistle signal is given starting the 2½ minute Time Limit).

506 Shooting
(a) Each archer shall shoot his arrows in ends of three arrows each.
(b) The maximum time permitted for an archer to shoot an end of three arrows shall be two and a half minutes. Any arrow shot either before the signal or after the signal denoting such time limit of two and a half minutes will forfeit the highest scoring arrow for that end (3 or 6 arrows as the case may be). However if it becomes necessary to change a string or make essential adjustment to equipment the Director of Shooting must be informed and extra time may be given.
(c) Excepting for persons who are permanently disabled, archers shall shoot from a standing position and without support, with one foot on each side of the shooting line.
(d) An arrow shall not be deemed to have been shot if:
(i) the archer can touch it with his bow without moving his feet from their position in relation to the shooting line.
(ii) the target face or buttress blows over (in spite of having been fixed and pegged down to the satisfaction of the judges). The judges will take whatever measure they deem necessary and compensate the adequate time for shooting the relevant number of arrows. If the buttress only slides down it will be left to the judges to decide what action to take, if any.
(e) While an archer is on the shooting line, he shall receive no assistance or information, by word or otherwise, from anyone, other than for the purpose of making essential changes in equipment.

507 Order of Shooting & Time Control
(a) Archers shall shoot one at a time on each target in rotation as follows: e.g. Three Archers per Target.
A–B–C
C–A–B
B–C–A
A–B–C etc.
If Archers shoot four per target the rotation shall be:
A, B–C, D
C, D–A, B
A, B–C, D etc.
(b) Two and a half minutes (2½ minutes) shall be the time allowed for an archer to shoot an end of three arrows.
A warning signal shall be given 30 seconds (½ minute) before the expiry of the 2½ minutes allowed.
(c) The 2½ minute Time Limit will be controlled by the Director of Shooting or by his Assistants.
(i) Plates – Yellow and Black Stripes.
(ii) Lights – Green, Amber and Red or
(iii) Digital clocks.
(d) Visual signals are to be placed on both sides of the field and, if necessary in the lane between Women's and Men's targets so that both right- and left-hand archers shall be able to observe them. They are to be placed in front of the shooting line on each side of the Field and in the clear lane at any distance shorter than 30 metres, but visible to all archers on the shooting line. Two plates, back to back, are essential in

the clear lane in order that the same side of the Plates (all yellow or black/yellow stripes) is displayed simultaneously to both men and women competitors.

(e) When the shooting is controlled by Plates:

The YELLOW and BLACK striped side will be turned towards the archers as a signal of warning that half a minute only is left of the 2½ minute Time Limit.

The YELLOW side of the Plate will be turned towards the archers at all other times.

Signals by whistle, and other Rules as in 507 (e) above are the same. The Plates are not to be less than 120 cm by 80 cm in size. They must be securely mounted to resist any wind and must be easy to turn quickly to show either side. One side of the Plates shall be striped with 20–25 cm wide stripes alternating in black and yellow. The stripes to be at an angle of about 45 degrees to the ground. The reverse side shall be all yellow.

(f) When the shooting is controlled by Lights:

(i) RED The Director of Shooting will give a two blast whistle ('whistle' may, anywhere in control of shooting, also mean 'bleep' or a hand operated or automatic sound signal which may be in use) as a signal that 'A' archers will occupy the shooting line all together.

GREEN on changing colour 20 seconds later, the Director of Shooting will give a one blast whistle as a signal for shooting to begin.

AMBER this light will show during shooting after 2 minutes as a signal that only half a minute is left.

RED indicates the 2½ minute Time Limit is up and two blasts on the whistle will be given as a signal that shooting is to stop – even if all three arrows have not been shot.

'A' archers still on the shooting line are to retire behind the waiting line.

'B' archers will move up and occupy the shooting line and wait for the Green light as above for shooting to begin: the whole will be repeated as above.

'C' archers are to follow.

At distances where 6 arrows (two ends of three arrows) are to be shot the above will be repeated before scoring. When the Red light comes on after one end of three arrows (or two ends of three arrows according to distances being shot) three blasts on the whistle will be given as a signal for archers to move forward to the Targets for scoring.

Lights. The colours shall be Green, Amber (Yellow) and Red in that order with the Red uppermost.

The Lights in the three places must be synchronized and at no time shall two different colours be on at the same time.

The Lights may be linked with an acoustical signal (bleep) to be operated electronically, but must also be able to be controlled manually as and when necessary.

(g) When timing is controlled by the use of Digital Clocks. The figures on the clock shall be not less than 30 cm in height and must be able to be clearly read a 180 m. distance. They must be able to be immediately stopped and reset as may be required. The clock must function on a count-down principle. All other requirements e.g. position, number etc. shall be the same as required for lights.

(h) Whenever the shooting line is vacated by all archers having finished their shooting of three arrows before the 2½ minute Time Limit has expired, the signal for the change will be given immediately.

(i) 20 seconds will be allowed for the archers to vacate and the next to occupy the shooting line. 20 seconds is also the time permitted to occupy the shooting line at the beginning of each end and will, as seen under (i) above, be indicated by a whistle signal of two blasts. No archer will occupy the shooting line except on the appropriate signal given when lights are operated.

(j) If the shooting is suspended during an end for any reason the Time Limit shall be adjusted accordingly.

(k) The order of shooting may be changed temporarily for the purpose of changing a string or making other essential adjustments to equipment. If however such attention to equipment should become essential while on the shooting line, the archer may step back and at the same time call the Technical Commission (T.C.) by using the flag or other device provided for the purpose. The Judges having verified the archer was justified in leaving the line, will arrange with the Director of Shooting for this archer to shoot the arrows left of that end before he gives the signal to move forward for scoring, an announcement to this effect being made over the loudspeaker.

508 Scoring

(a) One Scorer shall be appointed for each target.

(b) At distances of 90, 70 or 60 metres, scoring shall take place after every second end of three arrows.

At distances of 50 and 30 metres, scoring shall take place after every end of three arrows. After arrows have been scored and drawn from the targets, all arrow holes shall be suitably marked.

(c) Scorers shall enter in descending order the value of each arrow on Score Sheets as called out by the archer to whom the arrows belong. Other archers on that target shall check the value of each arrow called out.

Only arrows scoring Ten points shall be referred to as "Golds".

(d) Neither the arrows nor the face shall be touched until all the arrows on that target have been recorded.

(e) An arrow shall be scored according to the position of the shaft in the target face.

(f) If more than three arrows (or six as the case may be), belonging to the same archer, should be found in the target or on the ground in the shooting lanes, only the three lowest (or six lowest, as the case may be) in value shall be scored.

Should an archer be found to repeat this, he may be disqualified.

(g) Should the shaft of an arrow touch two colours, or touch any dividing line between scoring zones, that arrow shall score the higher value of the zones affected.

Should a fragment of a target face be missing, including a dividing line or where two colours meet, then an imaginary line shall be used for judging the value of any arrow that may hit such a part.

(h) Unless all arrow holes are suitably marked on each occasion when arrows are scored and drawn from the target, arrows rebounding from the target face shall not be scored.

(i) An arrow hitting:

(i) the target and rebounding, shall score according to its impact on the target, provided that all arrow holes have been marked and an unmarked hole or mark can be identified.

When a rebound occurs:

(a) with archers shooting one at a time on each target, the archer concerned will, after shooting his end of three arrows, remain on the shooting line with his bow held above the head as a signal to the Judges.

(b) with more than one archer shooting at a time on each target, the archer concerned will finish his end of three arrows and remain on the shooting line, while the other archer on that target will, when the rebound occurs, stop shooting but remain on the shooting line with the bow held above the head.

When all archers on the shooting line for that end have finished shooting their three arrows or the two and a half minutes time limit has expired, whichever is appropriate, the Director of Shooting will interrupt the shooting. The archer with the rebound arrow will advance to the target together with a Judge, who will judge the point of impact, take down the value and mark the hole and later participate in scoring of that end. The rebound arrow is to be left behind the target until that end has been scored. When the Field is again clear the Director of Shooting will give the signal for shooting to recommence. In case of (b) above with more than one archer shooting together, the other archer on the same target who remained on the shooting line while the rebound arrow was judged, will first complete his end of 3 arrows to be shot – no other archer is to occupy the shooting line meanwhile.

(ii) the target and hanging from it, shall oblige the archer or archers on that target to stop shooting just as if a bouncer had occurred, and signal in the same way. When the shooting of that end has been completed by the other archers on the line, a Field Officer shall remove the arrow (or if that is not possible mark the hole, note the score and leave the arrow at the target). The remaining arrows shall be shot by the archer(s) on that target before the Director of Shooting orders general shooting to recommence. The Field Officer concerned shall participate in the scoring of that end.

(iii) Another arrow in the nock and remaining embedded therein, shall score according to the value of the arrow struck.

(iv) Another arrow, and then hitting the target face after deflection, shall score as it lies in the target.

(v) Another arrow, and then rebounding from the target, shall score the value of the struck arrow, provided the damaged arrow can be identified.

(vi) A target other than an archer's own target, shall not score.
(vii) And passing through the target shall, provided all arrow holes have been marked and provided an unmarked hole can be identified, score according to the value of the hole in the target face.
(j) The Director of Shooting will ensure that, after scoring, no arrows are left in the targets before any signal is given for shooting to recommence. If this inadvertently happens, the shooting shall not be interrupted.
An archer may shoot that end with other arrows, or make up the arrows lost after shooting over that distance has been completed.
In such circumstances, a Judge shall participate in the scoring after that end, making sure that the arrows which remained in the target are checked back to the archer's score sheet before any arrows are withdrawn from the target.
(k) In the event of an archer leaving arrows, e.g. on the ground in the target area, he may use others provided he inform a judge before shooting. The Judge shall exercise such checks as they deem fit in each circumstance.
(l) An archer may delegate authority to score and collect his arrows to his Team Captain or to another archer on his own target.
(m) A scoring board or some such device with competitor's name and/or target number (1A, 1B, 1C or simply A, B, C and adding 1D/D if four archers on the target etc.) is permitted for displaying progressive total scores after each end. When any such device is being used it shall be placed below each buttress on the ground; it must be pegged or fixed securely to prevent movement by wind. It shall be changed by the scorer appointed and aided by the archers on that target after the arrows have been scored and drawn, before leaving the target.
(n) Score sheets shall be signed by the Scorer and the Archer, denoting that the Archer agrees with the score, and thereafter he may make no claim for any alteration of the score.
If the scorer is participating in the shooting, his score sheet shall be signed by some other archer on the same target.
(o) In the event of a tie in score, the results shall be determined as follows:
(i) For Individuals:
The Archer, of those tying, with the greatest number of scoring hits.
If this is also a tie, then the Archer of those so tying with the greatest number of Golds (Hits scoring 10 points).
If this is also a tie, then the Archer of those so tying with the greatest number of hits scoring 9 points.
If this is also a tie, then the Archers so tying shall be declared equal.
(ii) For Teams:
The Team, of those tying, having the Archer making the highest individual score.
If this is also a tie, then the Team of those so tying having the Archer making the second highest individual score.
If this is also a tie, then the Teams so tying shall be declared equal.
(p) At important tournaments the duty of the Scorers Committee will be:
(i) To record on a large scoreboard, after each end, the progressive totals of at least the first eight women and the first eight men.
(ii) To record on another large scoreboard, after each distance, the progressive totals for every competitor.
(iii) To provide daily results and progressive totals daily, and, after the last day of the Tournament, the Grand Total for Individuals and the Team results. Copies of these results shall be made available to: Team Captains, Members of the Administrative Council and Congress Representatives who are present, Members of the T.C., Director of Shooting, The Press.

509 Judging

At least three Judges shall be appointed.
(a) The duties of the Judges shall be:
(i) to check all distances and the correct layout of the shooting field/course; the dimensions of Target faces and buttresses; that the centre of the Golds are the correct height from the ground; that all the buttresses are set back at a uniform angle;
(ii) to check all the necessary field equipment;
(iii) to check all competitors' equipment, the day before the Tournament and at any time thereafter during the Tournament.
(iv) to check the conduct of the shooting;
(v) to check the conduct of the scoring;
(vi) to consult with the Director of Shooting on questions which arise regarding the shooting;

(vii) to handle any disputes or appeals which may arise;
(viii) in liaison with the Director of Shooting, to interrupt the shooting if necessary, because of weather conditions, a serious accident, or such occurrences, but to ensure if at all possible, that each day's programme is completed on that day;
(ix) to consider complaints or requests from Team Captains regarding Field Equipment and where applicable to take suitable action;
Collective decisions shall be made by a simple majority of votes. In case of a tie, the Chairman shall have a casting vote.
(x) Competitors and Officials are to conform with the F.I.T.A. Constitution and Rules as well as decisions and directives the Judges may find necessary according to the terms of reference for this Commission. An archer proved to have transgressed any Rules and Regulations knowingly may be ruled by the Judges not to be eligible to participate and be eliminated and will lose any position he may have gained.

510 Queries, Appeals and Disputes
(a) Scorers shall refer any query about the value of an arrow in a Target to the T.C. before any arrows are drawn. The ruling of the Judges shall be final.
(b) A mistake on a score sheet discovered before the arrows are drawn may be corrected, but the correction must be witnessed and initialled before the arrows are drawn, by one of the Judges and the archer concerned. Any other disputes concerning entries on a score sheet shall be referred to a Judge.
(c) Should a Target Face become unreasonably worn or otherwise disfigured or should there be any other complaint about Field Equipment, an archer or his Team Captain may appeal to the Judges to have the defective item replaced or remedied.
(d) Questions concerning the conduct of the shooting or the conduct of a competitor shall be lodged with the Judges the same day.
(e) Queries regarding daily published results shall be lodged with the Judges without any undue delay, and in any event must be lodged in time to allow corrections to be made before the prizegiving.
(f) In the event of a competitor not being satisfied with a ruling given by the Judges, he may, except as provided for in sub-paragraph (a) above, appeal through his Team Captain to the Jury in writing when a Jury exists.
Trophies or prizes which may be affected by a dispute shall not be awarded until the Jury ruling has been given.

511 Miscellaneous Equipment
The following equipment is recommended in relation to importance of the tournament.
(a) Numbers to be worn by each competitor:
1A, 1B, 1C, 2A, 2B, 2C, etc.
(b) A device to indicate the order of shooting: A.B.C.; C.A.B.; B.C.A.; etc. The letters shall be large enough to be read by all competitors from their shooting positions. Two or more such devices may be needed.
(c) One large scoreboard for progressive totals after each end, for at least the first eight women and the first eight men.
(d) Another large scoreboard for displaying the progressive scores of all competitors after each distance.
(e) Flags, or some suitable device, whereby Scorers at the target and archers at the shooting line can call for a member of the T.C.
(f) Flags, of any light material and of a colour easily visible (such as yellow) to serve as wind indicators, shall be placed above the centre of each Target, 40 cm above the Target Buttress or the Target Number, whichever is the higher. Such Flags shall be not more than 30 cm and not less than 25 cm square.
(g) Raised platform with seating facilities or high tennis chair for the Director of Shooting.
(h) Loudspeaker equipment. Recommended at large Tournaments (to make communications more effective between officials) is such equipment as Field Telephones, 'walkie-talkie' and the like.
(i) Sufficient chairs or benches behind the waiting line for all competitors, Team Captains and other officials.

B) INDOOR ARCHERY
521 The Indoor F.I.T.A. Rounds
There are two Indoor F.I.T.A. Rounds:
Round I 30 arrows shot from 18 metres
Round II 30 arrows shot from 25 metres
for both women and men.

522 Target Faces
Description:
(a) For Indoor Archery there are two Standard circular F.I.T.A. Target Faces 60 cm and 40 cm in diameter. Both these faces are divided by a thin line into five concentric colour zones arranged from the centre outwards as follows:
Gold (Yellow), Red, Light Blue, Black and White.
Each colour is in turn divided by a thin line into two zones of equal width thus making in all ten scoring zones of equal width measured from the centre of the Gold:
3 cm on the 60 cm target face
2 cm on the 40 cm target face
Such dividing lines, and any dividing lines which may be used between colours, shall be made entirely within the higher scoring zone in each case.
Any line marking the outermost edge of the White shall be made entirely within the scoring zone.
The width of the thin dividing lines as well as the outermost line shall not exceed 2 mm on both the 60 cm and the 40 cm target faces.
The centre of the target face is termed the 'pinhole' and shall be indicated by a small cross the lines of which shall not exceed 2 mm in width.
(b) **Scoring Values and Colour Specifications:**
These are according to Article 508.
(c) **Tolerance of Measurements:**
The permissible variations in dimensions of the target face in each of the ten zones shall be measured by the diameters of each separate circle enclosing each of the 10 zones. The tolerance of each such diameter shall not exceed plus/minus 1 mm on both the 60 cm and the 40 cm target face; i.e. measured through the centres outwards:

Zone	Diam. 60 cm Face	Toler. plus/ minus	Diam. 40 cm Face	Toler. plus/ minus
10	6 cm	1 mm	4 cm	1 mm
9	12	1	8	1
8	18	1	12	1
7	24	1	16	1
6	30	1	20	1
5	36	1	24	1
4	42	1	28	1
3	48	1	32	1
2	54	1	36	1
1	60	1	40	1

(d) **Size of Target Faces at each Round:**
For the 18 metres Indoor F.I.T.A. Round I: target face of 40 cm;
for the 25 metres Indoor F.I.T.A. Round II the target face of 60 cm shall be used.

523 Target Set Up
(a) The Centre of the Gold shall be 130 cm above the ground. If the 40 cm target faces are in two lines one above the other, the centre of the Gold shall be 100 cm and 160 cm respectively above the ground.
A tolerance of measurement shall not exceed plus/minus 2 cm.
(b) The Buttresses may be set up to any angle between vertically and about 15°, but a line of Buttresses shall be set up at the same angle.

524 Shooting & Scoring
(a) Each archer shall shoot his arrows in ends of three arrows each.
(b) Scoring shall take place after each end of 3 arrows.
(c) A scoring board or some such device with competitor's name and/or target number (1A, 1B, 1C or simply A, B, C and adding 1D/D if four archers on the target etc.) is permitted for displaying progressive/total scores after each end. When any such device is being used it shall be placed on the ground below the Buttress or fixed firmly to the Buttress. It shall be changed by the scorer appointed, aided by the archers on that target after the arrows have been scored and drawn, before leaving the target.

525 Other Rules & Regulations
In all other aspects the Target Archery Rules of Shooting will apply with the exception of Article 505 (k) (i.e. the two and a half minute Time Limit for shooting three arrows may not be extended at Indoor shooting).
If space does not permit a Waiting line then Article 503 (b) may be waived.
Notes:
1. Safety precautions behind the targets call for special attention.
2. Source of light whether natural or artificial and its effect on the target faces is important and should be considered.

C) FIELD ARCHERY
541 Terms
(a) Some of the Terms as used in Field Archery

UNIT – A 14 target course including all official shots.
ROUND – Two Units, or twice around one Unit – 28 targets.
FACE – Target face.
SPOT – The aiming centre of the face.
BUTT – Any object upon which a face is fixed.
POST – Shooting position.
SHOT – Used in connection with the post number, i.e. 1st, 2nd, 3rd or 4th shot, etc.
(b) Two 28 target Standard Rounds are recognized:
(i) The Field Round
(ii) The Hunters Round
with 112 arrows in each Round.

542 The Field Round

The Standard Field Round Unit consists of 14 shots – 4 arrows at each distance.
15, 20, 25 and 30 metres at a 30 cm. face total 16 arrows.
35, 40 and 45 metres at 45 cm. face total 12 arrows.
50, 55 and 60 metres at a 60 cm. face total 12 arrows.
And the following four posts – each arrow to be shot from a different post or at a different face:
35 metres at a 45 cm. face, all four arrows from the same distance (the fan shot) total 4 arrows.
6, 8, 10 and 12 metres at 15 cm. face total 4 arrows.
30, 35, 40 and 45 metres at a 45 cm. face total 4 arrows.
45, 50, 55 and 60 metres at a 60 cm. face total 4 arrows.
Total number of arrows in the Field Round Unit 56 arrows.
All 14 shots shall be mixed to give maximum variety.

543 The Field Round Faces

(a) There are four Standard circular faces:
60 cm, 45 cm, 30 cm and 15 cm diameters.
All four faces consist of:
- an outside ring, which shall be black
- an inner ring, which shall be white
- a centre circular spot, which shall be black

The white ring shall have a diameter half the diameter of the black outer ring, and the black circular spot shall have a diameter one sixth of the black outer ring, i.e.:
the target with 60 cm diameter – white inner ring 30 cm, black centre spot 10 cm;
the target with 45 cm diameter – white inner ring 22.5 cm, black centre spot 7.5 cm;
the target with 30 cm diameter – white inner ring 15 cm, black centre spot 5 cm;
the target with 15 cm diameter – white inner ring 7.5 cm, black centre spot 2.5 cm
(b) Animal pictures bearing the Field Round faces may also be used. Such faces need only be outlined but all lines shall be entirely within the scoring area outlined (the higher scoring area). The spot to be a contrasting colour and to be plainly visible.
(c) The scoring values are:
the centre black spot – 5 points
the inner white ring – 4 points
the outside black ring – 3 points.

544 The Hunters Round

The Standard Hunters Round Unit consists of 14 shots with:
one arrow from each of four different posts for each target:
Two targets with a 15 cm. face placed between 5 and 15 metres.
The total distance for the 8 arrows shall be 80 metres.
Four targets with a 30 cm. face placed between 10 and 30 metres.
The total distance for the 16 arrows shall be 320 metres.
Five targets with a 45 cm. face placed between 20 and 40 metres.
The total distance for the 20 arrows shall be 600 metres.
Three targets with a 60 cm. face placed between 30 and 50 metres.
The total distance for the 12 arrows shall be 480 metres.
Total number of arrows in the Hunters Round Unit – 56 arrows.
Total length of a Unit – 1480 metres.

545 The Hunters Round Faces

(a) There shall be four standard faces with exactly the same dimensions as for the Field Round but the faces shall be black with a white spot. The lines to be invisible from the posts but an exception may be made for the 15 cm. and the 30 cm. faces as the distances are so short.
(b) Animal pictures bearing the Hunters Round faces may also be used.
The inner ring shall be inside the animal figure.

The spot shall be a contrasting colour and be plainly visible.
(c) The scoring values are:
the centre white spot – 5 points
the inner black ring – 4 points
the outside black ring – 3 points.

546 Field Course Layout
(a) Two or more posts at any or all one-position shots may be used provided that the posts are equidistant from the target. Two posts to be placed side by side at every position where two archers are expected to shoot together.
(b) All posts shall be numbered together with the number of arrows to be shot.
(c) The distance **may** be stated.
Note: Organizers of Field Shoots may themselves decide whether the distances shall be marked or not marked in either Round.
(d) The butts shall measure not less than 75 cm square and at no point may the faces be less than 15 cm from the ground. All butts must be placed so that the full face is exposed to the archer.
(e) Faces shall not be placed over any larger face, nor shall there be any marks on the butt or foreground that could be used as points of aim.
(f) In the Field Round a 5 per cent variation in distances is permitted where necessary because of terrain, but any variations must be made up on another target in the same group.
(g) Direction arrows indicating the way round the Field Course should be placed as necessary to ensure safety.
(h) The official Field Course must be completed and ready for inspection not later than the morning of the day before the shooting starts.

547 Field Course Control and Safety
(a) A Field Captain shall be appointed to be in control of the Field Shoot.
(b) The duties of the Field Captain shall be:
(i) To satisfy himself that safety precautions have been observed in the layout of the Field Course.
(ii) To arrange with the Organizers for any additional safety precautions he may find advisable before shooting commences.
(iii) To address the competitors and officials on the safety precautions and any other matter concerning the shooting that he may judge to be necessary.
(iv) To see that a Target Captain and two scorers are appointed for each group.
(v) To designate the order in which groups are to shoot or the posts at which each group is to start shooting.
(vi) To ensure that one group does not hold up the following group.
Search for lost arrows must not delay groups, such arrows to be sought **after** shooting has finished.
(vii) To resolve disputes and queries that may arise in connection with the Rules or the conduct of shooting.

548 Archers Equipment
A. Instinctive or Bare Bow Class
1. This Article lays down the type of Equipment archers are permitted to use when shooting for F.I.T.A. purposes.
Items of Equipment not mentioned or covered in this Article are consequently not allowed to be used without prior approval of F.I.T.A. Congress. Further, it will be necessary to place before Congress any Equipment or part thereof for which approval is requested.
(a) **A Bow** of any type provided it subscribes to the accepted principle and meaning of the word Bow as used in Target Archery, e.g. an instrument consisting of a handle (grip), riser and two flexible limbs each ending in a tip with a string nock.
The Bow is braced for use by a single bow string attached directly between the two string nocks only, and in operation is held in one hand by its handle (grip) while the fingers of the other hand draw, hold back and release the string.
The Bow must be bare and free from any protrusions, marks or blemishes or laminated pieces, which could be used in aiming. The inside of the upper limb shall be without any trade marks.
(b) **A Bow String** made up of any number of strands of the material chosen for the purpose with a centre serving to accommodate the drawing fingers, a nocking point to which may be added serving(s) to fit the arrow nock as necessary and to locate this point one or two nock locaters may be positioned, and in each end of the Bow String a loop to be placed in the string nocks of the Bow when braced. The serving on the String must not end within the archer's vision at full draw. The Bow

String must not in any way offer aid in aiming through peephole, marking or any other means.
(c) **An Arrowrest and Arrowplate** which are part of the Bow (i.e. not moveable) and provided they do not offer any aid in aiming.
(d) **Arrows** of any type provided they subscribe to the accepted principle and meaning of the word Arrow as used in Target Archery. Arrows must not cause undue damage to faces and buttresses. The Arrows of each archer shall be marked with the archer's name, initials or insignia and shall have the same colour(s) in fletching.
Each arrow shall be numbered by the use of plainly visible rings of approximately 5 mm width and 5 mm spacing.
(e) **Finger Protection** in the form of finger stalls or tips, gloves, shooting tab or tape (plaster) to draw, hold back and release the string, provided they are smooth with no device to help to hold and/or release the String. A separator between the fingers to prevent pinching the arrow may be used. On the bow hand an ordinary glove, mitten or similar may be worn.
(f) **Accessories** such as bowsling, bracers, dress shield, quiver and tassel.
(g) **Ordinary Spectacles** as necessary or **Shooting Spectacles** provided they are fitted with the same lenses normally used by the archer and **Sun-glasses**. None must be fitted with microhole lenses, glasses or similar nor marked in any way which may assist in aiming.
(h) **Field Glasses** and other visual aids may be used between shots for spotting arrows, when shooting Rounds with marked distances.
2. The following equipment is not permitted:
(a) Field Glasses and other visual aids when shooting Rounds with unmarked distances
(b) Any aid for estimating distances
(c) Any memoranda that assist in improving scores
(d) Sights, draw check indicator and mounted stabilizers – **the Bow must be bare.**

B. Free style Class

1. This Article lays down the type of Equipment archers are permitted to use when shooting for F.I.T.A. purposes.
For Items of Equipment not mentioned or covered in this Article see Article 548 A 1 above.
(a) **A Bow** of any type provided it subscribes to the accepted principle and meaning of the word Bow as used in Target Archery, e.g. an instrument consisting of a handle (grip) riser and two flexible limbs each ending in a tip with a string nock. The Bow is braced for use by a single bow string attached directly between the two string nocks only, and in operation is held in one hand by its handle (grip) while the fingers of the other hand draw, hold back and release the string.
(b) **A Bow String** may be made up of any number of strands of the material chosen for this purpose, with a centre serving to accommodate the drawing fingers, a nocking point to which may be added serving(s) to fit the arrow nock as necessary, and to locate this point one or two nock locaters may be positioned, and in each of the two ends of the bow string a loop to be placed in the string nocks of the Bow when braced.
In addition one attachment which may not exceed a diameter of one centimetre in any direction on the string to serve as lip or nose mark. The serving on the String must not end within the archer's vision at full draw. The Bow String must not in any way offer aid in aiming through peephole, marking or any other means.
(c) **An Arrowrest**, which can be adjustable, any moveable **Pressure Button, Pressure Point** or **Arrowplate** and **Draw Check Indicator** may all be used on the Bow provided they are not electric or electronic and do not offer any additional aid in aiming.
(d) **A Bowsight or a Bowmark** for aiming, but at no time may more than one such device be used.
(i) **A Bowsight** as attached to the Bow for the purpose of aiming may allow for windage adjustment as well as elevation setting for aiming, but it is subject to the following provisions:
It shall not incorporate a prism or lens or other magnifying device, levelling or electric devices nor shall it provide for more than one sighting point. The length of any sight (ring, barrel, conical, etc.) shall not exceed the minimum inside diameter of the aperture. A hood is not to exceed a length of 1 cm irrespective of shape.
(ii) **A Bowmark** is a single mark made on

the Bow for the purpose of aiming. Such mark may be made in pencil, tape or any other suitable marking material. A plate or tape with distance marking may be mounted on the Bow as a guide for marking, but must not in any way offer any additional aid.
(e) **Stabilizers** on the Bow are permitted provided they do not:
(i) serve as a string guide
(ii) touch anything but the Bow
(iii) represent any obstacle to other archers as far as shooting is concerned.
Torque Flight Compensators may also be mounted.
(f) **Arrows** of any type provided they subscribe to the accepted principle and meaning of the word Arrow as used in Target Archery.
Arrows may not cause undue damage to faces and buttresses. The Arrows of each archer shall be marked with the archer's name, initials or insignia and shall have the same colour(s) in fletching.
Each arrow shall be numbered by the use of plainly visible rings of approximately 5 mm width and 5 mm spacing.
(g) **Finger Protection** in the form of finger stalls or tips, gloves, shooting tab or tape (plaster) to draw, hold back and release the string, provided they are smooth with no device to help to hold and/or release the String. A separator between the fingers to prevent pinching the arrow may be used.
On the bow hand an ordinary glove, mitten or similar may be worn.
(h) **Accessories** such as bracers, dress shield, bowsling, quiver and tassel.
(i) **Ordinary Spectacles** as necessary or **Shooting Spectacles** provided they are fitted with the same lenses normally used by the archer, and **Sun-glasses.** None must be fitted with microhole lenses, glasses or similar nor marked in any way which may assist in aiming.
(j) **Field Glasses** and other visual aids may be used between shots for spotting arrows, when shooting Rounds with marked distances.
2. The following equipment is not permitted:
(a) Field Glasses and other visual aids when shooting Rounds with unmarked distances
(b) Any aid for estimating distances
(c) Any memoranda that assist in improving scores

549 Shooting
(a) Archers shall shoot in groups of four if possible, but never less than three nor more than five.
(b) The archers shall be numbered in each group – A, B, C, and D – pre-fixed with 1, 2, 3, etc. indicating the number of each group (1A, 1B, 1C, 1D – 2A, 2B, 2C, 2D).
(c) The shooting shall take place in rotating order:
(i) Preferably two archers shall shoot together, one from each side of the post –
A ● B – C ● D
C ● D – A ● B
A ● B – C ● D, etc.
At the 15 cm. face archers may shoot one at a time.
(ii) Rotation of four archers shooting one at a time:
A – B – C – D
D – A – B – C
C – D – A – B
B – C – D – A
A – B – C – D, etc.
(iii) if there are three archers in a group:
A ● B – C
C ● A – B
B ● C – A
A ● B – C, etc.,
and similarly for five archers in a group.
(d) The order of shooting may be changed temporarily for the purpose of changing a string or making other minor adjustments to equipment.
(e) A broken bow may be replaced even by a borrowed bow.
(f) (i) Archers shall stand with both feet behind the relevant shooting line which is an imaginary line parallel to the target.
(ii) Archers waiting their turn to shoot shall stand well back behind the archers on the shooting line.
(iii) No archer shall approach the target until all have finished shooting except as permitted under Art. 550 (b) when shooting at the 30 cm. and 15 cm. faces.
(iv) Archers draw position, and relationship of arrow to drawing fingers must not change.
Draw position is the position or point archers choose to draw their hand with the bowstring before releasing.
The relationship of arrow to drawing fingers is the position of the drawing fingers as placed on the centre serving of the string in relation to the nocking point holding the arrow.
(g) An arrow shall not be deemed to have

been shot if the archer can touch it with his bow without moving his feet from their position in relation to the shooting line.
(h) Under no other circumstances may an arrow be reshot.
(i) 30 cm faces. Four faces shall be placed in the form of a square.
Every shooting position to have posts placed side by side.
Archers shooting from the left post shall shoot their first two arrows at the top left face and the remaining two arrows at the lower left face; archers shooting from the right posts shall shoot similarly at the top and lower right faces.
15 cm faces. Sixteen faces shall be placed in four vertical columns (1, 2, 3 and 4 from the left) of four faces (A, B, C and D from the top). Every shooting position to have two posts placed side by side. Archers shooting from the left post in the first detail shall shoot one arrow at each of the faces in column 1 starting at face A and then B, C and D from the appropriate posts; archers shooting from the right post in the first detail shall shoot their arrows in a similar manner at the faces in column 3.
The archers in the second detail shall shoot their arrows in a similar manner from the left post at faces in column 2 and the right post at faces in column 4.
(j) Arrows shall be shot in correct numerical rotation.
(k) A time limit of 1½ minutes per arrow shall be allowed from the time the archer takes his position at the post.
The time limit is to be enforced at the discretion of the Judges.
The archer to be cautioned by the Judges before the time limit be enforced.
(l) The Field Captain shall assign the post from which each group will commence shooting.
(m) All arrow holes to be suitably marked.
(n) Bouncers or arrows passing through the face, to be scored according to their point of impact on the face and provided that an unmarked hole or indentation can be identified.
(o) No archer shall relate to another archer the target distances on unmarked courses during the Tournament.

550 Scoring
(a) Two scorers shall be appointed in each group.
(b) Scoring shall take place after all archers in the group have shot their arrows, except on the 30 cm. face where scoring may take place after two archers have shot and after each archer has shot on the 15 cm. face.
(c) Scorers shall record the scores made on the score card alongside the correct number of the post. Where groups are assigned to stay at different posts they will complete the round up to and including the numbered post previous to the one at which they commenced.
(d) Scorers shall enter the value of each arrow on the score card as called out by the archer to whom the arrows belong. Other archers in the group shall check the value of each arrow so called.
Scorers to compare their scores before any arrows are drawn.
(e) Neither the arrows nor the face shall be touched until all arrows on that target have been recorded and scores checked.
(f) An arrow shall be scored according to the position of the shaft on the face.
(g) Should the shaft of an arrow touch two colours, or any dividing line between scoring zones, that arrow shall score the higher value of the zones affected.
(h) Provided all arrow holes are suitably marked, bouncers or arrows passing through the face to be scored according to their point of impact on the face and provided an unmarked hole or indentation can be identified.
(i) Another arrow in the nock and remaining embedded therein shall score according to the value of the arrow struck.
(j) In the case of a tie in scores, the result shall be determined as follows
(i) The archer, of those tying, with the greatest number of hit targets.
(ii) If this is also a tie, then the archer with the greatest number of scoring arrows (hits).
(iii) If this is also a tie then the archer with the greatest number of highest scoring zone hits.
(iv) If this is also a tie, then the archers so tying shall be declared equal.
(k) The Target Captain shall be the final judge of disputed arrows except at Tournaments.

551 Judging
(a) Judges shall be appointed with the Field Captain as Chairman. The duties of the Judges shall be:
(i) To check competitors' equipment

before the Tournament is due to start (time to be stated on the Tournament programme) and at any time thereafter during the Tournament.
(ii) To settle any query concerning the value of an arrow. Their ruling shall be final.
(iii) To check the conduct of the shooting and to resolve any disputes or appeals that may arise.
(iv) To consider requests from Target Captains regarding Field Equipment and, where applicable, to take suitable action.
(b) Questions concerning the conduct of the shooting or the conduct of a competitor shall be lodged with the Judges without any undue delay and in any event must be lodged before the prizegiving. The ruling of the Judges shall be final.
(c) At F.I.T.A. Championships their duties shall further be:
(i) To inspect the Field Course layout.
(ii) To satisfy themselves that safety precautions have been observed in the layout.
(iii) To check all competitors' equipment the day before the Tournament is due to start (Practice Day) and at any time thereafter during the Tournament.
(iv) And further, to deal with any general matters as indicated in Art. 547.
(v) To furnish a written Report on the Tournament to the F.I.T.A. Executive Committee, within four weeks, for publication.

D) CLOUT ARCHERY

561 Round
The Clout Round consists of 36 arrows shot from the following distances:
165 metres for Men
125 metres for Women
Shooting shall be in one direction only.
Six sighter arrows (two ends of three arrows) are permitted preceding the commencement of shooting. These shall be shot under the control of the Field Captain and shall not be scored.

562 The Clout Target
The Clout Target shall be circular, 15 metres in diameter and shall be divided into five concentric scoring zones arranged from the centre outwards and each measuring 1.5 metres in width. Each dividing line shall be entirely within the higher scoring zone.
The Clout Target may be marked out on the ground, or the scoring lines may be determined by a steel tape or non-stretch cord marked off at the dividing lines.
The centre of the Clout Target shall be marked by a brightly coloured distinctive triangular flag: the CLOUT. This flag shall not measure more than 80 cm in length and 30 cm in width. The flag to be affixed to a round pole of soft wood, firmly fixed vertically in the ground, so that the lower edge of the flag shall not be more than 50 cm from the ground.
Scoring values:
The values of each scoring zone of the Clout Target, starting from the centre outwards, are:
5 – 4 – 3 – 2 – 1

563 Equipment. Refer to Article 504.

564 Range Control and Safety. Refer to Article 505.

565 Shooting. Refer to Article 506.

566 Scoring.
Scoring shall take place after every second end of three arrows.
The Field Captain shall appoint one person to hold the Clout cord, and one person for each scoring ring to collect the arrows in the ring. After all arrows are collected they are sorted according to archer's individual markings, and the arrows shall remain in that scoring ring until scored.
Each competitor shall then call the value of his arrows, commencing with those of the highest value. The Field Captain shall check that all arrows are correctly called.
Arrows must remain in or on the ground untouched until withdrawn or removed, otherwise the arrows shall not be scored.
The value of the arrows that do not stick in the ground shall be determined by the position of their points as they lie.
Arrows sticking in the CLOUT shall score five.
No archer, except the appointed arrow gatherers, shall enter the Clout Target until his name has been called to record the value of his arrows.
Ties.
Ties in the Clout events shall be decided as follows:
First by the least number of misses; if the tie is still undecided, then the least number of ones, and so on. Should all arrows be

the same the archers so tying shall be declared equal.

E) FLIGHT ARCHERY

581 Flight Shoot

The Flight Shoot consists of six arrows shot for the greatest distance. For Club, Regional and National competitions the following classes may be used:
A. Target Bow Class
B. Flight Bow Class
The B Class may be divided into the following weight classes:
Men: 50 lbs, 65 lbs, 80 lbs,
Unlimited and Foot Bow
Women: 35 lbs, 50 lbs
Unlimited and Foot Bow
Shooting shall be in one direction only.

582 Range Layout

The base line or shooting line from which the arrows are shot, and from which measurements are made, shall be at least 20 metres long.
The Range Line, which is at right angles to the shooting line, must be clearly marked by stakes from zero to 100 metres beyond the existing record. From zero to 300 metres, the stakes will be every 100 metres. From 300 metres to the end of the Range line, the stakes shall be every 25 metres.
The landing area, defined as any ground on which the arrows are expected to land, must be at least 200 metres wide. This area must be free of obstructions and hazards, such as trees, buildings, fences, ditches, etc., and should provide turf (ground) favourable for arrows to land.

583 Equipment

(a) **Target Bows** A target bow is any bow with which the competitor has shot at least two standard target or field rounds.
(b) **Flight Bows** A flight bow may be any type of held bow, other than a crossbow or mechanically assisted bow.
(c) **Other Equipment** Inter-moving drawing and release aids are not permitted.
However the following traditional flight equipment may be used:
(i) Six-gold ring.
(ii) Flipper or strap, single or double.
(iii) Block.
(iv) Sipur.
(d) **Arrows** For target bow class the competitor must use his own standard length target arrows with which he has shot at least two target or field rounds.
For the flight classes, any type of arrow may be used.
In any flight competition the arrows must bear the following identification:
(i) Name of competitor; affixed by archer.
(ii) Numbered 1 to 6; affixed by archer.
(iii) Stamp indicating class in which used; affixed by officials.
The length of an arrow shall be determined by measurement from the floor of the nock to the tip of the pile.

584 Bow Weighing Scales

Bow weighing scales must be tested within thirty days of competition by a qualified agency and must carry a stamp of this certification of accuracy.

585 Weighing-in Requirements

Except for the target bow class, the unlimited class and the foot bow class, flight bows shall be weighed as follows:
(a) Bows shall be weighed just prior to commencement of shooting.
Weight of bow, length of arrow, and the class for which this combination is eligible, shall be recorded on a label affixed to the face of the bow.
(b) The weight of the bow shall be taken at two inches less than the length of the longest arrow, and again at one inch less than the length of this arrow. The difference in these weights shall be added to the last weight of the bow at full draw.
Weighing bows at full draw is optional with the competitor.
When an overdraw device is used and permits a draw in excess of 3 cm from the back of the bow, this excess shall be considered a portion of the arrow length for bow weighing purposes.

586 Range Control & Safety

There shall be a Flight Captain, whose decision shall be final, and an assistant Flight Captain, and such other assistance as may be deemed necessary to control the competition. The officials shall be responsible for the safety of onlookers who must at all times, when shooting is in progress, be not less than ten metres behind the shooting line.

587 Shooting

Except for the foot bow, the bow must be held in the unsupported hand. Each competitor must be at least two metres from the next competitor on the shooting line. He shall shoot his six arrows without interruption. Except for the foot bow class, competitors shall shoot from a standing position with both feet behind the base line or shooting line.

An arrow shall not be deemed to have been shot if the competitor can touch it with his bow without moving his feet from their position behind the shooting line. No competitor shall have more than six arrows with him at his position behind the shooting line.

588 Scoring/Measuring

(a) Distance measurements shall be made with a steel tape along the range line. The distance shot shall be measured to that point on the range line at which a line at right angles to the range line passes through the point where the arrow enters the ground; the line should pass through the pile end of the arrow.

(b) After all shooting has been completed, only the officials and the competitors are allowed beyond the shooting line.

(c) Each competitor is provided with six white sheets of paper 20 cm square on which his name appears. The sheets are numbered one to six.

As the competitor locates his arrows, the appropriate paper is placed over the arrow to identify it. When all six arrows are located, the competitor stands by his longest shot to facilitate measuring as only his longest shot is recorded.

An alternative method would be to provide each competitor with small 8 cm by 4 cm flags fastened to pointed dowels which could be stuck into the ground beside the arrow to identify it.

(d) Measuring shall commence at the furthest arrow. In the event a competitor shoots more than six arrows, the longest shot, or shots, are disqualified.

(e) Lost arrows must be reported to the Flight Captain and a full record made to identify the missing arrows before the next event is shot.

589 Championship Tournament Regulations

(a) **Flight Shoot.** The Flight Shoot consists of six arrows shot for the greatest distances.

There shall be one unlimited class for men and one unlimited class for women.

(b) **Range.** The landing area must be at least 200 metres wide and should stretch back from the end of the range line towards the base line at least 450 metres.

(c) **Equipment**

(i) **Bows.** A flight bow may be any type of hand bow, other than a crossbow or mechanically assisted bow.

(ii) **Arrows.** Any type of arrow may be used. Arrows must bear the name of the competitor and be numbered one to six.

(iii) **Other equipment** as under Article 583 (c).

(d) **Scoring.** After all shooting has been completed, only officials, scorers and competitors are allowed beyond the shooting line.

The competitors advance to retrieve their own arrows when identified and scoring/measuring is recorded. The competitors may not carry any arrows with them when moving beyond the shooting line. Each scorer is provided with small flags 8 cm by 4 cm fastened to pointed dowels, six for each competitor, with the competitor's name thereon and numbered from one to six. As the scorer locates the competitor's arrows the appropriate flag is stuck into the ground beside the arrow to identify it. If possible there should be one scorer for each competitor. To facilitate scoring, the scorer stands beside the competitor's longest shot as only the competitor's longest shot is recorded.

Part VI
JUDGING

601 Development of Judging

(a) The Judges Committee is responsible for educating, training and approving F.I.T.A. Judges, for specifying the rules controlling their activity and for supervising same.

(b) Every year the Judges Committee shall submit to council proposals for courses for new candidates or seminars for existing candidates and Judges that they intend to hold in the following year in time for the inclusion of the expenditures in the budget.

(c) Accreditation is given separately for each F.I.T.A. discipline but a judge can be approved for more than one discipline.

(d) At every F.I.T.A. championship, the Judges Committee shall arrange a meeting, with F.I.T.A. judges and judge-candidates present, in order to discuss matters pertaining to judging and to the application of the shooting rules.

602 Sections
Judges are grouped into two sections according to the languages they speak:
(a) **International judges,** of whom is requested an adequate knowledge of at least one of the official languages of F.I.T.A.
(b) **Regional Judges,** of whom is requested an adequate knowledge of a language that is commonly understood in at least two countries beside his own; language and countries must be stated in the application.

603 Applications
(a) Applications for Judge Candidates must be submitted to the chairman of the Judges Committee with copy to General Secretary on behalf of the applicants by their Member Associations and must indicate:
(i) name of the M.A.;
(ii) name, sex, age and address of applicant;
(iii) experience: in particular practical and technical experience in archery and possible experience in judging in other sports;
(iv) experience at F.I.T.A. Championships or Major Tournaments;
(v) attendance at courses held by the Judges Committee;
(vi) languages spoken;
(vii) any additional information that could assist the Judges Committee in evaluating the aptitude of the applicant.
(b) Member Associations may obtain application forms from the Chairman of the Judges Committee.
Renewal forms will be mailed directly to judges before the expiry of their term and must be returned to the chairman of the Judges Committee with copy to General Secretary.

604 Examinations
(a) The Judges Committee shall arrange, at F.I.T.A. Championships or if necessary at other major International Tournaments, meetings for applicants to take examinations for Judge-Candidates.
(b) The examining board should be formed by at least three members of the Judges Committee, if they were not all available up to two of them can be substituted by:
(i) members of the Constitution and Rules Committee;
(ii) members of the Target Archery and/or the Field Archery Committee, as applicable; in this order of preference.
(c) Under exceptional circumstances, the Chairman of the Judges Committee may delegate, for interviewing applicants, one or more persons who will submit to the Judges Committee a full report on each applicant together with proposals to be ratified by the Committee.
(d) The Judges Committee shall immediately notify the results of examinations to each applicant, his M.A. and the Secretary General of F.I.T.A.
(e) The Judges Committee may decline applications and re-appointments without giving any reason.

605 Judge-Candidates
(a) In order to become a F.I.T.A. Judge-Candidate, an applicant must:
(i) have been approved by his M.A., in an examination on F.I.T.A. Constitution and Rules;
(ii) have been a National Judge for at least two years;
(iii) pass a theoretical and practical examination at a meeting specially arranged and announced for that purpose by the Judges Committee.
(b) After passing the examination, a Judge-Candidate must serve for at least two years before becoming a F.I.T.A. Judge.
(c) An International Judge or, where this is deemed impractical by the Judges Committee, a M.A. shall supervise the activity of the Judge-Candidate over this period and submit at the end of each year a report, with observations, to the Judges Committee.
(d) Members of the Judges Committee, International Judges or representatives of M.A. acting as supervisors of Judge-Candidates shall always be allowed on the shooting fields and courses.

606 Judges
(a) After a Judge-Candidate has worked for two years, the J.C. shall consider the reports submitted by his supervisor and

(i) accredit him as a F.I.T.A. Judge from January 1st of the following year or
(ii) recommend a further period of at least one year as Judge-Candidate or
(iii) withdraw his accreditation as Judge-Candidate.
(b) The Judges Committee shall be responsible for the renewal of judges' accreditation.

607 Accreditation
(a) The period of accreditation for Judges and Judge-Candidates is two calendar years.
(b) The Judges and Candidate Judges shall be awarded different identity cards indicating name, member association, discipline section and years of accreditation.
(c) Judges are entitled to wear the F.I.T.A. Judge badge, which is available from the Treasurer, for all the period of their accreditation.
(d) An appeal against denial of accreditation as Judge or Judge Candidate may be lodged by the person concerned with council through the General Secretary.

608 List of Judges
(a) The Judges Committee shall transmit to the General Secretary, who will circulate it to all F.I.T.A. officers, Member Associations, Judges and Judge-Candidates, a list of all Judges and Judge-Candidates specifying the disciplines approved (Article 304).
(b) On request from Member Associations, the Judges Committee shall supply an advisory list of judges for International Calendar events.

609 National Judges
(a) All M.A.s must train and approve National Judges to serve at their tournaments valid for F.I.T.A. star badges and world records and at International Calendar tournaments.
(b) Training and approval procedures shall be held in conformity with the instructions of the Judges Committee.
(c) Every year M.A.s shall compile a list of their approved National Judges and send it to the General Secretary with the announcement of their F.I.T.A. Star Tournaments for that year.

Part VII
RECORDS

701 Definition
A new Record shall be established when a Score is at least one point higher than an existing Record.

702 World Championship Tournament Records
The following World Championship Records shall be recognized:
(a) **Individuals:**
Grand Total; Double FITA Round.
Each Distance; Double FITA Round.
(b) **Teams:**
Grand Total; Double FITA Round for the best three archers from the same Member Association, Women and Men respectively.

703 Confirmation of World Championship Tournament Records
World Championship Records shall be confirmed by Congress at the Session immediately following the Tournament.

704 World Records
The following World Records shall be recognized:
(a) **Individuals:**
(i) Total, Single FITA Round
(ii) Each Distance, Single FITA Round
(iii) Grand Total, Double Indoor FITA Round I (18 metres)
(iv) Grand Total, Double Indoor FITA Round II (25 metres)
(b) **Teams:**
Total, Single FITA Round for the best three archers from the same Member Association, Women and Men respectively.
Individual World Records may be established at World Championships, Olympic Games, Continental Championships, National Championships, or National or International Tournaments conforming to Article 306, organized by, or under the control of, Member Associations.
Team World Records may be established at World Championships, Continental Championships or any Tournament as above organized by, or under the control of Member Associations, at which there is competition between National Teams of three Women or three Men.

705 Confirmation of World Records

(a) World Records shall be subject to confirmation by the Executive Committee.

(b) Scores made at World Championships and Olympic Games shall be submitted to the Executive Committee by the General Secretary.

(c) Scores made at other Tournaments shall be sent to the General Secretary no later than 30 days after the tournament in question by the Member Association under the control of which the Tournament was organized, together with a declaration covering:

(i) The name or description, place and date of the Tournament.

(ii) Confirmation that the Tournament was shot under F.I.T.A. Rules.

(iii) Confirmation that an archer, in respect of whose scores Records are being claimed, was a member of a Member Association at the time.

(iv) Name, nationality and sex of archers.

(v) Details of the Record claimed, and supported by the original score sheet or a properly witnessed copy thereof.

(d) The Executive Committee shall not ratify a claim for a World Record until 30 days after the Tournament.

(e) Should a World Record be broken by two or more equal scores made on the same day, the archers shall be declared Joint World Record Holders.

(f) FITA Round World Record holders to be presented with a Diploma stating result and place of Record.

706 Continental/Regional Championship Tournament Records

The following Continental/Regional Championship Records shall be recognized:

(a) **Individuals:**

Total, Single FITA Round.

Each Distance, Single FITA Round

(b) **Teams:**

Total, Single FITA Round for the best three Archers from the same Member Association, Women and Men respectively.

707 Confirmation of Continental/Regional Championship Tournament Records

(a) Continental/Regional Championship Records shall be subject to confirmation by the Executive Committee.

(b) Scores shall be submitted to the General Secretary by the Organizing Committee giving:

(i) Name, nationality and sex of archers.

(ii) Details of the Record claimed, and supported by the original score sheet or properly witnessed copy thereof.

708 Olympic Games Records

The following Olympic Games Records shall be recognized:

Individuals:

Grand Total, Double FITA Round.

Each Distance, Double FITA Round.

709 Confirmation of Olympic Games Records

Olympic Games Records shall be confirmed by Congress at the Session immediately following the Tournament.

710 Publication of Records

Records for Women and Men shall be kept separate.

Details of new Records shall be circulated by the General Secretary to all Member Associations and Members of the Administrative Council.

Appendix

TARGET ARCHERY SHOOTING FIELD

RECOMMENDED ARCHERY FIELD LAYOUT

FITA Round – Major Tournaments

SIZE OF FIELD depends on the number of targets, i.e. number of competitors.

Women shoot at: 70m, 60m, 50m, 30m.

Men shoot at: 90m, 70m, 50m, 30m. Article 700.

Two Target BUTTRESSES, on stands, in each lane are moved forward for each distance. Each 2-target lane is a minimum of 5 metres wide.

LANES to be clearly marked on the ground by tape or whitewash.

CLEAR LANE to be between the Women's and Men's lanes, not less than 5 metres wide.

WAITING LINE to be indicated not less than 5 metres behind the Shooting Line.

SEATING shall be provided behind the Waiting Line for the men and women competitors.
Suitable BARRIERS shall be erected round the Field to keep back spectators. At least 10 metres away from each side of Field and behind the Waiting Line. At least 25 metres behind the 90 metres Target Line.

Large SCOREBOARDS to be placed so that they are visible to both Competitors and Spectators.
VISUAL SIGNALS – TIME CONTROL.
Note: At Club Shooting the Target Buttress Line is usually permanent and the Shooting Line is moved up at each distance.

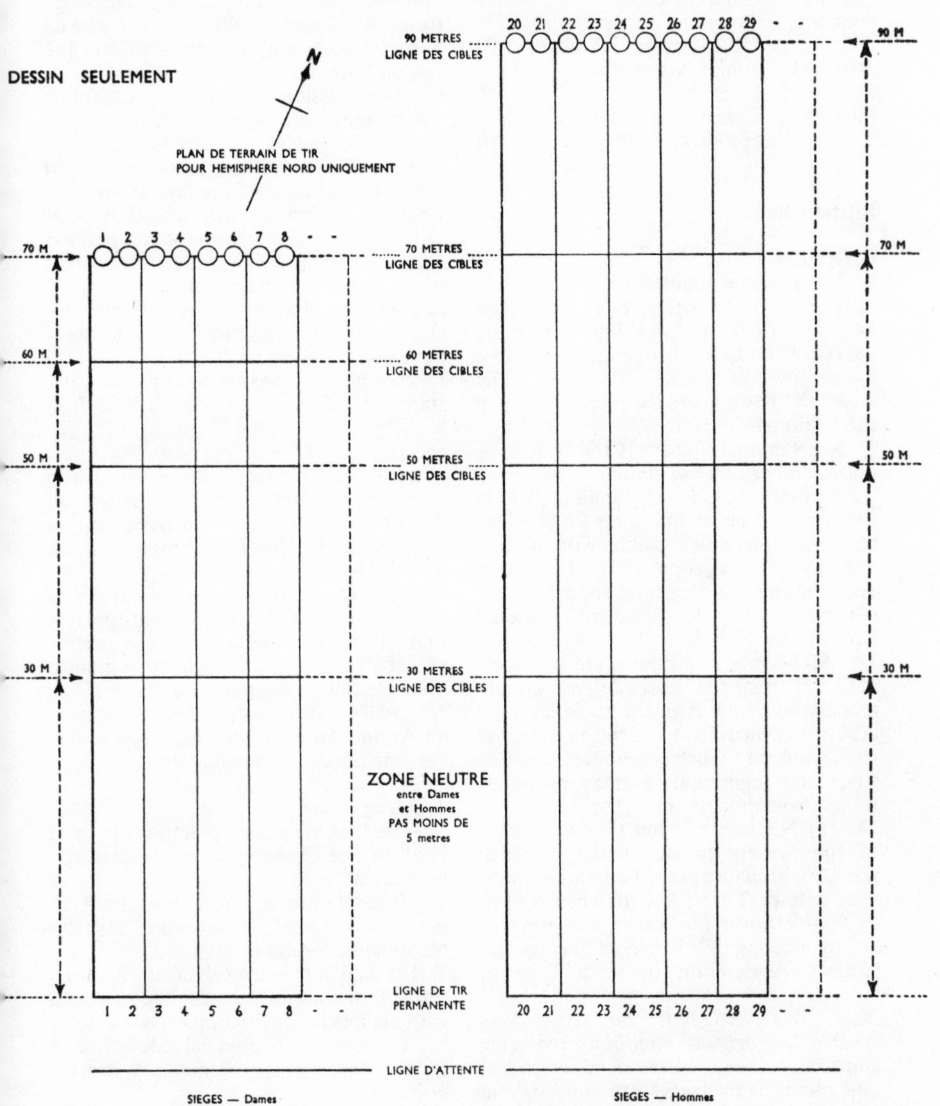

THE GRAND NATIONAL ARCHERY SOCIETY RULES OF SHOOTING

Contents

Introduction

GNAS Laws

3. The shooting regulations as prescribed in its Rules of Shooting shall be accepted as governing the relevant branches of the sport of archery throughout the area under the Society's jurisdiction. The Rules of Shooting are the responsibility of the National Council.

4. No Regional Society, County Association, archery club or similar organisation recognised by the Society shall include in its Constitution or Shooting Regulations any provisions which conflict with those of the Society. A copy of each County Associations and Regional Societies Constitution shall be deposited with National Council.

12. All Members, affiliated clubs, associated organisations, associations, county associations and regional societies shall accept the jurisdiction of the Society and shall conform to such conditions, shooting rules and regulations as may be determined from time to time.

14. (a) No archer, other than a member of the Society or one whose national society is affiliated to the Fédération Internationale de Tir à l'Arc may compete or officiate at any of the Society's meetings or at any meeting of a Regional Society or a County Association or at a Club or Association affiliated to a Regional Society. This clause does not apply to Ladies Paramount.

(b) No archer, other than a British National of the United Kingdom may be the holder of a British National Championship or of any of the challenge trophies offered at the British National Target Championship Meetings and the Grand National Archery Meeting.

(c) A professional archer may not hold a Championship title or challenge trophy nor may he receive any prize in connection with any tournament organised by or held under the auspices of the Grand National Archery Society or any affiliated body unless specifically offered for competition for professional archers only, not shooting in competition with amateurs.

A professional archer is one who uses his skill in shooting with the bow and arrow as a means of making his living.

Declaration of professionalism or reinstatement of amateur status shall be dealt with by the National Council at its discretion. (N.B. For purposes of international competition the attention of members is drawn to the Rules of Amateur Status laid down from time to time by the Fédération Internationale de Tir à l'Arc).

The implementation of any new Rules of Shooting or amendment to an existing rule that alters the intention of that existing rule shall be delayed for at least six months after ratification and publication by National Council except where it occurs at an Annual General Meeting when it shall become effective immediately.

Amateur Status

An amateur in archery practises the sport in all or one of the various branches as a leisure pursuit.

1. He shall observe the rules of the IOC, his International Federation and his National Federation.

2. He shall not have received any financial rewards or material benefits in connection with his sport participation except:

(a) He may be a physical education or sport teacher giving elementary instruction.

(b) Accept, subject to certain limitation:

(i) assistance administered through his

National Olympic Committee or National Federation.
(ii) compensation authorised by his NOC or National Federation, in case of necessity, to cover financial loss resulting from his absence from work.
(c) Accept prizes or trophies not to exceed 700 Swiss francs in value. Cash prizes are not allowed.
(d) Accept academic and technical scholarships.
3. Full details of amateur status and the IOC Eligibility Code, etc. are to be found in FITA Rules and Regulations Articles 201–205 inclusive.

Part I
TARGET ARCHERY

100 Target Faces
(a) The standard British target face is circular, 122 cm (4 ft) in diameter.
This British target face is composed as follows:
A circle in the centre 24.4 cm diameter, ringed by four concentric bands the breadth of each, measured radially being 12.2 cm.
The colours of the target face are: (from the centre outwards) gold, red, blue, black and white.
The centre of the gold is termed the 'pinhole'.
The standard FITA face is as above but each colour is divided into two zones of equal width by a line not exceeding 2 mm in width.
(b) Any dividing line which may be used between colours shall be made entirely within the higher scoring zone.
(c) Any line marking the outermost edge of the white shall be made entirely within the scoring zone.
(d) Tolerances on British faces are permitted as follows:
4 mm on the full 122 cm diameter
3 mm in any one zone of 12.2 cm
3 mm on the 24.4 cm diameter of the Gold

101 Range Layout
(a) The targets shall be set up at one end of the ground. They shall be inclined at an angle of about 15 degrees, with the pinholes 130 cm (4 ft 3 in) above the ground.
(b) Minimum spacing of target centres shall be:
Archers shooting singly 2.44 m (8 ft)
Archers shooting in pairs 3.05 m (10 ft)
Archers shooting in threes 3.66 m (12 ft)
(c) Each target shall be securely anchored so that it cannot blow off its stand. Likewise stands shall be anchored to prevent them from blowing over.
(d) All targets shall be clearly numbered.
(e) The shooting line (over which the archers shall take up their shooting positions) shall be measured from points vertically below the pinholes.
(f) Shooting marks, consisting of discs or other flat markers, shall be positioned opposite the targets at the appropriate distances. The shooting marks are to bear the number of the target opposite which they are placed.
(g) Lines at right angles to the shooting line and extending from the shooting line to the target line making lanes containing one, two or three bosses may be laid down.
(h) A waiting line shall be placed at least five yards behind the shooting line.
(i) On grounds where the public have right of access an area shall be roped off to indicate that no one can pass behind the targets within 50 yards of them. Where an efficient backstop netting, a bank or other similar device (not a hedge or penetrable fence) high enough for the top of the stop as seen from the shooting line to be at least as far above the top of the target as the gold is below the top of the target, then this distance may be reduced to 25 yards. The area to be roped shall extend from the ends of the 'safety line' so that no one can pass within 20 yards of the ends of the target line, 10 yards of the shooting line and 15 yards behind the shooting line.
(j) All tents and other shelters shall be placed at least 10 yards behind the shooting line, maintaining adequate room for the free passage of competitors and officials between the waiting line and the spectator line.
(k) Trade and refreshment areas shall be at least 25 yards behind the shooting line.

102 Equipment
Three types of bow are recognised:
(a) Bows and their accessories which conform in all respects to the following:
(i) A bow of any type may be used provided it subscribes to the accepted principle and meaning of the word bow as used in Target Archery; e.g. an article consisting of a handle (grip), riser and two flexible limbs each ending in a tip with a string nock.

The bow is braced for use by a single bowstring attached directly between the two string nocks only and, in operation, is held in one hand by its handle (grip) while the fingers of the other hand draw, hold back and release the string.

(ii) A bowstring may be made up of any number of strands of the material chosen for the purpose, with a centre serving to accommodate the drawing fingers, a nocking point to which may be added serving(s) to fit the arrow nock as necessary, and to locate this point one or two nock locators may be positioned and in each of the two ends of the bowstring a loop to be placed in the string nocks of the bow when braced.

In addition, one attachment which may not exceed a diameter of one centimetre in any direction is permitted on the string to serve as nose or lip mark.

The serving on the string must not end within the archer's vision at full draw. A bowstring must not in any way offer aid in aiming through 'peephole', marking or any other means.

(iii) An arrowrest, which can be adjustable, any movable pressure button, pressure point or arrowplate and draw check indicator may all be used on the bow provided they are not electric or electronic and do not offer an additional aid in aiming.

(iv) A bowsight, a bowmark or a point of aim on the ground for aiming is permitted, but at no time may more than one such device be used.

(1) A bowsight as attached to the bow for the purpose of aiming may allow for windage adjustment as well as elevation setting but it is subject to the following provision:

it shall not incorporate a prism or lens or other magnifying device, levelling or electric devices nor shall it provide for more than one sighting point.

An attachment to which the bowsight is fixed is permitted.

The length of any sight (ring, barrel, conical etc.) shall not exceed the minimum inside diameter of the aperture. A hood is not to exceed a length of 1 cm irrespective of shape.

(2) A bowmark is a single mark made on the bow for the purpose of aiming. Such mark may be made in pencil, tape or any other suitable marking material.

A plate or tape with distance markings may be mounted on the bow as a guide but must not in any way offer any additional aid.

(3) A point of aim on the ground is a marker placed in the shooting lane between the shooting line and the target. Such marker may not exceed a diameter of 7.5 cm and must not protrude above the ground more than 15 cm.

(v) Stabilisers and torque flight compensators on the bow are permitted provided they do not:

(1) serve as a string guide

(2) touch anything but the bow

(3) represent any obstacle to other archers as far as place on the shooting line is concerned.

(vi) Arrows of any type may be used provided they subscribe to the accepted principle and meaning of the word arrow as used in Target Archery, and that such arrows do not cause undue damage to target faces and buttresses.

An arrow consists of a shaft with head (point), nock, fletching and, if desired, cresting and/or numbers. The arrows of each archer shall be marked with the archer's name, initials or insignia and all arrows used for the same end of 3 or 6 arrows shall carry the same pattern and colour(s) of fletching, nocks and cresting (if any).

(vii) Finger protection in the form of finger stalls or tips, gloves, shooting tab or tape (plaster) to draw, hold back and release the string is permitted, provided they are smooth and with no device to help to hold and/or release the string.

Shooting tabs may be built up of several layers of any materials suitable for their use and allow for the part of the tab behind that used for drawing the string to be stiff using different materials for this build-up (the latter can be leather, plastic, metal, etc.) No shapes have been specified and no limitations in respect of size.

A separator between the fingers to prevent pinching the arrow may be used.

On the bow hand an ordinary glove, mitten or similar may be worn.

(viii) Field glasses, telescopes and other visual aids may be used for spotting arrows.

Ordinary spectacles as necessary or shooting spectacles provided they are fitted with the same lenses normally worn by the archer, and sun-glasses may be worn.

None may be fitted with microhole lenses,

glasses or similar marked in any way which can assist aiming.
(ix) Accessories are permitted such as bracers, dress shield, bowsling, belt or ground quiver, tassel and foot markers not protruding above the ground more than one centimetre.
(b) Crossbows which conform to the Rules and Conditions stated in Part V.
(c) Compound and other bows and their accessories which do not meet the requirements of para. 102(a) above.

103 Separate Styles and Conditions
(a) Bows conforming to 102(a) above.
(i) Free Style: As 102(a).
(ii) Barebow:
(1) As 102(a)(i) and the bow must be free from any protrusions, marks or blemishes or laminated pieces which could be used in aiming. The inside of the upper limb shall be without trade marks.
(2) As 102(a)(ii), except that there shall be no attachment to the string to act as a nose or lip mark or other marks to aid finger position selection.
(3) An arrowrest, arrowplate and pressure button are allowed. These may be adjustable.
(4) As 102(a)(vi) except that in Field Archery the arrows need be numbered by rings only, to be plainly visible, and at least 3mm wide and approximately 3mm spacing.
(5) As 102(a)(vii).
(6) As 102(a)(ix) except footmarkers.
(7) As 102(a)(viii) except that field glasses and other visual aids may not be used when shooting Field Rounds with unmarked distances.
(8) The following are not permitted:
Any aid for estimating distances
Any memoranda that assist in improving scores
Sights, draw check indicator and mounted stabilisers – the bow must be bare.
(iii) Traditional – As barebow except that (1) the arrows shall be made of wood except for the fletchings and they may be fitted with metallic piles and plastic nocks.
(2) the archers draw position, and the relationship of the arrow to the drawing finger must not change: i.e. face-walking and string-walking are not permitted.
(3) an arrowrest is permitted, but may not be adjustable, a pressure-button is not permitted.
(b) Crossbows (see Part V).
(c) Bows conforming to 102(c) above.
(i) Unlimited – No restrictions as to accessories, but the bow must be free and held in the hand.
(ii) Limited – The bow must be held in the hand and the string must be drawn, held back and released by the fingers of the other hand. A level, peepsight and pressure button are permitted but a scope is now allowed. A cable guard may be fitted.
(iii) Bowhunter – The bow must be held in the hand and the string must be drawn, held back and released by the fingers of the other hand. No marking or attachment may appear on the bow or string which may be used as an aid to aiming. A cable guard, one stabiliser not longer than 30.5 cm (12 in), a pressure button, and an adjustable arrowrest and plate are permitted.

104 Shooting
(a) Shooting, except in the case of permanently or semi-permanently disabled archers, shall be from an unsupported standing position, placing one foot on each side of the shooting line.
(b) (i) The order in which archers shall shoot at their respective targets shall be the order in which they appear on the target list and the drawing up of the target list shall be a matter for arrangement by the Tournament Organisers. Unless otherwise directed, No. 3 on each target shall be the Target Captain, and No. 4 the Lieutenant. The Captain shall be responsible for the orderly conduct of shooting in accordance with the Rules of Shooting.
(ii) The order of shooting in all Tournaments of Record Status shall rotate. For other Tournaments including Club Target Days, rotation shall be optional. (This rule does not apply to the Worcester Round).
(c) Six arrows shall be shot at an end. Each archer shall shoot three arrows and immediately retire and, when all on a target have shot, shall shoot three more. If an archer persists in shooting more than three arrows consecutively he may be disqualified by the Judge.
(d) In the event of an archer shooting more than six arrows at an end, the archer shall be penalised by losing the value of his best arrow(s) in the target, and such arrow(s) shall not be measured for a Gold prize.
(e) An arrow shall be deemed not to have

been shot, if the archer can touch it with his bow without moving his feet from their normal position in relation to the shooting line. In which case another arrow may be shot in its place. If another arrow is not available he may only retrieve his mis-nocked arrow with the Judge's permission.
(f) If from any cause an archer is not prepared to shoot before all have shot, such archer shall lose the benefit of that end.
(g) Archers arriving late shall not be allowed to make up any ends that they have missed.
(h) An archer shall retire from the shooting line as soon as his last arrow has been shot. The last archer on a target may, however, remain on the shooting line to keep company with another archer still shooting.
(i) Two and a half minutes shall be the maximum time for an archer to shoot three arrows, the time to start from when the archer steps on to the shooting line.
(j) Whilst an archer is on the shooting line, he shall receive no information by word or otherwise from anyone except the Judge or Field Captain(s).
(k) At any Meeting no practice is allowed on the ground the same day, except that one end of six arrows may be shot as sighters before the beginning of each day's shooting, but only after competitors have come under the Judge's orders at the Assembly. Such sighters shall not be recorded.
(l) If for any reason an archer is alone on a target he must notify the Judge who shall arrange for him to be transferred to another target or another archer to be transferred to join him.
(m) The maximum number of archers on a target shall be six.

105 Control of Shooting

(a) The Lady Paramount shall be the supreme arbitrator on all matters connected with the Tournament at which she officiates.
(b) At all times, whenever shooting takes place, it must be under the control of a Field Captain.
At larger meetings a Judge shall be appointed to take charge of the shooting. Field Captains, to whom the Judge may delegate his authority, may be appointed as necessary. If a Field Captain has not been appointed previously, the Judge may appoint any experienced archer to act in this capacity.
At Tournaments the Judge and Field Captains shall be non-shooting.
(c) The Judge shall be in sole control of the shooting and shall resolve all disputes (subject to the supreme authority of the Lady Paramount) in accordance with the Rules of Shooting.
(d) The Judge shall give the signal for assembly 15 minutes before the time appointed for shooting, and shall give the signal to start shooting. The Judge shall indicate when each end is completed, and no archer shall advance from the shooting line before receiving the signal.
(e) The Judge shall be responsible for deciding the value of all doubtful arrows when called by a Target Captain.
If an arrow or target face has been touched beforehand the arrow shall be ineligible for the higher value.
(f) The Judge shall be responsible for measuring arrows for the purpose of Gold prizes.
(g) The Judge shall be empowered to disqualify any archer if he observes any breach of the Shooting Rules or has any such breach reported to him by the Field Captain or by a Target Captain.
(h) The Judge may exchange, if shooting is being delayed by two slow archers on the same target, one of the slow archers with a quicker one from another target.
(i) The Judge may order the replacement of a faulty target, or may move the archers to another one.
(j) The Judge, in consultation with the Secretary or Organiser, shall be responsible for deciding the duration of intervals for meals, refreshments or suspension of shooting due to weather conditions, accidents or like occurrences – and further, make any other arrangement as needed in each case.
(k) The Judge shall exercise control over the use of loudspeakers and photographers so that the comfort and concentration of competitors is not disturbed. He shall also ensure that spectators are kept behind the spectator line and do not mingle with competitors. Spectators shall not go up to targets except with the permission of the Judge.
(l) At FITA Star Tournaments and World Record Status Tournaments there shall be an initial equipment inspection. At other FITA Round Tournaments an archer's

equipment shall be liable to inspection at any time.
(m) A bow may not be drawn except on the shooting line and in the direction of the target.
(n) Archers, other than those actually shooting or moving to and from the shooting line, shall remain behind the waiting line.

106 Scoring
(a) The scoring points for hits on the target face for GNAS Rounds are:
Gold 9, Red 7, Blue 5, Black 3, White 1.
The scoring points for hits on the target face for FITA Rounds are:
Inner Gold 10, Outer Gold 9, Inner Red 8, Outer Red 7, Inner Blue 6,
Outer Blue 5, Inner Black, 4 Outer Black 3, Inner White 2, Outer White 1.
The value shall be determined by the position of the arrow shaft.
(b) Archers shall identify their arrows by pointing at the nocks. Neither the arrow nor the target face shall be touched until the final decision as to score has been given and any such interference with the target or arrow shall disqualify the archer from scoring the higher value.
The Lieutenant will identify the arrows with the score called and will assist the Captain in any way that may be required No. 1 on the target shall identify the Lieutenant's score.
The duty of entering the scores on the score sheet may be shared by the archers on each target, but the Target Captain shall remain responsible for ensuring that scores are correctly recorded. The Target Captain and Lieutenant will check the score sheet and the Target Captain and the archer shall sign it as correct. The Lieutenant shall sign the Target Captain's score sheet. The attention of archers is drawn to their responsibility for ensuring that when signing score sheets the score, etc., that they sign for is correct.
(c) If an arrow touches two colours or any dividing line it shall be scored as being of that of the higher value.
(d) If any doubt or dispute shall arise it shall be decided by the Target Captain subject to appeal to the Judge.
(e) No alteration shall be made in the value of any arrow as entered on the score sheet, to the advantage of its owner, after such arrow has been drawn from the target.
Any alteration to the recorded score must be initialled by the Judge in a differing coloured ink prior to the withdrawal of the arrow from the target. No arrows shall be withdrawn from the target (without the express direction of the Captain) until all the archers' scores have been entered on the score sheet and the Captain is satisfied that they are correctly entered.
(f) If an arrow is observed to rebound from a target, the archer concerned shall draw the attention of the Judge to the fact after having shot his sixth arrow (or third if shooting in ends of 3 only) by retiring two paces from the shooting line and holding his bow above his head.
Upon the Judge satisfying himself that the claim is justified, the archer shall be permitted to shoot another arrow separately in the same end after all archers on that target have completed their normal shooting, such arrow to be numbered or preferably marked by the Judge.
To prevent frivolous bouncer claims, the archer is to be warned individually that if six original arrows were shot not including a bouncer, then his highest scoring arrow may, at the discretion of the Judge on repetition of a false claim, be deducted from that end's score. The Judge shall take part in that competitor's scoring to ensure that only the correct number of arrows are scored, and that the bouncer was not caused by striking another arrow already in the target. An arrow passing through a target cannot be scored.
(g) An arrow passing through the target face but remaining in the boss shall be withdrawn by the Captain or Lieutenant and shall be inserted from the back in the same place and at the assumed angle of original penetration until the pile is visible in the target face, when the score shall be determined.
(h) An arrow hitting and remaining embedded in another arrow shall be scored the same as the arrow struck.
(i) An arrow in the target, which has or may have been deflected by another arrow already in the target, shall be scored according to the position of its shaft in the target face.
(j) An arrow on the ground believed to have hit and rebounded from another arrow shall be scored the value of the struck arrow, if the latter is found in the target with its nock damaged in a compatible manner.

(k) If an arrow fails to enter the buttress and is hanging in the target face, it shall be pushed in by the Judge or shall be removed and the Judge will ensure that the appropriate score is recorded when scoring takes place.
(l) The FITA Rule that bouncers shall only be scored if arrow holes on the target face are marked applies to all FITA Rounds shot including those shot at Club Target Days, inter-county matches, etc. (see 108(c)).
(m) An archer may delegate another archer on the same target to record his score and pick up his arrows.
(n) An incapacitated archer may nominate an assistant, who shall be under the control and discipline of the Judge, to record his score and pick up his arrows.
(o) In the event of a tie for a score prize the winner shall be the one of those who tie who has the greatest number of hits. Should this result in a tie the prize shall be awarded to the archer among those who tie who has the greatest number of Golds. Should this number also be the same the archers shall be declared joint winners. Where the prize is for (i) most hits, or (ii) most Golds, ties shall be resolved on the above principle in the following order (i) highest score, most Golds, (ii) highest score, most hits.
(p) When a shoot (other than the annual Grand National Archery Meeting) is abandoned due to adverse weather conditions, the placings and prizes shall be awarded on the cumulative score at the conclusion of the last full end shot by the competitors, by instruction of the Judge.
(q) Bows which are recognised in Rule 102(b) & (c) MAY NOT BE USED IN DIRECT COMPETITION with bows recognised in Rule 102(a). Archers using bows recognised in Rule 102(b) & (c) shall not be eligible for any prize, medal, trophy or other award, classification, handicap or other distinction which has not been specifically devised or designated for archers using such bows.
The allocation of any prize, medal, trophy or other award shall be a matter for each individual tournament organiser. Classification, handicap or other distinction shall remain the sole prerogative of the Grand National Archery Society.

107 Dress Regulations

(a) At all Tournaments with National Record Status members of the Society shooting and officiating are required to wear the accepted dress.
(b) (i) Ladies are required to wear a dress or skirt or trousers (slacks) with suitable blouse.
(ii) Gentlemen are required to wear full length trousers and long or short sleeved shirts.
(iii) Sweaters/cardigans/blazers may be worn.
Each garment shall be plain dark green or white. There is no objection to wearing green and white garments together.
Waterproof clothing worn only during inclement weather is not subject to these regulations, but both white and green waterproofs are available and are recommended.
(c) Footwear must be worn by all competitors at all times during the Tournament.
(d) Advertising material must not be carried or worn. The name/emblem of an archer's Country, Regional or County Association or Club may be worn on the uniform or shooting clothes.
(e) Any archer not conforming to the above regulations shall be requested by the Judge and Organiser to leave the shooting line and will not be permitted to shoot.

108 Recognised Rounds for Record Classification and Handicap Purposes

(a) The following Rounds are recognised by the Society:
YORK
6 dozen arrows at 100 yards
4 dozen arrows at 80 yards
2 dozen arrows at 60 yards
ST GEORGE
3 dozen arrows at 100 yards
3 dozen arrows at 80 yards
3 dozen arrows at 60 yards
NEW WESTERN
4 dozen arrows at 100 yards
4 dozen arrows at 80 yards
WESTERN
4 dozen arrows at 60 yards
4 dozen arrows at 50 yards
NATIONAL
4 dozen arrows at 60 yards
2 dozen arrows at 50 yards
WINDSOR
3 dozen arrows at 60 yards
3 dozen arrows at 50 yards
3 dozen arrows at 40 yards

NEW NATIONAL
4 dozen arrows at 100 yards
2 dozen arrows at 80 yards
HEREFORD
6 dozen arrows at 80 yards
4 dozen arrows at 60 yards
2 dozen arrows at 50 yards
ALBION
3 dozen arrows at 80 yards
3 dozen arrows at 60 yards
3 dozen arrows at 50 yards
LONG WESTERN
4 dozen arrows at 80 yards
4 dozen arrows at 60 yards
LONG NATIONAL
4 dozen arrows at 80 yards
2 dozen arrows at 60 yards
LONG METRIC (Gentlemen)
3 dozen arrows at 90 metres
3 dozen arrows at 70 metres
AMERICAN
30 arrows at 60 yards
30 arrows at 50 yards
30 arrows at 40 yards
FITA (Gentlemen)
3 dozen arrows at 90 metres
3 dozen arrows at 70 metres
3 dozen arrows at 50 metres
3 dozen arrows at 30 metres
FITA (Ladies)
3 dozen arrows at 70 metres
3 dozen arrows at 60 metres
3 dozen arrows at 50 metres
3 dozen arrows at 30 metres
SHORT METRIC
3 dozen arrows at 50 metres
3 dozen arrows at 30 metres
LONG METRIC (Ladies)
3 dozen arrows at 70 metres
3 dozen arrows at 60 metres

(b) In every round the longer, or longest distance is shot first, and the shorter, or shortest distance last.

(c) When FITA and Metric Rounds are shot, FITA Rules apply.

At the Organiser's discretion a higher standard of control can be adopted from the minimum standards set out below.

(i) Club Target Days and Minor Tournaments without Record Status:

Arrow holes will not be marked.

Bouncers cannot be re-shot and will not score.

FITA Rules Articles 150 only shall apply.

(ii) All Tournaments with British Record Status:

Arrow holes will be marked.

If Visual Time Control is not available then Time Control must be applied in the following manner:

2 audible signals for archers in the first detail to take their position on the shooting line.

After 20 seconds one audible signal for shooting to commence.

After 2½ minutes (or earlier if shooting line is clear) 2 audible signals indicate that the archers remaining on the shooting line shall retire and the next detail take their place.

After 20 seconds one audible signal for the second detail to commence shooting.

And so continue until both details have shot their two ends (or one depending on the distances being shot) when 3 audible signals shall indicate that archers are to move forward to score and collect arrows.

At any time a competitor indicates a rebound then shooting is interrupted strictly in accordance with the procedure set out in FITA Rules Article 508(i).

(iii) FITA Star Tournaments:

Visual Time Control shall be adopted as set out in FITA Rules Article 507.

Automatic timing devices need not be incorporated into any adequately designed light system.

Rebounds shall be scored (FITA Rules Article 508(i)).

(iv) FITA Star Tournaments with World Record Status:

FITA requires conditions as near to World Championship standards as can reasonably be attained.

Visual Time Control shall be used.

(d) (i) A FITA Round may be shot in one day or over two consecutive days under FITA Rules.

(ii) All other Rounds to be shot in one day. (Except in accordance with Rule for Championships of more than one day's duration.)

(e) In addition any 'local' round made up of other numbers of arrows at specified distances may be used in Clubs and Tournaments provided the Rules of Shooting are adhered to in all respects and subject to their non-recognition by the GNAS for Record, Classification or Handicap purposes.

109 Club Events

(a) **Club Target Day**

(i) A Target Day is any day and time appointed under the Rules of the Club and previously announced to the Members.

(ii) There is no statutory limit to the number of officially appointed Target Days in any one week.
(iii) All scores made must be entered in the Club Record Book.
(iv) Target Days should commence punctually at the announced time.
(v) All shooting shall be in accordance with GNAS Rules of Shooting.
(vi) On any Club Target Day there shall be a minimum of two archers shooting, not necessarily on the same Target, each recording the other's scores in order that these scores may be recognised. An archer shooting alone may claim his score provided that it has been recorded throughout by a non-shooting archer.
(b) **Open Meeting**
An Open Meeting is an event run as a competition open to all Members of GNAS, and FITA Affiliated Members, with all the necessary organisation, advertising of the event, judging, etc., run under GNAS Rules of Shooting.
(c) **Tournament**
A Tournament is an Event at which awards are given. This may be an Open or Closed Meeting.

110 Six Gold Badge
(a) The award, which is for six consecutive arrows shot at one end into the Gold, is open to Members of the Society.
(b) The shortest distances at which it may be gained are:
Gentlemen – 80 yards Ladies – 60 yards
(c) In the FITA Round the badge will be awarded for six consecutive arrows at one end shot into the Gold zone at:
Gentlemen – 90 or 70 metres Ladies – 70 or 60 metres
(d) The Six Gold End must be made at a Meeting organised by the Society or by any of its associated bodies, or in competition at an Associated Club's Target Day, under GNAS Rules of Shooting.
(e) Claims for the award must be submitted to the GNAS Secretary on the appropriate form, accompanied by the original score sheet duly signed by the Club Secretary or Meeting Organiser.
(f) An Archer is entitled to only one Six Gold Badge but Junior holders of the Badge are also entitled to hold a Senior Badge.
(g) The shortest distance at which the Junior Six Gold Badge may be awarded is the middle distance in the National Championship Round for each age group.

111 FITA Star Badge
The award is open to Members of the Society according to qualifications and applications as laid down in FITA Rules. Claims for the award must be submitted to the GNAS Secretary on the appropriate form.

120 Regulations for the Grand National Archery Meeting
(a) The meeting shall consist of not less than three days' shooting, weather permitting, during which a Handicap Meeting may be held.
(b) A lady shall be invited to officiate as Lady Paramount by the Secretary after consultation with the National Council.
(c) The Judges shall be appointed by National Council.

121 Rounds
(a) The Ladies' Meeting shall consist of:
Two Hereford Rounds. Ladies may enter for the National Round only.
(b) The Gentlemen's Meeting shall consist of:
Two York Rounds.

122 Winners
The winners shall be those Archers obtaining the greatest scores over the Double Hereford and York Rounds respectively. In the event of a tie the archer making the greatest number of hits amongst those who have ties shall be the winner. In the event of this resulting in a tie the winner shall be the one of those who tie who has the greatest number of Golds. Should this number also be the same the archers shall be declared joint winners.

123 Shooting
If, owing to the state of the weather, the full number of arrows is not shot on the first or second day, the remaining arrows shall, if possible, be shot on the next day, providing that not more than eighteen dozen arrows are shot in any one day. The Judge in consultation with the Secretary (Organiser) and Field Captain shall decide whether any other Competitions shall be cancelled.

124 Challenge Trophies and Prizes
(a) The Challenge Trophies are open only to British Nationals of the United

Kingdom. Unless the winner is permanently resident in the United Kingdom the trophy shall remain in the custody of the Society. Any question as to the residence of the winner shall be decided by the National Council, whose decision shall be final.
(b) No awards shall be made unless one complete Round is shot, and if the Double Round be incomplete, the prizes and Challenge Trophies shall be awarded on the one round only that has been completed.
(c) Certain Challenge Trophies, i.e. those of the original National Round Championships, will be awarded on the two National Rounds. All Ladies will be competing for these.
(d) (i) The County Challenge Trophies shall be awarded to the County Teams making the highest aggregate scores at the Championship Meeting. The archer making the highest score in a winning team shall be entitled to hold the Trophy until the next meeting.
(ii) Each County's teams score shall consist of the four, or fewer highest scores made by the Ladies and Gentlemen respectively competing at the Championship Meeting.
(iii) Archers competing who are affiliated to the Society through one of its Affiliated Clubs (Associate Member) shall shoot for the County through which their GNAS Affiliation Fees are paid.
Archers competing who are Ordinary Members of the Society, or whose GNAS Affiliation Fees are paid through an Associated Organisation of GNAS shall notify the GNAS Secretary and the Secretary of the County concerned by 1st January in each year of the County for which they wish to shoot.
If, since the payment of GNAS Affiliation Fees, an Archer changes his Club because of a change in his private residence, and the new Club is situated in a different County he may, by notifying the GNAS Secretary and the County Secretaries concerned, shoot for his new County.
ALWAYS PROVIDING THAT IN THE YEAR 1st JANUARY–31st DECEMBER THE ARCHER DOES NOT SHOOT FOR THE CHAMPIONSHIP TITLES OF MORE THAN ONE COUNTY.
(e) No archer shall take more than one prize offered by the Society (the Challenge Trophies excepted) in any one Competition. Any archer who has won one or more of the Society's Medals is expected to wear one at least at every subsequent Championship or Handicap Meeting at which he shall compete.

140 Regulations for the British National Target Championship
(a) The Annual Championship shall consist of not less than two days shooting, weather permitting.
(b) A lady shall be invited to officiate as Lady Paramount by the Secretary after consultation with the National Council.
(c) The Judges shall be appointed by National Council.

141 Rounds
(a) The Ladies' Championship shall consist of two Hereford Rounds.
(b) The Gentlemen's Championship shall consist of two York Rounds.

142 Titles
The Championship Titles are open only to British Nationals of the United Kingdom and shall be awarded to the archers obtaining the greatest scores over the Double Hereford and York Rounds respectively. In the event of a tie the archer making the greatest number of hits amongst those who have ties shall be the Champion. In the event of this resulting in a tie the Champion shall be the one of those who tie who has the greatest number of Golds. Should this number also be the same the archers shall be declared joint Champions.

143 Shooting
If, owing to the state of the weather, the full number of arrows is not shot on the first day, the remaining arrows shall, if possible, be shot on the second day. If, owing to the state of the weather, a full Round cannot be shot the Judge in consultation with the Tournament Organiser and Field Captain shall determine at which point the Champions shall be declared.

144 Challenge Trophies
(a) The Challenge Trophies are open only to British Nationals of the United Kingdom. Unless the winner is permanently resident in the United Kingdom the trophy shall remain in the custody of the Society. Any question as to the residence of the winner shall be decided by the

National Council, whose decision shall be final.
(b) The Regional and County Challenge Trophies and/or medals shall be awarded to the respective teams making the highest aggregate scores at the Championship Meeting. The archer making the highest score in a winning team shall be entitled to hold the trophy until the next meeting. Each team's score shall consist of the four, or fewer, highest scores made by Ladies and/or Gentlemen competing at the Championship Meeting.
(c) The County and Region for which an archer shall shoot shall be determined by applying Rule 124(d)(iii).

160 Regulations for the UK Masters' Tournament
The UK Masters' Tournament is held annually, usually during the second weekend in June. The Tournament is by invitation only to:
(a) All Grand Master Bowmen, Master Bowmen and Junior Master Bowmen.
(b) Archers from FITA Member Associations.
(c) Archers nominated by the GNAS Target Selection Committee.

161 Rounds
A single FITA Round shall be shot over two consecutive days under FITA Target Archery Rules.

162 Titles
No titles are awarded.

163 Challenge Trophies
The Challenge Trophies are open to all competitors under the conditions stated in 124(a).

180 Indoor Target Archery

181 Recognised Rounds
The following Rounds are recognised by the Society:
(a) **Stafford Round:** 6 dozen arrows at 30 metres at an 80 cm target face.
(b) **Portsmouth Round:** 5 dozen arrows at 20 yards at a 60 cm target face.
(c) **Worcester Round:** 5 dozen arrows at 20 yards at a 40.64 cm (16 in) target face.
(d) **FITA Round I:** 30 arrows at 18 metres at a 40 cm target face.
(e) **FITA Round II:** 30 arrows at 25 metres at a 60 cm target face.
(f) In addition any 'local' round made up of other numbers of arrows at specified distances may be used in Clubs and Tournaments provided the Rules of Shooting are adhered to in all respects and subject to their non-recognition by the GNAS for record, classification or handicap purposes.

182 Regulations for the Stafford and Portsmouth Rounds
The Rules of Target Archery shall apply with the following exceptions.
(a) **Target Faces.** The target faces used shall be:
(i) Stafford Round: 80 cm diameter 10 zone at a distance of 30 metres (standard FITA target face).
(ii) Portsmouth Round: 60 cm diameter 10 zone at a distance of 20 yards (standard coloured and zoned).
(iii) Tolerances on 80 cm and 60 cm target faces shall not exceed 2 mm on any one zone and 3 mm on the diameter of each target face.
(b) **Range Layout.** Target centres shall be placed so as to allow archers to stand at a minimum of 0.91 m (3 ft) intervals while shooting.
(c) **Shooting**
(i) Archers may shoot singly or in pairs provided that Rule 182(b) is complied with. Archers shall rotate the order of shooting when shooting singly, and alternate when shooting in pairs.
(ii) An end shall consist of 3 arrows.
(iii) 3 Sighter arrows shall be shot.
(d) **Scoring**
The scoring points for hits on the target reading from the inner Gold to the outer White are 10, 9, 8, 7, 6, 5, 4, 3, 2, 1.

183 Regulations for the Worcester Round
The Rules of Target Archery shall apply with the following exceptions:
(a) **Target Faces**
(i) The target faces used shall be circular 40.64 cm (16 in) in diameter.
This target face is composed as follows:
A circle in the centre 8.13 cm (3⅓ in) diameter ringed by four concentric bands, the breadth of each measured radially being 4.064 cm (1 3/5 in).
The centre circle shall be coloured white and the four concentric bands black. The concentric bands shall be divided by white lines. Each of the white dividing lines shall be of no greater width than 1 mm (0.04 in).

(ii) Tolerances on target faces are permitted as follows:
2 mm (0.08 in) on each zone and 2 mm (0.08 in) on full 40.64 cm (16 in) diameter.
(b) **Range Layout**
(i) The centres of the target bosses on which the target faces are affixed shall be placed so as to allow archers to stand at a minimum of 0.91 m (3 ft) intervals while shooting.
(ii) The shooting line (over which the archers shall take up their shooting positions) shall be measured from points vertically below the centre of the target boss on which target faces are affixed.
(c) **Shooting**
(i) Five arrows shall be shot at an end. Each archer will shoot his five arrows before retiring from the shooting line.
(ii) In the event of an archer shooting more than five arrows at an end the archer shall be penalised by losing the value of his best arrow(s) in the target.
(iii) At any meeting no practice is allowed except that one end of five arrows may be shot as sighters.
(iv) The maximum number of archers on a target boss shall be four.
(v) Five minutes shall be the maximum time for an archer to shoot an end. The time to start from when the archer steps on to the shooting line.

(d) **Scoring**
The scoring points for hits on the target face are: 5, 4, 3, 2, 1, reading from the centre white circle.
(e) **Recognised Round**
(i) The Round shall consist of 12 ends (60 arrows).
(ii) The distance to be shot is twenty yards.
(iii) Each boss shall hold four target faces.
(iv) Target faces shall be arranged thus:
1 2
3 4
(v) Two archers of a group shall shoot five arrows when the second group shall then shoot their five arrows.
(vi) The first group of two archers shall shoot at the higher targets; the second group at the lower targets.
(vii) When all archers have shot 30 arrows those who have been shooting at the lower targets shall change to the higher targets and those who have been shooting at the higher targets shall shoot at the lower targets, thus:
Those who have been shooting on targets 1 and 2 shall shoot the remaining 30 arrows on targets 3 and 4 retaining their same shooting positions.

184 Regulations for the FITA Rounds I and II
(a) FITA Rules 521–525 will apply.
(b) **Shooting and Scoring**
(i) Each archer shall shoot his arrows in ends of three.
(ii) Two ends of sighter arrows are permitted each day preceding the commencement of shooting.
(iii) Scoring shall take place after each end of three arrows.
(c) **Other Rules and Regulations**
In all other aspects the rules of Target Archery shall apply except that the two and a half minute time limit for shooting three arrows may not be extended.
If space does not permit a waiting line may be omitted.

185 Regulations for the National Indoor Championship Meeting
(a) The Stafford Round shall be shot at the National Championship Meeting.
(b) Regulations for National Championship Meetings, Rules 140–144 apply as appropriate.
(c) National Records may be established according to Part VIII.

Part II
FIELD ARCHERY

200 Regulations
(a) GNAS Rules of Shooting 102, 103, 201–206 shall apply to GNAS recognised Rounds and any other traditional or local round run under the GNAS Rules of Shooting.
(b) At National Record Status and FITA Round events at and above County Championship level there shall be an initial equipment inspection. At such meetings an archer's equipment shall be liable to inspection at any time.

201 General Field Archery Rules
(a) Judges shall be appointed, working under a Field Captain to be in control of the shoot.
(b) The duties of the Field Captain and Judges shall be:
(i) to ensure that adequate safety pre-

cautions have been observed in the lay-out of the course and practice area (if any).
(ii) to address the assembled competitors before the shoot commences on safety precautions and any other appropriate matter including the method of starting the event, the starting points of each group, etc.
(iii) to ensure that all competitors are conversant with the rules of the competition and the method of scoring.
(iv) to resolve disputes or queries that may arise in interpretation of the rules or other matters.
(c) Each shooting group shall consist of not more than six and not less than three archers, one of which shall be designated Target Captain and two others as scorers.
(d) The Target Captain shall be responsible for the orderly conduct of shooting within the group, and have the ultimate responsibility for scoring the arrows.
(e) Each scorer shall be supplied with and complete a separate set of score cards for the shooting group and the duties of scorers shall be as follows:
(i) to write down the score of each competitor in the group.
(ii) to complete the score card at the end of the shooting.
(iii) to be responsible for deciding the value of each arrow, in the case of a dispute a Judge shall make the final decision.
(f) The score cards shall be signed by the scorer at the end of shooting, and by the archer as an acceptance of the final score.
(g) Should the two score cards not agree, then the lower score shall be taken as the result.
(h) The use of binoculars and other visual aids is not permitted in GNAS Field Archery rounds and FITA unmarked rounds.
(i) The archer's more forward foot must be in contact and behind the shooting post while shooting, except in the FITA Hunter, the FITA Field and the FITA Combination Rounds when the archer shall stand with both feet behind the relevant shooting line, which is an imaginary line parallel to the target through the shooting post.
(j) If, in competitions where the Targets have not been marked, an arrow is observed to bounce from, or is believed to have passed through the target face, the Field Captain or a member of the Technical Commission shall be called prior to any other arrows being shot at the target The Field Captain or member of the Technical Commission shall check it and if it appears that the arrow has bounced from or passed through the target face then another arrow may be shot at that target from the same position as the bouncing or passing through arrow was shot.
(k) An arrow shall be deemed not to have been shot, if the archer can touch it with his bow without moving his feet from their normal position in relation to the shooting line. In which case another arrow may be shot in its place. If another arrow is not available he may only retrieve his misnocked arrow with the Judge's permission.
(l) Archers waiting their turn to shoot shall stand well back behind the archers who are shooting.

202 Specific Rules Relating to the GNAS 'Recognised' Rounds

(a) **Foresters Round**
The standard Unit shall consist of the following 14 shots:
Three 24″ diameter faces at a distance of up to 70 yards.
Four 18″ diameter faces at a distance of up to 50 yards.
Four 12″ diameter faces at a distance of up to 40 yards.
Three 6″ diameter faces at a distance of up to 20 yards.
Targets. The target faces shall be of animal or bird design, and shall have inscribed on them an outer circle of fixed diameter, an inner circle of half that diameter, and a spot of one sixth that diameter.
Thus: 24″ Face 12″ Inner Circle. 4″ Spot
18″ Face 9″ Inner Circle. 3″ Spot
12″ Face 6″ Inner Circle. 2″ Spot
6″ Face 3″ Inner Circle. 1″ Spot
Shooting Rules. At a 24″ Target, four arrows are shot, one from each of four posts. At an 18″ Target, three arrows are shot one from each of three posts. At a 12″ Target, two arrows are shot one from each of two posts. At a 6″ Target, only one arrow is shot from one post. Multi-post shots may be equidistant from the target or 'walk-up' or 'walk-away'.
Scoring Aiming spot – 15 points
Inner circle – 10 points
Outer circle – 5 points
Range Marking. In either Marked or Unmarked distances.

(b) **Four Shot Foresters Round**

Shooting: On Forester animal faces, over unmarked Forester distances.

Shots: Four walk-up shots at each face.

Scoring: 15, 10 and 5 for spot, inner and outer respectively.

Unit: Fourteen faces in each unit (3 × 24″; 4 × 18″; 4 × 12″; 3 × 6″) – 112 shots, maximum possible score 1680.

Dimensions Spot: one-sixth of the outer diameter.
of Scoring Inner: half the outer diameter.
Zones:

(c) **Big Game Round**

The standard Unit shall consist of the following 14 shots, at the suggested ranges:

Three group 1 Targets at a distance of 70 to 40 yards.

Three group 2 Targets at a distance of 50 to 30 yards.

Four group 3 Targets at a distance of 40 to 20 yards.

Four group 4 Targets at a distance of 30 to 10 yards.

Targets. The target faces shall be of animal or bird design, with the scoring area divided into two parts. The high-scoring area, is the smaller area, situated in the 'heart/lung' region of the animal, and is known as the 'kill' zone. The low-scoring area, is the remainder of the animal within the marked perimeter, and is known as the 'wound' zone. Targets are classed into groups one, two, three and four, according to size.

Group 1. 40″ × 28″ – Bear, deer, moose, elk, caribou.

Group 2. 28″ × 22″ – Antelope, small deer, wolf, mountain lion.

Group 3. 22″ × 14″ – Coyote, javelina, turkey, fox, goose, wildcat, pheasant.

Group 4. 14″ × 11″ – Turtle, duck, grouse, crow, skunk, jackrabbit, woodchuck.

Any animal or bird consistent in size with a particular group may be used.

Shooting Rules. Three shots are permitted at each target, one from each of three posts, each successive post being closer to the target than the previous one.

Arrows shall be identifiable as to order of shooting. The archer shall stop shooting as soon as a hit is considered to have been made.

Scoring. The score is decided by the position of the arrow in the Target (i.e. in the 'kill' or 'wound' zone) and the number of arrows shot.

	Kill	Wound
1st arrow score	20	16
2nd arrow score	14	10
3rd arrow score	8	4

Only the score of the first scoring arrow counts.

Range Marking. In either Marked or Unmarked distances.

(d) **The National Animal Round**

The standard unit shall consist of 16 targets, and two units, mixed so that all the targets of one unit are not consecutive, shall comprise the round. The distances shall not be marked.

Targets. The target faces shall be of an animal or bird design, and shall have described upon them a circle of either 30, 22.5, 15 or 7.5 cm diameter according to the size of the animal picture and in the heart/lung region. The higher scoring area (the kill zone) shall be within the circle and the remainder of the animal shall be the lower scoring area (the wound zone).

The course shall be laid out so that each unit shall consist of the following targets set within the prescribed range, and the aggregate distance shot at each target face size shall be within the prescribed distances

No. of faces	Kill zone diam.	Distance range	Aggregate distance	Allowance (+ or –)
4	30 cm	55–30 m	320 m	16 m
4	22.5 cm	45–20 m	240 m	12 m
4	15 cm	35–10 m	160 m	9 m
4	7.5 cm	20– 5 m	80 m	4 m

The total distance shot shall be 800 m plus or minus 20 m for the whole unit.

Shooting. Two arrows shall be shot at each target, one from each of two posts set within the prescribed range.

Scoring. Kill zone – 10 points; wound zone – 5 points.

N.B. Swedish Big Game round faces fulfil the requirements set out above, and shall be used at National Record Status events.

(e) **The FITA Rounds**

(1) Rules as given in the FITA Constitution and Rules shall apply to the rounds listed below, when these rounds are shot at events with National Record Status, in respect of the following:

(i) the arrangement of the 15 and 30 cm faces.

(ii) the time permitted to shoot an arrow.

(iii) the 'Course Layout' (Article 546 dated 1/1/83).

(iv) the shooting order rotation.

(v) the inspection of archer's equipment.
(vi) the scoring of arrows.
(2) The FITA Hunter round.
(3) The FITA Field round.
(4) The FITA Combination round. This round shall consist of one Hunter (unmarked distances) unit and one Field (marked distances) unit laid out consecutively and not shot over the same ground. Binoculars or other visual aids are not permitted to be used or carried during the Hunter unit. This round is a GNAS round and is not recognised as such by FITA.

203 Other Rounds
Traditional or local rounds involving differing targets and methods of scoring may be shot in either Club or Open Competition providing that the GNAS rules affecting safety are observed and that the rules are made known to all competitors before shooting starts.

204 Separate Classes and Styles
(a) There shall be separate classes for Ladies, Gentlemen and Juniors (see Rule 704).
(b) Styles as defined in Rule 103.

205 Juniors
Where Juniors under 15 years of age shoot in a group containing archers above this age, the Juniors shall shoot last. For other Junior Rules see Part VII and 806(c).

206 Regulations for the National Field Archery Championship Meeting
(a) The Championship shall be held annually and shall consist of one Hunter round and one Field round shot over two days.
(b) The Championship shall be shot according to GNAS rule 202 (e).
(c) The National Championship Titles and awards shall be open to members of the GNAS only.
(d) The Open Championship Titles and awards shall be open to all competitors from FITA Member Associations.
(e) Unless the winner of any trophy is permanently resident in the UK the trophies shall remain in the custody of the Society at its Headquarters.
(f) The Judges for the event shall be appointed by National Council.

Part III
FLIGHT SHOOTING

300 Basis
(a) The three classes for which competitions may take place are:
A. Target Bows.
B. Flight Bows.
C. Free-style.
Ladies, Gentlemen and Juniors may compete equally in each class.
(b) The Classes may be subdivided into bow weights, as follows:
1–16 kg (35 lb)
2–23 kg (50 lb).
3–Unlimited.
Except for the target bow and unlimited classes flight bows shall be weighed as follows:
(i) Bows shall be weighed just prior to commencement of shooting. Weight of bow, length of arrow, and the class for which this combination is eligible, shall be recorded on a label affixed to the face of the bow.
(ii) The weight of the bow shall be taken at two inches less than the length of the longest arrow, and again at one inch less than the length of this arrow. The difference in these weights shall be added to the last weight of the bow at full draw.
Weighing bows at full draw is optional with the competitor. When an overdraw device is used and permits a draw in excess of one inch from the back of the bow, this excess shall be considered a portion of the arrow length for bow weighing purposes.
(c) For classes A and B only hand bows may be used and the bow must be held in the unsupported hand.
(d) If competitions for both Target and Flight Bows are being held on the same occasion, all shooting with Target Bows must be completed first.

301 Range Layout
(a) The Range Line, at right angles to the shooting line shall be clearly marked at 150 yards then at 50 yard intervals to at least 50 yards beyond the existing National Record Distance.
(b) Red warning flags shall be placed at each side of the range at 75 yards from the line of distance markers at a distance of 150 yards from the shooting line.

302 Equipment
(a) A Target Bow is any bow with which

the user has shot at least two standard Target or Field Rounds. In the event of a breakage, a similar bow may be used as replacement.
(b) Any type of bow, other than a cross-bow, may be entered for Classes B and C.
(c) In the Target Bow class competitors must use their own length standard Target arrows and normal tab or shooting glove.
(d) In Classes B and C any type of arrow may be used.
(e) Sipurs are not permitted in Class A.
(f) Mechanical releases, inter-moving drawing and/or release aids are prohibited.
The following may be used in Classes B and C:
Six-gold ring, Flipper or Strap (single or double), block sipur, and angle measuring device.
(g) In the event of a breakage a substitute bow or limb may be used providing it is checked for conforming to its class. In the event of this not being done the archer will automatically be transferred to the unlimited class.

303 Shooting
(a) Competitors should be at least six feet apart, and must not advance their leading foot over the shooting line.
(b) Each competitor may have one assistant or adviser, who must keep at least one yard behind the shooting line.
(c) (i) At least four ends, each of three arrows, will be shot.
(ii) After all classes have shot the first end competitors and officials will go forward. Competitors will stand by their furthest arrow. A marker with a label attached bearing the name of the competitor and class will then be placed at the pile end of the furthest arrow in each class.
(iii) Arrows will then be withdrawn.
(iv) Succeeding ends will then be shot and markers adjusted where necessary.

304 Control of Shooting
There shall be a Range Captain in charge who will act as Referee and Judge. His decision shall be final. He will also be responsible for the safety of spectators, who must at all times, when shooting is in progress, be not less than 10 yards behind the shooting line.

305 Measurements
Measurement of distances shall be made with a steel tape along the range line. The distances shot shall be measured to that point on the range line at which a line at right angles to the range line passes the point where the arrow enters the ground. If the arrow is lying on the ground the line should pass through the pile end of the arrow.

Part IV
CLOUT SHOOTING

400 Regulations
The Rules of Target Archery shall apply except as enumerated in the following paragraphs.
The Organisers shall take all reasonable steps to ensure that there be no risk occasioned to people, animals or property from arrows that miss the arget area by overshot or to either side (N.B. a distance of 75 yards from the Clout centre to the boundary of any land to which the public has access is deemed reasonable).

401 Targets
The centre of the Target shall be marked by a brightly coloured distinctive flag 12″ square, set as close as practicable to ground level on a smooth vertical stick. The stick should not project above the flag.

402 Shooting
(a) Shooting may be either 'two way' or 'one way'.
(b) Six sighter arrows shall be shot in each direction when shooting two ways.
(c) The Organiser, after considering general safety, archers' comfort and the duties of scorers, shall use his discretion as to the number of archers allocated to each target.

403 Scoring
(a) Scores shall be determined according to the distance of arrows at point of entry in ground from centre of flag stick.
Within a radius of 18 inches – 5 points
3 feet – 4 points
6 feet – 3 points
9 feet – 2 points
12 feet – 1 point
Arrows which have hit and remain embedded in the Clout shall score 5 provided they are not embedded in a lower scoring ring whereupon they shall score

according to the ring in which they are embedded.
(b) Rings of the above radii may be marked on the ground, the lines drawn being wholly within each circle.
(c) Where it is not practical to draw lines on the ground, scores shall be determined with a non-stretch cord or tape looped round the centre stick and clearly marked to measure the various radii. Where this method of measuring is used an area should be marked on the ground (conveniently a square or circle) which will contain the whole of the Clout scoring zone and which for all purposes included in (d) be termed the Target Area. The scorer should allow adequate time for all archers shooting to determine the position of the arrows in the said area before carrying out the following procedure. The scorer shall carry the taut cord round at ground level and one assistant scorer following the cord at each 'colour' shall withdraw and carry all arrows from the 'colour' for which he is responsible. An arrow lying loose on the ground shall be scored in accordance with the position of its point.
The arrows shall then be placed in distinct groups on or stuck into the ground at the appropriate section of the scoring cord and competitors will call their scores in the usual manner, picking up their arrows as they do so.
(d) No person other than the appointed scorers shall enter the target area until all arrows have been withdrawn and placed in their respective scoring groups. An arrow withdrawn by any other than an appointed scorer shall not be scored.

404 Round
(a) A Clout Round consists of 36 arrows.
(b) Distances to be shot shall be determined by the organisers. These would normally be:
for Gentlemen – 9 score yards
for Ladies – 7 score yards

405 National Championship Round
The National Championship shall be decided over a Double Clout Round.

Part V
CROSSBOW ARCHERY

500 Regulations
The Rules of Target Archery shall apply with the following exceptions:
(a) Crossbowmen shall shoot on separate targets from other archers and not compete with them.
(b) No person under 16 years of age may shoot unless in adult care and no person less than 12 years of age may shoot or manipulate a crossbow.

501 Equipment
(a) A crossbow stock and mechanism may be made from any material. No mechanical aids or rests are permitted. Prods may be made of any other material except metal. The length measured along the curves shall not exceed 36 inches.
(b) The draw-length shall be measured from the back of the prod to the string latch. Draw-weight shall not exceed 1280 lb/in with a maximum draw of 18 inches. (To determine the lb/in multiply the draw-length by the draw-weight). The draw-weight shall be marked on the prod, e.g. 70 lb at 18″.
(c) A string may be made of any non-metallic material.
(d) Bolts may be made of any material and of such design as not to cause unreasonable damage to the target. Bolt length is minimum 12 inches, maximum 15 inches. Three fletchings, feather or plastic, shall be fitted.
(e) Telescopic or magnifying sights are not allowed.
(f) Stirrups attached to the stock or ground are permitted, provided that Rule 501(b) is complied with.
(g) Pistol crossbows are not permitted.
(h) The use of safety catches is recommended and will become mandatory in 1983.

502 Recognised Rounds
(a) Windsor Round shot on a 60 cm FITA face scoring 9, 7, 5, 3, 1.
The Championship Round shall be a Double Windsor.
(b) American Round shot on a 60 cm FITA face scoring 10, 9, 8, 7, 6, 5, 4, 3, 2, 1.
(c) Western Round shot on an 80 cm FITA face scoring 10, 9, 8, 7, 6, 5, 4, 3, 2, 1.
(d) Any recognised GNAS or FITA Round.

503 Field Archery
(a) Current Field Archery Rules shall

apply with those exceptions detailed in 500(a) and (b).
(b) Targets shall be fixed below skyline.
(c) Field Rounds as recognised by GNAS or FITA shall be shot.

504 The Crossbow and the Law
When travelling on public transport or walking in a public thoroughfare it is essential that the prod be removed and the stock and prod be carried in a case or cover.

505 Safety Rules
If shooting is interrupted for any reason, crossbows shall be lowered immediately so that they are directed at the ground immediately in front of the shooting line and the bolt removed. Safety catches, where fitted, shall be applied.

Part VI
OTHER FORMS OF ARCHERY

600 Popinjay Shooting
Set-up for Popinjay

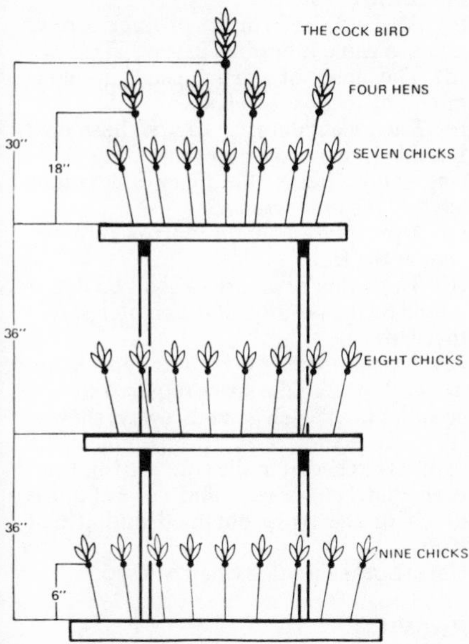

(a) The full complement of a Popinjay 'roost' shall consist of:
One Cock Bird
Four Hens
Minimum of twenty-four Chicks.

(b) Body size of all birds shall be 1½″ long ¾″ in diameter – only the plumage shall differ:
– that of the Cock Bird being most resplendent and 10″–12″ high.
– that of the Hen Birds being shorter 6″–8″ high and less colourful.
– that of the Chicks being shortest 3″–4″ high.
(c) The Chicks shall be perched on spikes 6″ long, not less than 4″ apart, in three rows, the vertical height between rows being not less than 3 feet. The Hen Birds shall be perched on spikes 18″ above the top row and shall be spaced not less than 8″ apart.
The Cock Bird shall be perched on a central spike not less than 30″ above the top row.
(d) The perches may be attached to, or hauled up a mast or wall to a height of 90 feet (measured to the Cock Bird).
Arrangements must be made to ensure, that when in position the perches are firmly held against movement by wind.
(e) All obstructions on and within the framework of perches must be softened with rubber or sponge rubber (or similar resilient material) to lessen the risk of arrow breakage.
(f) No hard and fast shooting position is dictated, although it should be pointed out to all competitors that a near vertical, close to mast attitude will offer a better target to the archer, inasmuch as a greater number of birds will be in line of the arrow flight path.
(g) Each and every part of the Popinjay Mast and Framework of Perches must be made to be safe from breakage and/or dislodgement by arrow or the elements.
(h) Whenever possible a shelter should be provided for competitors, a temporary structure approx. 7′6″ high covered on top with ½″ wire mesh is sufficient for this purpose. If no shelter is available competitors waiting to shoot must be made to wait outside the arrow fall-out area.

601 Arrows
Only arrows with blunts ¾″ to 1″ in diameter shall be used.

602 Shooting
(a) Archers will draw for order of shooting.
(b) Only one archer shall shoot at a time.

(c) Archers must shoot in rotation – only one arrow being shot per end.
(d) Disabled archers may shoot with the aid of a prop.

603 Mast Captain
A Mast Captain shall be appointed to ensure that shooting is conducted in a safe and proper manner. This person shall have the authority to terminate shooting, for instance – in the event of inclement weather or technical breakdown of the mast apparatus – and shall have authority to dismiss any competitor shooting dangerously or considered to be incapable of shooting safely. Assistants to the Mast Captain may be found necessary.

604 Scoring
(a) The scoring points for hits are:
Cock Bird – 5 points
Hen Bird – 3 points
Chick – 1 point
(b) Birds must be struck with the arrow and be dislodged and fall to the ground to score.

605 'Round'
Results may be determined by time limit or by a declared number of arrows.

606 Regulations for Tournaments
Popinjay Tournament Schedules shall bear the following information:
(a) Whether competition is determined by time limit or by number of arrows shot per person.
(b) Maximum number of archers that will be accepted.
Note: The GNAS Insurance Scheme does not cover for risks attendant on the erection and dismantling of Popinjay Masts.

620 Archery Golf
Regulations
(a) Only one bow shall be used throughout a round. In case of breakage it may be replaced.
(b) Any arrows may be used.
(c) The archer shall 'hole out' by hitting a white cardboard disc 4″ in diameter, placed on the ground at least one yard within the edge of the green level with the hole.
(d) An arrow landing off the fairway or in a bunker shall incur one extra stroke.
(e) The archer must stand immediately behind where his arrow lands to shoot the next arrow.
(f) A lost arrow incurs the normal penalty (as in golf) for stroke play but loses the hole in match play.
(g) The winner of the previous 'hole' takes the first shot for the next hole.
(h) The current Golf Rules and local Course Regulations shall apply in all cases not covered by the foregoing rules.

640 Archery Darts
Regulations
The Rules of Target Archery shall apply with the following exceptions:

Target Faces
Archery Darts Faces 76.2 cm (2′6″) in diameter shall be used.

General Rules
(a) The Targets shall be set up so that the centre of the Bull is at the centre of a 122 cm minimum diameter boss 130 cm from the ground.
(b) The minimum shooting distance shall be 13.7 m (15 yds).
(c) An End shall consist of three arrows unless a game is finished in less.
(d) The order of starting shall be determined by the toss of a coin.
(e) Each match must start and finish on a Double (the narrow outer ring). The inner ring counts treble; the inner Bull counts 50; and the outer Bull 25.
(f) A practice end of three arrows must be shot at the Bull.
(g) The value of an arrow shall be determined by the position of the greater part of the shaft.
(h) Scoring shall be by the subtraction method, so that the score required for the completion of each game is always shown.
(i) If the score required to complete the game is exceeded in the course of an End, then that End ceases, and no account is taken of the score obtained during that End.
Note: Local variations may be used.

Part VII
JUNIOR ARCHERY

700 General
(a) A Junior is under 18 years of age.
(b) Junior Archery shall be conducted in accordance with the Rules of Shooting

applicable to Seniors but the following special provisions shall apply.

701 Rounds
(a) In addition to the Rounds under Rule 108(a) the following are recognised:
BRISTOL I
6 dozen arrows at 80 yards
4 dozen arrows at 60 yards
2 dozen arrows at 50 yards
BRISTOL II
6 dozen arrows at 60 yards
4 dozen arrows at 50 yards
2 dozen arrows at 40 yards
BRISTOL III
6 dozen arrows at 50 yards
4 dozen arrows at 40 yards
2 dozen arrows at 30 yards
BRISTOL IV
6 dozen arrows at 40 yards
4 dozen arrows at 30 yards
2 dozen arrows at 20 yards
ST NICHOLAS
4 dozen arrows at 40 yards
3 dozen arrows at 30 yards
SHORT WINDSOR
3 dozen arrows at 50 yards
3 dozen arrows at 40 yards
3 dozen arrows at 30 yards
JUNIOR NATIONAL
(intended for girls under 13 and boys under 12 years of age):
4 dozen arrows at 40 yards
2 dozen arrows at 30 yards
METRIC I
3 dozen arrows at 70 metres
3 dozen arrows at 60 metres
3 dozen arrows at 50 metres
3 dozen arrows at 30 metres
METRIC II
3 dozen arrows at 60 metres
3 dozen arrows at 50 metres
3 dozen arrows at 40 metres
3 dozen arrows at 30 metres
METRIC III
3 dozen arrows at 50 metres
3 dozen arrows at 40 metres
3 dozen arrows at 30 metres
3 dozen arrows at 20 metres
METRIC IV
3 dozen arrows at 40 metres
3 dozen arrows at 30 metres
3 dozen arrows at 20 metres
3 dozen arrows at 10 metres
(b) In the Metric Rounds the two longer distances shall be shot on a 122-cm 10-zone target face and the two shorter distances on a 80-cm 10-zone target face under FITA Target Archery Rules. In all other Rounds the Standard British 122-cm 5-zone target face shall be used.
(c) (i) A Metric Round may be shot in one day or over two consecutive days.
(ii) All other Rounds shall be shot in one day.
(d) In addition, any 'local' Round made up of other numbers of arrows at specified distances may be used in Clubs and Tournaments provided the Rules of Shooting are adhered to in all respects and subject to their non-recognition by the GNAS for record, classification or handicap purposes.

702 National Championship Meeting
(a) The Meeting shall be of one day's duration and the following Rounds shall be shot:
Boys under 18 years of age – York
Girls under 18 years of age – Hereford
Boys under 16 years of age – Bristol II
Girls under 16 years of age – Bristol III
Boys under 14 years of age – Bristol III
Girls under 13 years of age – Bristol IV
Boys under 12 years of age – Bristol IV
An archer may enter for a Round in a higher age group than his own, but not for a Round in a lower age group.
(b) The winners of the York and Hereford Rounds shall be designated National Junior Boy Champion and National Junior Girl Champion respectively. The minimum age for competitors shall be 9 years on the day of the Championships.
(c) County Teams shall consist of the four, or fewer, highest scores made by Boys shooting the York and Girls shooting the Hereford Rounds.

703 National Indoor Championship Meeting
(a) The Championship shall consist of a Double FITA II Round, shot by all Sections.
(b) A FITA II Round consists of 30 arrows at a distance of 25 metres on a 60 cm 10-zone target face.
(c) There shall be the following Sections:
Section 1 Boys under 18
Section 2 Girls under 18
Section 3 Boys under 16
Section 4 Girls under 16
Section 5 Boys under 14
Section 6 Boys under 12
Section 7 Girls under 13

(d) The minimum age shall be 9 years on the day of the Championship.

704 Field Archery

(a) **Junior Posts**

(i) **Hunter Round**

Juniors (15/17) shall shoot from the same posts as Adults in all cases.

Junior (12/14) shall shoot two arrows from each of the two nearest shooting posts at the targets showing 45 cm and 60 cm faces.

Juniors (under 12) may shoot all four shots from the front post on ALL targets.

(ii) **Field Round**

Juniors (15/17) shall shoot from the same posts as Adults in all cases.

Juniors (12/14) may shoot all four shots from the front post on the 60 cm walk-up target; and, shall have a forward post provided, 15 metres in advance of the Adult posts on the fixed position targets at 60, 55, 50, 45 metres.

Note that this latter target is a 45 cm face.

Juniors (under 12) may shoot the same privilege shots as Juniors (12/14), and, in addition, may shoot from the front post at ALL walk-up targets.

(iii) **FITA Combination Round**

The rules regarding shooting posts for Juniors in the Hunter and Field Round shall apply to the appropriate unit in this Round.

(iv) **Foresters Round**

Juniors (15/18) shall shoot from the same posts as Adults in all cases.

Juniors (12/14) shall shoot from the same posts as Adults at the 6″ and 12″ faces, they shall shoot two arrows from the middle distance post and one arrow from the front post at the 18″ faces, and they shall shoot two arrows from each of the two nearest posts at the 24″ faces.

Juniors (under 12) shall shoot all arrows from the front peg at all targets.

(v) **Four-shot Foresters Round**

Juniors (15/17) shall shoot from the same posts as Adults in all cases.

Juniors (12/14) shall shoot two arrows from each of the two nearest shooting posts at the targets showing 18″ and 24″ faces.

Juniors (under 12) shall shoot all arrows from the front post at all targets.

(vi) **Big Game Round**

Juniors (15/17) shall shoot from the same posts as Adults in all cases.

Juniors (12/14) shall shoot two arrows from the middle distance post and one from the front post until a hit is scored.

Juniors (under 12) shall shoot up to three arrows all from the front post until a hit is scored.

(vii) **National Animal Round**

Juniors (15/17) shall shoot from the same posts as the adults in all cases.

Juniors (12/14) may shoot both arrows from the nearest shooting post at the 30 cm kill zone diameter faces.

Juniors (under 12) may shoot both arrows at the 30 cm and the 22.5 cm kill zone diameter faces from a single privilege post set at an appropriate distance.

705 Clout Shooting

The distances shall be:

Boys under 18 years: 140 yards
Girls under 18 years 120 yards
Boys under 16 years 120 yards
Girls under 16 years 100 yards
Boys under 14 years 100 yards
Girls under 13 years 80 yards
Boys under 12 years 80 yards

Part VIII RECORDS

800 National Record

A National Record may be established and submitted to National Council for ratification at:

(a) Any Meeting organised by FITA, FITA Members, GNAS, Regional Societies.

(b) Any Meeting which has applied to National Council by 31st December in respect of target archery, and before October 31st of the preceding year in respect of field archery, for prior recognition and has been granted such status. It shall be a condition that such meeting shall be open to all members of GNAS.

801 Submission of Claims

Claims for National Records shall be submitted to the GNAS Secretary on the appropriate form except for National Championships and UK Masters Tournament when the Secretary will submit claims to National Council.

The claim forms must be completed prior to the dispersal of the Meeting at which the record has been made, one copy shall be handed to the archer and one copy retained by the Tournament Organiser. Both copies must be sent to the Secretary

within 28 days of the date on which the record was made.
The claim form sent by the Tournament Organiser shall be accompanied by the original score sheet (or a photo copy) and the results sheet as circulated.

802 Target Archery
(a) A world record may be established for the FITA Round and each distance of the FITA Round according to qualifications laid down in FITA Rules.
Claims for World Records shall be submitted to the GNAS Secretary supported by the necessary documents for onward transmission to FITA for ratification.
(b) National Records may be claimed for any single or double round shot at recognised Record Status Meetings but where a Double Round is shot on the one day the second Round will not be accepted for Record purposes.

803 Field Archery
Record Rounds are restricted to National Animal Unmarked Hunter, Marked Field and FITA Combination Rounds.

804 Flight Shooting
(a) National records may be claimed in all classes. The measurements must be checked and witnessed by the Range Captain and one other responsible person. In addition the Range Captain must certify that the ground over which the shot was made was reasonably flat and level.
(b) A new record may be established when the measurement is at least one yard longer than an existing record.

805 Clout Shooting
National records may be established for 'one way' and 'two way' when shooting is at the following distances:
Gentlemen 9 score yards
Ladies 7 score yards

806 Junior Archery
(a) Junior National Records may be established at Record Status Meetings as set out above. In addition:
(b) **Target Archery**
National Records may be established according to age groups as shown. (There is nothing to prevent a junior holding a record in a Round of a higher age group.)
Under 18 Boys Bristol I, Metric I & distances Metric I
Under 18 Girls Bristol II, Metric II & distances Metric II
Under 16 Boys Bristol II, Metric II
Under 16 Girls, under 14 Boys Bristol III, Metric III, Short Windsor
Under 13 Girls, under 12 Boys Bristol IV, Metric IV, St Nicholas
(c) **Field Archery**
A National Record may be set up by any Junior shooting the requisite Round for his age group over a full 28 Target Course. (N.B. this does not include twice round a 14 Target Course.)
No Junior may hold a National Record in a Round for a higher age group unless he shoots to the conditions appropriate to that group. Records will not be kept for the Juniors (under 12) class in respect of the National Animal Round.
(d) **Clout Shooting**
Records may be established at each of the prescribed distances, both 'one way' and 'two way' shooting.

Part IX
CLASSIFICATION AND HANDICAP SCHEMES

900 Classification Regulations for all Disciplines
(a) The use of the Classification Scheme by Clubs is optional and the administration of it shall be in the hands of Club officials.
(b) Initial grading or subsequent upgrading occurs immediately the necessary scores have been made in the calendar year.
(c) The qualification holds for one year immediately following that in which it is gained. If it is not maintained during that year, reclassification shall be on the scores made during the year.
(d) The scheme shall apply only to those archers using equipment defined in Clause 102(a).

901 Target Archery
(a) To gain Class I, II or III a member must shoot during the calendar year and under GNAS Rules of Shooting, three Rounds of, or better than, the scores set out in Table A at a meeting organised by GNAS or a body affiliated to GNAS or at an Associated Club Target Day when a minimum of two archers are shooting together. Junior scores are shown in Table A on page 185.

(b) **Master Bowmen**
(i) Qualifying Rounds: York, FITA (Gentlemen); Hereford, FITA (Ladies).
(ii) Number of Rounds: Four, including at least one York/Hereford and one FITA.
(iii) Any two of the Rounds must be shot at a meeting organised by FITA, FITA Members, GNAS, a Regional Society or County Association. The remainder may be shot at any of the above or at any Associated Club Tournament or Target Day when a minimum of two archers are shooting together on the same target.
(c) **Grand Master Bowman**
(i) Qualifying Rounds: York, FITA (Gentlemen); Hereford, FITA (Ladies).
(ii) Number of Rounds: 2 FITA, 1 York/ Hereford.
(iii) All Rounds must be shot at Meetings organised by FITA, FITA Members, GNAS, or a Regional Society, including Regional Inter-County Tournaments whether such meetings are open or closed.
(d) **Junior Master Bowmen**
(i) Qualifying Rounds: York, Bristol I, Men's FITA, Ladies' FITA, Metric I (Boys); Hereford, Bristol II, Ladies' FITA, Metric I, Metric II (Girls).
(ii) Number of Rounds: Four of the Rounds must be shot, with a minimum of one and a maximum of three FITA/Metric Rounds.
(iii) One Round must be shot at a meeting organised by FITA, FITA Members, GNAS, a Regional Society or County Association. The other three Rounds may be shot at the above or at a Club Tournament or Target Day with a minimum of two archers shooting supervised by a Senior (see Table A on page 186).

902 Field Archery
(a) Qualifying Rounds: FITA Hunter, FITA Field and FITA Combination.
(b) Qualifying scores: As in Table C on page 186.
(There is no separate scheme for those under 15 years of age. Should such Juniors wish to enter the classification scheme they must shoot the full distance.)
(c) **Grand Master Bowman**
(i) Number of Rounds (each Round must be of the required standard):
2 Hunter, 2 Field
2 Hunter, 1 Field, 1 Combination
1 Hunter, 2 Field, 1 Combination
(ii) All Rounds must be shot at Meetings organised by FITA, FITA Members, GNAS, a Regional Championship Meeting, a Regional Inter-Counties Meeting, County Championship or any competition granted National Record Status (only two scores shot at the same venue may be used for this qualification).
(d) **Master Bowman**
(i) Number of Rounds (each Round must be of the required standard):
3 Hunter, 1 Field
2 Hunter, 2 Field
1 Hunter, 3 Field
2 Hunter, 1 Field, 1 FITA Combination
1 Hunter, 2 Field, 1 FITA Combination
(ii) Two Rounds must be shot at Meetings detailed in (c) (ii) above. The remainder may be shot at any of the above or at any Associated Club Open Tournament when a minimum of three archers are shooting together on one target.
(e) **Classes I, II & III**
N.B. Qualifying scores may be obtained by shooting the same Unit twice.
(i) Number of Rounds:
1st Class: As for Master Bowman
2nd & 3rd Class: Two Rounds, each of which must be of the required standard.
(ii) Rounds must be shot at any of the Meetings detailed in (d) (ii) above or at a Classification Shoot when a minimum of three archers are shooting together on the same target.

903 Flight Shooting
(a) Archers can qualify as Master Flight Shot or 1st Class Flight Shot at any Flight Shoot organised by GNAS, a Regional Society or County Association under GNAS Rules of Shooting.
(b) Archers can qualify as Grand Master Flight Shot at any of the above except that the County Association Meeting must be the County Championships.
(c) Minimum distances:

	Ladies	Gentlemen
Grand Master Flight Shot	450 yds	550 yds
Master Flight Shot	340 yds	440 yds
1st Class Flight Shot	275 yds	375 yds

904 Crossbow Shooting
Using the Windsor Round.
Qualifying Scores
Master Arbalist 780 3 scores (2 and 1)
Arbalist 1st Class 630 3 scores (1 and 2) see

Arbalist 2nd Class 480 3 scores (1 and 2) below

Qualifying Meetings

For the Master Arbalist 2 and for the 1st and 2nd Class Arbalist 1, scores must be made at a Meeting organised by FITA. FITA Members, GNAS, a Regional Society, or County Association. The remainder may be shot at any of the above or at any Associated Club Tournament or Target Day when a minimum of two archers are shooting together on the same Target.

905 Submission of Claim

(a) Claims for the title of Grand Master and Master in all disciplines shall be submitted to the GNAS Secretary on the appropriate form. The Secretary will, on behalf of the National Council:

(i) Satisfy himself as to the validity of the claim.

(ii) Notify the claimant and send him the appropriate badge.

(iii) Publicise the award.

(b) It shall be the responsibility of the archer concerned to submit the claim together with the following documents of proof.

(i) **Rounds shot at Club Meetings**. The original score sheet endorsed by an Officer of the Club to the effect that the Round was shot at a Club Tournament or Target Day.

(ii) **Rounds shot at any other Meeting**. The official Result Sheet sent out by the Organiser(s) of the Meeting.

(c) Any such claim shall also include a certificate that the archer was using a bow recognised as in Rule 102(a).

920 Handicap Scheme

Copies of the GNAS Handicap Tables, which include the Rules for the operation of the Scheme, can be obtained from the GNAS Secretary.

921 Handicap Improvement Medal

(a) The medals are Challenge Trophies and remain the property of the GNAS.

(b) One medal will be loaned on application to any Club having not less than ten shooting members, which has been an Associated Club of the Society for at least twelve months.

(c) In the event of a Club ceasing to function, the Secretary thereof will be personally responsible for returning the medal to the Society.

(d) The Club will notify to the Secretary the name and address of the winner of the medal each year immediately it has been awarded (giving old and new handicap figures) or, if it has not been duly competed for, will return it to the Society.

(e) (i) The medal is to be awarded to the member, lady or gentleman, who having been a member of the Club for not less than six months prior to January 1st attains the greatest improvement in handicap during the following calendar year provided that he or she shall have shot not fewer than twelve rounds on his or her own Club Target Days during that period, in addition to any eligible rounds shot elsewhere. If owing to adverse weather, no member has shot twelve rounds on Club Target Days during the period, the Club Committee has discretion to make the award on a slightly lesser number of rounds.

(ii) In the event of a tie, those who tied shall shoot it off on a day and round to be decided by the Club, or, at the Club's discretion, the medal may be awarded to the member with the greatest number of attendances during the period amongst those who have tied.

(f) The GNAS Handicap Regulations and Tables must be used for assessing all handicaps in connection with the award of these medals.

(g) The holder of the medal should wear it on all Club Target Days at which he or she is present. It is left to each Club to impose any penalty in this connection.

Table A Qualifying Scores—Junior

	Bristol 1 (Hereford)	Bristol 2	Bristol 3	Bristol 4	Metric I (Ladies' FITA)	Metric II	Metric III	Metric IV	York	FITA (Men)	St George
Boys under 18:											
MB	919				1009				735	923	
1st Class	781				871	977			581	775	491
2nd Class	629	817			711	830	1002		435	620	379
3rd Class	498	685	833		571	687	883		325	491	290
Boys under 16:											
1st Class	651	838			735	852	1020				
2nd Class	541	730	873		618	736	925				
3rd Class	436	617	770		504	614	817				
Boys under 14:											
1st Class		685	833				883				
2nd Class		572	727	896			771	1001			
3rd Class		483	637	817			677	925			
Boys under 12:											
1st Class			813	967			862	1068			
2nd Class			682	857			724	964			
3rd Class			548	733			582	844			
Girls under 18:											
MB	781	951			871	977					
1st Class	629	817			711	830					
2nd Class	498	685	833		571	687	883				
3rd Class	378	549	705		439	542	748				
Girls under 16:											
1st Class		685	833			687	883				
2nd Class		549	705			542	748				
3rd Class		420	570	755		408	606	865			
Girls under 13:											
1st Class			727	896			771	1001			
2nd Class			592	776			630	885			
3rd Class			484	668			513	779			

New Western	New National	Long Western	Long National	Albion	Western	National	Windsor	American	St Nicholas	Short Windsor	Long Metric (Men)	Short Metric	Long Metric (Ladies)	Junior National
362	254	509	362	629							314		409	
263	182	404	283	519	530	387	646	538			233	387	325	
191	131	316	218	420	440	318	551	459		663	172	319	252	
		419	294	535	544	397	660	550		753		398	337	
		345	239	453	471	341	584	486		691		342	276	
		274	188	371	393	283	501	417		619		285	218	
					440	318	551	459		663		319		
					363	260	467	389		588		263		
					303	217	400	333		523		221		
					424	306	535	445	543	648		308		458
					333	238	433	361	475	556		242		398
					249	177	335	280	398	456		182		331
		404	283	519	530	387	646	538				387	325	
		316	218	420	440	318	551	459		663		319	252	
		236	161	325	348	249	450	375		572		253	187	
		316	218	420	440	318	551	459		663		319		
		236	161	325	348	249	450	375		572		253		
		170	115	241	262	186	351	293		473		191		
					363	260	467	389	499	588		263		419
					275	196	367	306	424	490		201		354
					212	150	290	242	358	407		156		297

Table B Qualifying Scores—Senior

	York	FITA	ST George	New Western	New National	Long Metric	Short Metric	Hereford	Albion	Long Western	Long National	Western	National	Windsor	American
Gentlemen:															
GMB	1085	1223													
MB	1000	1153													
1st Class	798	980	646	512	368	431									
2nd Class	560	753	475	347	243	302	451	760	614	494	351				
3rd Class	342	512	304	202	139	181	331	519	436	330	228	455	330	568	473

	Hereford	FITA	Albion	Long Western	Long National	Long Metric	Short Metric	Western	National	Windsor	American
Ladies:											
GMB	1112	1198									
MB	1033	1121									
1st Class	843	933	672	551	395	443					
2nd Class	606	688	502	389	272	312	376	516	375	631	525
3rd Class	378	439	325	236	161	187	253	348	249	450	375

Table C Qualifying score tables

	GMB	MB	1st CLASS	2nd CLASS	3rd CLASS
Freestyle:					
Ladies	400	350	300	230	160
Gentlemen	440	400	350	270	180
Girls		300	250	180	100
Boys		350	300	230	150
Barebow:					
Ladies	350	300	230	160	110
Gentlemen	400	350	300	230	160
Girls		230	180	110	60
Boys		300	250	180	100
Traditional:					
Ladies	300	230	160	110	60
Gentlemen	350	300	230	160	110
Girls		180	110	60	40
Boys		230	180	110	60

N.A.A. (NATIONAL ARCHERY ASSOCIATION OF THE UNITED STATES) TARGET RULES OF SHOOTING (1981)

Contents

Foreword

The rules contained herein govern conduct in the National Archery Association Annual Tournament, and any F.I.T.A. Star Tournament, or Tryout Tournaments, Qualifying Tournaments, as well as all Six-Gold Tournaments, officially recognized by the National Archery Association of the United States. In the event of a conflict between N.A.A. rules and F.I.T.A. rules, the F.I.T.A. rules shall prevail in all N.A.A. sanctioned tournaments.

Because local conditions may prevent elaborate field arrangements, properties, or personal usage, minimum rules are stated and allowable tolerances indicated. In the interest of uniformity, local clubs and associations are urged to adopt these rules to govern local archery competition. Such local clubs or associations may adopt special regulations, or additional rules, providing that such additions do not conflict with, or in any way alter, any of the rules contained herein.

Decisions not regulated by the Official N.A.A. Target Archery Rules of Shooting, or by specific regulations of local clubs and associations, shall fall under the authority of the tournament officials involved.

PRIMARY RULES

Safety & Courtesy

Every precaution must be taken to ensure that the highest possible safety standards have precedence over all other considerations or rules. Any practices, attitudes, equipment, or conditions, which are in the least degree unsafe, are prohibited. It shall be the responsibility of every N.A.A. member to insist upon strict maintenance of safety standards at all times.

Official practice shall be from a common shooting line (for each division) and shall be controlled by whistle signals.

To ensure a fair enjoyment of archery competition by all contestants, a high standard of personal courtesy and sportsmanship is enjoined upon all. Discourteous and unsportsmanlike conduct is an unwarranted offense against other archers and an affront to the heritage, dignity, and tradition which is an integral part of the sport of archery. Persistence in discourteous or unsportsmanlike conduct, after one warning by a tournament official, shall be considered grounds for expulsion from the tournament without a refund.

1.0 Range Layout

1.1 The target field shall be laid out so that the shooting is from South to North. A maximum deviation of 45 degrees is allowed for N.A.A. Annual Tournaments. Local tournament deviation from this rule is allowed if required by local terrain.

1.2 The range shall be squared off and each distance accurately measured from a point vertically beneath the Gold on each target to the shooting line.

1.3 Points on the shooting line directly opposite each buttress shall be marked and numbered correspondingly.

1.4 At right angles to the shooting line (and extending from the shooting line to the target line), lines may be laid down to create lanes containing one, two, or three buttresses; *or* center lines or center point markers from the shooting line to each buttress may be used.

1.5 Each two-target lane is a minimum of 5 m wide *or* if center lines or markers are used, the minimum distance between centers is 2.5 m (see Conversion Table, page 7).

1.6 For a Star F.I.T.A., or any regional or national tournament, the shooting line shall remain stationary and the targets shall be brought forward from the longer to the lesser distances. For local tournaments the target line may remain stationary and the shooting line moved up at each distance.

1.7 Four (4) archers shall be the maximum number assigned to each target. Local, school, and club tournaments may exceed this number if absolutely necessary. The minimum number on a target shall be three (3).

1.8 A waiting line shall be indicated at least 5 m behind the shooting line.

1.9 Each target shall be set up at an angle of 15 degrees plus or minus 3 degrees.

1.10 Buttresses shall be pegged securely to the ground, to prevent their being blown over by wind. Any portion of a buttress likely to damage an arrow shall be covered.

1.11 Each target shall be numbered. The numbers (30 cm sq.) shall be clearly visible from 90 m and shall be attached either above or below the center of each buttress so as to be clear of the target face. At local tournaments, target numbers may be attached to the right leg of the target stand.

1.12 The center of the gold shall be 130 cm plus or minus 5 cm (or 51'' plus or minus 2''), above the ground.

1.13 At least every third target shall have a wind flag of a color easily visible from 90 m and mounted at least 40 cm above the top of the target. The size of the flag shall be from 25 to 30 cm square. Local tournaments may deviate from this rule. However, at a Star F.I.T.A. or a Qualifier, there shall be a wind flag on every target.

1.14 Suitable barriers shall be erected around the field to keep spectators off the shooting area. Such barriers should be at least 10 m behind the waiting line, at least 10 m away from each side of the field, and as far beyond the target base line as necessary to prevent members of the public from moving into the archer's line of vision or shooting.

1.15 The organizing committee shall provide lights, plates, or flags to be used for time control. Sufficient numbers of these items shall be provided so that they are clearly visible to the shooters.

1.16 Recommended – a raised platform for the Director of Shooting.

1.17 Recommended – a loudspeaker system for the use of the Director of Shooting.

1.18 Recommend – sufficient chairs or benches behind the waiting line for all competitors, Team Captains, and other officials.

Conversion Table

Centimeters-Meters	*Yards*	*Feet*	*Inches*
1 centimeter			0.3937
80 centimeters			31.50
122 centimeters			48.00
1 meter		3	3.37
5 meters	5	1	4.85
30 meters	32	2	5.10
50 meters	54	2	0.50
60 meters	65	1	10.20
70 meters	76	1	7.90
90 meters	98	1	3.30

2.0 Target Faces

Description

(a) There are two standard circular target faces: 122 cm and 80 cm diameters. Both these faces are divided into 5 concentric color zones arranged from the center outwards as follows: Gold (yellow), Red, Light Blue, Black, and White.

Each color is in turn divided by a thin line into 2 zones of equal width, thus making in all 10 scoring zones of equal width measured from the center of the Gold:

6.1 cm on the 122 cm target face

4 cm on the 80 cm target face

Such dividing lines, and any dividing lines which may be used between colors, shall be made entirely within the higher scoring zone in each case.

Any line marking the outermost edge of the White shall be made entirely within the scoring zone.

The width of the thin dividing lines as well as the outermost line shall not exceed 2 mm on both the 122 cm and the 80 cm target faces.

The center of the target face is termed the "pinhole" and shall be indicated by a small "x" (cross), the lines of which shall not exceed 2 mm.

(b) Scoring Values and Color Specifications:

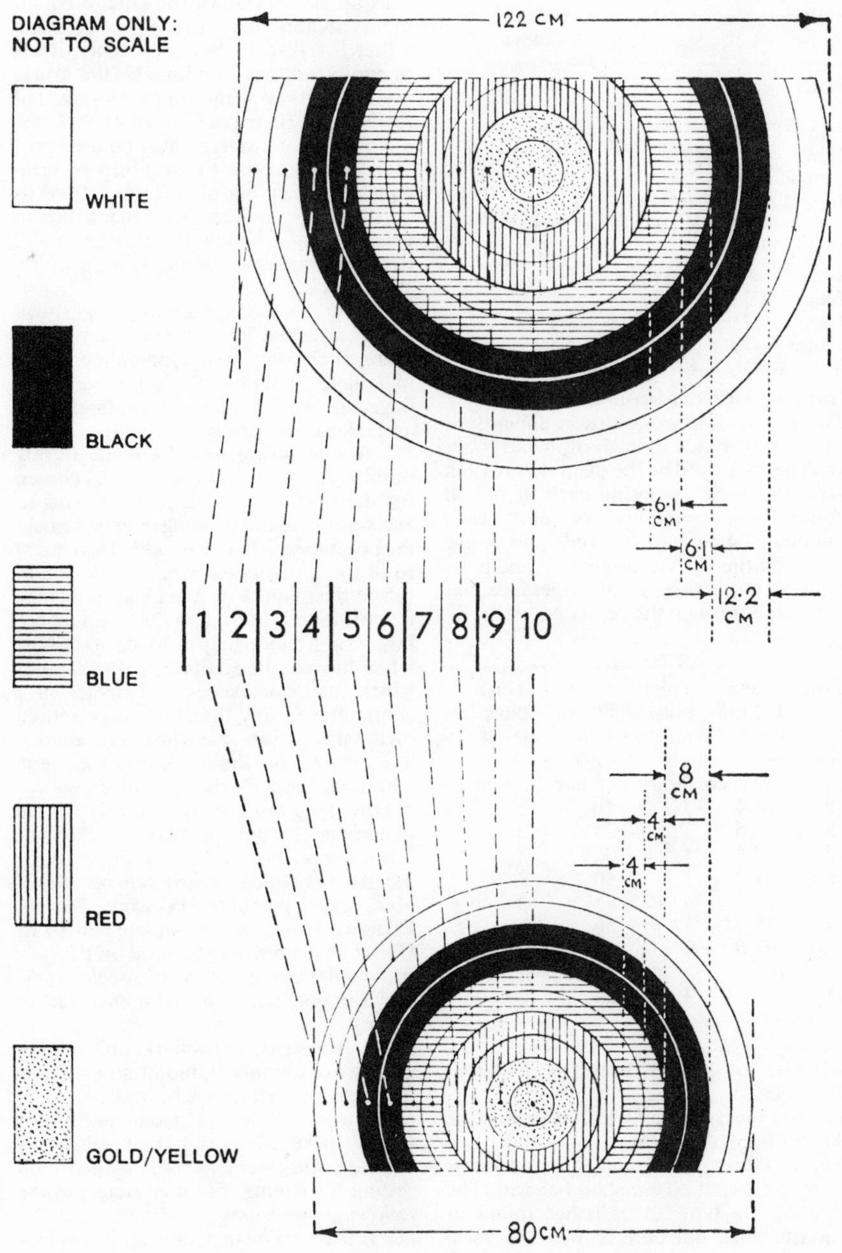
DIAGRAM ONLY:
NOT TO SCALE
WHITE
BLACK
BLUE
RED
GOLD/YELLOW
122 CM
6·1 CM
6·1 CM
12·2 CM
1 2 3 4 5 6 7 8 9 10
8 CM
4 CM
4 CM
80CM

Scoring Values Zone		Colors	Munsell Color Scale Notations
Inner	10	GOLD/ YELLOW	5Y 8/12
Outer	9		
Inner	8	RED	8.3R 3.9/13.5
Outer	7		
Inner	6	LIGHT BLUE	5B 6/8
Outer	5		
Inner	4	BLACK	N2
Outer	3		
Inner	2	WHITE	N9
Outer	1		

(c) Tolerance of Measurements

The permissible variations in dimensions of the target face in each of the 10 zones shall be measured by the diameters of each separate circle enclosing each of the 10 zones. The tolerance of each such diameter shall not exceed plus/minus 3 mm on the 122 cm target face and plus/ minus 2 mm on the 80 cm target face; i.e. measured through the center outwards:

Zone	Diam. 122 cm Face	Toler. plus/ minus	Diam. 80 cm Face	Toler. plus/ minus
10	12.2 cm	3 mm	8 cm	2 mm
9	24.4	3	16	2
8	36.6	3	24	2
7	48.8	3	32	2
6	61.0	3	40	2
5	73.2	3	48	2
4	85.4	3	56	2
3	97.6	3	64	2
2	109.8	3	72	2
1	122	3	80	2

(d) Size of Target Faces at Different Distances

For distances of 90, 70 and 60 meters, the Target Face of 122 cm shall be used.

For distances of 50 and 30 meters, the Target Face of 80 cm shall be used. The size of the buttress, whether round or square, must not be less than 124 cm in any direction to ensure that any arrow hitting the buttress and touching the outermost edge of the target face remain in the buttress.

3.0 Archer's Equipment

This article lays down the type of equipment archers may use when shooting either F.I.T.A. or N.A.A. events. Items of equipment not mentioned in this article are not allowed without prior approval of the N.A.A. Board of Governors.

3.1 A **bow** of any type may be used provided it subscribes to the accepted principle and meaning of the word 'bow' as used in target archery; e.g., an instrument consisting of a handle (grip), riser, and 2 flexible limbs each ending in a tip with a string nock.

The bow is braced for use by a single bowstring attached directly between the 2 string nocks only, and in operation is held in 1 hand by its handle (grip), while the fingers of the other hand draw, hold back, and release the string.

3.2 A **bow string** may be made of any number of strands of the material chosen for the purpose, with a center serving to accommodate the drawing fingers, a nocking point to which may be added serving(s) to fit the arrow nock as necessary, and to locate this point 1 or 2 nock locators may be positioned. In each of the 2 ends of the bow string, a loop may be made of the bow when braced. In addition, 1 attachment, which may not exceed a diameter of 1 centimeter in any direction, is permitted on the string to serve as a lip or nose mark. The serving on the string must not end within the archer's vision at full draw.

A bow string must not in any way offer aid in aiming through peephole marking or any other means.

3.3 **An arrowrest**, which can be adjustable, any movable **Pressure Button, Pressure Point**, or **Arrowplate** and **Draw Check Indicator** may be used on the bow provided they are not electric or electronic and do not offer any additional aid in aiming.

3.4 A **bow sight**, a bowmark, or a point of aiming are permitted, but at no time may more than 1 such device be used.

(a) A bow sight as attached to the bow for the purpose of aiming may allow for windage ajustment as well as elevation setting for aiming, but it is subject to the following provisions:

(1) It shall *not* incorporate a prism or lens or other magnifying, leveling or electric devices, nor shall it provide more than one sighting point.

(2) For Star F.I.T.A. and Qualifying

Tournaments the length of any sight (ring, barrel, conical, hood, etc.) shall not exceed the minimum inside diameter of the aperture.
A hood is not to exceed a length of 1 cm, irrespective of shape.
(3) An attachment to which the bow sight is fixed is permitted.
(b) A bowmark is a single mark made on the bow for the purpose of aiming. Such mark may be made in pencil, tape, or any other suitable marking material.
A plate or tape with distance marking may be mounted on the bow as a guide for marking, but must not in any way offer any additional aid.
(c) A point of aim on the ground is a marker placed on the shooting line and the target. Such marker may not exceed a diameter of 7.5 cm and must not protrude above the ground more than 15 cm.
3.5 **Stabilizers** on the bow are permitted provided they do not:
serve as a string guide;
touch anything but the bow;
represent any obstacle to other archers as far as place on the shooting line is concerned.
(The term, 'stabilizer', shall also include counterbalancing weights.)
3.6 **Arrows** of any type may be used provided they subscribe to the accepted principle and meaning of the word 'arrow' as used in target archery, and that arrows do not cause undue damage to target faces and buttresses.
An arrow consists of nock, shaft, and arrow head (point) with fletching and, if desired, cresting.
Each archer's arrows shall be marked **with the archer's name, initials, or insignia**, and shall have the same color(s) of fletching, nock, and cresting.
3.7 **Finger protection** in the form of finger stalls on tips, gloves, shooting tab, or tape (plaster) to draw, hold back and release the string are permitted, provided they are smooth with no device to help hold and/or release the string.
A separator between the fingers to prevent pinching the arrow may be used.
On the bow hand, an ordinary glove, mitten, or similar item may be worn.
Shooting tabs may be built up of several layers of suitable material (such as leather, plastic, metal a.o.) to stiffen the part of the tab behind that used for drawing the string. Note: No shapes have been specified and no limitations stated with respect to size.
3.8 **Field glasses**, telescopes and other visual aids may be used for spotting arrows.
However, ordinary spectacles as necessary or shooting spectacles provided they are fitted with the same lenses normally used by the archer, and sun glasses may be worn. None must be fitted with microhole lenses, glasses or similar, nor marked in any way to assist in aiming.
3.9 **Accessories** are permitted such as bracers, dress shield, bowsling, belt or ground quiver, tassel; foot markers not protruding more than 1 centimeter.
3.10 **Changing Equipment** – If it becomes necessary for an archer to use tackle which has not been inspected by the Field Officials, the responsibility is on the archer to show such tackle to a Field Official before using it. Any competitor contravening this rule may be disqualified.

4.0 Range Control & Safety
4.1 **Field Officials** shall be appointed by the Tournament Committee.
A. A Director of Shooting (D.O.S.) shall be appointed for all tournaments (for tournaments of fewer than ten targets, he may act also as a Judge). His duties shall include:
1. Control of shooting with a whistle;
2. Ensuring the 2½ minute time allowance for 3 arrows is enforced;
3. Exercising control over use of the loudspeaker;
4. Exercising control over newsmen and photographers so that the comfort and concentration of the competitors is not disturbed;
5. Seeing that spectators stay behind the restraining line at all times;
6. Seeing that Team Coaches and Managers remain behind the waiting line;
7. Being responsible for all safety precautions;
8. Act as Head Official and, in conjunction with the appointed Judges, controlling the tournament.
B. **Judges** sufficient in number to cover the targets being used. These Judges work under the direction of the D.O.S. and their responsibilities will include:
1. Checking all distances and field set up;
2. Inspecting archer's equipment before the tournament begins and at any time thereafter during the tournament: (At the

N.A.A. National Tournament this inspection shall take place the day before official scoring starts.)

3. Checking the conduct of shooting and scoring which includes making decisions on questionable arrows. The decision of the Judge on a questionable arrow shall be final;

4. Resolving disputes and queries in connection with the shooting, scoring and field equipment (targets, bows, etc.);

5. In liaison with the D.O.S., interrupting shooting if necessary, because of weather conditions, a serious accident, or like occurrence, but to ensure if at all possible, that each day's program is completed on the scheduled day.

4.2 **Whistle Signals** to be used in conjunction with lights or flags as follows:

2 blasts on the whistle – archers move from waiting line to the shooting line

1 blast – signal to shoot

3 blasts – signal to score arrows

4 or more blasts – to stop all shooting – emergency

4.3 Under the control of the Director of Shooting, two ends of three (3) sighter arrows are permitted preceding the commencement of shooting each day. No other trial shots in any direction are allowed on the shooting field during the days of competition. (If the rounds used in the competition are N.A.A. rounds, practice on the field may be permitted prior to and after the official round – at the option of the Tournament Committee.)

4.4 No archer may draw his bow, with or without an arrow except when standing on the shooting line.

If an arrow is used, the archer shall aim toward the target, but only after being satisfied that the field is clear both in front of and behind the targets. If, while drawing his bow with an arrow before the shooting starts or during breaks between distances, an archer looses an arrow, intentionally or otherwise, such an arrow shall count as part of the next end to be shot.

The scorer shall make a note to this effect on the archer's scoresheet and enter the values of all hits for that end (3, 5, or 6 arrows as the case may be), but the highest scoring arrow will be forfeited.

This also applies to sighter arrows shot before or after the signal indicating the 2½ minute allowed to shoot an end of three arrows. Such action must be initialled by the D.O.S. or one of the Judges *and* the archer concerned.

4.5 While shooting is in progress, only those archers whose turn it is to shoot may be on the shooting line. All other archers shall remain behind the waiting line with their tackle. After an archer has shot his arrows, he shall retire behind the waiting line immediately. (He may not spot his last arrow before leaving the line.)

4.6 No archer or official may touch the tackle of any archer without the latter's consent.

4.7 An archer who arrives after the shooting has started shall forfeit the number of arrows already shot, unless the D.O.S. is satisfied that he was delayed by circumstances beyond his control, in which case he may be allowed to make up the arrows lost after the distance then being shot has been completed.

4.8 The Director of Shooting has the authority to extend the 2½ minute time limit in exceptional circumstances. The most common occurrences and procedures are listed below. In any other unforeseen instance, the D.O.S., in conjunction with the Judges, shall make and announce their decision to the competitors. This decision is final.

Bounce-Outs – When a bounce-out occurs, the archer shooting the bounce-out will tell the archer shooting with him. This other archer will stop shooting, but remain on the shooting line, while the archer who had the bounce-out finishes his end. Both will then raise their bows overhead. An official will respond to the signal, and will signal the D.O.S. who then announces the problem and the number of arrows to be shot by the archer who did not complete the end.

After the official and the archer who shot the bounce-out have scored the arrow and returned behind the shooting line, the archer with arrows to shoot will be signalled by the D.O.S. to go to the line and shoot when the signal is given. A time limit of 50 sec. will be given for each arrow to be shot.

Equipment Failure – An archer with equipment failure will step back from the shooting line and raise his bow overhead. The other archer will continue shooting the end. At the completion of the end (3 arrows), the official responding to the signal will signal the D.O.S., who will make an announcement and the numbers of arrows to be shot. Upon completion of repairs, the D.O.S. will signal the archer to complete the end, allowing 50 sec. for each arrow. No other archer may occupy the line at this time.

Repairs must be completed within 5 minutes of completion of the end in progress when the failure occurred. The timing of this interval will be the responsibility of the Director of Shooting.

The Hanging Arrow – The archer who shot a hanging arrow will advise the other archer on his target and both will step back from the shooting line with bows held overhead. An official will respond and stop the shoot. The D.O.S. will make an announcement. The official and the archer who shot the hanger will advance to the target, score the arrow and remove it, following the same procedure as with a bounce out. Fifty (50) seconds will be allowed for each remaining arrow to be shot.

Pass-Through – If noted from the shooting line, it is handled the same way as a bounce-out.

Trouble at the Target, such as loose target face, fallen flag, etc. – Both archers will stop shooting, step back from the shooting line and signal official by raising bows overhead. The official will stop the shoot. The D.O.S. will make an announcement. Shooting will resume when officials have corrected the problem.

4.9 When time control is used, archers may not raise the bow arm until the signal for shooting to begin is given; i.e., when the light changes to green and/or the whistle is blown.

5.0 Shooting

5.1 Initial target assignments may be made according to any system designated by the Tournament Officials. Normal procedure is in the order of registration. There shall not be less than 3 nor more than 4 archers assigned to each target in use. Four (4) is the optimum number. (Schools, club and local tournaments may increase the maximum to 6 if necessary.)

5.2 Archers shall be reassigned targets after each round on the basis of their total score for the rounds completed. At Olympic Tryouts, there is no target reassignment.

5.3 The Director of Shooting shall control shooting and ensure the observance of the 2½ minute time allowance for an end of 3 arrows. Any arrow shot either before the signal or after the signal indicating the time limit will forfeit the highest scoring arrow for that end of 3, 5, or 6 as the case may be.

5.4 The D.O.S. shall control shooting with a whistle. (See Art. 4.2 and 4.3.) If shooting is suspended during an end for any reason, 1 blast on the whistle will be the signal for shooting to recommence.

5.5 Except for persons who are permanently disabled, archers shall shoot from a standing position and without support, with 1 foot on each side of the shooting line, or marker.

5.6 Whenever 2 archers are shooting together, neither shall stand closer than 18 inches (46 cm) from either the center marker nor the side boundary markers.

5.7 An arrow shall not be deemed to have been shot if:

the archer can touch it with his bow without moving his feet from their position in relation to the shooting line;

the target face or butt blows over (in spite of having been fixed and pegged down to the satisfaction of the Field Officials).

The Field Officials will take whatever measures they deem necessary to compensate the adequate time for shooting the relevant number of arrows.

5.8 While an archer is on the shooting line, he shall receive no assistance nor information, by word or otherwise, from anyone, other than for the purpose of making essential changes in equipment.

6.0 Scoring

6.1 Two (2) archers on each target shall act as scorekeepers and shall verify that scores agree after each end.

6.2 At 90, 70, and 60 meters, scoring may take place after every end of 3 arrows or every second end (6 arrows).

At 50 and 30 meters, scoring shall always take place after each end of 3 arrows. (Local or club shoots may modify this rule.)

For rounds other than F.I.T.A., scoring shall take place after either 5 or 6 arrows have been shot.

6.3 Scorers shall enter the value of each arrow on the score sheets as called out by the archer to whom the arrows belong. Other archers on that target shall check the value of each arrow called out.

6.4 Neither the arrows nor the face shall

be touched until all the arrows on that target have been recorded.

6.5 An arrow shall be scored according to the position of the shaft in the target face.

6.6 If more than 3 arrows (5 or 6 as the case may be), belonging to the same archer, should be found in the target or on the ground in the shooting lanes, only the 3 lowest (5 or 6 as the case may be), in value shall be scored.

Should an archer be found to repeat this, he/she may be disqualified.

6.7 Should the shaft of an arrow touch 2 colors, or touch any dividing line between scoring zones, that arrow shall score the higher value of the zones affected.

Should a fragment of a target face be missing (including a dividing line, or where 2 colors meet), then an imaginary line shall be used for judging the value on any arrow that may hit such a part.

6.8 Unless all arrow holes are suitably marked on each occasion when arrows are scored and drawn from the target, arrows rebounding from the target face shall not be scored. (Local clubs or schools may elect to count rebounds from the scoring face as 7 points if holes have not been marked, providing the rebound has been witnessed.)

6.9 An arrow hitting:

a. the target and rebounding, shall score according to its impact on the target. (See 6.8 above)

b. another arrow and remaining embedded therein, shall score according to the value of the arrow struck.

c. another arrow, and then hitting the target face after deflection, shall score as it lies in the target.

d. another arrow, and then rebounding from the target, shall score the value of the struck arrow, provided the damaged arrow can be identified.

e. the target face after rebounding off the ground, shall not score.

f. a target other than the archer's own target, shall not score.

g. and passing through the target shall score according to the value of the unmarked hole. (See 6.8 above)

6.10 The Director of Shooting will ensure that, after scoring, no arrows are left in the target before any signal is given to recommence. If this inadvertently happens, the shooting shall not be interrupted.

An archer may shoot that end with other arrows, or make up the arrows lost, after shooting over that distance has been completed. In such circumstances, one of the Judges shall participate in the scoring after that end, making sure that the arrows which remained in the target are checked back to the archer's score sheet before any arrows are withdrawn from the target.

6.11 In the event of an archer leaving arrows; e.g., on the ground in the target area, he may use others provided he informs the D.O.S. before shooting. The D.O.S. shall exercise such checks as he deems fit in such circumstances.

6.12 An archer may delegate authority to score and collect arrows to his Team Captain or to another archer on his own target. (In the case of a handicapped archer, he may request that someone be appointed by D.O.S. to score and collect his arrows.)

6.13 A scoring board or some such device with the competitor's name and/or target number is permitted for displaying progressive total scores after each end. When such a device is used, it shall be placed below each buttress *or* behind the waiting area. It must be pegged to the ground so that it will not move from the wind. It shall be changed by the scorer appointed and aided by the archers on that target after the arrows have been scored and drawn.

6.14 Score sheets shall be signed by the scorer and the archers, denoting that the archer agrees with the score, and thereafter no claim may be made to alter the score.

If the scorer is participating in the shooting, his score sheet shall be signed by some other archer on the same target.

6.15 In the event of a tie in score, the results shall be determined as follows:

a. For individuals:

Of those tying, the archer with the greatest number of scoring hits.

If this is also a tie, then the archer of those tying with the greatest number of 10's. If this is also a tie, then the archer with the greatest number of 9's. Should this be tied, then the archers shall be declared equal.

b. For teams:

Of those tying, the team with the archer having the highest individual score. If this is also a tie, then the team (of those tying) with the archer having the highest second score. If this is also a tie, then the teams shall be declared equal.

7.0 Appeals and Disputes

7.1 In the case of questionable arrows, either the scorers or the participants shall refer any question about the value of an arrow in the target to a Judge before the arrows are drawn. (See Art. 4.1B)

7.2 A mistake on a score sheet, discovered before the arrows are drawn, may be corrected, but the correction must be witnessed and initialed by one of the Judges and the archer concerned before the arrows are drawn. Any other disputes concerning entries on a score sheet shall be referred to a Judge by the archer.

7.3 Should a target face become unreasonably worn or otherwise disfigured, or should there be any complaint about field equipment, an archer may appeal to a Field Official to have the defective item repaired or replaced.

7.4 Questions concerning the conduct of the shooting or the conduct of a competitor shall be lodged with the Director of Shooting the same day.

7.5 In the event of a competitor not being satisfied with a ruling given by a Field Official, he may, except as provided in 7.1, appeal in writing to the Tournament Committee.

8.0 Eligibility and Classification

8.1 Archers shall be classed in the following groups:

Men	18 years old or over
Ladies	18 years old or over
Intermediate Boys	15 to 18 years old
Intermediate Girls	15 to 18 years old
Junior Boys	12 to 15 years old
Junior Girls	12 to 15 years old

Cadet Boys and Girls less than 12 years old

8.2 An archer must shoot in the highest class if the official start of the tournament shall be on or after the birthday which places him in the higher class.

8.3 An archer may by choice compete in a higher class and may also by choice return to his established class provided the choice is made before scoring begins. However, an archer may not shoot in a lower class.

8.4 No archer shall be barred from a tournament because of a physical handicap unless his or her shooting requires mechanical aids which, in the judgement of the Field Officials, would give him undue advantage over other archers, or if his or her participation makes it impossible for archers sharing the target to operate under the time sequence.

9.0 Target Archery Championship Rounds

All N.A.A. Approved Championship rounds will use the 10-ring face and be scored from the center out: 10, 9, 8, 7, 6, 5, 4, 3, 2, 1. Shooting shall be in one direction only and will commence at the longest distance and finish at the shortest distance. If a F.I.T.A. Round is included in the program, it shall be shot first and may be shot in one day or over two consecutive days. If the F.I.T.A. Round is shot over two days, the two longer distances shall be shot the first day and the two shorter distances on the second day.

When a tournament includes more than 1 round, archers shall be reassigned to targets in the order of their scores after the first round is completed. (See Art. 5.2)

9.1 Men and Intermediate Boys *F.I.T.A. Round*:

36 arrows at 90 m 122 cm face
36 arrows at 70 m 122 cm face
36 arrows at 50 m 80 cm face
36 arrows at 30 m 80 cm face

Ladies and Intermediate Girls *F.I.T.A. Round*

36 arrows at 70 m 122 cm face
36 arrows at 60 m 122 cm face
36 arrows at 50 m 80 cm face
36 arrows at 30 m 80 cm face

Junior Metric Round (Boys and Girls under 15 years)

36 arrows at 60 m 122 cm face
36 arrows at 50 m 122 cm face
36 arrows at 40 m 80 cm face
36 arrows at 30 m 80 cm face

Cadet Metric Round (Boys and Girls under 12 years)

36 arrows at 45 m 122 cm face
36 arrows at 35 m 122 cm face
36 arrows at 25 m 80 cm face
36 arrows at 15 m 80 cm face

9.2 900 Metric Round

30 arrows at 60 m 122 cm face
30 arrows at 50 m 122 cm face
30 arrows at 40 m 122 cm face

Junior 900 Round (under 15 years)

30 arrows at 50 m 122 cm face
30 arrows at 40 m 122 cm face
30 arrows at 30 m 122 cm face

Cadet 900 Round (under 12 years)

30 arrows at 40 m 122 cm face
30 arrows at 30 m 122 cm face
30 arrows at 20 m 122 cm face

9.3 James D. Easton (600) Round*

20 arrows at 60 m 122 cm face
20 arrows at 50 m 122 cm face

20 arrows at 40 m 122 cm face

9.4 Collegiate 720 Round

24 arrows at 50 m 80 cm face
24 arrows at 40 m 80 cm face
24 arrows at 30 m 80 cm face

9.5 Collegiate (600) Round*

20 arrows at 50 m 122 cm face
20 arrows at 40 m 122 cm face
20 arrows at 30 m 122 cm face

9.6 Indoor F.I.T.A. Round I

30 arrows at 18 m 40 cm face
Perfect Score – 300 points

9.7 Indoor F.I.T.A. Round II

30 arrows at 25 m 60 cm face
Perfect Score – 300 points

9.8 Clout Round – 36 arrows

165 m – men and intermediate boys
125 m – ladies and intermediate girls
110 m – junior and cadet boys and girls

* *Both these rounds have 5-arrow ends at each distance.*

10.0 Clout Rules of Shooting

10.1 The Clout Round consists of:
36 arrows at 165 m men and intermediate boys
36 arrows at 125 m ladies and intermediate girls
36 arrows at 110 m junior and cadet boys and girls

10.2 Two (2) sighter ends of 3 arrows each are permitted preceding the commencement of shooting. These shall be shot under the control of the Field Captain and shall not be scored.

10.3 The Clout target shall be circular, 15 m in diameter and shall be divided into 5 concentric scoring zones each measuring 1.5 m in width. Each dividing line shall be entirely within the higher scoring zone.
The Clout target may be marked on the ground *or* the scoring lines may be determined by a steel tape or non-stretch cord marked off at the dividing lines.

10.4 The center of the Clout Target shall be marked by a brightly colored distinctive triangular flag the CLOUT. This flag shall not measure more than 80 cm in length and 30 cm in width. The flag is to be affixed to a round pole of soft wood, firmly fixed vertically in the ground, so that the lower edge of the flag shall not be more than 50 cm from the ground.

10.5 Scoring values of each scoring zone starting from the center outward are:
5, 4, 3, 2, 1.

10.6 Equipment (See Article 3.0)

10.7 Range Control and Safety (See Article 4.0)

10.8 Shooting (See Article 5.0)

10.9 Scoring

a. Scoring shall take place after every second end of 3 arrows.

b. The Field Captain shall appoint one person to hold the Clout rope, and one person for each scoring ring to collect the arrows in that ring. After all arrows are collected, they are sorted according to the archer's individual markings, and the arrows shall remain in that scoring ring until scored.

c. Each competitor shall then call the value of his arrows, commencing with those of the highest value. The Field Captain shall check that all arrows are correctly called. Arrows must remain in or on the ground untouched until withdrawn or removed; otherwise, the arrows shall not be scored.

d. The value of the arrows that do not stick in the ground shall be determined by the position of their points as they lie.

e. Arrows sticking in the Clout Flag shall score 5.

f. No archer, except the appointed arrow gatherers, shall enter the Clout Target until his name has been called to record the value of his arrows.

g. Ties in the Clout events shall be decided as follows:
First – by the least number of misses; if the tie is still undecided, then the least number of ones, and so on.
Should all the arrows be the same, the archers so tying shall be declared equal.

11.0 The Team Round

11.1 The recommended round to be used for the Team Round is the James D. Easton Round. (See Art. 9.3)

11.2 An Official Team shall consist of not more than 8 archers who are active fellow members of at least 1 month's standing of an Archery Club affiliated with the N.A.A. The scores for the 4 highest scoring archers from a team shall be used to arrive at a team total. If less than 4 archers wish to compete as a team, their scores must count as a complete team. An Official Team must be so located geographically that members may meet reasonably often for practice.

11.3 Team Shoot entries, including names, must be registered with the Secre-

tary, or his designate, by the time announced in the program.
11.4 Groups of 4 archers who cannot qualify as an Official Team may register to compete as above, but shall not be eligible for Team Awards.
11.5 The Official Team making the highest aggregate score shall be the winner of the Team Award. The Highest Scoring Archer, whether on an Official Team or an unofficial team, shall be the individual winner.
11.6 Shooting and scoring and all rules shall be in accordance with the rules for regular target rounds, except that 1 of the 2 scorers for each target shall be from an adjacent target.
11.7 At the N.A.A. National Tournament, *State Teams* shall be recognized in the following manner. The scores of the top 4 individuals from each state in each class shall make up the State Teams. Men's and Ladies' State Teams shall be recognised at every N.A.A. National Tournament. Recognition of State Teams in other classifications shall be left to the discretion of the Tournament Committee.

12.0 F.I.T.A. Indoor Rules of Shooting
12.1 The 2 F.I.T.A. Indoor Rounds are:
Round I 30 arrows at 18 m 40 cm face
Round II 30 arrows at 25 m 60 cm face
12.2 Target set up:
a. The center of the Gold shall be 130 cm above the ground. If the 40 cm faces are in 2 lines – 1 above the other – the center of the Gold shall be 100 cm and 160 cm, respectively, above the ground.
b. The targets may be set up at any angle between vertical and 15 degrees, but a line of targets shall be up at the same angle.
12.3 Shooting and scoring:
a. Each archer shall shoot his arrows in end of 3 arrows each.
b. Scoring shall take place after each end of 3 arrows.
c. A Scoring Board is permitted. (See Art. 6.13 for details.)
12.4 Other rules and regulations:
a. Target Archery Rules of Shooting shall apply *except* the 2½ minute time limit may not be extended.
b. If space does not permit, the Waiting Line requirement may be waived.

13.0 Crossbows
13.1 Crossbowmen do not compete with longbowmen. They compete with and against each other for awards within their own division.
13.2 Rules are the same as for longbowmen except where in conflict with the rules given in this section.
13.3 The Crossbow Field Captain is specifically appointed to supervise the crossbowmen. His duties and authority correspond to that of the Field Captain for the longbowmen, his decision being final unless appealed to the Board.
13.4 The Crossbows and parts may be made of any safe material. The "traditional" type crossbow shall be used, namely, the bow shall be fitted to a stock in a horizontal position.
13.5 Bow Weight: In flight shooting, or in other events where the weight of the bow is a governing factor in the competition, the various classifications set up shall be figured in direct proportion to the longbow for that class at twenty-seven inches draw, using the inch-pound method to determine the class in which the bow may fall. For Target shooting, it is recommended that the bow be limited to 80 pounds for outdoor shooting and 50 pounds for indoor shooting.
13.6 Drawing: Crossbows shall be drawn by hand. No mechanical aids shall be permitted for spanning the bow, however, the Field Captain may permit a physically incapacitated contestant the use of a mechanical spanning aid in order to compete. Foot stirrups attached to the stock or foot plates on the ground will be allowed.
13.7 Arrows: (or Bolts) may be made of any material, but must not be of such design that they will unreasonably damage the target face or bast. They should be plainly marked for ease in scoring.
13.8 Safety: Crossbowmen will keep their weapons when drawn, whether loaded or not, pointed in the direction of the target. The Crossbow Field Captain may, at his discretion, reprimand or even bar from further competition a crossbow he considers dangerous to other shooters or spectators. All safety rules specified for longbowmen also pertain to crossbowmen.
13.9 Shooting: Crossbowmen stand to shoot and shall shoot "offhand." No rest or straps of any description shall be permitted. The Field Captain may permit a physically incapacitated contestant to shoot while seated.
13.10 Sights: Magnifying sights shall not be permitted. Level bubbles, prismatic

sights and other optical non-magnifying sights are allowed.

13.11 Spotting Aids: Binoculars or spotting scopes may be used at any time to locate hits. Spotting scopes may be left on the shooting line at the discretion of the Field Captain.

13.12 Infractions of Rules: The Crossbow Field Captain shall have the responsibility and authority to interpret and to decide questions of rules in accordance with regulations customs.

13.13 Target Backstops: (or Basts) shall be the same as those used by the longbowmen.

13.14 Targets: Target faces for the crossbow championship round shall be the standard 80 cm. F.I.T.A. target face. Crossbow archers use the same size target as do longbowmen for Clout, F.I.T.A. I & II Rounds. For crossbow events which had no counterpart in the Longbow Division, such as the King's and Queen's Rounds, the appropriate target faces shall be used.

13.15 Rounds: The National Championship for both Gentlemen and Ladies shall be determined by the highest total scores shot, by each sex, in the Quadruple International Crossbow Round. The tournament officials may, at their discretion, add such other events as it considers desirable, such as Clout, King's and Queen's Rounds, novelty rounds, etc., but the scores made in such events shall not count toward determining the championship.

13.16 International Crossbow Round:
30 arrows at 65 M (71.1 yds.)
30 arrows at 50 M (54.7 yds.)
30 arrows at 35 M (38.3 yds.)
An optional six practice arrows will be permitted prior to official scoring at each distance.
Perfect Score – 900.

13.17 Awards:
Gentleman: First, second, third place NAA medals for permanent possession.
Ladies: First, second, third place NAA medals for permanent possession.
The Fred Isles Cup; Gentleman's National Crossbow Champion.
The H. L. Bailey Trophy; Lady's National Crossbow Champion.
The Karl Traudt Award; The high single International Crossbow Round.
The Anderson Award; The Crossbow Clout Champion.
The Stevens Dagger: The King's Round Champion.
The Queen's Scepter: The Queen's Round Champion.

13.18 Heraldry: In addition to the foregoing awards, The National Crossbowmen of the United States have rules governing the decoration of pennons or gonfalons which may be displayed. These rules may be obtained from the National Crossbowmen thru the Secretary-Treasurer of The National Crossbowmen.

14.0 Appendix

14.1 Dress regulations for N.A.A. Championships – Target and Field

a. During the tournament the following white attire is permitted:
Ladies – Dresses, skirts, or slacks with suitable blouses or tops.
Gentlemen – Full-length trousers and long or short sleeved shirts.
Adverse weather conditions – The Director of Shooting may declare what will constitute proper attire!
Field Tournaments – The same rules apply.

b. Footwear must be worn by all competitors at all times during the tournament.

c. No advertising of any kind shall appear on the clothing worn by the competitors or officials.

d. At the N.A.A. National Tournament, competitor's number is to be worn on the middle of the back and be visible at all times while shooting is in progress.

Recommended Target Archery Field Layout

F.I.T.A. Round – Major Tournaments
Size of field depends on the number of targets, i.e. number of competitors.
Ladies shoot at:
70 m – 60 m – 50 m – 30 m
Gentlemen shoot at:
90 m – 70 m – 50 m – 30 m
(Art. 9.1 F.I.T.A. Rounds)
Two (2) Target *Buttresses*, on stands, in each lane are moved forward for each distance. Each 2-target lane is a minimum of 5 meters wide.
(Art. 1.5)
Lanes to be clearly marked on the ground by tape or whitewash.
(Art. 1.4)
Clear Lane to be left between the Ladies' and Gentlemen's lanes, not less than 5 meters wide.

Waiting Line to be indicated not less than 5 meters behind the Shooting Line.
(Art. 1.8)
Seating shall be provided behind the Waiting Line for the use of all competitors and officials.
(Art. 1.18)
Suitable *Barriers* shall be erected round the Field to keep back spectators. At least 10 meters away from each side of the Field and behind the Waiting Line. At least 25 meters behind the 90 meter Target Line.
(Art. 1.14)

Large *Scoreboards* are to be placed so that they are visible to both Competitors and Spectators.
(Art. 6.13)
Visual signals – time control
(Art. 1.15)

Note: At Club Shooting, the Target Buttress Line is usually permanent and the Shooting Line is moved up at each distance.

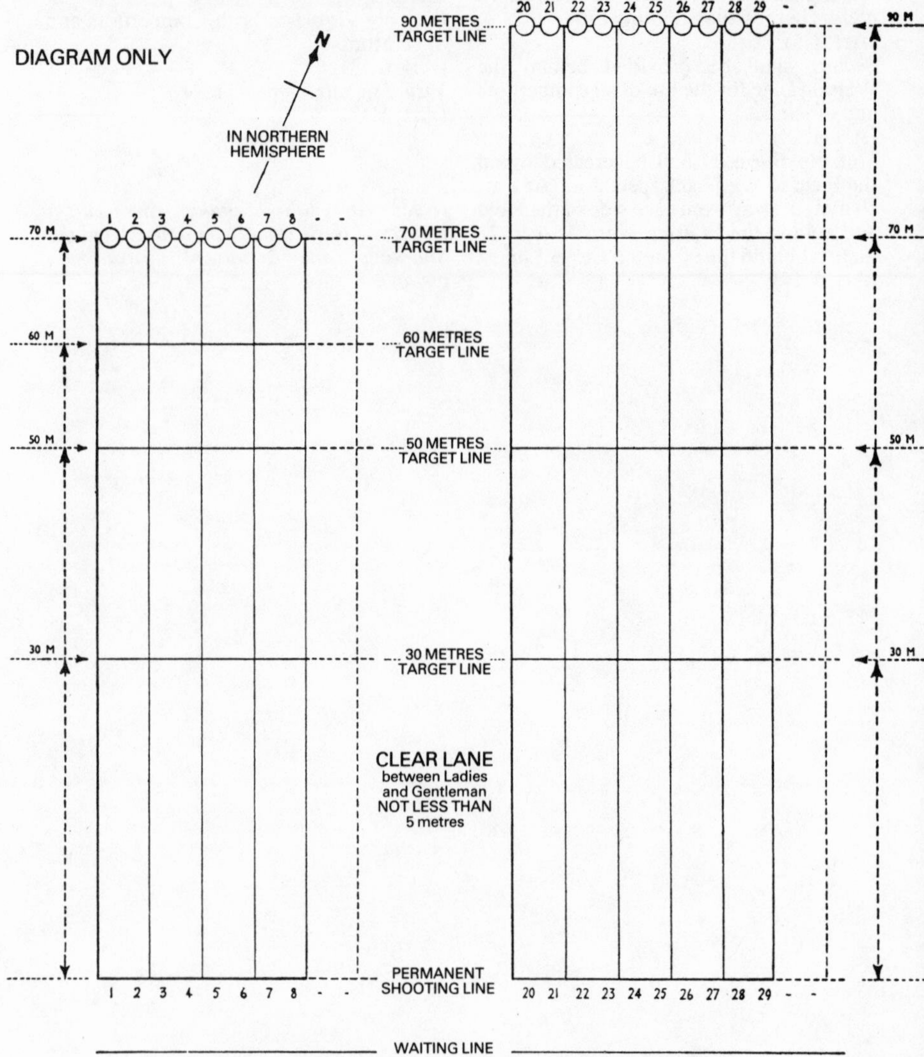
DIAGRAM ONLY
N
IN NORTHERN HEMISPHERE
20 21 22 23 24 25 26 27 28 29 - -
90 METRES TARGET LINE
90 M
1 2 3 4 5 6 7 8 - -
70 M
70 METRES TARGET LINE
70 M
60 M
60 METRES TARGET LINE
50 M
50 METRES TARGET LINE
50 M
30 M
30 METRES TARGET LINE
30 M
CLEAR LANE
between Ladies
and Gentleman
NOT LESS THAN
5 metres
PERMANENT SHOOTING LINE
1 2 3 4 5 6 7 8 - -
20 21 22 23 24 25 26 27 28 29 - -
WAITING LINE
SEATING — Ladies
SEATING — Gentleman

Appendix 2
Champions

CHAMPION ARCHERS OF GREAT BRITAIN

(At the Grand National Archery Meeting, which included British Championship)

	Gentlemen	*Ladies*
	(Single York Round)	
1844	Rev J. Higginson	—
	(Double York Round)	(Ninety-six arrows at 60 yards)
1845	P. Muir	Miss Thelwall
1846	R. G. Hubback	—
		(144 arrows at 60 yards)
1847	P. Muir	Miss E. Wylde
		(Seventy-two arrows at 60 yards and seventy-two at 50 yards)
1848	E. Maitland	Miss J. Barrow
	(Champion's medal awarded on points)	(Double National Round)
1849	H. A. Ford	Miss Temple
		(Seventy-two arrows at 60 yards and thirty-six at 50 yards)
1850	H. A. Ford	Mrs Calvert
		(Double National Round)
1851	H. A. Ford	Miss Villers
1852	H. A. Ford	Miss Brindley
		(Challenge Prize for ladies awarded on points)
1853	H. A. Ford	Mrs Horniblow
1854	H. A. Ford	Mrs Davison
1855	H. A. Ford	Mrs Davison
1856	H. A. Ford	Mrs Horniblow
1857	H. A. Ford	Miss H. Chetwynd
1858	H. A. Ford	Mrs Horniblow
1859	H. A. Ford	Miss Turner
1860	G. Edwards	Mrs G. Atkinson
1861	G. Edwards	Mrs G. Atkinson
1862	G. Edwards	Mrs Horniblow
1863	P. Muir	Mrs Horniblow
1864	G. Edwards	Miss Betham
1865	E. A. Holmes	Miss Betham
1866	G. Edwards	Miss Betham
1867	H. A. Ford	Mrs E. Lister
1868	W. Rimington	Miss Betham
1869	W. Rimington	Mrs Horniblow
1870	E. A. Holmes	Mrs Horniblow
1871	Capt C. H. Fisher	Mrs Horniblow
1872	Capt C. H. Fisher	Mrs Horniblow
1873	Major C. H. Fisher	Mrs Horniblow
1874	Major C. H. Fisher	Mrs Pond

1875	G. E. S. Fryer	Miss Hollins
1876	H. H. Palairet	Mrs W. Butt
1877	W. Rimington	Mrs W. Butt
1878	H. H. Palairet	Mrs Marshall
1879	R. Walters	Mrs Marshall
1880	H. H. Palairet	Mrs Horniblow
1881	H. H. Palairet	Miss Alice B. Legh
1882	H. H. Palairet	Mrs Piers Legh
1883	C. J. Longman	Mrs Piers Legh
1884	C. E. Nesham	Mrs Piers Legh
1885	C. E. Nesham	Mrs Piers Legh
1886	C. E. Nesham	Miss Alice B. Legh
1887	Major C. H. Fisher	Miss Alice B. Legh
1888	C. E. Nesham	Miss Alice B. Legh
1889	B. P. Gregson	Miss Alice B. Legh
1890	C. E. Nesham	Miss Alice B. Legh
1891	F. L. Govett	Miss Alice B. Legh
1892	G. E. S. Fryer	Miss Alice B. Legh
1893	B. P. Gregson	Mrs C. Bowly
1894	Eyre W. Hussey	Mrs C. Bowly
1895	G. E. S. Fryer	Miss Alice B. Legh
1896	G. E. S. Fryer	Miss Bagnall Oakley
1897	G. E. S. Fryer	Mrs C. Bowly
1898	C. J. Perry Keene	Miss Alice B. Legh
1899	Eyre W. Hussey	Miss Alice B. Legh
1900	R. Brooks-King	Miss Alice B. Legh
1901	Eyre W. Hussey	Mrs C. Bowly
1902	R. Brooks-King	Miss Alice B. Legh
1903	R. Brooks-King	Miss Alice B. Legh
1904	J. Penrose	Miss Alice B. Legh
1905	J. H. Bridges	Miss Alice B. Legh
1906	R. Brooks-King	Miss Alice B. Legh
1907	H. P. Nesham	Miss Alice B. Legh
1908	R. Brooks-King	Miss Alice B. Legh
1909	W. Dod	Miss Alice B. Legh
1910	R. Brooks-King	Mrs H. A. Wadworth
1911	W. Dod	Miss Q. Newall
1912	R. Brooks-King	Miss Q. Newall
1913	R. Brooks-King	Miss Alice B. Legh
1914	H. P. Nesham	Mrs S. H. Armitage
1919	T. H. Langford Sainsbury	Miss M. Hyde
1920	C. K. Philips	Mrs R. Sandford
1921	W. A. Inderwick	Miss Alice B. Legh
1922	Major G. A. E. Chapman	Miss Alice B. Legh
1923	R. Brooks-King	Mrs Boddam Whetham
1924	W. A. Inderwick	Mrs Shillito
1925	Major J. J. B. Farley	Miss N. E. Wallace
1926	H. A. Cox	Miss N. E. Wallace
1927	H. A. Cox	Miss V. M. Rushton
1928	H. A. Cox	Mrs J. H. Atkinson
1929	H. A. Cox	Mrs J. H. Atkinson
1930	Major F. S. Williams-Thomas	Mrs R. Sandford
1931	Major F. S. Williams-Thomas	Mrs J. H. Atkinson
1932	Major F. S. Williams-Thomas	Mrs R. Sandford
1933	Major F. S. Williams-Thomas	Mrs C. W. Nettleton
1934	J. H. Davey	Miss V. M. Rushton
1935	H. A. Cox	Mrs J. H. Atkinson
1936	J. H. Davey	Miss E. Browett

1937	Group-Capt A. Shekleton	Mrs M. L. Bates
1938	Rev D. Lloyd Wilson	Mrs Lindner
1939	Capt A. H. Mole	Mrs L. Nettleton
1946	C. B. Edwards (Double Hereford Round)	Mrs S. Macquoid
1947	C. Downing	Mrs P. de Wharton Burr
1948	F. L. Bilson	Mrs P. de Wharton Burr
1949	H. A. Hooker	Miss B. J. Waterhouse
1950	R. J. Beal	Mrs G. A. Arthur
1951	J. B. Arch	Mrs Marion Felix
1952	W. Bickerstaff	Mrs T. C. Morgan
1953	T. C. Morgan	Miss A. B. Dennett
1954	J. B. Collyer	Mrs J. K. Flower
1955	H. A. Oram	Mrs J. K. Flower
1956	G. A. Brown	Miss J. Warner
1957	R. D. Matthews	Mrs J. K. Flower
1958	R. D. Matthews	Mrs J. C. Reynolds
1959	R. Hall	Mrs L. Fowler
1960	G. A. Brown	Miss J. F. Taunton
1961	F. W. Bing	Miss S. M. Lyons
1962	R. Hall	Miss V. Wooler
1963	R. P. Bishop	Mrs A. Brien
1964	R. D. Matthews	Miss S. D. Kemp
1965	R. D. Matthews	Miss C. Britton
1966	J. I. Dixon	Mrs J. Hills
1967	G. Sykes	Mrs J. Hills
1968	R. D. Matthews	Mrs S. S. Simester
1969	R. D. Matthews	Miss L. A. Thomas
1970	T. H. Wareing	Miss L. A. Thomas

(From this year a separate British National Championship was instituted, divorced from the Grand National Archery Meeting for the first time for 126 years)

1971	R. C. Hemming	Miss L. A. Thomas
1972	R. C. Hemming	Mrs B. A. Strickland
1973	R. D. Matthews	Miss P. M. Edwards
1974	R. D. Matthews	Miss P. M. Edwards
1975	R. D. Matthews	Miss P. M. Edwards
1976	M. Blenkarne	Mrs N. Bottomley
1977	M. T. Deacon	Miss P. M. Edwards
1978	M. Blenkarne	Miss J. Abbott
1979	M. Blenkarne	Miss S. Willcox
1980	M. Blenkarne	Miss D. Salter
1981	M. Blenkarne	Mrs V. John
1982	P. Armstrong	Miss P. M. Edwards
1983	S. Hallard	Mrs E. Robinson

CHAMPION ARCHERS OF THE UNITED STATES

When these contests started the Championship was awarded on points, for hits on the target, and not on the score. Men shot the double York Round (*qv*) and ladies the double Columbia Round (*qv*).

1879	Will H. Thompson	Mrs Spalding Brown
1880	L. L. Peddinghaus	Mrs T. Davis
1881	Frank H. Walworth	Mrs A. H. Gibbes
1882	Homer S. Taylor	Mrs A. H. Gibbes
1883	Col. Robert Williams Jr	Mrs Lyda Scott Howell
1884	Will H. Thompson	Mrs George S. Hall

1885	Col. Robert Williams Jr	Mrs Lyda Scott Howell
1886	William A. Clark	Mrs Lyda Scott Howell
1887	William A. Clark	Mrs A. M. Phillips
1888	Will H. Thompson	Mrs A. M. Phillips
1889	Louis W. Maxson	Mrs A. M. Phillips
1890	Louis W. Maxson	Mrs Lyda Scott Howell
1891	Louis W. Maxson	Mrs Lyda Scott Howell
1892	Louis W. Maxson	Mrs Lyda Scott Howell
1893	Louis W. Maxson	Mrs Lyda Scott Howell
1894	Louis W. Maxson	Mrs Albert Kern
1895	W. R. Robinson	Mrs Lyda Scott Howell
1896	D. F. McGowan	Mrs Lyda Scott Howell
1897	William A. Clark	Mrs J. S. Barker
1898	Louis W. Maxson	Mrs Lyda Scott Howell
1899	M. C. Howell	Mrs Lyda Scott Howell
1900	A. Rankin Clark	Mrs Lyda Scott Howell
1901	Will H. Thompson	Mrs C. S. Woodruff
1902	Col Robert Williams Jr	Mrs Lyda Scott Howell
1903	Wallace Bryant	Mrs Lyda Scott Howell
1904	George P. Bryant	Mrs Lyda Scott Howell
1905	George P. Bryant	Mrs Lyda Scott Howell
1906	Henry B. Richardson	Mrs E. C. Cooke
1907	Henry B. Richardson	Mrs Lyda Scott Howell
1908	Will H. Thompson	Miss Harriet A. Case
1909	George P. Bryant	Miss Harriet A. Case
1910	Henry B. Richardson	Miss Julia V. Sullivan

(From 1911 two equal Championships were shot: for men (a) a double American Round and (b) a double York Round; for ladies (a) a double Columbia Round and (b) a double National Round.)

1911	a) Dr Robert P. Elmer	a) Mrs J. H. Taylor
	b) Homer S. Taylor	b) Mrs J. H. Taylor
1912	a) George P. Bryant	a) Mrs J. H. Taylor
	b) George P. Bryant	b) Mrs J. H. Taylor
1913	a) Dr Robert P. Elmer	a) Mrs L. C. Smith
	b) Dr J. W. Doughty	b) Mrs P. S. Fletcher
1914	a) Dr Robert P. Elmer	a) Mrs B. P. Gray
	b) Dr Robert P. Elmer	b) Mrs B. P. Gray

(From 1915 a single Championship was awarded on the hits and scores for both double rounds combined in a single total.)

1915	Dr Robert P. Elmer	Miss Cynthia M. Wesson
1916	Dr Robert P. Elmer	Miss Cynthia M. Wesson
(1917 and 1918: no tournament)		
1919	Dr Robert P. Elmer	Miss Dorothy D. Smith
1920	Dr Robert P. Elmer	Miss Cynthia M. Wesson
1921	James S. Jiles	Miss Dorothy D. Smith
1922	Dr Robert P. Elmer	Miss Dorothy D. Smith
1923	William H. Palmer	Miss Norma L. Peirce
1924	James S. Jiles	Miss Dorothy D. Smith
1925	Dr Paul W. Crouch	Miss Dorothy D. Smith
1926	Stanley F. Spencer	Miss Dorothy D. Smith
1927	Dr Paul W. Crouch	Mrs Robert Johnson
1928	William H. Palmer Jr	Mrs Beatrice Hodgson
1929	Dr E. K. Roberts	Mrs Audrey Grubbs
1930	Russell B. Hoogerhyde	Mrs Audrey Grubbs

(From 1931 hits were no longer counted and the Championship has since been awarded on the combined scores of the two double rounds.)

1931	Russell B. Hoogerhyde	Mrs Dorothy (Smith) Cummings
1932	Russell B. Hoogerhyde	Miss Ilda Hanchette
1933	Ralph R. Miller	Miss Madeline Taylor
1934	Russell B. Hoogerhyde	Mrs G. de Sales Mudd
1935	Gilman Keasey	Mrs Ruth Hodgert
1936	Gilman Keasey	Mrs Gladys M. Hammer
1937	Jack Wilson	Miss Jean A. Tenney
1938	Pat Chambers	Miss Jean A. Tenney
1939	Pat Chambers	Miss Belvia Carter
1940	Russell B. Hoogerhyde	Miss Ann Weber
1941	Lawrence A. Hughes	Miss Careta Dillinger
(1942 to 1945: no tournament)		
1946	Wayne Thompson	Miss Ann Weber
1947	Jack Wilson	Miss Ann Weber
1948	Lawrence A. Hughes	Miss Jean Lee
1949	Russ Reynolds	Miss Jean Lee
1950	Stanley Overby	Miss Jean Lee
1951	Russ Reynolds	Miss Jean Lee
1952	Robert Larson	Mrs Ann Corby
1953	William Glacken	Mrs Ann Corby
1954	Robert Rhode	Miss Laurette Young
1955	Joe Fries	Mrs Ann Clarke
1956	Joe Fries	Mrs Carole Meinhart
1957	Joe Fries	Mrs Carole Meinhart
1958	Robert Bitner	Mrs Carole Meinhart
1959	Bert Vetrovsky	Mrs Carole Meinhart
1960	Robert Kadlec	Mrs Ann Clarke
1961	Clayton Sherman	Miss Vicki Cook
1962	Robert Pender	Miss Nancy Vonderheide
1963	Ed Rohde	Miss Nancy Vonderheide
1964	Dave Keaggy Jr	Miss Vicki Cook
1965	George Clauss	Miss Nancy Pfeifer
1966	Hardy Ward	Mrs Helen Thornton
1967	Ray Rogers	Miss Ardelle Mills
1968	Hardy Ward	Miss Vicki Cook
1969	Ray Rogers	Mrs Doreen Wilber
1970	Joe Thornton	Mrs Nancy Myrick
1971	John Williams	Mrs Doreen Wilber
1972	Kevin Erlandson	Miss Ruth Rowe
1973	Darrell Pace	Mrs Doreen Wilber
1974	Darrell Pace	Mrs Doreen Wilber
1975	Darrell Pace	Miss Irene Lorensen
1976	Darrell Pace	Miss Luann Ryon
1977	Richard McKinney	Miss Luann Ryon
1978	Darrell Pace	Miss Luann Ryon
1979	Richard McKinney	Miss Lynette Johnson
1980	Richard McKinney	Miss Judi Adams
1981	Richard McKinney	Miss Debbie Metzgar
1982	Richard McKinney	Miss Luann Ryon
1983	Richard McKinney	Mrs Nancy Myrick

COMMONWEALTH GAMES

In 1982, target archery was included for the first time in the Commonwealth Games.

	Men	*Ladies*
1982	Mark Blenkarne (GBR)	Miss Neroli Fairhall (NZ)

EUROPEAN CHAMPIONSHIPS
(Inaugurated 1968)

1968	Mrs M. Maczynska	Poland	K. Laasonen	Finland
1970	Mrs A.-L. Berglund	Sweden	V. Sidoruk	USSR
1972	Miss K. Lossaberidze	USSR	G. Jervill	Sweden
1974	Mrs B. Gould	Gt Britain	R. Schiffl	West Germany
1976	Miss O. Rulenko	USSR	R. Svensson	Sweden
1978	Miss V. Kovpan	USSR	K. Laasonen	Finland
1980	Miss N. Butuzova	USSR	M. Vervink	Belgium
1982	Miss N. Butuzova	USSR	V. Esheyev	USSR

WORLD TARGET ARCHERY CHAMPIONSHIPS

Ladies			*Teams*
1931 Lwow	Mrs J. Spychajowa-Kurkowska	Poland	
1932 Warsaw	Mrs J. Spychajowa-Kurkowska	Poland	
1933 London	Mrs J. Spychajowa-Kurkowska	Poland	Poland
1934 Bastad	Mrs J. Spychajowa-Kurkowska	Poland	Poland
1935 Brussels	Mrs I. Catani	Sweden	Great Britain
1936 Prague	Mrs J. Spychajowa-Kurkowska	Poland	Poland
1937 Paris	Mrs E. Simon	Great Britain	Great Britain
1938 London	Mrs N. Weston Martyr	Great Britain	Poland
1939 Oslo	Mrs J. Spychajowa-Kurkowska	Poland	Poland
1946 Stockholm	Mrs P. de Wharton Burr	Great Britain	Great Britain
1947 Prague	Mrs J. Spychajowa-Kurkowska	Poland	Denmark
1948 London	Mrs P. de Wharton Burr	Great Britain	Czechoslovakia
1949 Paris	Miss B. Waterhouse	Great Britain	Great Britain
1950 Copenhagen	Miss J. Lee	USA	Finland
1952 Brussels	Miss J. Lee	USA	USA
1953 Oslo	Mrs J. Richards	USA	Finland
1955 Helsinki	Mrs K. Wisniowska	Poland	Great Britain

(FITA series introduced: double round of thirty-six arrows each at 70, 60, 50 and 30 metres)

1957 Prague	Mrs C. Meinhart	USA	USA
1958 Brussels	Mrs S. Johansson	Sweden	USA
1959 Stockholm	Mrs A. Corby	USA	USA
1961 Oslo	Miss N. Vonderheide	USA	USA
1963 Helsinki	Miss V. Cook	USA	USA
1965 Vasteras	Miss M. Lindholm	Finland	USA
1967 Amersfoort	Mrs M. Maczynska	Poland	Poland
1969 Valley Forge	Mrs D. Lidstone	Canada	USSR
1971 York	Miss E. Gapchenko	USSR	Poland
1973 Grenoble	Miss L. Myers	USA	USSR
1975 Interlaken	Miss Z. Rustamova	USSR	USSR
1977 Canberra	Miss L. Ryon	USA	USA
1979 Berlin	Miss J. Kim	South Korea	South Korea
1981 Punta Ala	Miss N. Butuzova	USSR	USSR
1983 Long Beach	Miss Kim Jin Ho	South Korea	South Korea

Gentlemen			*Teams*
1931 Lwow	M. Sawicki	Poland	France
1932 Warsaw	L. Reith	Belgium	Poland

1933	London	D. Mackenzie	USA	Belgium
1934	Bastad	H. Kjellson	Sweden	Sweden
1935	Brussels	A. van Kohlen	Belgium	Belgium
1936	Prague	E. Heilborn	Sweden	Czechoslovakia
1937	Paris	G. De Rons	Belgium	Poland
1938	London	F. Hadas	Czechoslovakia	Czechoslovakia
1939	Oslo	R. Beday	France	France
1946	Stockholm	E. Tang Holbek	Denmark	Denmark
1947	Prague	H. Deutgen	Sweden	Czechoslovakia
1948	London	H. Deutgen	Sweden	Sweden
1949	Paris	H. Deutgen	Sweden	Czechoslovakia
1950	Copenhagen	H. Deutgen	Sweden	Sweden
1952	Brussels	S. Andersson	Sweden	Sweden
1953	Oslo	B. Lundgren	Sweden	Sweden
1955	Helsinki	N. Andersson	Sweden	Sweden

(FITA series introduced: double round of thirty-six arrows each at 90, 70, 50 and 30 metres)

1957	Prague	O. K. Smathers	USA	USA
1958	Brussels	S. Thysell	Sweden	Finland
1959	Stockholm	J. Caspers	USA	USA
1961	Oslo	J. Thornton	USA	USA
1963	Helsinki	C. T. Sandlin	USA	USA
1965	Vesteras	M. Haikonen	Finland	USA
1967	Amersfoort	R. Rogers	USA	USA
1969	Valley Forge	H. Ward	USA	USA
1971	York	J. C. Williams	USA	USA
1973	Grenoble	V. Sidoruk	USSR	USA
1975	Interlaken	D. Pace	USA	USA
1977	Canberra	R. McKinney	USA	USA
1979	Berlin	D. Pace	USA	USA
1981	Punta Ala	K. Laasonen	Finland	USA
1983	Long Beach	R. McKinney	USA	USA

WORLD FIELD CHAMPIONS

	Women		*Men*		*Class*
1969	Miss R. Dabelow	USA	W. Cowles	USA	Instinctive
	Mrs I. Danielsson	SWE	R. Branstetter, Jr	USA	Free style
1971	Miss E. Schewe	USA	E. Moore	USA	Instinctive
	Mrs S. Johansson	SWE	S. Lieberman	USA	Free style
1972	Mrs I. Grandquist	SWE	L. Berggren	SWE	Instinctive
	Miss M. Bechdolt	USA	J. C. Williams	USA	Free style
1974	Miss E. Schewe	USA	L. Berggren	SWE	Instinctive
	Miss L. Lessard	CAN	D. Brothers	USA	Free style
1976	Mrs S. Sandford	GBR	J. Virtanen	FIN	Instinctive
	Mrs A.-M. Lehmann	GER	T. Persson	SWE	Free style
1978	Miss S. Kobuchi	JPN	A. Rosenberg	SWE	Instinctive
	Mrs A.-M. Lehmann	GER	D. Pace	USA	Free style
1980	Miss S. Konttila	FIN	A. Rosenberg	SWE	Instinctive
	Miss C. Jussila	FIN	G. Bjerendahl	SWE	Free style
1982	Miss A. Dardenne	FRA	A. Rosenberg	SWE	Instinctive
	Miss C. Jussila	FIN	T. Quick	SWE	Free style

OLYMPIC MEDAL WINNERS

			Double FITA Round	*Total*
MUNICH				
	GOLD			
1972	Mrs Doreen Wilber	USA	1198+1226	2424
	Mr John Williams	USA	1268+1260	2528
	SILVER			
	Mrs Irena Szydlowska	POL	1224+1183	2407
	Mr Gunnar Jervill	SWE	1229+1252	2481
	BRONZE			
	Mrs Emma Gapchenko	URS	1201+1202	2403
	Mr Kyosti Laasonen	FIN	1213+1254	2467
MONTREAL				
	GOLD			
1976	Miss Luann Ryon	USA	1217+1282	2499
	Mr Darrell Pace	USA	1264+1307	2571
	SILVER			
	Miss Valentina Kovpan	URS	1182+1278	2460
	Mr Hiroshi Michinaga	JPN	1226+1276	2502
	BRONZE			
	Miss Zebiniso Rustamova	URS	1202+1205	2407
	Mr Giancarlo Ferrari	ITA	1220+1275	2495
MOSCOW				
	GOLD			
1980	Miss Keto Lossaberidze	URS	1257+1234	2491
	Mr Tomi Poikolainen	FIN	1220+1235	2455
	SILVER			
	Miss Natalia Butuzova	URS	1251+1226	2477
	Mr Boris Isachenko	URS	1217+1235	2452
	BRONZE			
	Miss Paivi Meriluoto	FIN	1217+1232	2449
	Mr Giancarlo Ferrari	ITA	1215+1234	2449

IInd OLYMPIAD, PARIS, 1900

50 metres competition		
Concours d'ensemble	*Gold medal*	
Cordon doré (large target)	Mackintosh	Australia
Chapelet (small target)	Herouin	France
Concours individuel		
Chapelet (small target)	Mougin	France
33 metres competition		
Concours d'ensemble		
Cordon doré (large target)	H. van Innis	Belgium
Concours individuel		
Chapelet (small target)	H. van Innis	Belgium
A la perche (popinjay) 30 metres	Foulon	France

IIIrd OLYMPIAD, ST LOUIS, 1904

Double York Round—men	*Olympic range medals*	
100yd	Col R. Williams	USA
80yd	Will H. Thompson	USA
60yd	E. Frentz	USA

Double American Round—men		
60yd	H. B. Richardson	USA
50yd	Cyrus Dallin	USA
40yd	C. S. Woodruff	USA

Team contest (Ninety-six arrows at 60 yards)

	Olympic team and individual medals
Potomac Archers	Will H. Thompson
	Col R. Williams
	L. W. Maxson
	G. C. Spencer

Double National Round—women		
	Olympic range medals	
60yd	Mrs H. Pollock	USA
50yd	Miss E. C. Cooke	USA

Double Columbia Round—women		
50yd	Mrs C. S. Woodruff	USA
40yd	Miss Leonie Taylor	USA
30yd	Miss Mabel Taylor	USA

Team contest (Ninety-six arrows at 50 yards)

	Olympic team and individual medals
Cincinnati Archery Club	Mrs M. C. Howell
	Mrs H. Pollock
	Mrs C. S. Woodruff
	Miss L. Taylor

IVth OLYMPIAD, LONDON, 1908

Double York Round—men		
Gold Medal	W. Dod	GB
Silver Medal	R. Brooks-King	GB
Bronze Medal	H. B. Richardson	USA
Special merit certificate	M. Berton	France

Double National Round—women		
Gold Medal	Miss Q. F. Newall	GB
Silver Medal	Miss C. Dod	GB
Bronze Medal	Mrs Hill-Lowe	GB

50 metres competition		
Gold Medal	M. Grisot	France
Silver Medal	M. Vernet	France
Bronze Medal	M. Cabaret	France
Special Merit Certificate	R. O. Backhouse	GB

VIIth OLYMPIAD, ANTWERP, 1920

Target competition (Thirty arrows at 50 metres, fifteen arrows at 33 metres and fifteen arrows at 28 metres)

50 metres team competition	Belgium	
33 metres team competition	Belgium	
28 metres team competition	Netherlands	

Individual competition—men

50 metres	L. Brulé	France
33 metres	H. van Innis	Belgium
28 metres	H. van Innis	Belgium

Individual competition—women

	Miss Q. F. Newall	GB

A la Perche (popinjay)
(Twenty arrows, 31 metres mast)

Team competition	Belgium	
Individual competition		
'High birds' shooting	E. van Meer	Belgium
'Small birds' shooting	E. Clostens	Belgium

Appendix 3
Equipment Suppliers (U.K.)

The following are among the leading retailers in the UK:

The Archery Centre
Highgate Hill
Hawkhurst
Kent

Chiltern Archery
Hunters Lodge
Buckland Village
Nr Aston Clinton
Buckinghamshire HP22 5LH

Les Howis (Marksman) Bows Ltd
Main Street
Cuckney
Nr Mansfield, Nottinghamshire NG20 9JL

Longshot Archery Co.
Hampton Court Road
Hampton Court
KT8 9BX

Macclesfield Archery Centre
143–5 Park Lane
Macclesfield
Cheshire SK11 6UB

Pro Shop Archery Specialists
11a Windsor Road
Walton-le-Dale
Preston
Lancashire

Quicks, The Archery Specialists
18–22 Stakes Hill Road
Waterlooville
Portsmouth PO7 7HY

Severn Products
The Butts
Boreley
Ombersley
Worcestershire

Targetcraft Archery Centre
The Old School
Bedford Road
Marston Moreteyne
Bedfordshire MK43 0ND

Wales Archery Specialist
Crick Manor
Crick
Nr Newport
Gwent NP6 4UW

Appendix 4
Equipment Suppliers (U.S.A.)

Leading makers and suppliers of equipment in the USA include:

Bear Archery
Rural Route 4
4600 Southwest 41st Blvd.
Gainesville, Florida 32601

Easton Aluminum Inc.
7800 Haskell Avenue
Van Nuys, Ca. 91406

Hoyt/Easton Archery
11510 Natural Bridge Rd.
Bridgeton, Mo. 63044

Nishizawa, USA
24665 Glenwood Drive
Los Gatos, Ca. 95030

Precision Shooting Equipment Inc.
P.O. Box 5487
Tucson, Az. 85703

Yamaha International Archery Div.
6600 Orangethorpe Avenue
Buena Park, Ca. 90620

Appendix 5
Association & Society Addresses

Fédération Internationale de Tir à l'Arc
FITA Executive Bureau
Via Cerva n. 30
20122 Milan
Italy

Grand National Archery Society
National Agricultural Centre
Stoneleigh
Kenilworth
Warwickshire CV8 2LZ

National Archery Association of the United States
1750 East Boulder Street
Colorado Springs
CO 80909
USA

British Crossbow Society
9 Atalanta Street
Fulham
London SW6 6TU

National Field Archery Society
67 Seaburn Road
Toton
Beeston
Nottinghamshire NG9 6HN

Crossbow Archery Development Association
Frost Street
Wolverhampton WV2 2RB

Index of Bibliographical References

Many of the authors whose works are cited in this book have written more extensively on archery subjects than the following entries may suggest. The works here listed are those needed to be consulted in compiling the encyclopaedia. Some works have been reprinted in recent years, but the majority of these re-issues are now out of print; original editions only are cited.

Acker, W. R. B., *Japanese Archery* (Rutland, Vt. & Tokyo, 1965), 72, 100

Ascham, R., *Toxophilus*, 1545 (from edition of W. A. Wright, *English Works of Roger Ascham*, Cambridge, 1904), 9, 15, 20, 25, 45, 55

Avon-Coffrant, F., *Tir à l'Arc* (Paris, 1977), 105

Bilson, F., *Crossbows* (Newton Abbot, 1974), 41, 48

Blackmore, H. L., *Hunting Weapons* (London, 1971), 85

Clover, P. (ed.), *Bowman's Handbook*, 5th edition (Portsmouth, 1968), 52, 57, 58, 96

Credland, A. G., 'The Bullet Crossbow in Britain', *Journal of the Society of Archer-Antiquaries* (1972), 33, 84–5

'Crossbow Guns and Musket Arrows', *Journal of the Society of Archer-Antiquaries* (1977), 78

Edwards, C. B., *An Archer's Notes* (Leeds, 1949), 49.

The 'Tox' Story (1968), 92.

Elmer, R. P., *Target Archery* (New York, 1946), 9, 38, 46, 74, 79, 91, 111, 113

English, F. L., 'The Exterior Ballistics of the Arrow', *Journal of the Franklin Institute* (Philadelphia, 1930), 22

Ford, H., *Archery: Its Theory and Practice* (London, 1856), 15, 44, 61, 63

Gibson, G., 'Origins of William Tell', *Journal of the Society of Archer-Antiquaries* (1975), 103

Grose, F., *Treatise on Ancient Armour* (London, 1786), 88

Hamilton, T. M., *Native American Bows* (York, Pa., 1972), 22, 84

Hansard, G. A., *The Book of Archery* (London, 1840), 65

Hardy, R., *Longbow: A Social and Military History* (Cambridge, 1976), 65, 74

Harmuth, E., *Die Armbrust* (Graz, 1975), 27

Harris, P. V., *The Truth About Robin Hood* (1973), 67

Hay, I., *The Royal Company of Archers, 1676–1951* (Edinburgh & London, 1951), 92

Haynes, M., 'Rigors for Riggers', *Bow & Arrow* (Covina, Ca., 1967), 39

PERIODICALS